Wall Street Words

David L. Scott

Wall Street Words

Houghton Mifflin Company · Boston · 1988

The inclusion of any word in this book is not an expression of the Publisher's opinion as to whether or not it is subject to proprietary rights. Indeed, no word in this book is to be regarded as affecting the validity of any trademark.

This publication is designed to provide accurate and authoritative information in regard to the subject matter covered. It is sold with the understanding that the Publisher, author, and contributors are not engaged in rendering legal, accounting, or other professional advice, with respect to this publication. If, as a direct result of information supplied through this publication, legal advice or other expert assistance is required, the services of a competent professional person should be sought. The opinions of the contributors of the investment "tips" that appear in this publication are personal, and do not necessarily represent the opinions of the Publisher, the author, or the institutions with which the contributors are affiliated.

Charts by Mary Reilly

Library of Congress Cataloging-in-Publication Data

Scott, David Logan, 1942–
    Wall Street words.

    Bibliography: p. 403
    1. Investments—Dictionaries. 2. Securities—Dictionaries. 3. Stock-exchange—Dictionaries.
I. Title.
HG4513.S37   1988   332.6′03′21   87–21444
ISBN 0–395–43747–4

Manufactured in the United States of America

Contents

Special Consultants & Reviewers

Contributors of Investment "Tips"

Barry Allen
Senior Investment Consultant
Massachusetts Mutual Life
 Insurance Company
Springfield, MA

Anthony L. Bartolini, Esq.
Law Offices
Dechert Price & Rhoads
Philadelphia, PA

David M. Blitzer
Vice President & Chief Economist
Standard & Poor's Corporation
New York, NY

Michele R. Bourgerie, CPA
National Director of Personal
 Financial Planning
Arthur Young
New York, NY

Bonnie Briskin
Stockbroker
Tucker, Anthony & R.L. Day, Inc.
Boston, MA

Jin Wook Choi, Ph.D.
Advisory Economist, Economic
 Analysis & Planning
Chicago Board of Trade
Chicago, IL

George Domolky
Portfolio Manager
Fidelity Management & Research
 Company
Boston, MA

Allan R. Emkin
Vice President
Wilshire Associates
Santa Monica, CA

Mitchell S. Farkas
Vice President
Manager, CMA Marketing
Merrill Lynch, Pierce, Fenner &
 Smith Inc.
New York, NY

Steven Flagg
Research Coordinator
PaineWebber Incorporated
New York, NY

Stephanie R. Goldsborough
Treasury Officer, Private Investment
 Group
Maryland National Bank
Baltimore, MD

Reg Green
Editor, *Mutual Fund News Service*
San Francisco, CA

Kathleen Hegenbart
Vice President
Financial Consultant
Shearson Lehman Brothers
Newton Centre, MA

Steven J. Hueglin
Executive Vice President
Gabriele, Hueglin & Cashman
New York, NY

Neal Litvack
Marketing Manager, Retail Services
Fidelity Management & Research
  Company
Boston, MA

Richard Mazur
Vice President, Research Marketing
PaineWebber Incorporated
New York, NY

Thomas J. McAllister, CFP
President
McAllister Financial Planning
Indianapolis, IN

Merrill Lynch
  Asset Management, Inc.
Princeton, NJ

Irwin H. Metzger
Vice President
Merrill Lynch, Pierce, Fenner &
  Smith Inc.
New York, NY

J. Kendrick Noble, Jr.
First Vice President
PaineWebber Incorporated
New York, NY

Henry Nothnagel
First Vice President—Retail Marketing
Chicago Board Options Exchange
Chicago, IL

Ray Ozyjowski
Regional Sales Coordinator
PaineWebber Incorporated
New York, NY

T. Boone Pickens, Jr.
Founder & General Partner
Mesa Limited Partnership
Amarillo, TX and
Founder & Chairman
United Shareholders Association
Washington, DC

Marilyn J. Pitchford, CPA
Partner
Arthur Young
Boston, MA

J. Blaine Reeve, CFA
Senior Vice President
Commerce Union Bank
Nashville, TN

Katherine L. Robinson
Assistant Vice President
Kidder, Peabody & Company
Boston, MA

John T. Scully
General Partner
Post 63 Partners
Pacific Stock Exchange
San Francisco, CA

Robert G. Segel
Managing Director
Tucker, Anthony & R. L. Day, Inc.
Boston, MA

Gene Walden
Contributor, *Investor's Daily*,
  Financial Planning, and
  Corporate Report
Minneapolis, MN

Herbert F. Wass
Vice President
Federal Reserve Bank of Boston
Boston, MA

Rudolph D. Watz, CLU, ChFC
Vice President & Director of
  Retirement Plans
Value Line Securities, Inc.
New York, NY

Martin E. Zweig
Editor
The Zweig Forecast
New York, NY

Preface

The stock market is but a mirror which . . . provides an image of the underlying or *fundamental* economic situation. Cause and effect run from the economy to the stock market, never the reverse.

—John Kenneth Galbraith
The Great Crash, 1929

When we reach for words to describe the business of life and the world of business, we tend to invade the Seven Liberal Arts, and sometimes call upon the Seven Deadly Sins.

—Robert Warren Kent, Ph.D.
Money Talks

The language of Wall Street, like the market's performance, reflects ongoing changes in the economy and in society as a whole. Investing—always a dynamic field fraught with risk—has never sustained more radical changes than those witnessed in the last few years. Investors have been confronted with a host of new products and services in volatile, highly competitive markets, complex new avenues of investment opportunity in a global economy, and a substantially altered federal tax code. They have observed scandal and corruption on Wall Street resulting in greater regulation of the securities markets, increased use of sophisticated communications technology, and a rash of corporate mergers, takeovers, buybacks, and restructurings. *Business Week* recently noted that "terrified of the new world of options, stock indexes, and program trading, individuals have been seeking the sanctuary of professional investment managers." *Wall Street Words*, a reference book of over 3,600 investment terms and 87 "tips" from 32 experts, addresses the individual investor's need to understand the language of the changing market in order to make reasoned, prudent decisions in the marketplace. It is to the individual investors that *Wall Street Words* is dedicated; yet the book is an essential reference source for the professionals in the field—the brokers, dealers, traders, analysts, planners, consultants, bankers, and others who drive the markets.

Although a small core of investing vocabulary has remained virtually unchanged through the years, overall it has been dramatically expanded and altered by a steady influx of new terms and new meanings, many of which are not readily understandable to the uninitiated. This book—the only one of its kind that is based on the terminology encountered in transcripts from *Wall $treet Week with Louis Rukeyser* and other financial broadcasts, *The Wall Street Journal*, *Business Week*, *Forbes*, *Barron's*, *Fortune*, *Investor's Daily*, and various newsletters—tracks the words of stock and bond trading, options and futures trading, brokerage, financial planning, technical analysis, banking and investment banking, accounting and finance, economics and business law, taxation, insurance, and corporate structure/operations. *Wall Street Words* contains many terms not found in other works of this type, e.g., *preopening indication, auction-rate preferred stock, CARS, LIONS, automated stock trading, electronic funds transfer, sweep account, flip-over pill, suicide pill, ethical fund*, and *vulture fund*.

The words are entered in strict alphabetical order with brief phrasal meanings, often followed by full sentences expanding on the meanings. Many entries are supplemented with "case study" paragraphs that provide actual accounts of the strategies, maneuvers, procedures, laws, concepts, or actions represented by the entry words and their meanings. For instance, at *program trading* you will find a detailed account of this activity and a description of its impact on the markets; at *Tax Reform Act of 1986*, an analysis of the initial and projected effects of the new legislation; at *insider trading*, a case history; and at *greenmail*, another case history with reportage of aftereffects. These paragraphs, unique to *Wall Street Words*, are intended to offer the investor information not readily obtained in a single reference source, certainly not one devoted to the language that is "heard on the Street."

Still another unique feature of the book is the inclusion of brief "tips" from the experts, such as the ones found at *clone fund, bear market, bond swap, cash value life insurance, concept company, devaluation, interest rate futures, load fund, no-load fund, put, takeover*, and *zero-coupon bond*. These "tips," appearing throughout the book near the entries to which they relate, have been prepared by brokers, traders, bankers, financial planners, attorneys, accountants, securities analysts, economists, financial writers, and chief executive officers. The writers of the "tips" answer some of the questions most often asked by individual investors.

Wall Street Words is the culmination of three years' research and writing, augmented by the work of a number of other people, especially my editor, Anne Soukhanov. Anne is America's most organized, thoughtful, and convincing person; to say that this book would not have been possible without her is a classic understatement. She took my original idea and crafted it into something that I feel is much better. I would also like to thank the contributors of the investment "tips." Their insights give *Wall Street Words* its distinctive character. To John T. Scully, Robert S Pirie, and Gerald C. Meyers, who read the proofs and offered valuable advice before publication, thanks. My gratitude to Houghton Mifflin Reference Department editors David R. Pritchard, Pamela B. DeVinne, Susan M. Innes, James P. Marciano, and Rosemary E. Previte who checked and corrected proof, and to production manager Christopher Leonesio who directed the book through keyboarding into final pages. And now, as the triple witching hour draws near, I would like to thank the Graduate Research Advisory Committee at Valdosta State College, which provided financial assistance for this project.

David L. Scott, Ph.D.

Valdosta, Georgia
January 1988

A

a **1.** —Used in the dividend column of stock transaction tables in newspapers to indicate a cash payment in addition to regular dividends during the year: *2.75a.* **2.** —Used in money market mutual fund transaction tables in newspapers to indicate a yield that may include capital gains and losses as well as current interest: *AmCap Reserv a.*

A **1.** —Used in earnings reports in newspapers to identify the primary market of a firm's common stock as the American Stock Exchange. **2.** An upper-medium grade assigned to a debt obligation by a rating agency. Such a rating indicates a strong capacity to pay interest and repay principal; however, this capacity is susceptible to impairment in the event of adverse developments.

AA/Aa A high grade assigned to a debt obligation by a rating agency. Such a rating indicates a very strong capacity to pay interest and repay principal. An AA rating indicates only slightly lower quality than the top rating of AAA.

AAA The highest grade assigned to a debt obligation by a rating agency. Such a rating indicates an unusually strong capacity to pay interest and repay principal. —Also called *triple A.*

abandonment —See EXPIRATION.

ABC Agreement An agreement between a firm that finances a seat on the New York Stock Exchange and the employee who purchases the seat. The agreement, approved by the Exchange, permits the member to (1) transfer the seat to another employee of the member firm, (2) keep the seat and purchase a second membership for another individual designated by the lending firm, or (3) sell the membership with proceeds given to the member firm. ABC Agreements are used because of an exchange restriction against organizations rather than individuals being members.

above par Designating a security that sells at more than face value or par value. For example, a $1,000 par bond trading at a market price of $1,050 is selling above par. A fixed-income security is most likely to sell above par if market rates of interest have declined since the time the security was issued. Bonds purchased above par will result in capital loss to the buyer if held to maturity and redeemed at face value. —See also BELOW PAR; PREMIUM 2; PREMIUM BOND.

abusive tax shelter A tax shelter in which an improper interpretation of the law is used to produce tax benefits that are clearly disproportionate to economic reality.

Accelerated Cost Recovery System (ACRS) An accounting technique for calculating the depreciation of tangible assets on the basis of the estimated-life classifications into which the assets are placed. ACRS was initiated by the Economic Recovery Act of 1981. The goal was to make investments more profitable by sheltering large amounts of income from taxation during the early years of an asset's life. The initial law established classifications of 3, 5, 10, and 15 years; these classifications were subsequently modified to longer ones in order to reduce depreciation and increase the government's tax revenues. The classification into which an asset is placed determines the percentage of the cost potentially recoverable in each year. —See also ACCELERATED DEPRECIATION; STRAIGHT-LINE DEPRECIATION.

accelerated depreciation A method of writing off the cost of a capital asset in which the largest deductions are taken in the early years of the asset's life. The purpose of using accelerated depreciation is to delay taxes to a future date so that cash savings from the deferral can be reinvested to earn additional income. —See also ACCELERATED COST RECOVERY SYSTEM; STRAIGHT-LINE DEPRECIATION.

acceptance —See BANKER'S ACCEPTANCE.

accommodative monetary policy The Federal Reserve policy of increasing the supply of money to make credit more readily available. An accommodative monetary policy tends to lower interest rates, especially the short-term ones, at the time credit is made plentiful, but such a policy is likely to result eventually in increased inflation and interest rates. —See also MONETARY POLICY; MONETIZE THE DEBT.

account 1. The client of a broker, brokerage firm, or broker-dealer. The client may be a business, an individual investor, or an institutional investor. 2. The record of a client's transactions and investment position. —See also ACCOUNT STATEMENT.

accountant's opinion —See OPINION.

account executive —See REGISTERED REPRESENTATIVE.

accounting period —See FISCAL PERIOD.

Accounting Principles Board (APB) A group of accountants appointed by the American Institute of Certified Public Accountants to determine accounting principles for financial recordkeeping. The APB was terminated in 1973 with the founding of the Financial Accounting Standards Board. —See also APB OPINION.

account number A unique code assigned to each investor's account at a brokerage firm.

accounts payable Amounts of money owed to others. Accounts payable are current liabilities incurred in the normal course of business as a firm purchases supplies, with payment due at a later date. If a firm pays cash for all of its purchases, no accounts payable will appear on the firm's balance sheet.

accounts receivable Money owed to a business by customers who have bought goods or services on credit. Accounts receivable is a current asset that continually turns into cash as customers pay their bills. —Also called *receivables*.

accounts receivable turnover   The number of times in each period that a firm converts credit sales into cash. A high turnover indicates effective granting of credit and collection from customers by the firm's management. Accounts receivable turnover is calculated by dividing the average amount of receivables into annual credit sales. —Also called *receivables turnover*. —See also ACTIVITY RATIO; AGING; COLLECTION PERIOD.

account statement   A periodic statement to the investor showing the investor's investment position at a given point in time and transactions for the investor's account during a given period of time. Unless an investor's account is inactive, an account statement is generally sent at the beginning of each month. Statements for inactive accounts are sent quarterly.

accredited investor   An investor with sufficient income or wealth to be exempted from the 35-person limit in contributing funds to a private limited partnership. An accredited investor must have an annual income of over $200,000 or a net worth of $1 million, or the investor must purchase $150,000 or more of the offering with the investment representing 20% or less of his or her net worth.

accretion   The accumulation of capital gains on discount bonds with the expectation that the securities will be redeemed at maturity. Excluding municipals, the amount of annual accretion is taxable on an original issue discount bond even though only a small amount of interest or no interest at all is paid each year. —See also IMPUTED INTEREST.

accrual accounting   A method of accounting that recognizes expenses when incurred and revenue when earned rather than when payment is made or received. Thus, it is the act of sending the goods or receiving an inventory item that is important in determining when transactions are posted on financial statements. For example, using accrual accounting, sales are recorded as revenue when goods are shipped even though payment is not expected for days, weeks, or months in the future. Most firms use the accrual basis of accounting in recording transactions. —See also CASH BASIS ACCOUNTING.

accrued expense   An expense incurred but not yet paid. A firm incurs certain expenses such as wages, interest, and taxes that are paid only periodically. From the time the expenses are incurred until the date they are paid, they build up in a firm's balance sheet as accrued expenses.

accrued interest   Interest owed but not yet paid. Accrued interest is listed as a liability on corporate balance sheets. It is also added to the price at which bonds are traded. For example, if a 12% coupon bond is now trading at a price of $950 and the last record date for an interest payment was 2 months ago, the buyer must pay the seller $20 (2 months' interest at 1% per month on $1,000 principal) in accrued interest in addition to the quoted price. This additional expense will be recovered when the new owner receives six months' interest after holding the bond only four months.

accrued market discount The gain in the value of a bond that occurs because the bond has been bought at a discount from face value. For example, a $1,000-par bond maturing in 10 years and selling at $800 can be expected to rise gradually in price over its remaining life. The accrued market discount is the portion of any price rise caused by the gradual increase (as opposed to an increase caused by a fall in interest rates).

accumulate To purchase a relatively large amount of stock in a firm over a period of time. —See also DISTRIBUTE.

accumulated depreciation The total amount of depreciation that has been recorded for an asset since its date of acquisition. For example, a computer with a 5-year estimated life that was purchased for $2,000 would have accumulated depreciation of $800 [($2,000/5) × 2] and a book value of $1,200 ($2,000 − $800) after 2 years of using straight-line depreciation. —Also called *depreciation reserve.*

accumulated dividend —See DIVIDENDS IN ARREARS.

accumulated earnings tax A federal tax on a company's retained earnings that are considered in excess of what is reasonable. The purpose of an accumulated earnings tax is to make it more difficult to defer or lower the tax rate (i.e., change from ordinary income to capital gains) on income that would ordinarily be paid to stockholders in dividends. For example, stockholders in high tax brackets generally prefer that earnings be retained rather than paid in dividends so that they can avoid current taxation at ordinary rates. The position of the Internal Revenue Service is that if the funds are not actually needed by the firm and are only being retained for tax reasons, the accumulated earnings should be taxed.

accumulation area In technical analysis, a rectangular-shaped chart formation caused by insiders and other knowledgeable investors who purchase shares of stock from the public. If an accumulation area can be identified, it indicates a time to buy. An accumulation area is generally characterized by little price movement and relatively heavy volume. —See also DISTRIBUTION AREA; RECTANGLE; REVERSAL PATTERN.

acid-test ratio —See QUICK RATIO.

acquisition The purchase of an asset, such as a plant, a division, or even an entire company. For example, General Motors made a major acquisition in 1984 when it purchased Electronic Data Systems Corporation in order to gain expertise in the computer services market.

ACRS —See ACCELERATED COST RECOVERY SYSTEM.

acting in concert Two or more investors acting together to achieve a common goal. For example, a number of relatively large investors may accumulate a major position in a security in an attempt to influence management decisions.

active Pertaining to a security in which there is a great deal of trading. Active securities appeal to many investors because they are easier to trade without affecting the price. In over-the-counter trading, an active security normally has a smaller spread between the bid and ask price. —See also MOST-ACTIVE STOCKS.

⚠ In September of 1986 the stock of USX Corp. (formerly United States Steel), amid rumors of an impending takeover or of possible corporate restructuring, became what is called very active. Over 15 million shares, or 6%, of all USX's outstanding stock were traded, thus making it the most active stock on the New York Stock Exchange (NYSE) on September 17. The extent of the activity in USX is illustrated by the fact that trading in its stock represented approximately 10% of all trades on the NYSE that day. During the day, a 4-million-share block as well as a 2-million-share block changed hands.

active bond crowd Members of the New York Stock Exchange who trade frequently in active bonds. —See also CABINET CROWD.

active box —See OPEN BOX.

active investment management The management of an investment portfolio that involves active trading of securities in an attempt to produce above-average returns on a risk-adjusted basis. Active management is predicated on the belief that it is possible to beat the market averages consistently. —See also PASSIVE INVESTMENT MANAGEMENT.

active market A securities market or the market for a particular security in which trading is relatively heavy. An active market not only results in more profits for brokers but also helps institutional investors wishing to acquire or dispose of large positions without affecting price.

activity The amount of relative trading volume in a security.

activity ratio A measure of how rapidly a firm is able to convert various accounts into cash or sales. In general, the sooner management can convert assets into sales or cash, the more effectively the firm is being run. —See also ACCOUNTS RECEIVABLE TURNOVER; COLLECTION PERIOD; FIXED ASSET TURNOVER; INVENTORY TURNOVER; TOTAL ASSET TURNOVER.

actual In commodities, the physical asset (i.e., the commodity) as opposed to a futures contract on that asset.

A/D —See ADVANCE-DECLINE LINE.

additional paid-in capital Stockholder contributions in excess of the stock's stated or par value. For example, if a firm issues stock with a par value of $1 per share but sells the stock to investors at $10 per share, the firm's financial statements will show $1 in common stock and $9 in additional paid-in capital for each share issued. —Also called *capital surplus; paid-in surplus.*

add-on Funds that are added to a certificate of deposit after the date of purchase at the same rate of interest as the one on the original certificate. Some savings institutions permit add-ons that provide a real benefit to investors during a period of declining interest rates.

adjustable-rate preferred stock —See FLOATING-RATE PREFERRED STOCK.

adjusted basis The cost or basis at which an asset is acquired, adjusted for certain occurrences since the day of acquisition. For example, stock dividends, stock splits, and dividends deemed to be return on capital result in a downward adjustment in the cost basis of a security. Conversely, commissions result in an upward adjustment in the cost basis. Adjusted basis is used in calculating gains and losses for tax purposes. —See also BASIS 2.

adjusted debit balance   The amount owed a broker by a customer adjusted by paper profits on short sales and balances in a special miscellaneous account. Adjusted debit balance is used to determine if a customer is permitted to withdraw cash or securities from a margin account.

adjusted exercise price   The strike price of put and call options on Government National Mortgage Association (GNMA) pass-through certificates. Because GNMA contracts composed of mortgages at interest rates other than a benchmark rate must be adjusted in price to achieve the benchmark, the exercise prices of options on the contracts must also be adjusted to achieve an exercise price producing GNMA contracts yielding the benchmark interest rate.

adjusted gross income   An individual's gross income less certain allowed business-related deductions, which include alimony payments, contributions to a Keogh retirement plan, and in some cases, contributions to an IRA. Adjusted gross income and gross income will be the same for many taxpayers. —See also ADJUSTMENTS TO INCOME.

adjustment   1. —See DIVIDEND ADJUSTMENT.   2. —See INTEREST ADJUSTMENT.

adjustment bond   —See INCOME BOND.

adjustment in conversion terms   An alteration in the terms under which a convertible security may be exchanged. For example, if an issuer implements a two-for-one split (resulting in a doubling of the number of shares) in the common stock into which its convertible security may be exchanged, the issuer will nearly always be required to reduce the convertible's conversion price by half. Automatic price adjustments also may be scheduled over the life of a convertible security. Scheduled increases in the conversion price on specific dates would be an example of an automatic adjustment.

adjustments to income   Reductions from a taxpayer's gross income in arriving at adjusted gross income. These adjustments are permitted even if the taxpayer does not itemize deductions during a tax year. Allowable adjustments of particular interest to investors are interest penalties on early savings withdrawals and payments into IRAs and Keogh plans. —See also ADJUSTED GROSS INCOME.

ADR   —See AMERICAN DEPOSITORY RECEIPT.

ad valorem tax   A tax that is computed as a percentage of the value of specific property. For example, many states levy an annual tax on the market value of an investor's securities as of a certain date. —Also called *property tax*.

advance-decline index A cumulative total of the daily number of stock issues advancing in price less the daily number of issues declining in price. Technical analysts use the advance-decline index as a measure of breadth in order to determine the strength of market movements. Movement of the advance-decline index in the same direction as the market confirms the market movement and indicates that the movement will continue.

advance-decline line (A/D) A line on a graph representing the advance-decline index over a period of time. The direction of the advance-decline line is used to confirm movements in a stock or the market.

advance refunding —See PREREFUNDING.

adverse opinion An opinion by a firm's auditors that the firm's financial statements do not accurately present its operating results or financial position. This unusual opinion is a strong warning that investors should be wary. —See also CLEAN OPINION; DISCLAIMER OF OPINION; OPINION; QUALIFIED OPINION; SUBJECT TO OPINION.

Advisers Act —See INVESTMENT ADVISERS ACT OF 1940.

advisors' sentiment The view of market forecasters regarding the future course of security prices. Strong bullish sentiment indicated by investment advisors is often considered a bearish sign, while strong, bearish sentiment is considered a bullish sign. This contrarian technical indicator is based on the theory that when most advisors expect a certain market movement, the opposite movement is most likely to occur. —See also SENTIMENT INDEX.

Should investors take advisors' sentiment seriously? Why?

As with any profession, its members include the good, the poor, and the indifferent. It takes a lot of watching to differentiate one category from the other. However, the aggregate opinion of advisors is invaluable. When their sentiment runs to heavy one-sided extremes, it tends to be wrong. So—beware of the crowd if the consensus approaches unanimity.

Martin E. Zweig, Editor
The Zweig Forecast, *New York, NY*

---

advisory account A brokerage account in which the broker may make limited investment decisions without consulting the customer. Securities traded in the account are confined to those that meet the customer's investment goals. —See also DISCRETIONARY ACCOUNT.

affiliate   One organization that is related to another organization through some type of control or ownership. For example, a U.S.-based company may have a foreign affiliate that handles overseas sales.

affiliated person   A person who is in a position to influence a firm's management decisions. Affiliated persons normally include directors, officers, owners of over 10% of the firm's outstanding stock, and family members or close associates of these groups. —Also called *control person.*

after-hours trading   Trading in securities after the exchanges are closed. After-hours trading often refers to trading a listed security in the over-the-counter market after the exchanges have been closed for the day. This fairly common practice is not illegal.

aftermarket   —See SECONDARY MARKET.

aftertax profit   —See NET INCOME.

aftertax yield   The rate of return on an investment after taxes have been calculated and subtracted. Aftertax yield, as opposed to pretax yield, is generally a preferred basis for comparing investment alternatives.

Why should an investor concentrate on aftertax, rather than pretax yield?

Taxes, after all, are a fundamental cost to the investor and reduce the yield on an investment as surely as any other cost or expense. Therefore, the tax burden on an investment will always be an important factor in determining an investor's true yield. Some investments (for example, municipal bonds) produce income which is not currently subject to federal (and sometimes state and local) income taxes. Thus, it would not be accurate to ignore income taxes when comparing the yield on a municipal bond that produces a 5% return free of income taxes with a corporate bond that produces an 8% return but is subject to federal and state income taxes which may well reduce the 8% yield to 5% or lower. In addition, some investments are subject to state and local taxes other than income taxes such as personal property taxes. Such taxes also erode the yield on an investment and should be taken into account. In short, when comparing investment yields, an aftertax yield comparison will give a more accurate comparison.

Anthony L. Bartolini, Esq.
Dechert Price & Rhoads, Philadelphia, PA

AFUDC   —See ALLOWANCE FOR FUNDS USED DURING CONSTRUCTION.

against the box   —See SHORT AGAINST THE BOX.

aged fail   A contract between broker-dealers that remains unsettled 30 days after the settlement date. A security subject to an aged fail may no longer be counted as an asset by the receiving firm.

agency   **1.** A security issued by a federal agency or federally-sponsored corporation. —See also FEDERAL AGENCY SECURITY; FEDERALLY-SPONSORED CORPORATE SECURITY. **2.** A relationship between an agent and a principal in which the agent acts for and represents the principal on the basis of the principal's instructions.

agent   An individual or organization that acts on behalf of and is subject to the control of another party. For example, in executing an order to buy or sell a security, a broker is acting as a customer's agent.

aggregate exercise price   In options trading, an option contract's exercise price multiplied by the number of securities specified in the contract. For example, a call option on 100 shares of ITT common stock at an exercise price of $65 has an aggregate exercise price of 100 × $65, or $6,500. The aggregate exercise price of an option on an asset other than stock is calculated in a similar manner.

aggressive   Relating or referring to an investment philosophy that seeks above-average returns by accepting above-average risks. An example of an aggressive investment posture would be confining one's investments to the common stocks of companies in young industries with high growth potential. Likewise, seeking high current yields by purchasing bonds issued by financially weak companies is an example of aggressive investing.

aging   A technique for evaluating the composition of a firm's accounts receivables to determine if irregularities exist. For example, a financial analyst may use aging to determine if a firm carries many overdue debtors that may never pay their bills. Aging involves grouping a firm's accounts receivables according to the length of time that the accounts have been outstanding. —See also ACCOUNTS RECEIVABLE TURNOVER; ACTIVITY RATIO; COLLECTION PERIOD.

agreement among underwriters   A contract signed by members of an underwriting syndicate that specifies the syndicate manager, member liability, and life of the group. —Also called *underwriting agreement*.

AICPA   —See AMERICAN INSTITUTE OF CERTIFIED PUBLIC ACCOUNTANTS.

airport revenue bond   Tax-exempt debt issued by a city, county, state, or airport authority with debt service guaranteed either by general revenues generated by the airport or by lease payments for facilities used by a particular airline. The second type of airport revenue bond depends on the financial strength of the private company and may be more risky (depending on the individual airline) than a bond guaranteed by an airport's general revenues.

all-holders rule   A Securities and Exchange Commission rule prohibiting bidders and target companies from excluding a stockholder or a group of stockholders from a tender offer. —See also EXCLUSIONARY TENDER OFFER.

allied member An officer, a partner, or a stockholder of a member firm of the New York Stock Exchange who is not individually a member. Allied members, bound by special rules, may not trade on the Exchange floor.

alligator An option spread in which the commissions are so large a part of any potential profit that the investor gets eaten alive. Obviously, alligator spreads are of greater benefit to the broker than to the investor.

allocate 1. To spread systematically a single monetary amount over a number of time periods. For example, depreciation allocates the cost of a capital asset over its useful life. 2. To distribute cost or revenue over a number of operations or products. For example, a business must decide how to allocate the costs of running its headquarters over all its operations to determine the profitability of each of those operations.

all-or-none offering A securities offering in which the entire issue must be sold or the securities will be withdrawn from distribution. With an all-or-none offering, no sales are considered final until the issuer has determined that the entire issue has been distributed.

all-or-none order A limit order either to buy or to sell a security, in which the broker is directed to attempt to fill the entire amount of the order or none of it. An all-or-none order differs from a fill-or-kill order in that, with an all-or-none order, immediate execution is not required.

When is an all-or-none order appropriate?

All-or-none can be used to prevent a partial execution resulting in a minimum commission that is inordinately high in relation to the dollar amount of the transaction. The disadvantage of this type of order is the lack of standing on the specialist's book; i.e., the order is usually the last to be executed since it is restricted to amount and remains behind all unrestricted orders at a specified price. The risk of losing a desired trade must be weighed against the savings on commissions.

John T. Scully, General Partner
Post 63 Partners, The Pacific Stock Exchange Incorporated
San Francisco, CA

---

allotment Securities apportioned to members of an underwriting syndicate for resale to investors.

allowance for doubtful accounts A balance sheet account established to offset expected bad debts. If a firm has made a sufficient provision in its allowance for doubtful accounts, reported earnings will not be penalized by bad debts when the bad debts occur. If uncollectible accounts are larger than expected, however, the firm will have to increase the size of the account and reduce reported income. —Also called *allowance for bad debts; reserve for bad debts.*

allowance for funds used during construction (AFUDC) A special income for utilities resulting from an unusual accounting technique that permits firms to calculate income on funds expended in construction projects even though no income is actually earned. Although income is expected to accrue in future years, the utilities move a portion of the expected future income to the present, a technique that results in an overstatement of reported current earnings. Thus, a high proportion of AFUDC to total net income indicates poor current earnings quality and a cause for investor concern.

alpha The mathematical estimate of the return on a security when the return on the market as a whole is zero. Alpha is derived from a in the formula $R_i = a + bR_m$ which measures the return on a security (R_i) for a given return on the market (R_m) where b is beta. —See also BETA; CAPITAL ASSET PRICING MODEL; CHARACTERISTIC LINE.

alternative minimum tax (AMT) A federal tax on taxable income as adjusted for specific tax preference items such as passive losses from tax shelters and interest paid on certain municipal bonds. The intent of the tax is to ensure that nearly all individuals pay at least some tax on their incomes. The alternative minimum tax is most likely to apply to individuals with high incomes when a relatively large portion of the income is sheltered from taxation under normal reporting. —Also called *minimum tax.* —See also PRIVATE ACTIVITY BOND.

alternative order A customer order that instructs a broker to complete one of two possible transactions, but not both. For example, an investor holding shares of USX Corp. acquired at $45 may have a price target of $75 but may wish to limit any losses to a maximum of $5 per share. The investor would place a limit order to sell at $75 and a stop order to sell at $40. Whichever occurs first will trigger a transaction and cancel the other part of the order. —Also called *one-cancels-the-other order.*

AMBAC —See AMERICAN MUNICIPAL BOND ASSURANCE CORPORATION.

American Association of Individual Investors An organization that sponsors publications, seminars, and other educational programs for individual investors. This group, established in 1979, has its headquarters in Chicago.

American currency quotation In foreign exchange trading, the value of a foreign currency in terms of the U.S. dollar. For example, if the West German mark is worth 40¢, the American currency quotation would be expressed as .40, meaning there are .4 dollars to the mark. —Also called *multiplier.* —See also EUROPEAN CURRENCY QUOTATION.

American depository receipt (ADR) A negotiable receipt on securities that are being held in custody overseas. ADRs are traded in place of the foreign securities in order to alleviate some difficulties (e.g., transferring certificates overseas or converting currencies) in buying and selling foreign securities.

American Institute of Certified Public Accountants (AICPA) A professional association for Certified Public Accountants providing guidance to members on accounting techniques and standards. The AICPA determines how financial data are calculated and reported to stockholders.

American Municipal Bond Assurance Corporation (AMBAC) A subsidiary of MGIC Investment Corporation, an insurer of residential mortgages, that guarantees interest and principal payments on municipal bond issues. The insurance normally results in a higher bond rating and a correspondingly lower interest rate when the insured bonds are initially sold. —See also MGIC INDEMNITY CORPORATION; MUNICIPAL BOND INSURANCE ASSOCIATION.

American Stock Exchange (AMEX, ASE)® A trademark for an organized exchange in New York City that provides facilities for trading securities of national interest. Since its listing requirements are less stringent than those of the New York Stock Exchange, the AMEX often trades in the securities of younger and smaller firms with fairly volatile price movements. Approximately 1,500 securities are traded on the AMEX. —See also CURB EXCHANGE.

American Stock Exchange Market Value Index A market index composed of all the common stocks and warrants listed on the American Stock Exchange and weighted according to the market value (price × shares listed) of each security. The Index indicates the market movements of more volatile securities, including numerous oil and high technology issues, that tend to be listed on this Exchange. The current version of the Index was established in 1973 with a base of 100. —Also called *ASE Index*.

Americus Shareowner Service Corporation A private corporation that artificially divides shares of certain blue-chip firms into income and capital appreciation components. Stockholders place shares in trust with Americus, at which time Americus issues these stockholders new unit shares. A PRIME unit has the right to all dividends and to appreciation up to a predetermined level. SCORE shares have the right to all capital appreciation above a predetermined level. PRIME and SCORE are traded on the American Stock Exchange. Americus permits the holders of certain stocks to choose between dividends and appreciation.

AMEX® —See AMERICAN STOCK EXCHANGE®.

amortize To write off gradually and systematically a given amount of money over a specific number of time periods. For example, an accountant amortizes the cost of a long-term asset by deducting a portion of that cost against income in each period. Likewise, an investor will normally amortize the premium each year on a bond purchased at a price above its principal.

AMT —See ALTERNATIVE MINIMUM TAX.

analyst —See FINANCIAL ANALYST.

A-network —See NETWORK A.

animals Zero-coupon receipts on U.S. Treasury securities that have been repackaged and sold to investors under names such as CATS®, TIGR℠, and LIONS. —Also called *felines*. —See also COUPON STRIPPING.

annualized Pertaining to a variable that has been mathematically converted to a yearly rate. Inflation and interest rates are generally annualized since it is on this basis that these two variables are ordinarily stated and compared. As an example, disregarding the effects of compounding, the earning of a 3% return on an investment during a 4-month period is equal to 9% (12/4 × 3%) on an annualized basis.

annual meeting The annual gathering of a corporation's directors, officers, and shareholders during which new directors are elected, shareholder resolutions are passed or defeated, and operating and financial results of the past fiscal year are discussed.

Annual reports: how to read between the lines.

To the trained eye, the pages of a corporate annual report offer not only a revealing look at the company's past, but a glimpse into its future. Most securities experts turn first to the back section of the report, where all the financial information is located. Look over the auditor's report—usually a straightforward, two-paragraph letter commenting on the company's financial reporting practices. If the letter goes beyond two paragraphs, that could mean something's askew. Read the letter carefully. Next, look at the income statement, which generally covers the company's income for the past three years. A strong company should show annual increases in both sales and per-share income. A quick glance at the balance sheet will give you a better idea of where the company draws its income, and where it spends it. Other key indicators include book value (shareholders' equity divided by total liabilities), net working capital (current assets minus current liabilities), current ratio (current assets divided by current liabilities), approximate return on equity (subtract net income from shareholders' equity and divide the balance into net income). A strong company will generally show increases in all four of these. In reading through the text in the front of the report, look for information on new products and strategies that could contribute to the company's future success.

Gene Walden, Contributor
Investor's Daily, Financial Planning, *and* Corporate Report
Minneapolis, MN

---

annual report A firm's annual statement of operating and financial results. The annual report contains an income statement, a balance sheet, a statement of changes in financial position, an auditor's report, and a summary of operations. Since many annual reports are prepared with public relations as a prime focus, serious investors should obtain a copy of a firm's 10–K report in order to obtain detailed financial data.

annuitant The recipient of an annuity.

annuity A stream of equal payments, as to a retiree, that occur at predetermined intervals (i.e., monthly or annually). The payments may continue for a fixed period or for a contingent period, such as the recipient's lifetime. Although annuities are most often associated with insurance companies and retirement programs, the payment of interest to a bondholder is also an example of an annuity. —See also ANNUITY CERTAIN; CONTINGENT ANNUITY; DEFERRED ANNUITY; HYBRID ANNUITY; IMMEDIATE ANNUITY; JOINT AND SURVIVOR ANNUITY; PERPETUITY; REFUND ANNUITY; STRAIGHT LIFE ANNUITY; TAX-SHELTERED ANNUITY; VARIABLE ANNUITY.

annuity bond —See CONSOL.

annuity certain An annuity that provides a fixed number of payments. If the annuitant dies prior to the completion of the contract, payments continue to the annuitant's designated beneficiary.

annuity due An annuity in which payments are made at the beginning of each period. —See also ORDINARY ANNUITY.

antidilution clause A stipulation of virtually every convertible security that requires an adjustment in the conversion terms in the event of certain occurrences such as stock splits, stock dividends, and new stock issues that would dilute the value of the conversion privilege. As an example, a bond convertible into 40 shares of stock would have its terms changed to conversion into 120 shares if the stock split 3 for 1.

anti-dilutive Pertaining to the conversion of convertible securities into common stock when such conversion would result in an increase in the fully diluted or primary earnings per share. For example, using warrants to acquire common shares of stock when the amount of funds required to exercise the warrant exceeds the value of the stock is anti-dilutive. Anti-dilutive conversions are not considered in calculating earnings per share.

antigreenmail provision A provision in a firm's charter that prohibits management from purchasing a large shareholder's stock at a premium price without extending the same offer to other shareholders. —See also GREENMAIL.

antitakeover measure An action by a firm's management to make a takeover by another party more difficult or impossible. Examples of antitakeover measures include a fair price amendment, staggered terms of office for directors, and a requirement for an increased number of affirmative votes from shareholders to approve a takeover. —See also SHARK REPELLENT; SHOW STOPPER.

⚠ The 1980s might well be called the Era of the Raiders. In order to fight off potential takeovers, many companies adopted preventive strategies, and Beard Oil Company's maneuvers are typical. For example, in 1986 Beard's shareholders approved a number of antitakeover meas-ures, among them being staggered terms of office for the directors. The annual election of all directors was changed to a system by which two of the six directors would be elected to three-year terms every third year. In addition, the shareholders authorized a significant increase in the amount of common and preferred stock that the firm could sell. They approved a new requirement by which an 80% shareholder vote would be necessary in order to permit a merger proposed by any share-holder owning 10% or more of the company's stock if over 25% of the board of directors had disapproved of the merger. Beard shareholders also ratified an arrangement whereby management was required to obtain their approval if it desired to buy out a holder having over 5% of the company's stock.

antitakeover statute   A state law that makes it easier for a firm based in that state to fend off a takeover hostile to the firm's management. Such a statute may actually penalize shareholders since acquisition-minded firms or individuals may be less likely to make an offer for the firm's stock.

antitrust laws   Federal and state statutes designed to promote compe-tition among businesses. Antitrust laws in the United States originated from the laissez-faire excesses that took place in the early 1900s. Effec-tiveness of antitrust laws is heavily dependent upon enforcement by the powers in charge—primarily the U.S. Justice Department. Thus, the success of antitrust laws has varied over time. —See also CELLER-KEFAU-VER ANTIMERGER ACT; CLAYTON ACT; FEDERAL TRADE COMMISSION ACT OF 1914; SHERMAN ANTITRUST ACT.

APB   —See ACCOUNTING PRINCIPLES BOARD.

APB opinion   A determination by the Accounting Principles Board as to the way a certain financial transaction is to be treated for reporting purposes. For example, APB Opinion 15 sets forth the ways in which convertible issues and common stock equivalents are to be used in cal-culating earnings per share. In 1973 further APB opinions were halted when the Accounting Principles Board was superseded by the Financial Accounting Standards Board. —See also FASB STATEMENT.

application of funds statement   —See STATEMENT OF CHANGES IN FINAN-CIAL POSITION.

appreciation   An increase in value, as of an asset. —Often used to distinguish securities that are likely to provide profits because of in-creases in price as opposed to dividend payments.

approved list   —See LEGAL LIST.

arb   —See ARBITRAGEUR.

arbitrage   The simultaneous purchase and sale of substantially identical assets in order to profit from a price difference between the two assets. As a hypothetical example, if CBS stock trades at $115 on the New York Stock Exchange (NYSE) and at $114 on the Midwest Stock Exchange (MSE), an investor could guarantee a profit by purchasing the stock on the MSE and simultaneously selling the same amount of stock on the NYSE. Of course, the price difference must be sufficiently great to offset commissions. Arbitrage may be employed by using various security combinations including stock and options, convertibles and stock, and so forth. —See also BASIS TRADING; RISK ARBITRAGE.

arbitrage bond A municipal bond issued for the purpose of investing the proceeds in securities with higher yields than those paid by the municipal bond. Generally, the arbitrage involves purchasing U.S. Treasury bonds that are used to prerefund an outstanding issue prior to the outstanding issue's call date.

arbitrageur One who engages in arbitrage. —Also called *arb.*

⚠️ In November of 1986 the Securities and Exchange Commission (SEC) announced that Ivan F. Boesky, one of America's most successful, best known, and wealthiest arbitrageurs, had agreed to plead guilty to one felony count and pay $100 million to settle SEC charges of insider trading. The news produced large trading activity in the securities markets with major declines in junk bonds and stocks involved in actual and possible takeover attempts. Boesky was also barred for life from working in the securities industry. Ivan Boesky's settlement with the SEC apparently ended the career of a successful arbitrageur who had been instrumental in many of the takeovers and buyouts occurring in the early and mid-1980s. During that time, arbitrageurs became the darlings of the financial press as they amassed enormous sums of money to invest in special situations involving takeover candidates. These funds were used in establishing positions in so-called undervalued firms. Once the investment positions were made public by the arbitrageurs, other investors including firms interested in acquiring the undervalued companies were attracted to the stock. As a result, the arbitrageurs were often able to sell the stock to the target firms in buybacks (greenmail) or to other firms in takeovers. In a few instances the arbitrageurs continued to purchase shares and actually took control of the companies. The Boesky settlement put an immediate damper on some of the takeover speculation that had been a major factor driving the securities markets. It also brought calls for additional regulation of the markets.

arbitration The mandatory method of settling disputes between exchange employees and member firms by an impartial third party. Disputes between customers and member firms can be settled by arbitration if requested by the customers. —See also BOARD OF ARBITRATION.

arrearage An overdue payment. —See also DIVIDENDS IN ARREARS.

articles of incorporation The document that a firm files with state authorities in establishing a corporation. This document contains the firm's name and address, the type and amount of stock to be authorized and issued, the type of business activity, a delineation of corporate powers, and other information. —Also called *charter.*

ascending triangle In technical analysis, a triangle-shaped chart formation in which the left side is nearly vertical, the top is nearly horizontal, and the third side slopes upward to the right connecting the other two sides. An ascending triangle is generally viewed as a bullish indicator, especially when the price breaks upward through the top side on high volume. —See also DESCENDING TRIANGLE; TRIANGLE.

ASE —See AMERICAN STOCK EXCHANGE®.

ASE Index —See AMERICAN STOCK EXCHANGE MARKET VALUE INDEX.

ask The price at which a security is offered for sale. —Also called *offer.* —See also BID 1.

assay A test to determine the purity of gold, silver, or other precious metals. Metals used for delivery of futures contracts must be assayed to verify that they meet standards established by the exchange on which the contracts trade.

asset Something of monetary value that is owned by a firm or an individual. Assets include tangible items such as inventories, equipment, and real estate, as well as intangible items such as property rights or goodwill. The balance sheet is the financial statement listing assets. —See also CURRENT ASSET; INTANGIBLE ASSET; LIABILITY; TANGIBLE ASSET.

asset allocation The assignment of investment funds to broad categories of assets. For example, an individual allocates funds to bonds and equities. Likewise, an investment manager may allocate clients' funds to common stocks representing various industries.

asset play A stock with a market price considerably lower than the value of the firm's assets on a per-share basis. For example, a paper company may operate in an extremely competitive market and earn minimal profits. However, a financial analyst may feel that investors are concentrating on poor earnings and are pricing the stock such that extensive and valuable timber and real estate holdings are not reflected in the stock's current market price. Thus, the stock is an asset play.

asset redeployment The reallocation of underutilized assets in an attempt to make a firm more profitable. For example, a company might sell a relatively unprofitable subsidiary and use the funds to strengthen another part of its business. Many corporate takeover attempts are based on the premise that assets will be redeployed once the acquisition has been completed.

asset stripping The sale of selected assets of an acquired company, generally to raise enough money to pay off some of the debt incurred in financing the acquisition.

asset turnover —See TOTAL ASSET TURNOVER.

asset value —Used to refer to the stock of a company having valuable assets that are not necessarily fully reflected in the stock price. This situation may occur when the assets are not producing much current income. —See also ASSET PLAY; UNDERVALUED COMPANY; VALUE INVESTING.

assign To decide which writer of an option or futures contract (the party that is short the security) will be required to perform the terms of the contract. Assignments are normally made in a random manner by clearing corporations and brokerage companies when the holders of the contracts ask for delivery of the asset specified in the contract. —See also UNWELCOME ASSIGNMENT.

assignment   The transfer of a registered security from one owner to another.

associate member   A firm that has certain advantages of membership on the American Stock Exchange without actually owning a seat. Although an associate member may place orders through regular members, an associate member is not permitted to trade for its own account on the Exchange floor. —See also REGULAR MEMBER.

at-risk rule   A rule that limits tax write-offs to the amount of money directly invested (and thus, at risk) in an asset. The purpose of an at-risk rule is to prohibit investors from deriving tax benefits exceeding the amount of money actually invested.

at-the-close order   A specialized order to a broker in which the customer specifies that execution take place at the closing price of the day. In practice, execution is permitted during a closing period of 30 to 60 seconds before the bell.

at-the-money   Pertaining to a call option or put option that has a strike price equal to the price of the underlying asset.

at-the-opening order   A specialized order to a broker in which the customer specifies that execution take place at the opening price of the day.

auction market   A market in which buyers and sellers gather to transact business through announced bid and ask prices. The organized securities exchanges are auction markets. —See also DEALER MARKET.

auction-rate preferred stock   A special type of floating-rate preferred stock on which dividend payments are determined through periodic auctions conducted by the issuer. This kind of stock differs from floating-rate preferred stock on which the dividends are tied to a short-term interest rate.

audit   An examination of an organization's financial documents in order to determine if the records and reports are valid and if the information is fairly presented. An independent audit is normally conducted by a Certified Public Accountant who then issues an opinion as to whether the statements accurately and fairly represent the firm's operations and financial position. —See also EXTERNAL AUDIT; INTERNAL AUDIT; OPINION.

audit committee   A subcommittee of a corporation's board of directors that selects the firm's external auditors. The audit committee is responsible for hiring the auditors, resolving disputes with the auditors, and evaluating and disclosing the auditors' reports.

audited statement   A financial statement prepared as per generally accepted auditing standards. —See also UNAUDITED STATEMENT.

auditor   A person who examines the financial records and reports of an organization. If the person is an employee of the organization being audited, he or she is known as an internal auditor. If the auditor is not an employee of the organization, he or she is called an external auditor.

auditor opinion —See OPINION.

audit trail A record of business transactions permitting an interested party to trace an organization's activities to original documents. Audit trails are used to verify account balances.

Autex An electronic network alerting broker-dealers to the interests of other broker-dealers in buying or selling large blocks of securities. For example, a broker may have an institutional customer interested in disposing of 100,000 shares of a stock. Rather than dumping such a large order on the exchange specialist, the broker could use the Autex system to determine if other broker-dealers are interested in, or have customers interested in acquiring that block of stock.

authority A government organization created to perform a certain function. For example, a state or region may establish a public power authority to provide low-cost electricity to people living in a certain geographical area. The activities of an authority and its fund-raising methods are ordinarily limited.

authority bond A bond issued by an authority with interest and principal payable only from revenues generated by the authority. The quality of the authority bond is only as good as the quality of the projects sponsored by the authority. —See also REVENUE BOND.

authorization to transfer A form signed by a customer permitting a broker to transfer funds from a segregated account to a nonsegregated account, both of which belong to that customer. The purpose of the transfer is normally to cover a shortage of funds in a margin account with funds that the customer has in a separate account.

authorized capital stock The number of shares of capital stock that a business may issue. Authorized capital stock is stated in a firm's articles of incorporation; changes in it may occur only if approved by the stockholders. The number of shares authorized often greatly exceeds the number actually issued. In this way, management can issue more shares to raise additional funds or it can use the shares for making an acquisition. —Also called *shares authorized*. —See also ISSUED CAPITAL STOCK; OUTSTANDING CAPITAL STOCK.

Automated Search and Match A New York Stock Exchange system designed to uncover individual affiliations that might indicate possible insider trading. The system contains public data on approximately 500,000 business executives and 75,000 companies and subsidiaries.

automated stock trading The trading of securities without direct assistance from a broker or specialist. Generally, automated stock trading involves investor trading of securities via computer. Security bid and ask prices are listed and are continually updated with executions occurring automatically when the orders are entered. While fully automatic trading has been restricted primarily to professional and institutional investors, increasing numbers of brokerage firms are now offering some automation for individual investors. —Also called *computerized investing*. —See also INSTINET®; NATIONAL SECURITIES TRADING SYSTEM; SOES.

automatic dividend reinvestment —See DIVIDEND REINVESTMENT PLAN.

automatic reinvestment The automatic purchase of additional shares of an open-end investment company with any dividends and capital gains distributions that are made by the firm. This option (in lieu of actually receiving the payments) permits a mutual fund shareholder to increase his or her holdings in the fund. Taxes still must be paid on the amount reinvested even though no funds are received directly. —See also DIVIDEND REINVESTMENT PLAN.

Should mutual fund shareholders choose automatic reinvestment, and if so, why?

Many financial experts agree that most successful investing programs begin with a plan for investing regularly. Making periodic investments is a systematic way of saving for future financial goals, such as an early retirement, the purchase of a new home, or a child's education. Many firms now provide the service of automatically transferring funds from a bank account—either monthly or quarterly—to a fund account. They also send confirmation of the transaction. To discontinue the service at any time, one simply needs to make the request in writing.

Neal Litvack, Marketing Manager
Fidelity Investments, Boston, MA

---

automatic withdrawal A feature of some mutual funds allowing a shareholder to specify that the fund remit fixed payments at periodic intervals. The payments are composed of dividends, interest, and capital gains received by the fund, and, if these are insufficient, liquidation of some shares owned by the shareholder.

AUTOPER An electronic trading and reporting system used by the American Stock Exchange for small orders. AUTOPER allows a specialist to execute an order and report the trade automatically.

available asset A person's or a firm's asset that is not being used as collateral for a loan and is therefore available for general use or for sale.

average —See AVERAGES.

average collection period —See COLLECTION PERIOD.

average cost Total cost divided by units of production. Thus, if a firm produces 10,000 units of output for a total cost of $25,000, the average cost of each unit is $25,000/10,000 units, or $2.50. Average cost is made up of costs remaining unchanged over a wide range of output and costs varying directly with output. Firms with the lowest average cost in an industry are in an advantageous competitive position in the event of severe competition and price cutting. —See also FIXED COST; MARGINAL COST; VARIABLE COST.

average-cost method A method of valuing inventory in which unit cost is calculated by dividing the number of units available for sale into the total cost of goods available for sale. —See also FIRST-IN, FIRST-OUT; INVENTORY VALUATION; LAST-IN, FIRST-OUT; LOWER OF COST OR MARKET.

average down To purchase shares of the same security at successively lower prices in order to reduce the average price at which the stock was acquired. If an investor purchases 100 shares of Westinghouse common stock at $40 per share and the price subsequently falls to $30 per share, the purchase of an additional 100 shares would reduce the investor's average cost to $35 per share. Opponents of this strategy argue that the investor is simply throwing good money after bad money and would be better advised to sell the stock, having realized that a mistake had been made to begin with. —See also AVERAGE UP.

average life —See HALF-LIFE.

averages Stock price measures calculated and distributed by a number of organizations including Dow Jones, Standard & Poor's, and organized securities exchanges. The two major stock price measures are the Dow Jones Averages and the Standard & Poor's 500. —Also called *average; market averages; market index; stock average.* —See also INDEX.

average up To purchase shares of the same security at successively higher prices. When averaging up, the investor accumulates an increasingly larger position in a security while keeping the average cost of the position lower than the security's current market price. Such an investor will earn significant profits only if the stock price continues to rise. The investor will suffer substantial losses if the stock price quickly drops after he or she has established a large position at increasingly higher prices. —See also AVERAGE DOWN.

averaging —See DOLLAR-COST AVERAGING.

away —Used to refer to a market, quotation, or trade not originating with a particular dealer. For example, a dealer might quote a stock at 15 away, meaning that the price comes from a different market maker.

away from the market —Used to refer to a security order at a price not immediately available. A limit order to buy 100 shares of Chrysler at $37 is away from the market if Chrysler stock is currently trading at $41 per share.

B

b —Used in the dividend column of stock transaction tables in newspapers to indicate payment of a stock dividend in addition to the indicated cash dividend: *1.50b*.

B **1.** —Used in earnings reports in newspapers to identify the Boston Stock Exchange as the primary market of a firm's common stock. **2.** A low, speculative grade assigned to a debt obligation by a rating agency. A rating of B indicates that there is considerable uncertainty as to the ability to pay interest and repay principal over a long period.

Ba —See BB.

Baa —See BBB.

baby bond A bond with a principal amount under $1,000. Baby bonds may be issued by firms hoping to attract investors who do not have funds to purchase bonds with $1,000 principal. On occasion, bonds of less than $1,000 principal are issued as part of a corporate refunding. Because baby bonds are unusual, they may be more expensive to trade.

backdating The permitting of a mutual fund shareholder to use previous purchases of the fund's shares in qualifying for reduced commission charges on subsequent purchases. Backdating is used when a fund offers declining proportional sales charges on larger purchases.

back-end load —See DEFERRED SALES CHARGE.

backing away The failure of a market maker to honor a previous bid for a minimum quantity of a security. The National Association of Securities Dealers considers backing away unethical.

back office The physical location within a business where records are kept and processed. In the case of a brokerage firm, the back office includes the section where individual account records are kept, checks are processed, and security certificates are sent. —Also called *operations department*.

back up To swap a debt security of one maturity for another security with a shorter maturity.

backwardation —See INVERTED MARKET.

bad delivery Delivery of a security that fails to meet all the standards required to transfer title to the buyer. —See also GOOD DELIVERY; RECLAMATION.

bail out To sell a security, generally at a loss, in anticipation of a further price decline.

bailout The financial rescue of a faltering business or other organization. Government guarantees for loans made to Chrysler Corporation constituted a bailout.

balanced budget A budget in which the expenditures incurred during a given period are matched by revenues.

balanced fund An investment company that spreads its investments among stocks and bonds. Essentially, a balanced fund is a middle-of-the-road fund that balances its portfolio to achieve both moderate income and moderate capital growth.

balance of payments The flow of money payments between one country and other countries. Balance of payments is more inclusive than balance of trade because balance of payments includes foreign investment, loans, and other cash flows as well as payments for goods and services. A country's balance of payments has a significant effect on its currency value in relation to other currencies. It is of particular interest to individuals owning foreign investments or owning domestic investments in companies dependent upon exports.

Why are valuable assets often hidden on a firm's balance sheet?

Because the balance sheet is stated at historical cost rather than current market, land and buildings bought in 1950, for example, may appear to be worth virtually nothing compared with identical real estate bought at today's inflated fair market values. Certain intrinsic assets are hidden and may not even be on the balance sheet. For example, the costs of patents and technology developed by a computer manufacturer will generally be written off, and the costs incurred in developing name recognition as an industry leader are never really known. The value of these hidden assets may never be quantified until a business is sold. An astute investor, knowledgeable about companies in a particular industry, may be able to spot a bargain by simply knowing the accounting treatment of significant items or knowing how long a company has operated in its present facilities. It may be hard to define value, but if you know what to look for, you know when it's there. Interestingly enough, the corporate headquarters of a large company may not recognize the real value of one of its smaller divisions, especially if corporate overhead allocations have reduced division profits over the years. If a decision is made to streamline operations, the division may be a natural target for sale. The employees running the division often have the best knowledge of asset values and business potential, as well as the adverse effects of corporate allocations (they have complained to headquarters about the allocation for years). If the employees have an entrepreneurial bent, they may be well advised to capitalize on their knowledge of unrecognized value by structuring a buy-out of the division.

Marilyn J. Pitchford, CPA
Arthur Young, Boston, MA

---

balance of trade The net amount of exports less imports for a specific period of time. If the net amount is positive, i.e., exports exceed imports, the balance is generally considered favorable. Conversely, a negative balance is said to be unfavorable. A country's balance of trade position has great impact on economic activity and the profits of companies operating in the country. —See also TRADE DEFICIT; TRADE SURPLUS.

balance sheet The financial statement of a business or institution that lists the assets, debts, and owners' investment as of a specific date. Assets are listed in the order of how soon they will be converted into cash, and debts in the order of how soon they must be paid. Since balance sheets do not list items at their current monetary value, they may greatly overstate or understate the real value of certain corporate assets and liabilities. —Also called *statement of financial condition; statement of financial position.* —See also CONSOLIDATED BALANCE SHEET.

balloon interest Higher interest on the longer maturity bonds of a serial bond issue.

balloon payment A final payment on a loan that is significantly larger than the payments preceding it. For example, a bond issuer may redeem 3% of the original issue each year for 20 years and then retire the remaining 40% in the year of maturity.

BAN —See BOND ANTICIPATION NOTE.

bank discount basis A method of quoting the yield on a debt security in which the amount of discount from face value is divided by the security's face value with the result annualized. For example, a $10,000 face amount bond due in 2 months and selling for $9,900 would be quoted at ($100/$10,000) (360/60), or 6%. While this is a common way of quoting yields on certain securities such as Treasury bills and commercial paper, it actually understates the effective rate paid. —Also called *discount basis; discount yield.* —See also EQUIVALENT BOND YIELD.

banker's acceptance A short-term credit instrument created by a non-financial firm and guaranteed by a bank as to payment. Acceptances are traded at discounts from face value in the secondary market on the basis of the credit quality of the guaranteeing banks. These instruments have become a popular investment for money market funds. —Also called *acceptance.*

bank grade —See INVESTMENT-GRADE.

bank holding company A corporation that owns the stock of one or more banks and thus exercises control over the bank or banks. —See also HOLDING COMPANY.

Banking Act of 1933 —See GLASS-STEAGALL ACT.

bank line —See LINE OF CREDIT.

banknote Currency issued and guaranteed by a bank. The sole issuer of banknotes in the United States is the Federal Reserve Bank.

bankruptcy In the legal sense, the condition of a firm when its debts (i.e., what it owes) exceed its assets (i.e., what it owns) or when the firm is unable to pay its bills. Formal bankruptcy may result in reorganization and continued operation of the firm or it may require liquidation and distribution of the proceeds. In either case, most security owners, especially shareholders, are likely to suffer losses. Stock transaction tables indicate that a company is in bankruptcy proceedings by appending the symbols *vi* or *q* immediately before the name of the stock. —See also CHAPTER 7; CHAPTER 11; REORGANIZATION.

Banks for Cooperatives (COOP) Twelve regional, privately owned, government-sponsored banks that make loans to farm cooperatives. The loans are financed primarily by the sale to investors of debt securities issued by the Federal Farm Credit Bank.

bar chart A graph displaying an economic variable (normally a stock price) with time measured on the horizontal axis and the value of the variable measured on the vertical axis. In a bar chart of a stock price, the high and low prices for the period are connected by a vertical line. A short horizontal slash is drawn across the bar at the closing price. Bar charts are the graphs most frequently used by technicians. —Also called *vertical line chart*. —See also CHARTING; LINE CHART; POINT-AND-FIGURE CHART.

Barron's Confidence Index A measure of investor confidence calculated by dividing the yield on intermediate-grade bonds into the yield on high-grade bonds. A rising ratio indicates that investors are demanding a lower premium in yield for increased risk, thus expressing confidence in the economy and the securities markets. A rising Index is considered bullish for stocks; a falling Index is considered bearish for stocks. —See also CONFIDENCE INDICATOR; STANDARD & POOR'S CONFIDENCE INDICATOR.

base year The year on which an index is based. Normally, the base year is set at an index value of 100 (sometimes 10). The consumer price index of 316 in January 1985 indicated that, on average, an item costing $100 in 1967 (the base year), cost $316 in 1985. —See also INDEX.

basis **1.** In futures trading, the difference between the futures price and the spot price. The basis will narrow as a contract moves closer to settlement. **2.** In taxation, the acquisition cost of an asset, adjusted for capital distributions (i.e., stock dividends). A security's basis is used in calculating gains and losses for tax purposes. —Also called *tax basis*. —See also ADJUSTED BASIS.

basis book A book of tables that converts bond yields for given maturity lengths and coupon rates to equivalent dollar prices. —Also called *bond basis book*.

basis grade The specified grade for a commodity in order for the commodity to be acceptable for delivery on a futures contract.

basis point One one-hundredth of a percent (1/100 of 1%). Basis point is used to measure yield differences among bonds. For example, there is a 30 basis point difference between two bonds if one yields 10.3% and the other yields 10.6%. —See also SPREAD 4.

basis price **1.** The price of a security quoted in terms of its yield rather than its dollar price. Bonds are often quoted on a basis price reflecting yield to maturity since this particular information is of greatest importance to an investor deciding to buy or sell. **2.** The price selected by a specialist at which to execute an odd-lot order on an inactive stock. The large spread on inactive stocks often results in a basis price that splits the difference between the bid and ask.

basis risk The risk that a commodity contract's basis will move against the investor. For example, an investor may buy a spot contract and sell short a higher-priced futures contract on the same commodity in expectation of a narrowing of the basis but may find that the basis widens instead.

basis trading An arbitrage operation in which an investor takes a long position in one security and a short position in a different but similar security in an attempt to profit from a change in the basis between the two securities. For example, an investor might purchase a call with an April expiration and simultaneously sell short a call with a different expiration or strike price on the same stock. The investor expects that the values of the two positions will change over time such that a profit will ensue. Basis trading is undertaken when the investor feels one security is priced too high or too low relative to the price of another security. Because of this the profit on one side of the trade should more than cancel out the loss on the opposite side of the trade. Basis trading may involve baskets of securities as well as individual securities. Thus, an investor may purchase an index or a group of securities and simultaneously sell short an index or a group of securities. —Also called *relationship trading.* —See also PROGRAM TRADING.

batch trading A trading system for securities in which orders accumulate over a period of time and then, at specified times, are executed all at once. An example of batch trading in the United States occurs on opening transactions when orders received after the previous day's close are executed all at one time. Otherwise, batch trading is not used in the U.S. securities markets. —See also CONTINUOUS TRADING.

BB/Ba A higher-speculative grade assigned to a debt obligation by a rating agency. Such a rating indicates significant speculative elements and a moderate ability to pay interest and repay principal.

BBB/Baa A medium-grade assigned to a debt obligation by a rating agency. Such a rating indicates an adequate ability to pay interest and repay principal; however, adverse developments are more likely to impair this ability than would be the case for bonds rated A and above. A BBB or Baa rating is the lowest category in which a bond can be considered investment grade.

BD form A document containing information on a firm's officers and capital that is filed by broker-dealers with the Securities and Exchange Commission.

bear An investor who believes a security (or some other asset) or the security markets in general will follow a broad downward path. An investor can often be a bear on a particular security but not on the general market, and vice versa. —See also BULL.

bearer bond A debt instrument having no owner's name on the issuer's books and no name inscribed on the certificate. Since no record of ownership exists, bearer bonds are favored by investors wishing to illegally avoid gift, estate, and local taxes. Issuance of new municipal bonds in bearer form was prohibited beginning in 1983. —Also called *coupon bond*. —See also COUPON CLIPPING.

bearer form —Used to refer to any security not registered to an owner on the books of the issuing organization. Essentially, a security in bearer form is owned by the person holding the security. —See also REGISTERED SECURITY.

How to avoid being mauled—and even turn a profit—in a bear market. What are the best types of investment choices in such a market?

A bear market is upon us when we experience a prolonged period of falling prices. Some ways to avoid being mauled by such an animal are these:

1. Spread your risk over at least five or six different investment positions and types of investment. For example, a real estate limited partnership should do well in a rising interest rate environment which may offset a decrease in bond prices.
2. Choose less volatile stocks, the value of which will hold better in a down market. While you may not have as high an upside potential, you may not have as much downside risk.
3. Set objectives for your portfolio. On the day you buy, have an agreement with your financial consultant as to where you want to sell on both the upside and the downside, and stick with it.

Remember it's a market of stocks, not just a stock market. Correct picks and strategies in a bear market can still make money.

Kathleen Hegenbart, Vice President, Financial Consultant
Shearson Lehman Brothers, Newton Centre, MA

---

bearer stock Ownership certificates not registered in a name. As is the case with other bearer securities, bearer stock is a negotiable certificate that can be transferred between owners without endorsement. Bearer stock is popular in Europe but not in the United States.

bear hug A buyout offer so favorable to stockholders of an acquisition target company that there is little likelihood they will refuse the offer. Not only does a bear hug offer a price significantly above the market price of the target company's stock, but it is likely to offer cash payments as well. —See also TAKEOVER.

bearish Feeling that a particular stock or the market as a whole is headed for a period of generally falling prices. —See also BULLISH.

bear market An extended period of general price declines, in an individual security or other asset, such as silver or real estate, a group of securities, or the securities market as a whole. Nevertheless, even during widespread bear markets, it is possible to have bull markets in particular stocks or groups of stocks. For example, stocks of gold-related companies often move against major trends in the security markets. —See also BULL MARKET.

bear raid A concerted effort to drive down the price of a stock by selling many shares short. The bear raid was popular among speculators in the early 1900s. A bear raid would frequently be accompanied by rumors and stories unfavorable to the target company, planted in business publications. The goal of the raid was to involve other investors in a selling stampede that would drive the stock's price down to a bargain level.

> ⚠️ While bear raids are now illegal and are really considered relics, *The Wall Street Journal* nevertheless reported in 1986 an instance in which a broker-dealer went out of business following an apparent bear raid. On October 1 of that year the firm, Yves Hentic & Co., was put out of business by its clearing agent when it was unable to meet capital requirements. Hentic, a large holder of a security that it had underwritten earlier during a several-week period in which the price of the security had declined dramatically, suffered collapse of its own capital position. Wall Streeters speculated that the sharp decline of the stock held by Hentic from $8 a share in September to a low of $2.50 on the day Hentic was put out of business, actually resulted from a bear raid made by hedge funds that were selling the stock short.

bear spread In futures and options trading, a strategy in which one contract is bought and a different contract is sold such that the person undertaking the spread makes a profit if the price of the underlying asset declines. Two contracts are utilized to limit the size of the potential loss. An example of a bear spread is the purchase of a call option and the simultaneous sale of another call option with a lower strike price and the same expiration date as the option purchased. A fall in the price of the underlying stock will tend to result in a declining value of each option. Because the option sold carried a higher price than the option purchased, the investor could expect to make a profit equal to the difference between the two options if a major price decline in the stock should occur. —See also BULL SPREAD.

bear trap An accumulation of shares being sold short by bears trying to drive down the price of a stock. The bear trap occurs when the bears find they must repurchase the shares from an individual or a group at an artificial price determined by the seller.

beat the averages To obtain superior investment returns, generally on a risk-adjusted basis, compared with popular stock price averages such as the Dow Jones Industrial Average or the Standard & Poor's 500. Professional portfolio managers are generally judged by their ability to beat the averages, although many studies indicate that it is virtually impossible to do so consistently on a risk-adjusted basis.

beginning inventory Goods available for sale at the beginning of an accounting period. —See also ENDING INVENTORY.

bell The device that sounds to mark the open and close of each trading day on an organized securities exchange.

bells and whistles Special features that are added to ordinary investments in order to make them stand out and attract investors' notice. Examples of bells and whistles include put features on bonds and floating dividends on preferred stock. Often the value of the features is more apparent than real. —Also called *kickers*; *wrinkles*.

Which bells and whistles are worth all the noise?

Bells and whistles, the special features added to the structure of an investment to attract interest, can provide value-added if the feature (or features) meets your investment needs. But first, ask yourself if the investment stands alone on its own merit without the bells and whistles. Remember, the quality of the content of the package is more important than the wrapping paper.

Kathleen Hegenbart, Vice President, Financial Consultant Shearson Lehman Brothers, Newton Centre, MA

---

bellwether stock A stock that tends to lead the market and signals the general direction of security prices. For many years General Motors was looked to as the market's bellwether stock, but more recently the stock of International Business Machines Corporation seems to fill this role.

belly up Pertaining to or being in bankruptcy. —Used of a firm.

below par Designating a security that sells at less than face value or par value. For example, a $1,000 par bond with a market price of $850 is below par. Likewise, a $100 par preferred stock with a market price of $80 is below par. Fixed-income securities normally trade below par because market rates of interest are higher than they were when the securities were issued. —See also ABOVE PAR; DISCOUNT; DISCOUNT BOND.

beneficial owner The owner of a security registered in another name. For example, investors often leave securities in trust with their brokerage firms. While the brokerage firm is shown on the issuer's books as the owner of record, the investor is the beneficial owner.

best-efforts basis **1.** An agreement by an investment banker to do its best to oversee, but not guarantee, the sale of a security issue in the primary market. —See also UNDERWRITER. **2.** An investor's market order to buy or sell a security in which the brokerage firm agrees to obtain the best possible price.

beta A mathematical measure of the sensitivity of rates of return on a portfolio or a given stock compared with rates of return on the market as a whole. A high beta (over 1.0) indicates moderate or high price volatility. A beta of 1.5 forecasts a 1.5% change in the return on an asset for every 1% change in the return on the market. High-beta stocks are best to own in a strong bull market but are worst to own in a bear market. —See also ALPHA; CAPITAL ASSET PRICING MODEL; CHARACTERISTIC LINE; PORTFOLIO BETA.

bid **1.** The price that a potential buyer is willing to pay for a security. —See also ASK. **2.** An offer to purchase something.

bid wanted (BW) Notice by a security owner that a security position is available for sale and that purchase offers will be considered. A bid wanted announcement is the initial step in seeking an interested buyer, with the final price to be negotiated later.

Big Bang The date October 27, 1986, on which the London security markets were significantly deregulated. The deregulation eliminated fixed commissions on security trades and put an end to the prohibition against securities firms acting as brokers and dealers.

Big Blue International Business Machines Corporation. The term derives from the firm's logo, normally appearing in blue.

Big Board The New York Stock Exchange, the largest organized exchange in the United States.

Big Eight The eight large, national public accounting firms in the United States: Arthur Anderson; Arthur Young; Coopers & Lybrand; Deloitte, Haskins & Sells; Ernst & Whinney; Peat, Marwick, Mitchell; Price Waterhouse; and Touche Ross.

Big Four The four major brokerage companies that dominate trading in equities and bonds in Japan. The Big Four includes Daiwa Securities Ltd., Nikko Securities Ltd., Nomura Securities Ltd., and Yamaichi Securities Ltd.

Big MAC A bond issued by the Municipal Assistance Corporation for the City of New York.

BIGS —See MUNICIPAL CONVERTIBLE.

Big Three The three major automobile manufacturers in the United States: Chrysler, Ford, and General Motors.

bill **1.** —See TREASURY BILL. **2.** —See DUE BILL.

black Pertaining to a firm or the operations of a firm deemed profitable. The term *black* derives from the black ink used to show a profit on financial statements. —See also RED.

Black and Scholes Model A relatively complicated mathematical formula for valuing stock options. The Black and Scholes Model is used in an attempt to determine if a particular option should be selling at a price other than the one at which it currently trades. —See also OPTION PRICING MODEL.

Black Friday September 24, 1869, when stock market operator Jay Gould nearly cornered the gold market. Although eventually broken by government selling of the metal, the corner resulted in massive failures on Wall Street during the confusion. Gould made considerable profits on the manipulation, but his brokers declared bankruptcy.

Black Thursday October 24, 1929, when security prices plunged in one of the most memorable days in the history of the New York Stock Exchange. During the afternoon, Richard Whitney, Vice President of the Exchange, went to the floor with large buy orders in a successful attempt to stem the decline. Unfortunately, his success was short-lived.

Black Tuesday October 29, 1929, the date of the greatest frenzy on the New York Stock Exchange during the Great Crash. Security prices plunged, volume surged to over 16 million shares, and the ticker tape ran hours behind trading on the floor.

blanket bond —See BLANKET FIDELITY BOND.

blanket certification form —See FORM FR–1.

blanket fidelity bond Insurance against losses from employee actions such as forgery or unauthorized trading. —Also called *blanket bond; fidelity bond.*

Do brokerage firms send blanket recommendations to their clients too late for real effectiveness?
• •

When a blanket recommendation is made, it could be construed as a short-term trading idea or as a long-term investment idea. Usually the brokerage system is informed when the recommendation is made, and key clients—those likely to act on the suggestions—have already been notified. If it is a long-term trading idea, it is still considered timely even though you may pay 10–15% higher on the investment idea than you would have when the original recommendation was made. Your intention for a return over the long term should be higher than 10–15%.

Bonnie Briskin, Stockbroker
Tucker, Anthony & R.L. Day, Inc., Boston, MA

blanket recommendation   A recommendation to buy or sell a security that is sent by a brokerage firm to all its customers. Firms do not consider individual investors' objectives before sending out a blanket recommendation.

blank stock   Stock with voting powers, preferences, and rights determined by the issuer's board of directors after the shares have been purchased by subscribers.

block   A large amount of a security. Generally, a security position must total 10,000 shares or more to qualify as a block.

blocked account   —See RESTRICTED ACCOUNT.

block house   A brokerage firm that specializes in assisting with trades of large blocks of securities. Block houses generally work with institutional clients such as mutual funds and pension funds that take large security positions.

block positioner   A securities dealer willing to take a large long or short position in a stock or bond. The block positioner expects to profit on a position by selling at a price higher than the one at which the block was purchased, but will often hedge by using arbitrage or options.

block trade   A trade of 10,000 shares or more. Because of the large amount of money involved, a block trade is nearly always between two institutions.

blotter   An accounting book of original entry used in the back office of brokerage firms for recording clearances, fails, trades, and so forth.

blowout   The nearly immediate sale of a new security issue because of great investor demand. —See also HOT ISSUE.

blue chip   A very high quality investment involving a lower-than-average risk of loss of principal or reduction in income. The word *blue chip* is generally used to refer to securities of companies having a long history of sustained earnings and dividend payments.

Blue List®   A trademark for a Standard & Poor's weekday publication devoted to offerings of municipal bonds.

Blue Room   A relatively small trading room on the floor of the New York Stock Exchange containing three posts, and located adjacent to the main trading room.

blue skying   Determining if a new issue of securities meets the requirements for distribution in the various states where the issue will be sold.

blue sky laws   State regulations covering the offering and sale of securities within state boundaries. Although the laws differ among states, most include provisions relating to fraudulent activities and the licensing of people selling securities. The term *blue sky laws* derives from an effort to protect investors from unwittingly buying a piece of "blue sky."

B-network   —See NETWORK B.

board broker   An employee of the Chicago Board Options Exchange who handles option orders that cannot be immediately executed because of price limits away from the current market price.

board of arbitration   A group of three to five people selected to arbitrate disputes between securities firms. The board's rulings are final for those disputes in which both parties have agreed to arbitration.

board of directors   The body of people responsible for supervising the affairs of a corporation. The board of directors generally sets broad corporate policy rather than participating in day-to-day managerial decisions, although selection of the chief executive officer is the board's responsibility. Members are elected by the firm's stockholders and may or may not be stockholders themselves. —See also CHAIRMAN; INSIDE DIRECTOR; INTERLOCKING DIRECTORATES; OUTSIDE DIRECTOR.

board of governors   1. An elected body of members of a stock exchange who oversees affairs of the exchange. 2. A body of people appointed by the President of the United States to the Federal Reserve to oversee the nation's money system. Decisions by the board have great impact on the securities markets. —See also FEDERAL OPEN MARKET COMMITTEE.

board room   1. A room or section of a room in a brokerage office in which security prices are displayed. 2. The room in which a firm's board of directors meets.

bond   1. A long-term promissory note. Bonds vary widely in maturity, security, and type of issuer, although most are sold in $1,000 denominations (or $5,000 denominations for municipal bonds). 2. A written obligation that makes a person or an institution responsible for the actions of another.

bond anticipation note (BAN)   A short-term municipal security with principal repayment to be made with the proceeds derived from a long-term municipal bond issue that is to be sold at a later date. Essentially, BANs represent debt that is used until long-term funding is available.

bond bank   A bond pool sponsored by a state.

bond basis book   —See BASIS BOOK.

bond broker   A broker executing trades in bonds on an organized exchange or in the over-the-counter market.

Bond Buyer's Index   An index of yields for AA-rated and A-rated municipal bonds, widely used by dealers to evaluate yields on new municipal bond issues. The Index is published by *The Bond Buyer*, a daily publication specializing in fixed-income securities.

bond calendar   —See CALENDAR.

bond conversion   The exchange of a convertible bond for another asset, generally shares of common stock. —See also CONVERTIBLE SECURITY.

bond discount   —See UNAMORTIZED BOND DISCOUNT.

bond dividend   A dividend paid in the dividend payer's bonds. —See also LIABILITY DIVIDEND.

bondholder   An individual or institution owning bonds in a corporation or other organization.

bond pool   A municipal bond offering in which a sponsor sells an issue of bonds with proceeds used by a number of cities or other tax-exempt organizations. The pool permits small cities with low borrowing requirements to reduce the underwriting and interest costs inherent in a small issue. Because of the varying credit risks associated with cities in a single bond pool, nearly all bond pools are insured as to payment of interest or principal. —Also called *pool financing*.

bond power   A form, separate from a bond certificate, that permits the owner of the bond to transfer ownership to another investor without endorsing the bond certificate. —See also STOCK POWER.

bond premium risk   —See RISK PREMIUM.

bond rating   The grading of a debt security with respect to the issuer's ability to meet interest and principal requirements in a timely manner. The three major rating services—Fitch, Moody's, and Standard & Poor's—each use triple A as the highest rating and grade down through Bs and Cs from there. (D is used only by Fitch.) Debts rated AAA, AA, A, and BBB are considered investment grade. Higher rated bonds provide lower returns as the price the investor pays for greater safety. —See also INTEREST COVERAGE; STOCK RATING.

How can I obtain a tax benefit from a bond swap?

Bond swaps are done for many reasons (e.g., to improve income, improve quality, change maturity schedule, or enhance diversification). Thus, if the bond swap is worthwhile it will be done for various economic reasons rather than simply for tax benefits. (Of course, there is nothing wrong with obtaining a tax benefit at the same time.) A tax benefit is often realized when an investor sells bonds that had been acquired during a period when interest rates were lower than they are at the time of the swap. Because interest rates have risen, bond prices have fallen, and the seller is able to generate a tax-deductible capital loss. The tax savings may be viewed as an ancillary benefit derived from the bond swap. A word of caution is in order, though: if you are considering a bond swap that will generate a tax-deductible capital loss, do not swap into a security classified by the Internal Revenue Service as basically identical to the one you sold, until the appropriate time period has passed. Otherwise, the loss will be disallowed for tax purposes.

Stephanie R. Goldsborough, Treasury Officer
Maryland National Bank, Baltimore, MD

bond ratio   The proportion of a firm's long-term financing represented by debt. The bond ratio is calculated by dividing a firm's total outstanding debt by long-term debt and owners' equity. The bond ratio differs from a debt ratio in that debt ratio calculations include short-term as well as long-term debt. —See also COMMON STOCK RATIO.

bond room   The room below the main trading floor of the New York Stock Exchange in which bonds listed on the Exchange are traded.

bond sinking fund   —See SINKING FUND PROVISION.

bond swap   The selling of one bond issue while simultaneously buying another issue in order to take advantage of differences in interest rates, maturity, risk, marketability, and other factors. In some instances, especially with municipals, bond swaps are undertaken in order to realize losses for tax purposes. —See also INTERMARKET SPREAD SWAP; RATE ANTICIPATION SWAP; REVERSE SWAP; SUBSTITUTION BOND SWAP; TAX SWAP.

book   **1.** A specialist's information on limit orders to buy and sell the security in which the specialist makes a market. The orders are left by other exchange members who wish to undertake a trade at a price that differs from the current market price. The book provides the specialist with an estimate of the demand and supply for the stock in which he or she is a market maker. —Also called *specialist's book.* **2.** —See BOOK VALUE PER SHARE.

book-entry security   A security for which the purchaser receives a receipt rather than an engraved certificate. Although a certificate may actually exist in some instances, it is held in one location as ownership changes. The U.S. government, which issues Treasury bills only in book-entry form, uses this method as a way to reduce paperwork expenses. —See also DEPOSITORY TRUST COMPANY.

⚠️ In June of 1986, the State of Utah issued slightly over $91 million worth of book-entry securities in the form of general obligation bonds due to mature annually beginning in 1988. The bonds, fully registered in the name of a nominee, were kept by the Depository Trust Company in New York City. Thus, purchasers would not receive certificates representing their ownership in the bonds because all the certificates were to be kept in a single location. However, interest and principal payments were to be sent to the beneficial owners by participants of the Depository Trust Company. Utah chose book-entry securities as a means of reducing issue costs.

book value   **1.** The net dollar value at which an asset is carried on a firm's balance sheet. For example, a building purchased for $900,000 that over a period of years has been depreciated by $200,000 has a book value of $700,000. Book value, an accounting concept, often bears little relation to an asset's market value. —Also called *carrying value; depreciated cost.* **2.** —See BOOK VALUE PER SHARE.

book value per share   Common stockholders' equity on a per-share basis. Book value per share is calculated by subtracting liabilities from assets and dividing the remainder by the number of outstanding shares of stock. —Also called *book; book value.* —See also MARKET TO BOOK.

borrowing power **1.** A firm's ability to borrow significant amounts of money. This term is often applied to companies having valuable assets but few outstanding debts. **2.** The amount of money that may be borrowed in a margin account.

Boston Stock Exchange (BSE) One of the smaller regional securities exchanges that offers facilities for the trading of stocks and bonds.

BOT —Used on transaction slips to indicate the side of a trade in which securities are bought. —See also SLD 2.

bottom The lowest price to which a stock, market index, or another asset will sink. —See also TOP.

bottom line —See NET INCOME.

bought deal —See FIRM COMMITMENT.

boutique —See INVESTMENT BOUTIQUE.

box The physical location in which brokerage firms and banks place securities for safekeeping. —See also FREE BOX; OPEN BOX.

box spread A combination of four options consisting of one money spread on calls (one long, one short, same expiration, different strike price) and one money spread on puts (one long, one short, same expiration, different strike price). A box spread locks in a specific dollar return at expiration (all four options have the same expiration), with the goal being to acquire the position at a sufficiently low outlay that a favorable return is guaranteed.

bracket creep The movement of a taxpayer into higher tax brackets as his or her taxable income increases over time. Bracket creep occurs because of the progressive nature of the federal income tax structure in which extra income is taxed at higher and higher rates. As a result of bracket creep, more and more individuals seek tax-advantaged investments. Bracket creep was reduced significantly by 1986 tax reform that reduced the number of tax brackets.

bracketing The order in which underwriters' names appear in a securities offering. The names are generally listed in the order of importance in a particular offering. —See also MAJOR BRACKET; MEZZANINE BRACKET; TOMBSTONE.

breadth of market The underlying strength of stock market movements in an upward or a downward direction. Determining breadth of market is important to technical analysts when they forecast whether a given market movement is likely to persist. Among numerous measures of market breadth, the advance-decline index is one of the most popular. —Also called *market breadth*.

break **1.** A sharp price decline in a particular security or in the market as a whole. A break normally occurs when unexpected negative information is made public and investors rush to sell. **2.** A discrepancy on the books of a brokerage firm.

break **1.** To dissolve an underwriting syndicate. **2.** —See BUST.

breakaway gap   In technical analysis, a gap in a price chart caused by a stock price breaking out of a trend on high volume. A breakaway gap is bullish if the price movement is upward and bearish if the price movement is downward. —See also EXHAUSTION GAP; RUNAWAY GAP.

breakeven   **1.** The level of output or sales necessary to cover fixed expenses. Companies in industries such as automobile and steel manufacturing that have high fixed costs and resultingly high breakevens are likely to exhibit large fluctuations in earnings. **2.** The price at which a security position can be closed out with no profit or loss.

breakeven analysis   A mathematical procedure for analyzing the relationships among a firm's fixed costs, profits, and variable costs. Financial analysts are particularly interested in how changes in output and sales will translate into changes in earnings.

breakeven time   The number of years that a convertible security must be held in order for its extra current income to cover the excess of its market price over its value in terms of common stock (i.e., annual interest on the bond less annual dividends on the stock). For example, a 10% coupon bond selling for $1,000, convertible to common stock with a market value of $600 and paying no dividend, would have a breakeven time of $400/$100, or 4 years.

breaking the syndicate   The termination of a syndicate of investment bankers organized to underwrite an issue of securities. Following the breaking of the syndicate, its individual members are free to dispose of remaining securities without price restrictions.

breakout   The advance of a stock price above a resistance level, or the fall of a stock price below a support level. A breakout, especially one on relatively heavy volume, indicates to technicians that the security is about to make a major price movement in the direction indicated by the breakout. Thus, if a breakout is upward, a major upward price movement can be expected. A breakout on relatively low volume is suspect. —See also BREAK THROUGH; CONGESTION AREA.

breakpoint   The cumulative level of purchases of shares in a mutual fund that is required before an individual purchaser can qualify for a reduced sales commission. —See also LETTER OF INTENT; RIGHT OF ACCUMULATION.

break through   To penetrate a resistance level on the upside or a support level on the downside. —See also BREAKOUT.

breakup   The division of a company into separate parts. The most famous breakup to date was the 1984 division of American Telephone & Telegraph Company (AT&T). The AT&T breakup was intended to increase competition in the communications industry.

breakup fee   A provision in a takeover agreement requiring a firm to pay the investment banker a large sum of money if another firm takes over the target company. A breakup fee tends to discourage other firms from making bids for the target.

breakup value The market value of all the individual parts of a firm if the firm were to be broken up and the individual parts operated independently. If the breakup value of a firm exceeds the market value at which its stock trades, the firm may be managed and operated inefficiently. In such a case, the stockholders would see increased value in their holdings if parts of the firm were divested. Many takeovers originate when raiders spot firms with breakup values that exceed the prices at which those firms' stocks are traded.

bridge loan A short-term loan taken out until permanent financing can be arranged. —Also called *swing loan*.

broad tape The machine over which Dow Jones & Company provides current business news to brokerage houses and other subscribers. The broad tape is named for the wide size of the paper on which the news is printed, compared with the size of ticker tape.

broker 1. An individual or a firm that brings together buyers and sellers but does not take a position in the asset to be exchanged. Some observers feel that a broker, compared with a dealer, is more likely to provide an unbiased opinion on a security since less self-interest is involved in the transaction. —See also DEALER. 2. —See REGISTERED REPRESENTATIVE.

Criteria to keep in mind when selecting a broker.

The nature of the firm by which the broker is employed is an important factor. One needs to know that one's assets are protected and that the firm has a good reputation. You must be able to trust your broker and to know that he or she has your goals, objectives, and best interest in mind. Your broker should take the time to discuss your objectives with you. The broker should also ensure that you understand all the activities that occur in your account. Before selecting a broker, ask around and get referrals.

Bonnie Briskin, Stockbroker
Tucker, Anthony & R.L. Day, Inc., Boston, MA

broker call loan —See CALL LOAN.

broker comparison —See COMPARISON.

broker-dealer A firm that brings buyers and sellers together in its function as a broker and that also takes positions of its own in selected securities while fulfilling its function as a dealer. Many firms that are commonly called *brokers* or *brokerage firms* are actually broker-dealers.

brokered CD A certificate of deposit of a commercial bank or savings and loan that is sold through a middleman (normally a brokerage firm) rather than being sold directly by the savings institution itself. Small investors can frequently obtain rates paid on very large certificates through brokered CDs, which are generally sold in $1,000 units.

brokers' loan Funds borrowed by a broker, mainly from banks, for various purposes including customers' purchases of securities on margin, an underwriter's purchase of a new security issue for resale, and a specialist's inventory of securities. —See also CALL LOAN.

BSE —See BOSTON STOCK EXCHANGE.

bucket shop An illegal operation in which buy and sell orders are accepted but no executions actually take place. Rather, the operators expect to profit when customers close out their positions at a loss. A bucket shop is similar in concept to a bookie who does not lay off bets and accepts the risk of a bettor winning.

bull An investor who believes the price of a particular security or security prices in general will follow a broad upward trend. An investor can often be a bull on a specific security but not on the general market, and vice versa. —See also BEAR.

bulldog bond A sterling-denominated bond issued by a non-British firm or institution. An example of a bulldog bond is one denominated in sterling and issued in England by a U.S.-based company. Purchase of a bulldog bond by a U.S. investor would entail extra risks but also potential rewards stemming from possible changes in the value of sterling in relation to the dollar.

bullet immunization Immunizing a bond portfolio so as to fund a single liability.

bullion Refined gold or silver in bulk (i.e., ingots) rather than in the form of coins.

bullish Feeling that a particular stock or the market as a whole is headed for a period of generally rising prices. —See also BEARISH.

bull market An extended period of generally rising prices in an individual item (e.g., stock or gold), a group of items (i.e., commodities or oil stocks), or the market as a whole. Since security prices are often subject to reversals, it is sometimes difficult to know whether there has been a temporary interruption or a permanent end to a bull market. Thus, whether a bull market is actually in progress at any given time is often subject to individual interpretation. —See also BEAR MARKET.

bull spread In futures and options trading, a strategy in which one contract is bought and a different contract is sold such that the person undertaking the spread makes a profit if the price of the underlying asset rises. Two contracts are used in order to limit the size of the potential loss. —See also BEAR SPREAD.

bunch To combine a number of odd-lot orders into round-lot orders so as to avoid an odd-lot differential.

burn and churn —See CHURN.

business cycle The somewhat irregular but recurring periods of change in economic activity over time. A business cycle is generally divided into four stages: expansion, prosperity, contraction, and recession. The given stage in which the economy operates has a significant impact on a firm's profitability and prospects. This impact is especially severe with respect to firms that experience large swings in sales and profits. Many analysts believe that stock prices tend to lead the business cycle. Therefore, it is felt that bull markets begin before a period of expansion and that bear markets begin before a period of contraction.

business day A day on which the securities markets are open.

business fundamentals The general economic background including earnings, sales, wage rates, taxes, and inflation. Improving business fundamentals are generally viewed as bullish for stocks, although existing stock prices at any given point already include some of the expected improvement of the business fundamentals.

business risk The risk that a business will experience a period of poor earnings and resultant failure. Business risk is greatest for firms in cyclical or relatively new industries. Business risk affects holders of stock and bonds, since a firm may be unable to pay dividends and interest.

bust To cancel an order after it has been filled. Cancellation normally occurs only under unusual circumstances such as an error or a misunderstanding. —Also called *break*.

busted convertible A convertible bond on which the stock into which the bond is convertible has fallen so far below the conversion price that the convertible bond trades in the market as regular debt. For example, if a convertible bond is convertible into stock at a price of $40 per share when the stock sells at only $7 per share, the conversion feature has such little value that the bond will be priced to offer a yield to investors nearly the same as a bond of similar risk and maturity but without any conversion feature.

bust-up takeover The acquisition of a firm in which the acquiring company sells certain assets or segments of the acquired firm in order to raise funds and repay debt used to finance the purchase. Such a takeover is most often undertaken when the target firm has a significant amount of undervalued assets and the acquiring company has little cash.

butterfly spread A combination of two long and two short call options, all with the same expiration date. The two short options carry the same strike price, which is sandwiched between a higher and a lower strike price on the long options. A hypothetical example of a butterfly spread would be to sell two April GM $60 and buy an April GM $50 and an April GM $70. The butterfly spread is designed to be profitable if the price of the underlying asset remains within a narrow trading range.

buy A bargain-priced asset. For example, an analyst may feel that a particular firm owns valuable assets overlooked or undervalued by the financial community; in that instance, the firm's stock is considered a buy.

buy To purchase a security or another asset. —See also SELL.

buy-and-hold strategy The investment strategy of purchasing securities and holding them over extended periods of time. Investors using the buy-and-hold strategy select companies on the basis of their long-term outlook. Such investors are not influenced by short- or intermediate-term movements in the price of a security.

buy-and-write strategy The investment strategy of purchasing stock and writing call options. A buy-and-write strategy is a fairly conservative approach to generating maximum current income from option premiums and dividends. —See also COVERED WRITER.

buy a spread In options trading, to establish a spread position in which the premium on the option purchased exceeds the premium on the option sold. A typical example would be to buy a call on Amoco with a $60 strike price for a premium of $300 and to sell an Amoco call with a $65 strike price for $125 (both expire on the same date).

buy back To repurchase an asset or security. For example, a company may decide to buy back shares of its own stock from an investor in order to reduce the possibility of a takeover. —See also GREENMAIL.

buyback A company's repurchase of a portion of its own outstanding shares. The purpose of the buyback may be to acquire a block of stock from the hands of an investor unfriendly to the target firm's management, who is considering taking over the firm. Conversely, the buyback may be an attempt to increase earnings per share by reducing the number of outstanding shares. Regardless of the purpose of the buyback, the result is increased risk for the firm because of reduced equity in the firm's capital structure. —Also called *stock repurchase plan*. —See also PARTIAL REDEMPTION; SELF-TENDER.

⚠️ The mid-1980s saw a rash of buybacks among American corporations. These buybacks were spearheaded by the large oil companies in attempts to increase the market prices of their common stock and thereby fend off takeovers. Included in this group were Phillips Petroleum, Unocal, and Atlantic Richfield, each of which bought back $4 billion or more in common stock. In fact, Phillips repurchased nearly 50% of its outstanding shares. Other firms, including Amoco, Exxon, and IBM, repurchased lesser amounts of their stock. To a great extent, the buybacks were financed by issuing additional debt; however, some firms raised cash by selling assets or generated the funds through normal operations. Critics of the buyback programs say that corporations using their funds for the purchase of securities instead of investing in new plants and equipment are setting the stage for eventual economic decay.

buyers' market A market in which the supply of an asset swamps demand to the point that prices fall below the level expected under normal circumstances. For example, during the last quarter of 1985, state and local governments issued tax-free bonds in record numbers to beat the year-end deadline for new restrictive rules on tax-free issues to take effect. This huge supply of bonds created a buyers' market and drove interest rates on tax-free bonds to a level approaching the rates on taxable U.S. Treasury securities. —See also SELLERS' MARKET.

buy in   One broker's purchase of securities that another broker has failed to deliver on time.

buying climax   A period of sharp upward movement in the stock market accompanied by very high volume. A buying climax often signals the end of a bull market or, at the least, an overbought market that can be expected to fall. —See also SELLING CLIMAX.

buying panic   A period of rapidly rising stock prices on very large volume as investors, speculators, traders, and institutions attempt to establish investment positions without regard to price. Buying panics occur when individuals and institutions believe they must buy securities at once before prices rise further. —See also SELLING PANIC.

buying power   1. The amount of liquid funds available for investing. A large amount of buying power indicates that significant funds from investors are available to fuel a bull market. 2. The funds in an investor's brokerage account that may be used for purchasing securities. An investor's buying power includes cash balances plus the loan value on securities held in the account.

buy minus   Pertaining to an order to purchase a security only when the last change in the security's price is downward. A buy minus order may be used to acquire a position in a security during a short-term price decline.

buy on margin   To buy securities by putting up only part of the purchase price and borrowing the remainder. The word *margin* refers to the portion the investor puts up rather than the portion that is borrowed. The loan is normally arranged by the investor's broker. The securities must be kept in the account. —See also INITIAL MARGIN REQUIREMENT; MAINTENANCE MARGIN REQUIREMENT.

What are the risks inherent in buying securities on margin?

Here one borrows money from a broker to buy securities using securities as collateral so that more can be bought at one time. It's called leveraging and it is wonderful! In an up market! You make more money since you put more money out at risk. (It's wonderful for your broker too; the broker makes more commissions and charges you interest.) BUT, if the market goes against you it can be *just awful*, since you owe the borrowed money in full, with interest, no matter what happens to the price of the stock or bond. TIP: Margin is a little like booze: the more you drink the better you feel. Until the morning after.

Thomas J. McAllister, CFP
McAllister Financial Planning, Indianapolis, IN

buy out   **1.** To purchase all the stock of a company or all the stock of a company owned by one investor or by a group of investors. For example, corporate management may decide to buy out an investor in order to halt a potential takeover. **2.** To terminate a contract before its scheduled termination date by reaching a monetary agreement satisfactory to the parties involved.

buyout   **1.** The purchase of a company. —See also LEVERAGED BUYOUT. **2.** The purchase of all the stock of a company, owned by a single investor or by a group of investors.

buy side   The portion of the securities business in which institutional orders originate. In most instances the buy side is limited to institutional buyers such as pension fund portfolio managers. Individual investors are usually excluded from the buy side because they are not considerd formal participants in the securities business. —See also SELL SIDE.

buy signal   An indication provided by a technical tool, such as a bar chart or trading volume, that a particular security or securities in general should be purchased. For example, a stock achieving a new high price on heavy trading volume is often interpreted as a buy signal. —See also SELL SIGNAL.

buy stop order   A customer order to a broker to buy a security if it sells at or above a stipulated (stop) price. This specialized order can be used to protect an existing profit or to limit the potential loss on a security that has been sold short. —See also SELL STOP ORDER; STOP ORDER 1.

buy the book   An order to purchase all of a security offered at the current ask price. The purchase is made from the specialist, dealers, and other holders willing to sell at the specified price.

BW   —See BID WANTED.

bylaws   Stockholder-approved regulations governing the conduct of a business. Bylaws typically include election rules for directors, rules for the selection of auditors, and rules for amending existing bylaws.

C

c   **1.** —Used in the dividend column of stock transaction tables of newspapers to indicate that the listed dividend is a liquidating dividend: *City Inv 7.50c.* **2.** —Used in money market mutual fund transaction tables in newspapers to indicate funds that are chiefly or wholly exempt from federal income taxes: *Fld Tax Exmpt c.*

Caa   —See CCC.

cabinet crowd   New York Stock Exchange members trading inactive bonds. —Also called *inactive bond crowd.* —See also ACTIVE BOND CROWD.

cabinet security An inactive security listed on an exchange. Limit orders for inactive securities are kept in metal cabinets until they are removed for execution or cancellation.

cabinet trading The trading of inactive bonds through the matching of buy and sell limit orders recorded on cards stored in cabinets in the New York Stock Exchange bond room.

CAES —See COMPUTER ASSISTED EXECUTION SYSTEM.

cage —See CASHIER'S DEPARTMENT.

calendar A list of upcoming bond issues. A full calendar indicating a large number of issues may force the issuers to offer higher interest rates in order to compete for buyers. —Also called *bond calendar.*

calendar spread In options and futures trading, the purchase of one contract and the sale of another contract identical to the first except for the delivery or expiration date. An example of calendar spread would be the purchase of a December call with a strike price of $20 and the sale of a June call with the same $20 strike price. The purpose of a calendar spread is to profit from a change in the price difference as the securities move closer to maturity. —Also called *horizontal spread; time spread.*

call **1.** An option that permits the owner (option holder) to purchase a specific asset at a predetermined price until a certain date. For example, an investor may purchase a call option on General Electric stock that confers the right to buy 100 shares at $25 per share until October 17. Calls are sold for a fee by other investors who incur an obligation. —See also PUT 1; SYNTHETIC CALL. **2.** The forcing of an option writer to sell shares of stock at a price stipulated in the contract. Most calls take place just before the expiration of the options. **3.** An issuer's right to repurchase an issue of bonds at a predetermined price before maturity. The feature is used when interest rates fall, so that the bonds can be repurchased and a new issue with a lower rate sold. A call feature is normal for nearly all long-term bond issues, and it operates to the detriment of bond owners. —See also CALL PRICE; CALL PROTECTION; EXTRAORDINARY CALL; OPTIONAL CALL; SINKING FUND CALL. **4.** Redemption of an issue of bonds before maturity by forcing the bondholders to sell at the call price.

callable bond A bond that is subject to redemption by its issuer before maturity.

callable preferred stock An issue of preferred stock that may be repurchased by the issuer at a specific price (normally at par value or slightly above). The option to repurchase the preferred stock is held by the issuer, not the investor. Calls can be expected when market rates of interest have fallen significantly below the yield on the preferred stock at the time the stock was issued.

called away —Used to refer to the forced sale of a security by an investor because of the action of another party. For example, the writer of a call option has the underlying stock called away when the call owner exercises the option. Likewise, a bondholder may have bonds called away by the issuer if interest rates decline and the issuer decides to redeem a portion of the issue before maturity.

call feature —See CALL PROVISION.

call loan A loan that may be terminated at any time by either party. For investors, a call loan means bank loans to stockbrokers for the purpose of carrying customer margin borrowing, using securities as collateral. The rate of interest, similar to that on other high quality short-term loans, varies over time. Brokerage firms normally charge customers the rate on call loans plus an additional percent or so depending on the amount borrowed. —Also called *broker call loan.* —See also BROKERS' LOAN.

call option —See CALL 1.

call premium The difference between the principal amount of a security and the price at which the security can be called by the issuer. During the first few years a call is permitted, the premium is generally equal to one year's interest. Thereafter, the premium gradually declines to zero at maturity. Calls for sinking fund requirements are normally made at par rather than at a premium.

call price The price at which an issuer may, at its option, repurchase a security for redemption before the security's maturity. For bonds, the call price often declines over the life of the security until it reaches par value at maturity. —Also called *redemption price.* —See also EXTRAORDINARY CALL; OPTIONAL CALL; SINKING FUND CALL.

> In late 1980 Eastern Air Lines issued a new debenture as part of an exchange offer for two of its outstanding debenture issues. The new debenture had a coupon of 11¾% and a maturity date of 2005. The call price at which the debenture could be redeemed was initially 111.7500% of principal in 1981, decreasing by .5875% annually until the year 2000, following which the call price would remain at face value until maturity. Thus, in 1991, ten years following the first potential call at 111.7500% of principal, the call price would drop by 5.875% (10 × .5875% annually) to 105.875% of principal.

call protection The prohibition against an issuer's calling a bond from an investor during the early years of the security's life. Municipals and industrial bonds normally have ten years of call protection while protection on utility debt is often limited to five years. A longer period of call protection is advantageous to the investor since calls nearly always occur during periods of reduced interest rates. —Also called *cushion.* —See also CALL 3; NONCALLABLE; NONREFUNDABLE.

call provision The stipulation in most bond indentures that permits the issuer to repurchase securities at a fixed price or at a series of prices before maturity. This provision operates to the detriment of investors since calls normally occur on high-interest bonds during periods of reduced interest rates. Thus, an investor whose bond is called must find another investment that will most likely provide a lower return. Certain preferred stock issues are also subject to call. —Also called *call feature.*

---

*Why should I check a bond's call provision before
buying it? Which types of bonds have these provisions?*
• •

Bond issuers seem to call their bonds in when bond investors
least want to receive their principal back—after interest rates
have already dropped. If you pay close attention to a bond's
call provisions, however, you can avoid experiencing losses of
principal (i.e., you can avoid paying big premiums for high-
coupon bonds which are about to be called in at lower premium prices, or worse yet, at par). Furthermore, if you are a
short maturity buyer (let's use three years for an example), you
may be able to earn a higher yield for the three-year period by
purchasing a longer cushion bond that is callable in three years
instead of buying a bond that matures in three years. Reason:
the market will generally reward you with a higher yield to the
call on the cushion bond (due to the *uncertainty* of its actually
being called in three years) versus the yield which the market
will provide you on a similar bond that will *definitely* mature in
three years. It is important to mention that if you invest in a
cushion bond and it is not called, you will be faced with the
choice of (a) holding a longer bond than you may have intended to hold or (b) liquidating at market value.

*Stephanie R. Goldsborough, Treasury Officer
Maryland National Bank, Baltimore, MD*

---

call spread   An option position in which a call is purchased while
another call on the same security is sold short. The two calls have
different strike prices, different expiration dates, or both. —Also called
option spread. —See also SPREAD 1.

call watch   A service provided by independent organizations that monitor the actions of bond issuers in order to inform clients (such as financial
advisors, trustees, and individual investors) that their bonds have been
called for redemption before maturity. A call watch is particularly valuable for holders of bearer bonds for which no records of ownership are
maintained by the issuers.

cancel former order   A customer order to a broker that cancels and
replaces a previous unfilled order with a new order. For example, a
customer may cancel a former limit order to buy stock at $15 per share
and replace it with a market order.

cancellation   A broker's notice to a customer than an erroneous trade
credited to the customer has been voided. For example, if a brokerage
firm mistakenly purchases 200 shares of stock for the account when the
customer has entered an order for only 100 shares, the firm will send
the customer a cancellation for the 200-share trade to void the original

confirmation and then will send a new confirmation showing the correct trade.

cancel order A customer order to a broker that cancels a previous unfilled order given by the customer.

cap **1.** An upper limit on the interest rate to be paid on a floating-rate note. —See also COLLAR. **2.** —See CAPITALIZATION.

capital appreciation An increase in the market value of a security.

capital appreciation bond —See ZERO-COUPON BOND.

capital asset An asset with an expected life of over one year and one that is not bought and sold in the normal course of business. Buildings and machinery are examples of capital assets.

capital asset pricing model (CAPM) A mathematical model that attempts to explain how securities should be priced, based on their relative riskiness in combination with the return on risk-free assets. This model, which yields beta, the widely used measure of risk, has been subject to a number of criticisms; nevertheless, it is considered a very important element of modern investment and portfolio theory. —See also CAPITAL MARKET LINE.

capital dividend A dividend considered to be paid from paid-in capital rather than from current earnings or retained earnings. Capital dividends are generally not taxable to a stockholder when paid; rather, they are used to adjust the basis of the security downward such that a larger capital gain or a smaller capital loss will result at the time the security is sold. A capital dividend is somewhat akin to tearing boards off a house to use as firewood. If the process goes on too long the house itself will go. —Also called *return of capital.*

capital expenditure Funds used to acquire a long-term asset. A capital expenditure results in depreciation deductions over the life of the acquired asset. —Also called *capital outlay.*

capital flight The shifting of funds out of a country to avoid confiscation, controls, or depreciation. Capital flight results in further deterioration of a currency's exchange rate.

capital gain The excess by which proceeds from the sale of a capital asset exceed the cost basis.

capital gains distribution Payments to investment company shareholders based on gains from securities in the firm's portfolio that have been sold. These gains are passed through to the shareholders and are taxed to the shareholders. Distributions normally occur once each year. —See also INCOME DIVIDEND.

capital gains tax The tax applicable to gains and losses from the sale of capital assets. Prior to 1987 certain capital gains and losses received special treatment for tax purposes. Beginning in 1987, investors were no longer permitted to exclude a portion of gains and losses in calculating federal income taxes.

capital intensive Pertaining to a firm or industry that requires large amounts of fixed assets and/or cash to operate. Steel, automobile manufacturing, and mining are capital intensive industries.

capitalization The amounts and types of long-term financing used by a firm. Types of financing include common stock, preferred stock, retained earnings, and long-term debt. A firm with capitalization including little or no long-term debt is considered to be financed very conservatively. —Also called *cap; capital structure; total capitalization.* —See also COMPLEX CAPITAL STRUCTURE; LARGE-CAPITALIZATION STOCK; MARKET CAPITALIZATION; RECAPITALIZATION; SMALL-CAPITALIZATION STOCK.

capitalization rate The rate used to convert an income stream into a present value lump sum. For example, a capitalization rate of 10% and an income stream of $2,000 annually provide a present value of $2,000/.10, or $20,000. The capitalization rate for a particular flow of income is a function of the rate of interest on Treasury bills (the risk-free rate) and the risk associated with the flow of income. A riskier investment has a higher capitalization rate and a resultantly lower present value.

capitalize To calculate the current value of a future stream of earnings or cash flows. For example, in order to calculate the current price at which a bond should sell, a financial analyst must capitalize the interest payments and principal repayment that will be made to the investor.

capital lease The long-term lease of a capital asset. To the lessee, a capital lease is the same as owning the asset. Accounting rules require that the leased asset and the present value of the lease payments be recorded on the lessee's balance sheet. For the lessor, a capital lease is treated as a sale of the asset. —Also called *financial lease.*

capital loss The excess by which the cost basis of a capital asset exceeds the proceeds from its sale.

capital market The market for long-term funds where securities such as common stock, preferred stock, and bonds are traded. Both the primary market for new issues and the secondary market for existing securities are part of the capital market.

capital market line The line used in the capital asset pricing model to illustrate the rates of return for efficient portfolios depending on the risk free rate of return and the level of risk (as measured by beta) for a particular portfolio. The capital market line shows a positive linear relationship between returns and portfolio betas. —Also called *market line.* —See also ALPHA; BETA; SYSTEMATIC RISK.

capital outlay —See CAPITAL EXPENDITURE.

capital shares One of two types of stock issued by a dual purpose fund in which the owner is entitled to all of the capital value but none of the current income of the fund. Capital shares appeal primarily to aggressive investors seeking capital growth. —See also INCOME SHARES.

capital spending Spending for long-term assets such as factories, equipment, machinery, and buildings that permits the production of more goods and services in future years. Capital spending increases a country's material wealth.

capital stock   Shares of ownership in a business. These shares include common stock of various classes and any preferred stock outstanding. If a firm has only a single class of capital stock outstanding, *common stock* and *capital stock* are often used interchangeably. —See also AUTHORIZED CAPITAL STOCK; OUTSTANDING CAPITAL STOCK; STOCK CLASS.

capital structure   —See CAPITALIZATION.

capital surplus   —See ADDITIONAL PAID-IN CAPITAL.

CAPM   —See CAPITAL ASSET PRICING MODEL.

carload   In commodities trading, a railroad car or truckload of grain that ranges from 1,400 to 2,500 bushels.

carryback   A business operating loss that may be carried back (up to three years) for tax purposes. A carryback is used to recover taxes already paid on income earned in previous years. For example, if a firm experiences a year of large losses following a period of profitable operations, it may use the losses to cancel out profits from previous years on which taxes have already been paid. Taxes paid on profits canceled by the carryback are then refunded to the firm by the Internal Revenue Service. —Also called *carryover; tax loss carryback.*

carryforward   1. A business operating loss that may be carried forward up to 15 years for tax purposes. Thus, a loss in one year would be carried forward to a future year and used to offset profits up to the amount of the carryforward. Carryforwards are especially useful to firms operating in cyclical industries such as transportation. —Also called *tax loss carryforward.* 2. In taxation of individuals, net capital losses exceeding the annual limit of $3,000 that may be carried to subsequent years so as to offset capital gains or ordinary income. There is no limit to the amount of capital losses that may be used to offset capital gains in any one year, only in the amount of losses in excess of gains that may be used to offset income. —Also called *carryover.*

carrying charges   1. The cost of owning and storing a commodity during a period of time. This cost influences the difference between the futures price and the expected future spot price. 2. —See COST OF CARRY.

carrying value   —See BOOK VALUE 1.

carryover   —See CARRYBACK; CARRYFORWARD.

CARS   —See CERTIFICATE FOR AUTOMOBILE RECEIVABLES.

cartel   A group of companies or countries acting together to control the supply and price of certain goods or services. Cartels are formed to produce higher profits than would ordinarily be the case.

cash   Coins and currency on hand and in checking account balances. Since cash is a nonearning asset, firms normally attempt to keep their cash balances to the minimum level required to sustain operations.

cash account   A brokerage account requiring that cash payments on purchases and deliveries on sales be made promptly. (Settlement is officially five business days after the transaction date.) The cash account is the most popular type of brokerage account even though it permits no investor borrowing (i.e., buying on margin). —Also called *special cash account*. —See also MARGIN ACCOUNT.

cash basis accounting   A method of accounting in which receipt and payment of cash are the basis for recording transactions. Thus it is not the date on which goods and services are received that matters as in the accrual method, but the dates on which the cash changes hands for the transactions. Cash basis accounting is typically used for tax purposes by individuals but not by corporations. —See also ACCRUAL ACCOUNTING.

cash contract   A fairly unusual security transaction in which settlement with payment and security delivery are to occur on the same day as the trade date. This type of trade often occurs during the last week of a calendar year when sellers wish to settle early in order to realize a gain for tax purposes. —Also called *cash trade*. —See also REGULAR-WAY CONTRACT; SELLER'S OPTION CONTRACT.

cash cow   A business or a segment of a business that produces significantly more cash than it consumes. As an example, a firm may sell a product that requires minimal advertising and promotional expenditures but continues to generate revenues year after year. Firms sometimes use cash cows to provide cash for financing other segments of their business.

cash dividend   A dividend paid in cash (i.e., by check) to holders of a firm's stock. Although the amount is normally based on profitability, it may temporarily exceed net income. Certain legal and contractual restrictions may limit a firm's ability to pay cash dividends.

What are the advantages or disadvantages of investing in firms that pay large cash dividends?

An investment in stocks paying high cash dividends will require that tax be paid currently. Alternatively, an investment in growth stocks that frequently pay low or no dividends will defer a greater portion of the tax bite until the stock is sold. Large cash dividends are typically associated with no growth or limited growth companies that may or may not be suitable for your overall investment strategy. If you are in a high marginal tax bracket, the effective aftertax yield of an investment paying cash dividends may be lower than other investment alternatives.

Michele R. Bourgerie, CPA
Arthur Young, New York, NY

cash equivalent **1.** An asset such as property or stock that has a realizable cash value equivalent to a specific sum of money. **2.** An asset so easily and quickly convertible to cash that holding the asset is esentially equivalent to holding cash. A Treasury bill is a cash equivalent.

cash flow The amount of net cash generated by an investment or a business during a specific period of time. Cash flow is calculated by adding noncash charges such as depreciation to net income after taxes. Because cash is the fuel that drives a business, many analysts consider cash flow to be a company's most important financial statistic. In addition, firms with big cash flows are frequently takeover targets because acquiring firms know that the cash can be used to help pay off the costs of the acquisitions.

cash flow per share A firm's cash flow divided by the average number of shares of capital stock outstanding. Cash flow per share is frequently used in valuing a firm's stock by analysts who feel the amount of net cash produced by the firm is a more valid measure of value than reported earnings per share.

cashier's check A check drawn by a bank on itself. A cashier's check is made out to a designated institution or person and must be paid for before issuance. —See also CERTIFIED CHECK.

cashier's department The division of a broker-dealer operation in which security certificates are processed, checks are sent or received, and dividend and interest records are kept. Essentially, the cashier's department handles the broker-dealer's money and paperwork. —Also called *cage.*

Cash Management Account (CMA)® A trademark for computer-supported financial services for the receiving, investing, paying, and lending of money involving brokerage services including but not limited to the subscription and redemption of shares of mutual investment, etc. It is an integrated financial service accessible by a debit card and checks combining a stock brokerage account with a bank account and a mutual fund account. This comprehensive, innovative type of brokerage account was introduced by Merrill Lynch, Pierce, Fenner, and Smith in 1977.

cash management bill A very short-term security (10 to 20 days from date of issue until maturity) issued by the U.S. Treasury in order to manage its cash balances. A cash management bill is issued in minimum denominations of $1 million and is bought by institutional investors.

cash market The market in which trades are made for the immediate sale or purchase of a particular item. —Often used in commodities trading to differentiate transactions involving immediate or nearly immediate delivery from transactions requiring delivery at a future time. —Also called *spot market.*

cash on delivery —See DELIVER VERSUS PAYMENT.

cash price A price quotation in a cash market. In the case of securities trading, this term is used to distinguish a transaction from regular five-day delivery. It may be desirable for tax or dividend reasons. In commodities trading, a cash price implies immediate or nearly immediate delivery as opposed to settlement in a specified future month. —Also called *spot price.*

cash ratio Cash and cash equivalents in relation to current liabilities. A firm's cash ratio is a demanding test of its liquidity. —See also CURRENT RATIO; QUICK RATIO.

cash reserves Investment funds being held in short-term assets such as Treasury bills and certificates of deposit while awaiting more permanent investment opportunities. Large cash reserves, indicating a big pool of funds that eventually will be used, may force up the prices of selected investments at the time the funds are invested.

cash secured put A put for which the writer deposits cash equal to the option's exercise price. For example, the writer of a put option on 100 shares of Sears stock at $35 per share would deposit $3,500 since the writer has agreed to buy $3,500 of Sears common stock in the event that the put is exercised. Funds for a cash secured put may be placed in short-term income-earning securities such as Treasury bills.

cash settlement Settlement of a futures contract in cash rather than in the asset underlying the contract. For example, stock index futures call for cash settlement because it is not feasible actually to deliver an index or the securities constituting an index.

Is cash-value life insurance a good investment? Why? For whom?

For many years this was a lousy investment pushed by excellent sales forces, often using deceptive practices to mask how poor it really was. In recent years the situation has changed, with the widespread offering by major companies of universal life and interest sensitive whole life, both of which pay competitive interest rates on the cash-value portion of the policy. These policies can be an appropriate, even an excellent, investment because of the lack of federal taxation on the internal earnings of the policies. And if they are held until death no tax is ever paid on these earnings. If the owner ever needs funds he or she can borrow from the policy rather than cashing it in, thereby continuing to avoid taxation. TIP: Cash-value life insurance is an *investment* and should be treated as such. If you just need protection, buy term.

Thomas J. McAllister, CFP
McAllister Financial Planning, Indianapolis, IN

---

cash surrender value The money paid by an insurance company to a policyholder canceling an annuity or cash-value life insurance policy. Cash value accumulates when premiums and interest on any previous cash value exceed the cost of insurance. Generally, the cash value that a policyholder receives upon cancellation is not taxable unless it exceeds the sum of the premiums paid. —Also called *surrender value.*

cash trade —See CASH CONTRACT.

cash-value life insurance A type of life insurance in which part of the premium is used to provide death benefits and the remainder is available to earn interest. Thus, cash-value life insurance is both a protection plan and a savings plan. This insurance entails a significantly higher premium than protection-only insurance and, depending on the issuer and the policy, may pay a relatively small return on savings compared with other investments. —Also called *permanent insurance; whole life insurance.* —See also TERM INSURANCE.

CATS® —See CERTIFICATE OF ACCRUAL ON TREASURY SECURITIES.

CBOE —See CHICAGO BOARD OPTIONS EXCHANGE.

CBT —See CHICAGO BOARD OF TRADE.

CCAB —See MUNICIPAL CONVERTIBLE.

CCC/Caa A very speculative grade assigned to a debt obligation by a rating agency. Such a rating indicates default or considerable doubt that interest will be paid or principal repaid.

CD —See CERTIFICATE OF DEPOSIT.

Celler-Kefauver Antimerger Act A 1950 federal act that updated the Clayton Act by severely restricting anticompetitive mergers resulting from acquisition of assets. —See also ANTITRUST LAWS.

central assets account —See SWEEP ACCOUNT.

central bank A bank administered by a national government. A central bank issues money and carries out the country's monetary policy. The Federal Reserve System is the central bank of the United States.

central limit order book (CLOB) A central system that contains limit orders for securities from specialists and market makers. Such a system consolidates the limit orders in a central location and bridges the gap in establishing a national market system. A hard CLOB executes orders immediately; a soft CLOB provides data to facilitate trading but does not include automatic executions. Establishment of a CLOB has generally been opposed by securities exchanges standing to lose significant volume to such a system.

CEO —See CHIEF EXECUTIVE OFFICER.

certainty equivalent The minimum sum of money required to make an individual indifferent to receipt of the sum of money and the probable outcome of an uncertain event. For example, suppose you are told to draw one card from a full deck of cards. If you draw a red card you win $100 and if you draw a black card you win nothing. If you would accept $40 to forego the selection and possibility of winning, $40 is the certainty equivalent of the outcome of the event. Certainty equivalents are used in evaluating risk.

certificate Evidence of ownership of a bond or shares of stock. A certificate contains detailed information relating to the issuer and the owner, including the issuer's name, particulars of the issue, the number of shares or the principal amount of the bonds, and the name and address of the owner. The back of a certificate may contain further details about the issue along with a provision for transferring ownership. —Also called *stock certificate*. —See also BOOK-ENTRY SECURITY.

certificate for automobile receivables (CARS) A short-term debt security backed by automobile loans, originating when lenders have the automobile loans packaged and resold to the public, thereby providing the lenders with more funds for use in additional lending. CARS are relatively safe and pay short-term interest rates slightly above Treasury securities of similar maturity.

Certificate of Accrual on Treasury Securities (CATS)® A trademark for investment services in the field of zero-coupon treasury receipts. This investment vehicle was originated by Salomon Brothers and Bache. —See also COUPON STRIPPING.

certificate of deposit (CD) A receipt for a deposit of funds in a financial institution that permits the holder to receive interest plus the deposit at maturity. Early withdrawal of CDs issued after October 1, 1983, results in a penalty of 30 days' loss of interest on maturities of a year or less, and loss of 90 days' interest on maturities of over 1 year. —See also ADD-ON; JUMBO CERTIFICATE OF DEPOSIT; NEGOTIABLE CERTIFICATE OF DEPOSIT; REAL ESTATE CERTIFICATE OF DEPOSIT; TERM CERTIFICATE; ZERO-COUPON CERTIFICATE OF DEPOSIT.

When are certificates of deposit a good investment?

A certificate of deposit is typically appropriate for an individual whose objective is current income and a high level of safety. A major attraction of a certificate of deposit is that each depositor's funds are insured to $100,000 by the Federal Deposit Insurance Corporation or the Federal Savings & Loan Insurance Corporation, agencies of the U. S. government. Another advantage of a certificate of deposit is that the interest rate is often compounded, producing a higher effective yield than the stated annual rate. Certificates of deposit are particularly appealing in periods of high interest rates when an investor will expect to receive a competitive rate of return for a specified period of time. To compensate for the reduced liquidity, a certificate of deposit should produce a yield higher than that available through investment in a government obligation with a similar maturity.

Robert G. Segel
Tucker, Anthony & R. L. Day, Inc., Boston, MA

certificate of indebtedness A United States Treasury debt obligation with an original maturity of one year or less and a fixed coupon rate of interest. The certificate of indebtedness differs from a Treasury bill, which is sold at a discount from face value and which has no coupon.

certified check A check drawn on an individual's account in which the financial institution from which the check is drawn certifies that sufficient funds are available to cover the amount of the check when cashed.

certified financial planner (CFP) A professional financial planner who has completed a series of correspondence courses and has passed examinations in subject areas such as insurance, securities, and taxes. The designation is awarded by the Institute of Certified Financial Planners. —See also CHARTERED FINANCIAL CONSULTANT.

Certified Public Accountant (CPA) An accountant who has met certain state requirements as to age, education, experience, residence, and accounting knowledge. Accountants must pass an extensive series of examinations before becoming CPAs. In most instances, only CPAs are permitted to render opinions on the fairness of financial statements.

cf —Used in bond transaction tables in newspapers to indicate that the certificate of a bond has matured but is still trading: *VarCp 10s99cf.*

CFA —See CHARTERED FINANCIAL ANALYST.

CFP —See CERTIFIED FINANCIAL PLANNER.

CFTC —See COMMODITY FUTURES TRADING COMMISSION.

chairman The highest-ranking executive in a corporation. The chairman leads the board of directors in setting broad corporate goals and determining if managers are, in fact, pursuing and achieving those goals. In large corporations the chairman is not ordinarily involved in day-to-day operational activities although it is likely that he or she was the chief executive officer before attaining the position of chairman. In some corporations, the chairman also serves as the president and the chief executive officer. —Also called *chairman of the board.* —See also CHIEF EXECUTIVE OFFICER; DIRECTOR.

change —See NET CHANGE.

Chapter 7 A bankruptcy option in which a bankrupt firm is liquidated after the courts have determined that reorganization is not worthwhile. A trustee is charged with liquidating all assets and distributing the proceeds to satisfy claims in order of priority. In Chapter 7 bankruptcies the creditors often receive a fraction of their claims and the stockholders receive nothing.

Chapter 11 A bankruptcy option in which a trustee is appointed to reorganize the bankrupt firm. Although security holders are likely to find their existing claims reduced or replaced with different claims, it is expected that the firm will continue operating. Both creditors and owners must vote approval of the plan before the reorganization can be confirmed by court action and become effective. —See also REORGANIZATION PLAN.

characteristic line A straight line on a graph that shows the relationship over time between returns on a stock and returns on the market. The line is used to illustrate a stock's alpha (the vertical intercept) and beta (the line's slope) and to show the difference between systematic and unsystematic risk.

charge off —See WRITE OFF.

charitable contribution deduction An itemized income-tax deduction for donations of assets to Internal Revenue Service-designated organizations. Certain qualifications, such as a contribution limit of 50% of a taxpayer's adjusted gross income, apply. Of particular interest to investors is the ability to donate appreciated property (i.e., securities that have increased in value since acquisition) and to deduct the entire market value of the donated assets without obligation to pay taxes on the capital gains. Likewise, it is generally unwise from a tax standpoint to donate assets that have decreased in value since the date of acquisition. Donations of appreciated property may subject the taxpayer to the alternative minimum tax. —See also DEDUCTION.

Making maximum use of the charitable contribution deduction when donating securities.
• •

In order to maximize a charitable deduction using securities, one should treat as gifts only appreciated securities. The donor effectively escapes taxation on the gain, receiving a deduction equal to the fair market value of the security at the time the gift is made. A word of caution: the gain that escapes taxation is treated as a preference item for purposes of the alternative minimum tax. Securities with a capital loss should not be donated. If they are donated instead of being sold, the donor gives up the loss which may be used to offset capital gains, and up to $3,000 can be used to offset taxable income.

Michele R. Bourgerie, CPA
Arthur Young, New York, NY

---

charitable lead trust A trust that pays income to a charity for a specific length of time, at which point the remainder is left to designated beneficiaries (usually family members). The purpose of the charitable lead trust is to reduce taxes on the deceased's estate while at the same time keeping control of the estate's assets in the family.

charitable remainder trust A trust that provides an income to one or more individuals for a specified length of time, at which point the remainder of the trust is left to a designated charity. A charitable remainder trust produces the opposite results compared with a charitable lead trust, which pays income to a charity and leaves the principal to another party.

A charitable remainder trust can produce substantial tax benefits and is particularly suitable for use by a married couple with no children.

chart   A pictorial display of data. Charts are used to observe the historical values of variables and, frequently, to spot trends that may provide insights for use in projecting future values. —Also called *graph*. —See also BAR CHART; LINE CHART; POINT-AND-FIGURE CHART.

charter   —See ARTICLES OF INCORPORATION.

chartered financial analyst (CFA)   A financial analyst who has met certain standards of experience, knowledge, and conduct as determined by the Institute of Chartered Financial Analysts. The successful candidate must pass three examinations covering economics, security analysis, portfolio management, financial accounting, and standards of conduct.

chartered financial consultant (ChFC)   A professional financial planner who has completed a series of courses and examinations in subject areas such as economics, insurance, real estate, and tax shelters. The designation is awarded by American College of Bryn Mawr, Pennsylvania. —See also CERTIFIED FINANCIAL PLANNER.

chart formation   A series of graphed stock prices or other market variables that form a recognizable pattern which may be used to forecast future movements of the charted variable. Chart formations are not always as clearly defined as their users would like; thus, the ability to recognize and use the charted data does vary among technicians. —Also called *formation; pattern*. —See also INVERTED FORMATION.

charting   The graphing of market variables—particularly stock prices and market averages. Technicians also chart other variables including commodity prices, interest rates, and trading volume in an attempt to determine trends and project future values. —See also BAR CHART; LINE CHART; POINT-AND-FIGURE CHART.

chartist   A person (as a market technician) who attempts to determine future stock price movements by analyzing past price movements as recorded on a chart. Two chartists may have different projections after viewing the same chart.

chart service   A firm selling graphs of security prices. A chart service records prices for a large number of securities or commodities and publishes charts at periodic intervals (generally on a monthly basis) for sale to investors. Subscribing to a chart service saves an investor considerable time; however, the charts often arrive a few days after the date of the last entry.

chattel mortgage   A mortgage loan using personal property such as automobiles, paintings, inventories, or real estate leases (but not real estate ownership) as security.

cheap   Pertaining to or being a security that sells at a market price below what is expected, given fundamental factors such as earnings, assets, and management ability. Whether or not a security is cheap is a subjective judgment. —See also EXPENSIVE.

cheap money —See EASY MONEY.

checking the market Scanning market maker quotations to find the lowest ask or highest bid for a security.

checkwriting privilege The privilege of writing checks against shares held in a mutual fund. This option, providing improved liquidity for the investor, is generally offered free of charge. The dollar amount of each check is normally subject to a minimum—often $250 or $500—depending on the policy of the fund.

ChFC —See CHARTERED FINANCIAL CONSULTANT.

Chicago Board of Trade (CBT) An organized exchange established in 1848 to trade forward grain contracts. The CBT now provides trading in a wide variety of futures and options.

Chicago Board Options Exchange (CBOE) A securities exchange established in 1973 as the nation's first organized floor for trading standardized options. Although its success spawned option trading on a number of other exchanges, the CBOE remains the most active option exchange in the country. Unlike most exchanges that use a specialist system of trading, the CBOE uses market makers who compete among themselves for trades. —See also BOARD BROKER.

Chicago Mercantile Exchange (CME) An organized exchange, established in 1919, which is a marketplace for the trading of futures contracts in various agricultural commodities. The International Money Market, which trades financial instruments, is a division of the CME. —Also called *Merc*.

chief executive officer (CEO) The person responsible to a company's board of directors for carrying out its policies. Essentially, the CEO is the highest-ranking executive managing the firm on a day-to-day basis. —Also called *chief operating officer.* —See also CHAIRMAN.

How can I spot churning in my account?

When an inordinate, unwarranted, or unexpected amount of activity goes on in an account, it may be considered churning. Another, easier, way to spot churning is if the broker is making more money than the client. Check your monthly statements regularly and carefully.

Bonnie Briskin, Stockbroker
Tucker, Anthony & R. L. Day, Inc., Boston, MA

---

churn To trade securities very actively in a brokerage account in order to increase brokerage commissions rather than customer profits. Brokers may be tempted to churn accounts because their income is directly related to the volume of trading undertaken by the customers. Churning is illegal and unethical; suspected churning should be reported to the brokerage firm's office manager. —Also called *burn and churn; overtrade.*

Cincinnati Stock Exchange An almost completely automated securities exchange on which members enter orders directly rather than going through a specialist. Although this Exchange is a technological leader, its volume of transactions is relatively small compared with the other regional exchanges. —See also NATIONAL SECURITIES TRADING SYSTEM.

circle To find interested buyers of a new security issue before determining the final price. A potential customer will be given a preliminary price (e.g., the interest rate of a bond or the selling price for stock) and will then commit to purchase if the issue is actually priced at the preliminary estimate. A different price permits the customer to back out or to get the first chance to buy the issue at the new price. —See also INDICATION OF INTEREST.

class —See STOCK CLASS.

class action lawsuit A lawsuit in which one party or a limited number of parties sue on behalf of a larger group to which the parties belong. For example, investors may bring a class action suit against a brokerage firm that has actively promoted a tax shelter without having adequately disclosed the attendant risks. —See also SHAREHOLDER DERIVATIVE SUIT.

Clayton Act A 1914 federal law designed to promote competition by prohibiting or severely restricting practices such as the acquisition of competitors, price discrimination, secret rebates, and interlocking directorates. —See also ANTITRUST LAWS; CELLER-KEFAUVER ANTIMERGER ACT; FEDERAL TRADE COMMISSION ACT OF 1914; SHERMAN ANTITRUST ACT.

clean opinion The opinion of a firm's auditors that its financial statements are fairly presented in accordance with generally accepted accounting principles. A clean opinion does not necessarily mean that the firm is financially strong or that its future is favorable since even financially weak firms generally receive clean opinions. —Also called *standard opinion; unqualified opinion.* —See also ADVERSE OPINION; DISCLAIMER OF OPINION; QUALIFIED OPINION; SUBJECT TO OPINION.

clean trade A security transaction by a block positioner that exactly matches customer buy and sell orders. Thus, the positioner does not find it necessary either to acquire securities or to sell from inventory in order to complete the transaction.

clear To pay for securities delivered into an account and accept funds for securities delivered out of the account.

clear Designating a trade in which the seller delivers securities and the buyer delivers funds in the prescribed manner, on time. —See also FAIL; FAIL FLOAT; GOOD DELIVERY.

clearing fee A charge by a clearing house for clearing securities trades using its own facilities.

clearing house A corporation established by an exchange in order to facilitate the execution of trades by transferring funds, assigning deliveries, and guaranteeing the performance of all obligations. —See also CLEARING-HOUSE STATEMENT.

clearing-house statement A statement of security or commodity trades submitted by a member firm to a clearing house. The statement indicates the net balance (i.e., short or long) in each security or commodity and the net amount to be paid or received to reconcile the member's account.

clearing member A member of a clearing house. Membership in a clearing house permits the member firm to use the house for clearing security trades.

clientele effect The tendency of different securities to attract different types of investors, depending on the dividend policy of the issuer. For example, certain investors are attracted to stocks (e.g., electric utility stocks) with high dividend yields, while other investors in high income tax brackets prefer stocks with lower dividend yields but more capital gains potential.

Clifford trust A temporary trust (established to last at least 10 years and 1 day or until the death of the beneficiary) in which assets are irrevocably transferred to the trust and income from the trust is given to the beneficiary. When the trust is terminated, the principal passes back to the creator. Clifford trusts are used almost exclusively by people with dependent children or dependent parents. Income from trusts created before March 1, 1986 is taxed at the creator's rate until the minority child reaches 14 years of age. At that time the child's tax rate will apply. For trusts created after March 1, 1986, the income will be taxed at the donor's rate even after the minority child has reached 14 years of age. Tax reform passed in 1986 eliminated most of the tax advantages of Clifford trusts.

climax —See BUYING CLIMAX; SELLING CLIMAX.

clip To detach interest coupons from a bearer bond. These coupons must be presented to a bank, a brokerage house, or the issuer's agent in order for the holder of the bearer bond to receive interest payments.

CLOB —See CENTRAL LIMIT ORDER BOOK.

clone fund A mutual fund started by another mutual fund having grown so large that its management feels the fund is limited as to the investments it can make. For example, a very large fund would generally be unable to establish investment positions in small or new corporations. Thus, a new, smaller fund with the same goals as the older, bigger fund is started. Although the parent fund and clone fund have the same investment objectives, they purchase different securities and generally operate under different managements.

close 1. The end of a session of trading. 2. The last price at which a security trades during a trading session. The last price is reported in the financial media and is of particular importance to the valuation of investment portfolios. —Also called *closing price; last.*

What are clone funds, and are they as good as the real thing?

Rocky vs Rocky II. Clone mutual funds are replicas of existing funds. They are set up for several reasons. The managers of a fund may conclude that if it becomes any bigger it will be too unwieldy (this was true of the Windsor Fund). Or the group may want to introduce a new pricing structure (the Massachusetts Financial Services Lifetime funds differ from their originals simply in that the up-front commission charge was discarded in favor of an annual fee). Or a new fund may have similar but slightly different objectives (National Real Estate Stock Fund and National Real Estate Income Fund both buy real estate securities but put a different emphasis on capital appreciation versus income). Finally, when a group successfully pioneers a new type of fund, imitators inevitably follow (Benham Target Maturities broke new ground for investors planning for retirement with a series of zero-coupon bond funds. The following year the Scudder group followed suit).

There is no reason in principle why the clone should perform worse than the original. Over the years, the well-performing Pioneer Fund has generally been beaten by the even better performing Pioneer II. The investor should keep in mind, however, that the two funds are different. They may have different portfolio managers, perhaps some difference in investment outlook and, certainly, different portfolios. The simple rules then, when looking at a new clone fund, are first, take into account what the original has done—clearly that is a crucial piece of evidence. But second, do not rely exclusively on that evidence.

Reg Green, Editor
Mutual Fund News Service, *San Francisco, CA*

close a position To eliminate an investment position. The most common way to close a position is to sell a security that is owned. An investor might also close a position by purchasing stock to replace shares borrowed for a short sale.

closed corporation —See CLOSELY HELD COMPANY.

closed-end investment company An investment company that issues a limited number of shares and does not redeem those that are outstanding. Closed-end investment companies are fairly rare; their shares trade on the exchanges or in the over-the-counter market. Thus, like stock of other publicly traded companies, share prices are determined by the pressures of supply and demand rather than by the value of underlying assets. —Also called *publicly traded fund.* —See also MUTUAL FUND; REGULATED INVESTMENT COMPANY.

closed-end mortgage A mortgage with a prohibition against additional borrowing using the same lien. The prohibition against additional borrowing protects the existing creditors from having the security diluted. —See also MORTGAGE BOND; OPEN-END MORTGAGE.

closely held company A firm whose shares of common stock are owned by relatively few individuals and are generally unavailable to outsiders. —Also called *closed corporation*.

closet indexing Investing in a widely diversified portfolio of securities to achieve a performance level nearly identical to that of a broadbased market average while claiming to provide active management based on market expertise.

closing price —See CLOSE 2.

closing purchase —See CLOSING TRANSACTION 2.

closing quote The final bid and ask price stated by the market maker or specialist at the end of a trading session.

closing sale —See CLOSING TRANSACTION 2.

closing transaction **1.** The final transaction for a particular security during a trading day. —See also OPENING TRANSACTION 1. **2.** An option order that will eliminate or decrease the size of an existing option position. An investor who repurchases three options that have been sold short is entering into a closing transaction. —Also called *closing purchase; closing sale*. —See also CLOSE A POSITION; OPENING TRANSACTION 2.

CMA® —See CASH MANAGEMENT ACCOUNT.

CME —See CHICAGO MERCANTILE EXCHANGE.

CMO —See COLLATERALIZED MORTGAGE OBLIGATION.

CMX —See COMMODITY EXCHANGE OF NEW YORK.

CNS —See CONTINUOUS NET SETTLEMENT.

Code of Procedure Rules of the National Association of Securities Dealers (NASD) for settling disputes among members or complaints against NASD members by outsiders.

codicil A legal change to a will.

Coffee, Sugar and Cocoa Exchange (CSCE) An organized exchange established in 1882 (with cocoa having been added in 1979) that provides facilities in New York City for the trading of futures contracts on coffee, sugar, and cocoa. Options on sugar futures are also traded there.

coil —See TRIANGLE.

cold call A broker's initial telephone call to a heretofore unknown person during which the broker seeks to enlist that person as a customer.

collar A maximum and minimum rate of interest that will be paid on the par value of a floating-rate note. —See also CAP 1.

collateral Assets pledged as security for a loan. In the event that a borrower defaults on the terms of a loan, the collateral may be sold, with the proceeds used to satisfy any remaining obligations. High quality collateral reduces risk to the lender and results in a lower rate of interest on the loan.

collateralize To pledge an asset as security for a loan. A loan to a broker is collateralized by pledging securities.

collateralized mortgage obligation (CMO) A security issued by the Federal Home Loan Mortgage Corporation that is similar to a Freddie Mac pass through but that provides interest and principal payments in a more predictable manner. CMOs are classed according to expected maturity ranges at the time of issue. The greater certainty of payment size is offset by slightly lower yields, compared with ordinary pass throughs.

collateral trust bond A long-term debt obligation with a claim against securities (i.e., stock, bonds, and notes) rather than against physical assets. These bonds are issued primarily by holding companies that own mainly securities of subsidiaries.

collectible An asset of limited supply that is sought for a variety of reasons including, it is hoped, an increase in value. Stamps, antiques, coins, and works of art are among the many things normally classified as collectibles. Collectibles are often regarded by investors as a hedge against inflation; their values tend to appreciate most when general prices are rising. The collectibles market represents a very tricky investment for inexperienced investors.

collection period The number of days, on average, that a firm requires to collect a credit sale. The length of the collection period indicates the effectiveness with which a firm's management grants credit and collects from customers. A short period is desirable because the firm obtains cash more quickly for reinvestment or for paying its own bills. The collection period is calculated by dividing accounts receivable by average daily credit sales. —Also called *average collection period*. —See also AC-COUNTS RECEIVABLE TURNOVER; ACTIVITY RATIO; AGING.

combination option An option composed of one or more calls and one or more puts. While the original combination is sold as a single unit, each part may be sold or exercised individually. Examples of combination options are spreads, straddles, straps, and strips.

combination security A security that combines the attributes of two or more individual securities. An example of a combination security is a convertible bond that is part debt and part common stock.

COMEX —See COMMODITY EXCHANGE OF NEW YORK.

comfort letter A statement from a Certified Public Accountant declaring no indication of false or misleading information in the financial statements being used in connection with a securities offering.

commercial paper A short-term unsecured promissory note issued by a finance company or a relatively large industrial firm. The notes are generally sold at a discount from face value with maturities ranging from 30 to 270 days. Although the large denominations ($25,000 minimum) of these notes usually keep individual investors out of this market, the notes are popular investments for money market mutual funds. —Also called *paper*. —See also PRIME PAPER.

commingled fund   An investment fund consisting of assets of several individual accounts. A commingled fund is established to reduce the cost and effort required to manage accounts separately.

commingled securities   Customers' securities stored together with a brokerage firm's securities.

commission   The fee levied by a broker to undertake a trade on behalf of a customer. Since the amount of the commission for a particular trade is no longer fixed, it can vary considerably among firms. —See also DISCOUNT BROKERAGE FIRM; FULL-SERVICE BROKERAGE FIRM.

commission broker   An employee of a member firm of an organized securities exchange who transacts orders for the firm or its customers on the exchange floor. Orders flow to the commission broker from the firm's trading desk or its registered representatives.

commission house   A firm whose primary business is to execute its customers' orders to buy and sell securities for a fee. Commission houses earn the name from acting as brokers rather than as dealers.

Committee on Uniform Securities Identification Procedures (CUSIP)   A 15-person board that established a standard identification numbering system (CUSIP numbers) for all stock certificates and registered bonds issued in the United States. Each security has its own assigned CUSIP number that is used to improve the efficiency of clearing operations.

commodity   A generic, largely unprocessed, good that can be processed and resold. Commodities traded in the financial markets for immediate or future delivery are grains, metals, and minerals. They are generally traded in very large amounts. —See also FUTURES CONTRACT.

commodity-backed bond   A rare bond with interest payments and/or principal repayment tied to the price of a commodity such as silver or oil. Although such a bond carries a relatively low interest rate at the time of issue, it gives the investor a hedge against inflation since the price of the commodity is likely to rise. These bonds are normally issued by firms having a stake in the commodity used to back the security. —Also called *gold bond*.

⟨$⟩ In June of 1986 Standard Oil Company (formerly Standard Oil of Ohio) planned to issue a complicated oil-indexed debt unit consisting of 10 securities: eight $1,000 discounted bonds maturing in the year 2001 and two notes with values dependent on the price of oil. Neither note was to pay interest unless oil prices exceeded $25 per barrel. The redemption value of each note was also tied to the price of oil shortly before maturity. One note maturing 4½ years from the date of issue carried a maturity value of $1,000 plus $170 for each dollar above $25 per barrel that oil prices averaged during the 20-day period before redemption. The second note, with a maturity of 5¾ years, could be redeemed for $1,000 plus $200 for each dollar above $25 per barrel that oil prices averaged. At redemption, both premiums were limited to a maximum oil price of $40. Holders were permitted to redeem the notes on the first or the fifteenth of any month in the year of maturity. The bond and notes of each unit could be transferred separately a short time after the issue date. Because of an initially weak display of interest among investors, the units were withdrawn by Standard Oil before the issue date.

commodity brokerage firm —See FUTURES COMMISSION MERCHANT.

Commodity Exchange of New York (CMX, COMEX) An organized exchange operating in New York City that offers facilities for the trading of futures and futures options in metals.

Commodity Futures Trading Commission (CFTC) A federal agency, established in 1974, that regulates and supervises the trading of commodity futures and commodity options. Additional regulation is effected by the exchanges on which the contracts are traded. —See also NATIONAL FUTURES ASSOCIATION.

commodity option An option either to buy or to sell a commodity futures contract at a fixed price until a specified date. —See also CALL 1; PUT 1.

commodity product spread A spread involving two commodities: one, a primary commodity; and the other, a byproduct of the primary commodity. For example, an investor might purchase a contract for soybeans and sell short a contract for soybean oil.

Common Market —See EUROPEAN ECONOMIC COMMUNITY.

common-size statement A financial statement with variables expressed in percentages rather than in dollar amounts. For example, items on an income statement are shown as a percentage of revenue or sales, and balance sheet entries are displayed as a percentage of total assets. Common-size statements are used primarily for comparative purposes so that firms of various sizes can be equated. —Also called *one hundred percent statement*.

common stock A class of capital stock that has no preference to dividends or any distribution of assets. Common stock normally conveys voting rights and is often termed *capital stock* if it is the only class of stock that a firm has outstanding (i.e., the firm has neither preferred stock nor multiple classes of common stock). Common stockholders are the residual owners of a corporation in that they have a claim to what remains after every other party has been paid. The value of their claim depends on the success of the firm. —See also COMMON STOCK EQUIVALENT; STOCK CLASS.

common stock equivalent A security viewed as basically the same as common stock, generally because the equivalent security may be exchanged for shares of common stock. Common stock equivalents include convertible bonds, convertible preferred stock, options, and warrants. Common stock equivalents are used in calculating earnings per share even though the calculation overstates the actual number of shares outstanding.

How can one compare firms by using a common-size statement?

Certain regulated companies, such as banks, are required to analyze account balances, in percentage terms, to provide a profile of the bank's stability and performance compared with benchmarks established for the industry. Common-size statements would normally disclose account information in two columns: the first column would be in dollars and the second in percentages. This is a static analysis, in that income and expense items are shown as a percentage of current year sales, not as percentage increases or decreases over prior years. Trends exist among companies of comparable size in an industry. Statistical analysis invites comparison, and the marketplace will compare individual companies with industry averages. If cost of goods sold for companies with sales in the range of $20–$50 million should average 50% of sales, a company with a 70% factor indicates a problem. A judgment can be made about the temporary nature (a strike at a plant) or the permanent nature (poor management) of the problem by reviewing common-size statements for the last several years. Common-size statements are useful to investors and to the management of a company. Management can also use these statements as a tool for budget purposes to make sure, for example, that research and development is adequate to develop new products to meet future sales projections. For the investor, common-size statements are only valid when comparing a company with its peers; as a business grows, its percentages will change. A large manufacturing company should achieve better economies of scale than a small manufacturer, and a small service company will have a lower overhead rate than its larger counterpart.

Marilyn J. Pitchford, CPA
Arthur Young, Boston, MA

common stock fund   A mutual fund that limits its investments to shares of common stock. Common stock funds vary in risk from relatively low to quite high, depending on the types of stocks in which the funds invest.

common stock ratio   The portion of a firm's capitalization represented by owners' equity. A relatively high common stock ratio is the mark of a conservatively financed company.

community property   Property owned jointly by a husband and wife. The legal concept in community property states that, with the exception of gifts and inheritance, all property acquired by husband and wife during a marriage is equally owned by each spouse. The community property statute is very important in the event that the marriage is dissolved or one spouse dies.

comp —See COMPARISON.

company risk The risk that certain factors affecting a specific company may cause its stock to change in price in a different way from stocks as a whole. For example, the profits and stock price of a firm selling an unusually large part of its output to foreign customers are subject to factors (such as changes in foreign exchange rates) that are less important to other companies.

comparative financial statements Financial statements, one current and the other of the previous accounting period, presented together for comparative purposes.

comparison A confirmation from one broker to another with respect to the details of a security trade. —Also called *broker comparison; comp.*

compensating balance The funds that a corporate borrower must keep on deposit in a financial institution in order to satisfy the terms of a loan agreement. The deposit may be in a checking account, savings account, or certificate of deposit, depending on the nature of the agreement. The net effect of a compensating balance requirement is an increase in the effective cost of the loan because the borrower is unable to utilize all the funds on which interest is paid.

competitive bidding 1. A method by which a corporation or government organization wishing to sell securities in the primary market selects an investment banker on the basis of the best price offered via competitive bids by the investment bankers. Municipal governments and public utilities are often required to ask for competitive bids on new security issues. —See also NEGOTIATED OFFERING. 2. The bidding on U.S. Treasury securities in which an investor stipulates a particular price or yield.

competitive trader —See FLOOR TRADER.

completed-contract method A method of recognizing revenues and costs from a long-term project in which profit is recorded only when the project is complete. Even if payments are received while the project is in progress, no revenues are recorded until its completion. The completed-contract method, a conservative way of accounting for long-term undertakings, is utilized for certain types of construction projects. —See also PERCENTAGE-OF-COMPLETION METHOD.

complex capital structure A corporate capital structure containing securities other than straight debt and stock. Thus, a firm having securities outstanding such as convertible bonds, convertible preferred stock, options, rights, or warrants is said to have a complex capital structure. Potential dilution of earnings resulting from a complex capital structure occurs in firms that report earnings per share on a primary and a fully diluted basis.

compliance department A securities exchange staff charged with ensuring that activity on the exchange complies with the rules of the exchange and those of the Securities and Exchange Commission.

composite tape   A security price reporting service that includes all transactions in a security on each of the exchanges and in the over-the-counter market. A composite tape is supposed to provide a complete picture of a security's price and volume activity rather than limiting the information only to that which occurs on a single exchange.

compounding period   The time period between the points when interest is paid or when it is added to principal. For example, a three-month compounding period (quarterly compounding) indicates that the interest is paid or is calculated at three-month intervals.

compound interest   Interest paid on interest from previous periods in addition to principal. Essentially, compounding involves adding interest to principal and any previous interest in order to calculate interest in the next period. —See also FREQUENCY OF COMPOUNDING; SIMPLE INTEREST.

comptroller   —See CONTROLLER.

Compustat®   A trademark for goods and services including computer programming services; namely, systemizing statistical and financial information and preparing data cards and tapes based on such information, and reports consisting of printed cards and prerecorded computer tapes bearing statistical and financial information sold as a unit. The service is provided by Investors Management Services, a subsidiary of Standard & Poor's.

computer assisted execution system (CAES)   A system for the automatic execution of broker-dealer limit and market orders by market makers in the over-the-counter market. Broker-dealers may designate a particular market maker or may have the order automatically routed to the market maker offering the best price.

computerized investing   —See AUTOMATED STOCK TRADING.

Is "concept" more important overall than assets or income, when one evaluates concept companies?

Concept companies rely on investor psychology rather than fundamentals. If an investor can spot a concept or fad before it actually becomes popular, there is the possibility for gains. Warning: fundamentals become secondary for a concept stock. The perfect example would be the recent tremendous rise in the prices of the stock of condom manufacturers where the *concept* was that these manufacturers would profit from the AIDS epidemic.

Richard Mazur, Vice President, Research Marketing
Steven Flagg, Research Coordinator
PaineWebber Incorporated, New York, NY

concept company   A firm that attracts investors more on the basis of the type of business it is in or by the direction in which its management says it is moving than on its current earnings or dividends. For example, a company involved in sophisticated biomedical research that has the potential of making a major scientific breakthrough and large profits could qualify as a concept company. In the early 1970s, firms operating nursing homes were concept companies that eventually lost favor with many investors. Concept companies of the 1980s include firms engaged in computer software development, genetic engineering, and medical technology.

concession   The dollar discount from a security's retail selling price received by members of an underwriting syndicate. For example, a syndicate member paying $995 for a bond to be sold at par (i.e., at $1,000) is receiving a $5 concession. —Also called *selling concession.*

conditional rating   —See PROVISIONAL RATING.

conduit theory   The theory that since regulated investment companies merely act as conduits in passing dividends, interest, and capital gains to stockholders, these income items should not be taxed once to a company and then again to the company's stockholders. If an investment company complies with certain federal regulations, the income is taxed only to the stockholders receiving the distributions. —Also called *pipeline theory.* —See also SUBCHAPTER M.

confidence indicator   A measure of investors' faith in the economy and the securities market. A low or deteriorating level of confidence is considered by many technical analysts as a bearish sign. —See also BARRON'S CONFIDENCE INDEX; STANDARD & POOR'S CONFIDENCE INDICATOR.

confirmation   **1.** Written acknowledgment of a security trade, listing important details such as the date, the size of the transaction, the price, the commission, taxes, and the amount of money involved. A confirmation is generally mailed the day after a trade takes place. —See also CANCELLATION.   **2.** The reaction of one technical indicator (such as the movement of a stock price average) that strengthens a signal given by another indicator.

congestion area   In technical analysis, a horizontal band on a point-and-figure chart resulting from a stock price fluctuation within a narrow price range. Since a congestion area indicates an equality of supply and demand, the technicians wait until the stock breaks out of the upper or lower bound before committing funds. —See also BREAKOUT; HORIZONTAL COUNT.

conglomerate   A company engaged in varied business operations, many of which seem unrelated. A conglomerate is supposed to have reduced risk, since its various operations are affected differently by business conditions over time. In addition, it is possible for a conglomerate to redistribute its corporate assets depending on which operations show the most promise. Conglomerates were popular among investors during the 1960s but investors' interest in them faded during the 1970s and the 1980s.

consent dividend   Retained earnings credited to paid-in surplus by a personal holding company. The consent dividend is taxed to stockholders as an ordinary dividend; however, this tax liability is partially offset by the stockholders' increasing the cost basis of the stock by the same amount.

consol   A debt instrument having no scheduled return of principal and thereby perpetual interest payments and no maturity. Consols fluctuate widely in price with changes in long-term interest rates. They have never been popular in the United States. —Also called *annuity bond; perpetual bond*. —See also PERPETUITY.

consolidated balance sheet   A balance sheet in which assets and liabilities of a parent company and its controlled subsidiaries are combined, thereby presenting balance sheet items for the parent and its subsidiaries as if they were a single firm.

consolidated bond   A single bond issue used to replace two or more outstanding issues.

consolidated income statement   An income statement that combines the income statements of two or more organizations. As with other consolidated statements, a consolidated income statement eliminates any funds owed to or due from firms within the same group.

consolidated mortgage   A mortgage made to replace two or more outstanding mortgages.

consolidated quotation system (CQS)   An electronic system for disseminating the bid, ask, and size for a security in each market in which the security is traded. CQS was developed in 1978 by the National Association of Securities Dealers and the organized exchanges.

consolidated tape   An integrated reporting system of price and volume data for trades in listed securities in all markets in which the securities trade. Thus, the consolidated tape would report trades in General Motors stock not only from its principal market on the New York Stock Exchange, but also from all the other markets in which it trades. —See also NETWORK A; NETWORK B.

consolidation   A combination of two or more firms into a completely new company. Assets and liabilities of the firms are absorbed by the new company. —See also MERGER.

consortium   A group of organizations participating in a joint venture. Airbus Industrie, a European airplane manufacturer, is a consortium of four public and private corporations in Britain, France, Spain, and West Germany.

constant dollar plan   A formula plan for investing in which a constant amount of money is kept in stocks with the remainder in bonds or short-term securities. Essentially, this plan forces the investor to sell stocks in rising markets and purchase them in falling markets.

constant dollars   Dollars reported in unchanged value compared with the value reported on a previous date. For example, a company may have raised its dividends on each share of common stock from $2.00 in 1976 to $5.00 in 1986. However, after investors have adjusted for consumer price increases during the 10-year period, the 1986 dividend amounts to only $2.50 in constant dollars. In this case, the 1986 dollars are constant in terms of their 1976 purchasing power.

constant ratio plan   A formula plan for investing in which the market value of all stocks in an investor's portfolio is kept at a predetermined level. The remainder is kept in other investments. Thus, stocks must be sold if they rise in value more rapidly than other investments and sold if they fall in value more rapidly than other investments in the portfolio. As an example, an investor may decide upon a portfolio of 70% stocks and 30% bonds.

construction loan   A short-term mortgage with funds used to finance the construction of a real estate project before permanent long-term financing is obtained. Some real estate investment trusts specialize in these loans because their returns are often relatively high. Construction loans are often more risky than long-term mortgages.

construction work in progress (CWIP)   The amount of funds a company has tied up in construction projects. This asset is of particular importance to electric utilities because state regulators often disallow all or a portion of CWIP from earning a return.

constructive dividend   A corporate payment to a stockholder characterized by the Internal Revenue Service as a dividend distribution even though the corporation calls it something else. For example, a small firm may pay an employee, who is also a stockholder, an excessive salary so that the payment can be used as a tax-deductible expense rather than as an aftertax dividend payment. The Internal Revenue Service may determine that part of the payment is a constructive dividend and then disallow it as a tax-deductible expense.

constructive receipt   Receipt of items considered to be income for a given tax period even though payment is not received until later. For example, a dividend paid and mailed on December 29, 1986, but not received by stockholders until after the first of the following year is considered taxable income for 1986 because the stockholders are considered to have constructive receipt of the dividend.

consumed-income tax   A tax levied only against the part of income that is spent. Proponents of this type of taxation contend that exempting the portion of income that is saved will encourage savings, will provide funds for investment, and will make the economy more productive.

consumer price index (CPI)   A measure of the relative cost of living compared with a base year (currently 1967). The CPI can be a misleading indicator of inflationary impact on a given person because it is constructed according to the spending patterns of an urban family of four.
—See also GNP DEFLATOR; PRODUCER PRICE INDEX.

consumption tax   A tax levied on individual commodities or services and included as part of the retail price of those commodities or services paid by consumers. For example, a 25¢ tax levied on a pack of cigarettes is a consumption tax. Consumption taxes are advocated by many people as an inducement to increased savings in the economy. These people argue that the present taxation of income penalizes savers and rewards spenders. —See also EXCISE TAX; VALUE-ADDED TAX.

contango   In futures or options trading, a market in which longer-term contracts carry a higher price than near-term contracts. The premium accorded to longer maturities is a normal condition of the market and reflects the cost of carrying the commodity for future delivery. —See also INVERTED MARKET.

contingent annuity   A series of payments scheduled to begin at the time of a specified event. For example, an individual's death may set in motion an annuity payable to a designated person or organization.

contingent issue   An issue of securities to be distributed only when a specified event has occurred or when a given standard has been met. For example, the poison pill defense against hostile takeovers involves issuance of additional securities in the event that the raider acquires a certain percentage of the takeover target's outstanding stock.

contingent liability   An obligation that may occur, but that is not likely to occur because the event causing the obligation is improbable. For example, an award from a lawsuit against a firm in which there is little likelihood that the plaintiff will recover is a contingent liability of the defendant.

contingent order   A specialized security order in which the broker is instructed to take some action in the event that something else has already occurred. An example would be an order to sell call options on Westinghouse common stock only after shares of Westinghouse have been purchased at a specified limit price.

contingent takedown option   An option to purchase a fixed-income security at a predetermined price until a specific date. The price is normally at par since the bond to be purchased is a new issue. Contingent takedown options typically originate as sweeteners in new debt issues to lower the interest cost to the issuers.

continuing operations   Parts of a business that are expected to be maintained as an ongoing segment of the overall business operation. Income and losses from continuing operations are reported separately if any segments have been discontinued during the accounting period. —Also called *going lines.*

continuous compounding   Compounding of interest using the shortest possible interval of time. While continuous compounding sounds impressive, in practice it results in virtually the same effective yield as daily compounding.

continuous net settlement (CNS)   The settlement of securities transactions among brokers and dealers in which all transactions are netted out by the National Securities Clearing Corporation in order to minimize the movement of physical certificates and money balances. With continuous net settlement, only net settlement balances need be moved. For example, if during a day of trading, Merrill Lynch purchases 1,000 shares of Amoco for one customer and sells 1,000 shares of Amoco for another customer, Merrill Lynch will have a zero net settlement in this stock, with no movement of securities required.

continuous trading A trading system for securities in which transactions take place whenever a sell limit order equals or is less than a buy order or a buy limit order equals or is more than a sell order. Essentially, continuous trading occurs when dealers and brokers attempt to execute orders as soon as they have been received. Except for opening transactions, continuous trading is the way securities are bought and sold in the United States. —See also BATCH TRADING.

contra broker The broker on the opposite side of a transaction. To a broker acting as an agent to buy, the contra broker is the selling broker. Conversely, to a broker on the sell side, the contra broker is the broker on the buy side.

contract **1.** In futures trading, an agreement between two parties to make and take delivery of a specified commodity on a given date at a predetermined location. **2.** In options trading, an agreement by the writer either to buy (if a put) or to sell (if a call) a given asset at a predetermined price until a certain date. The holder of the option is under no obligation to act.

contract grades In commodities trading, the standards that a commodity must meet in order to be used for delivery on a futures contract. For example, the Chicago Board of Trade requires silver deliveries to take place with 1,000- or 1,100-ounce bars assaying not less than .999 fine.

contract month The month in which a futures contract requires delivery of the commodity. Most contracts are offset or closed before this time so that no delivery is necessary.

contract sheet A ledger sheet prepared by the Securities Industry Automation Corporation that lists transaction information of broker-dealers by security. Contract sheets summarize the information that participating broker-dealers require to settle their accounts with other broker-dealers and with the Securities Industry Automation Corporation.

contract size In futures and options, the size or amount of the asset to be delivered. For example, stock options nearly always specify 100 shares, while a silver futures contract on the Chicago Mercantile Exchange stipulates 5,000 troy ounces.

contractual plan A program in which an investor in a mutual fund agrees to invest a fixed amount of money at regular intervals in accumulating shares. For example, an individual may contract to invest $100 per month with a selected fund regardless of what the market does or at what price the fund's shares sell throughout the period. —See also DOLLAR-COST AVERAGING; LOAD SPREAD OPTION.

contrarian An investor who decides which securities to buy and sell by going against the crowd. For example, a contrarian would tend to purchase the stock of steel companies when steel stock prices are depressed and most investment counselors are advising against them. Contrarians operate on the premise that when stocks are very popular they are overbought, and when they are very unpopular they are oversold.

contributed capital Funds or property transferred to a company by its stockholders. The contribution may be made in return for stock, in which case the payment is recorded as paid-in capital, or it may be a donation, in which case it is recorded as donated capital.

contributory pension plan A pension plan in which the participating employees are required to support the plan with contributions. —See also NONCONTRIBUTORY PENSION PLAN.

controlled account —See DISCRETIONARY ACCOUNT.

controller An organization's chief accounting officer who is responsible for establishing and maintaining the organization's accounting system. —Also called *comptroller*.

controlling interest Ownership of sufficient outstanding corporate stock to control the actions of the firm. Controlling interest often involves ownership of significantly less than 51% of a firm's outstanding stock because many owners fail to participate in decision making.

control person —See AFFILIATED PERSON.

control stock —See SUPERVOTING STOCK.

control value The value of shares in a firm when the number of shares available is sufficient to control the firm. If one person or a group owns 60% of a firm's outstanding stock, the control shares are worth more on a per-share basis than the remaining 40% of outstanding shares.

conventional option A put or call option contract negotiated independent of the organized option exchanges. Before 1973 and the opening of the Chicago Board Option Exchange, all options originated through private negotiations. The disadvantage of conventional options is their lack of liquidity owing to a limited secondary market.

convergence The coming together of futures prices and spot prices as a futures contract nears expiration.

conversion equivalent The price at which common stock would have to sell in order to make a convertible security worth its market price in common stock value alone. The equivalent is calculated by dividing the conversion ratio into a convertible security's market price. A $1,000 face amount bond trading at $1,200 and convertible into 40 shares of stock has a conversion equivalent of $1,200/40 shares, or $30 per share.

conversion factors The rates used to adjust differences in bond values for delivery on a Treasury bond futures contract. Because the contract calls for the equivalent of an 8% coupon, 20-year maturity bond, it is necessary to convert other securities that are acceptable for delivery.

conversion parity The condition of a convertible security when it sells at a price equal to the value of the underlying asset into which it may be exchanged.

conversion period The time during which a convertible security may be exchanged for other assets. Most conversion periods extend for the lives of the convertible securities (until maturity for bonds) although some periods are limited. A conversion period occasionally may be extended by the issuer.

conversion premium The excess at which a convertible security sells above its conversion value. The conversion premium normally declines as a convertible security rises in market price. A bond trading at $1,400 and convertible into 50 shares of common stock with a current market price of $22 each sells at a conversion premium of $1,400 − $1,100, or $300.

conversion price The price per share at which common stock will be exchanged for a convertible security. The principal amount of a convertible security divided by the conversion price equals the number of shares that will be received upon exchange. The conversion price is normally adjusted downward for events such as stock splits and dividends. —See also ADJUSTMENT IN CONVERSION TERMS.

conversion privilege —See EXCHANGE PRIVILEGE.

conversion ratio The number of shares of stock into which a convertible security may be exchanged. The ratio for a convertible bond is calculated by dividing the conversion price into the principal amount of the bond.

conversion value The market value of the underlying asset(s) into which a convertible security may be exchanged. Generally, conversion value is the number of shares that can be obtained times the market price per share. A bond that can be converted into 30 shares of stock with a market price of $20 each has a conversion value of $600.

convertible —See CONVERTIBLE SECURITY.

convertible floating-rate note A floating-rate note that gives the holder the option of exchanging it for a longer-term debt security with a specified coupon. Unlike a regular floating-rate note, the convertible feature protects investors against declining interest rates.

convertible security A security that, at the option of the holder, may be exchanged for another asset, generally a fixed number of shares of common stock. Convertible issues frequently are fixed-income securities such as debentures and preferred stock. Their prices are influenced by changes in interest rates and the values of the assets into which they may be exchanged. Convertible securities vary in price to a greater degree than straight debt but to a lesser degree than the underlying asset. —Also called *convertible*. —See also BOND CONVERSION; BUSTED CONVERTIBLE; CONVERSION PREMIUM; CONVERSION PRICE; CONVERSION RATIO; CONVERSION VALUE; DIVIDEND ADJUSTMENT; INTEREST ADJUSTMENT.

What are the advantages and disadvantages of choosing convertible securities?

· ·

A convertible security is any security (usually a bond or preferred stock) other than a common stock that may be exchanged for common stock at the owner's option without putting up additional funds. Conversion terms are specified. Such a security is a hybrid: it provides greater safety than the common stock in the event of bankruptcy, it draws dividends or interest payments ahead of common dividends, but it sells at a price close to the price of the stock into which it is convertible when the stock is doing well (and thus above its basic investment value) with greater risk and lower yield than nonconvertible bonds and preferred stocks. Thus, convertible securities are for investors who wish to hedge their bets.

J. Kendrick Noble, Jr., First Vice President
PaineWebber Incorporated, New York, NY

---

convexity   A mathematical measure of the sensitivity of a bond's price to changing interest rates. A high convexity indicates a greater responsiveness of a bond's price to interest rate changes.

cooling-off period   The required waiting period between the time a firm files a registration statement for a new security issue with the Securities and Exchange Commission and the time the securities actually can be issued. The cooling-off period is normally 20 days, although the Securities and Exchange Commission may alter it for individual issues. —Also called *twenty-day period; waiting period.* —See also EFFECTIVE DATE.

COOP   —See BANKS FOR COOPERATIVES.

corner   Significant control over a sufficient portion of a particular security so that it is possible to control the security's price. Others wishing to purchase the security (especially to cover short positions) are forced to buy it at an artificially high price. Corners were popular in the early 1900s when the securities markets were virtually unregulated. —See also NATURAL CORNER.

corner   To acquire a big enough position in a particular security or commodity so that control over its price and supply is achieved.

corporate   Pertaining to a bond issued by a corporation as opposed to a bond issued by the U.S. Treasury or a municipality.

corporate bond fund   An investment company that invests in long-term corporate bonds and passes the income on these securities to its stockholders. Although these funds vary in value with changes in long-term interest rates, they normally provide a current return in excess of money market funds. Corporate bond funds are of interest primarily to investors seeking high current income or to those betting on a substantial fall in long-term interest rates.

corporate equivalent The yield required on a taxable bond selling at par to provide the same aftertax yield to maturity of a bond selling at a premium or discount. For example, a $1,000 par, 10% coupon bond selling for $900 and due to mature in 5 years provides a yield to maturity of 12.8%. However, after taxes have been paid at a rate of 28% on the $100 gain ($1,000 − $900) and 28% on the $100 annual interest payments, the aftertax yield to maturity is slightly under 10%. The corporate equivalent yield is 10%/(1 − tax rate) or 13.9%.

Corporate Financing Committee A council of the National Association of Securities Dealers that determines the fairness of markups made by underwriters on securities issues.

corporate raider —See RAIDER.

corporation A form of organizing a business in which the business is granted a state charter recognizing it as a separate legal entity having its own rights, privileges, and liabilities distinct from those of the individuals forming the business. A corporation acquires assets, enters into contracts, sues or is sued, and pays taxes in its own name. Corporations issue shares of stock to individuals supplying ownership capital and issue bonds to individuals lending money to the business. The corporate form of business is desirable for a variety of reasons including increased ability to raise capital. Most large firms, especially those engaged in manufacturing, are organized as corporations. All stocks sold in the primary market and traded in the secondary market are shares of corporate ownership. —See also INCORPORATE; LIMITED LIABILITY; PARTNERSHIP; PROPRIETORSHIP; UNLIMITED LIABILITY.

corpus **1.** The principal of a bond. For example, securities dealers create zero-coupon treasury receipts by purchasing a regular treasury bond and separating the interest coupons from the corpus. —See also COUPON STRIPPING. **2.** The principal amount of an estate or trust.

CORR —Used on the consolidated tape to indicate a correction in a reported transaction: *CORR.LAST.GY 50 WAS 51.*

correction A sharp, relatively short price decline that temporarily interrupts a persistent upward trend in the market or the price of a stock.

correlation A measure of how closely two variables move together through time. For example, all utility stocks tend to have a high degree of correlation because their share prices are influenced by the same forces. Conversely, gold stock price movements are not closely correlated with utility stock price movements because the two are influenced by very different factors. The concept of correlation is frequently used in portfolio analysis. —See also SERIAL CORRELATION.

correspondent A financial organization such as a securities firm or a bank that regularly performs services for another firm not having the requisite facilities or the access to perform the services directly. For example, a member of a securities exchange may execute a trade for a nonmember firm.

cost Expenditure of funds or use of property to acquire or produce a product or service. —See also AVERAGE COST; FIXED COST; HISTORICAL COST; MARGINAL COST; REPLACEMENT COST; VARIABLE COST.

cost accounting The field of accounting that measures, classifies, and records costs. A cost accountant might be required to establish a system for identifying and segmenting various production costs so as to assist a firm's management in making prudent operating decisions.

cost-benefit analysis The comparison of benefits and costs in decision making. Dollar values are assigned to benefits and costs in most cost-benefit analyses.

cost center A segment of a business or other organization in which costs can be segregated, with the head of that segment being held accountable for expenses. Cost centers are established in large organizations to identify responsibility and to control costs.

cost depletion Depletion calculated as a percentage of the original cost of a natural resource that is consumed during a period. —See also PERCENTAGE DEPLETION.

cost of capital The overall percentage cost of the funds used to finance a firm's assets. Cost of capital is a composite cost of the various individual sources of funds including common stock, debt, preferred stock, and retained earnings. The overall cost of capital depends on the cost of each source and the proportion that the source represents of all capital employed by the firm. The goal of an individual or business is to limit investment to assets providing a higher return than the cost of capital used to finance those assets.

cost of carry Direct costs paid by an investor to maintain a security position. For example, an individual purchasing securities on margin must pay interest expenses on borrowed funds. Likewise, an investor selling stock short is responsible for making dividend payments to the buyer. —Also called *carrying charges*. —See also NEGATIVE CARRY; POSITIVE CARRY.

cost of goods sold The cost of purchasing materials and preparing goods for sale during a specific accounting period. Costs include labor, materials, overhead, and depreciation.

Council of Economic Advisors A group of three economists appointed by the President of the United States to advise the executive branch on domestic and foreign economic issues. The influence of the Council has varied widely, depending on the views of the President in office and the use he wishes to make of its advice.

coupon 1. The annual interest paid on a debt security. A coupon is normally stated in terms of the rate paid on a bond's face value. For example, a 9% coupon, $1,000 principal amount bond would pay its owner $90 in interest annually. A coupon is set at the time a security is issued and, for most bonds, stays the same until maturity. **2.** The detachable part of a coupon bond that must be presented for payment every six months in order to receive interest. —See also CLIP; COUPON CLIPPING.

coupon bond —See BEARER BOND.

coupon clipping The removal of interest coupons attached to a bearer bond in order that they might be taken to a bank or sent to a paying agent for collection. Coupon clipping is necessary because owners of bearer bonds do not automatically receive interest checks in the mail every six months.

coupon-equivalent rate An alternative measure of yield that is used to make securities normally quoted on a discount basis comparable with those quoted on the more normal return on the amount invested. Stating interest at the coupon-equivalent rate is useful for securities, such as Treasury bills and commercial paper, sold at discounts from face value. As an example, a $10,000 ninety-one day Treasury bill selling for $9,750 is normally quoted at

$$\frac{\$10,000 - \$9,750}{\$10,000} \times \frac{360 \text{ days}}{91 \text{ days}} = 9.89\%$$

However, the coupon-equivalent rate calculated on the amount of money invested is

$$\frac{\$10,000 - \$9,750}{\$9,750} \times \frac{360 \text{ days}}{91 \text{ days}} = 10.14\%$$

—See also BANK DISCOUNT BASIS.

coupon-equivalent yield The stated rate of return on bonds without accounting for any compounding. Since bonds nearly always pay interest twice a year, the coupon-equivalent yield must be compounded semiannually to produce the effective annual yield, a measure used by many banks in advertising certificates of deposit. For example, a 12% coupon, $1,000 principal amount bond pays $60 in interest each 6 months, resulting in an effective yield of 12.36% because the first $60 payment each year can be reinvested to earn an additional $3.60 during the latter half of the year.

coupon stripping The purchase of ordinary bonds (normally, U.S. Treasury bonds) that are then repackaged such that the receipts to interest and principal payments are sold separately. The effect is to transform a regular-interest paying security into zero-coupon receipts of varying maturities. Sold under a variety of names such as CATS®, LIONS, and TIGR℠, these investments have proved popular for tax-sheltered accounts such as IRAs. Generic names for them include *animals* and *felines*. —Also called *stripping*. —See also CORPUS 1.

covariance A statistical measure of the extent to which two variables move together. Covariance is used by financial analysts to measure the degree to which return on two securities is related. In general, a high covariance indicates similar movements and lack of diversification. —See also RISK; VARIANCE.

covenant A clause in a loan agreement intended to protect the lender's claim by keeping the borrower's financial position approximately the same as it was at the time that the loan agreement was made. Essentially, covenants spell out exactly what the borrower may do and must do in order to satisfy the terms of the loan. For example, the borrower may be prohibited from issuing more debt by using certain assets as collateral. Likewise, the borrower may be required to issue reports to bondholders on certain dates. —Also called *protective covenant; restrictive covenant.* —See also INDENTURE; NEGATIVE COVENANT; POSITIVE COVENANT.

cover —See SHORT COVER.

coverage ratio A measure of a corporation's ability to meet a certain type of expense. For example, *dividend coverage* measures a corporation's ability to meet its current dividend with available net income. In general, a high coverage ratio indicates a better ability to meet the expense in question. —See also DIVIDEND COVERAGE; FIXED-CHARGE COVERAGE; INTEREST COVERAGE; PREFERRED DIVIDEND COVERAGE.

covered option A call option sold short by an investor owning the underlying stock. In case the option is later exercised against the short seller of the option, the seller is covered by the stock that is owned. —See also NAKED OPTION.

covered writer The seller or writer of a call option who owns the underlying asset that may be required for delivery. Covered writers are normally conservative investors seeking extra current income. —See also BUY-AND-WRITE STRATEGY.

CPA —See CERTIFIED PUBLIC ACCOUNTANT.

CPI —See CONSUMER PRICE INDEX.

CQS —See CONSOLIDATED QUOTATION SYSTEM.

crash An extended major decline in the securities markets.

credit 1. The ability to borrow or to purchase goods and services with payment delayed beyond delivery. 2. An accounting entry resulting in an increase in liabilities or owners' equity or a decrease in assets. —See also DEBIT. 3. The balance in an account.

credit balance Cash and the market value of securities held in a brokerage account. —See also DEBIT BALANCE; FREE CREDIT BALANCE.

credit-balance theory The technical indicator that uses the level of credit balances in investors' brokerage accounts. Most technical analysts consider large credit (cash) balances bullish because credit balances represent potential buying power that will eventually be used for purchasing securities. —See also DEBIT-BALANCE THEORY.

credit crunch A period of time during which borrowed funds are difficult to obtain and, even if they can be found, interest rates are very high. Credit crunches were particularly severe before 1980 when the ceilings on interest rates that financial institutions could pay resulted in a drying up of deposits. —See also REGULATION Q.

credit department —See MARGIN DEPARTMENT.

credit enhancement An addition to a bond issue that improves the issue's safety of principal and interest. For example, the purchase of insurance guaranteeing payments on a bond issue is credit enhancement.

credit line —See LINE OF CREDIT.

creditor One to whom funds are owed. Holders of bonds and debentures are creditors to whom funds are owed by the issuers. —See also DEBTOR; SECURED CREDITOR; UNSECURED CREDITOR.

credit rating A grading of a borrower's ability to meet financial obligations in a timely manner. Credit ratings are set by lenders and by independent agents for companies, individuals, and specific debt issues. —See also BOND RATING.

credit risk The risk that a borrower will be unable to make payment of interest or principal in a timely manner.

credit spread Simultaneous sale of one option and purchase of another option, resulting in a credit to the investor's account. Thus, more funds are received from the sale than are required for the purchase. —See also DEBIT SPREAD.

credit union A nonprofit cooperative financial institution providing credit to its members who share a common bond. Credit unions often pay slightly higher rates of interest on passbook-type savings accounts and charge lower rates on consumer loans.

creeping tender offer The purchase of a target firm's stock at varying prices in the open market rather than through a formal tender offer. Most shares are often acquired in large blocks from arbitrageurs, frequently resulting in the exclusion of small stockholders from the offer. The purpose of a creeping tender offer is to gain control of a firm's stock more cheaply and quickly than an ordinary tender offer permits. —See also WILLIAMS ACT.

cross To match, by a single broker or dealer, a buy order and a sell order. For example, a floor broker may have an order to buy 500 shares of IBM at $120 and another order to sell 500 shares of IBM at the same price. Subject to certain rules, the floor broker may cross the order by matching the sell and the buy orders. Crossing of stock is common in large blocks.

crossed trade The matching of a buy order with a sell order when the trade is not reported to the exchange on which it occurred. Crossed trades are prohibited.

cross hedge In futures trading, an offsetting position in a futures contract for an existing position in a related commodity in the cash market. An example would be the sale of a contract on wheat for delivery in two months in order to offset an existing cash position in oats.

crowd Members on the floor of an exchange who are clustered around a pit or a specialist's post waiting to execute trades. —See also FOREIGN CROWD.

crowding out Large borrowing by the federal government—a process that soaks up lendable funds, drives up interest rates, and eliminates from the credit markets many private firms wishing to borrow money from those markets. The government is able to crowd out private borrowers because its credit rating is so high and because it is willing to pay the interest rate demanded by the market. Small firms and companies with poor credit ratings are most adversely affected by crowding out.

crown jewel A prized asset of a company. —Often used to refer to a part of a business that is sought by another firm or an investor in a takeover attempt that is hostile to the target firm's management. —See also SCORCHED EARTH.

> ⚠️ Following its 1986 bankruptcy filing, LTV Corporation indicated that it might try to reorganize around its profitable aerospace and defense business. LTV operated the United States's second-largest steel business and had a large energy-products operation, but the aerospace and defense division had long been considered its crown jewel. In 1985, LTV suffered an operating loss in its steel and energy-products operations of $253 million on sales of nearly $6 billion, but its aerospace and defense business produced an operating profit of $164 million on sales of $2.25 billion. Thus the value of the aerospace and defense unit was used as collateral for bank loans and unpaid pension contributions.

crown jewel lockup agreement —See LOCKUP AGREEMENT.

CRSP tapes A magnetic computer tape of monthly and daily stock prices. The service is provided by the Center for Research in Security Prices at the University of Chicago.

crush A combination commodity trade in which soybean futures are purchased and soybean meal or oil futures are sold. —See also REVERSE CRUSH.

CSCE —See COFFEE, SUGAR AND COCOA EXCHANGE.

cum dividend —Used to refer to a stock trading such that buyers qualify to receive the next dividend payment. Stocks trade cum dividend until the fifth business day before the record date. —See also EX-DIVIDEND.

cum rights —See RIGHTS ON.

cumulative Designating preferred stock and income bonds on which all dividends must be paid in full before any payment of dividends to common stockholders. Thus, any dividends that are passed eventually must be brought up to date before common stockholders may receive payments. Nearly all issues of preferred stock are cumulative. —See also DIVIDENDS IN ARREARS; NONCUMULATIVE.

cumulative voting A type of corporate voting right in which a stockholder receives one vote per owned share times the number of directors' positions up for election. The stockholder may allocate votes among the different positions as he or she wishes. For example, an owner of 200 shares is permitted a total of 1,200 votes if 6 positions are to be voted on. These 1,200 votes may be cast for a single director, may be split between 2 directors, or may be allocated equally among all 6 directors. Cumulative voting, making it easier for smaller interest groups to be represented, is required by some states. —See also MAJORITY VOTING.

Curb Exchange An early name for what is now the American Stock Exchange. The term derived from the market's beginnings on a street in downtown New York.

currency option An option that gives the owner the right to buy (call) or to sell (put) a specific amount of a foreign currency at a predetermined price until a certain date. A currency option is identical in concept to a stock option. The only difference between the two is that foreign currency, rather than shares of stock, is the underlying asset in the option.

current asset Cash or an asset expected to be converted into cash within one year. In addition to cash, current assets include marketable securities, accounts receivable, inventories, and prepaid expenses. Current assets are typically not very profitable but tend to add liquidity and safety to a firm's operation. —Also called *gross working capital.*

current coupon Pertaining to a bond with an interest coupon very close to the coupons being carried on new issues of the same maturity. Therefore the bond must be selling at a price close to its par value. —Also called *full coupon.*

current issue The most recently issued Treasury security of a particular type. For 13-week Treasury bills that are auctioned each Monday, the current issue is the bill issued on the most recent Monday.

current liability A debt due within a year. Current liabilities include accounts payable, short-term loans from financial institutions, current maturities of long-term debt, dividends declared but not paid, and expenses incurred but not paid. Current liabilities are generally met using current assets.

current market value The value of an individual's portfolio when the securities are appraised at current market prices.

current maturity The length of time before a security matures. For example, a bond issued 15 years ago that had an original maturity of 20 years, has a current maturity of 5 years. The current maturity, rather than the original maturity, is important in valuing a bond.

current production rate The maximum interest rate payable on current Ginnie Mae pass throughs. The current production rate is normally ½ of 1% under the rate of interest charged on mortgages backing the pass throughs, with the difference covering service charges to the firm processing the mortgages. —See also GOVERNMENT NATIONAL MORTGAGE ASSOCIATION.

current ratio A measure of a firm's ability to meet its short-term obligations. The current ratio is calculated by dividing the current liabilities into current assets. Both variables are shown on the balance sheet. A relatively high current ratio compared with those of other firms in the same business indicates high liquidity and generally conservative management although it may tend to result in reduced profitability. —See also CASH RATIO; LIQUIDITY RATIO 1; QUICK RATIO; WORKING CAPITAL.

current yield   The annual rate of return received from an investment, based on the income received during a year compared with the investment's current market price. For example, a bond selling at $800 and paying annual interest of $80 provides a current yield of $80/$800, or 10%. —Also called *rate of return; running yield.*

curtesy   A widower's portion of his wife's assets that were acquired during the course of their marriage. Curtesy normally amounts to one third of the assets. —See also DOWER.

cushion   —See CALL PROTECTION.

cushion bond   A high-coupon bond that sells at a price only slightly above par because of a call provision permitting the issuer to repurchase the security near its current price. A cushion bond has an abnormally high current yield, little chance for a price rise, and considerable protection against falling prices caused by increased interest rates.

Can a cushion bond pad the conservative investor's backside against the impact of rising interest rates?

A cushion bond can protect a conservative investor against rising interest rates because the higher the coupon rate on a bond, the less dramatic the price change for a given shift in that bond's yield to maturity. This makes sense when one considers how much bigger a percentage change 25 basis points is when yields are 5%, as opposed to yields at 10%. Furthermore, the longer the maturity period, the greater the price change for a particular move in that bond's yield to maturity. Since cushion bonds are by definition premium-priced bonds that trade on a yield to the call basis, as opposed to a yield to maturity basis, their price swings account for shifts in interest rates for shorter time periods. Thus their price swings should be less dramatic when interest rates rise.

Stephanie R. Goldsborough, Treasury Officer
Maryland National Bank, Baltimore, MD

cushion theory   The idea that a large short position in a stock will eventually exert upward pressure on the stock's price as investors purchase the stock to cover their short positions. The rise in the price of a stock that has been the object of substantial short selling will be quicker as investors cover short positions to stem losses.

CUSIP —See COMMITTEE ON UNIFORM SECURITIES IDENTIFICATION PROCEDURES.

CUSIP number A unique identification number assigned to stock and bond certificates to improve the efficiency of clearing operations. —See also COMMITTEE ON UNIFORM SECURITIES IDENTIFICATION PROCEDURES.

custodian An organization, typically a commercial bank, that holds in custody and safekeeping someone else's assets. These assets may be cash, securities, or virtually anything of value.

custodian account An account controlled by a custodian rather than the owner of the assets. Custodian accounts are often used for minors or other individuals unable or unwilling to handle their own assets.

custody The service of a financial institution in which a customer's securities are held for safekeeping. For a fee the institution collects dividends, interest, and proceeds from security sales and disburses funds according to the customer's written instructions.

customer's loan agreement An agreement permitting brokerage firms to borrow customers' margined securities to cover certain delivery failures or other customers' short sales. A customer's loan agreement must be signed by the customer before borrowing can take place. —See also MARGIN AGREEMENT.

customer's man —See REGISTERED REPRESENTATIVE.

cut out The deletion or withholding of a trade from clearance.

cv —Used in the yield column of bond transaction tables in newspapers to indicate that a bond is convertible into some other asset—generally shares of common stock: *STERLBN 6½% cv.*

CV —Used on the consolidated tape to indicate a convertible security: *AXPr. CV 25.*

CWIP —See CONSTRUCTION WORK IN PROGRESS.

CXL —Used on the consolidated tape to indicate that a transaction reported earlier has been canceled: *CXL.5 SLS.BK.GY 49.*

When should I invest in cyclical stocks?

With the proper crystal ball, you should buy cyclical stocks six months before the earnings in the target group begin to move up, and sell the group six months before the earnings turn down. *Note*: Most crystal balls are cloudy!

Richard Mazur, Vice President, Research Marketing
Steven Flagg, Research Coordinator
PaineWebber Incorporated, New York, NY

cyclical Pertaining to a variable, such as housing starts, car sales, or the price of a certain stock, that is subject to regular or irregular up-and-down movements.

cyclical stock Common stock of a firm whose profits are heavily influenced by cyclical changes in general economic activity. As investors anticipate changes in profits, cyclical stocks often reach their high and low levels before the respective highs and lows in the economy.

D

d **1.** —Used in the daily or weekly low column of stock transaction tables in newspapers to indicate that the price of the security reached a new 52-week low: *d16.* **2.** —Used in mutual fund transaction tables in newspapers to indicate that the shares trade ex-distribution. **3.** —Used in bond transaction tables in newspapers to indicate a deep-discount bond: *OcciP d8.95s94.* **4.** —Used in over-the-counter stock transaction tables in newspapers to indicate the dividend in the previous or indicated year. No regular dividend is paid: *Brady A .05d.*

Daily Bond Buyer A comprehensive publication providing detailed information on the bond market, especially the muncipal bond segment. This weekday paper includes data on yields, new issues, underwriters, and nearly everything else of interest to professional bond buyers.

daily trading limit In commodities, the range of prices within which trades may take place during a day. The limit is normally determined on the basis of the previous day's settlement price.

daisy chain Manipulative trading among a small group of individuals or institutions, intended to give the impression of heavy volume. As outsiders see the unusual trading activity and are drawn into the chain, the traders who started the daisy chain then sell their positions, leaving the new investors with overpriced securities.

D&O Coverage —See DIRECTORS' AND OFFICERS' LIABILITY INSURANCE.

dated date The date on which a newly issued bond begins accruing interest. The buyer of a bond in the primary market must pay the issuer interest accruing between the dated date and the settlement date in addition to the principal amount of bonds purchased. This additional interest is returned to the buyer when the issuer makes the first interest payment. For example, a new bond issue with a dated date of July 1 and a settlement date of July 20 would require purchasers to pay 19 days' interest in addition to the face value of the bonds.

date of acquisition For accounting and tax purposes, the effective purchase date of an asset.

day order   A customer order to buy or sell a security which will expire automatically at the end of the trading day on which it is entered. —Used when a customer prefers to reconsider an order that is not executed on the day it was placed. —See also GOOD-TILL-CANCELED ORDER.

day trade   A trade opened and closed on the same trading day. A purchase and sale of the same security on the same day is an example of a day trade. Likewise, a short sale followed by a covering purchase on the same day is a day trade.

day trader   A speculator who buys and sells securities on the basis of small short-term price movements. The day trader is thought to add a measure of liquidity to the market.

dealer   An individual or a firm that buys assets for and sells assets from its own portfolio as opposed to bringing buyers and sellers together. In practice, many firms operate as broker-dealers and perform both services depending on the market conditions and on the size, type, and security involved in a particular transaction. Dealers are sometimes able to offer investors better prices but they may tend to make recommendations based on their own ownership positions. —See also BROKER.

dealer loan   A short-term secured bank loan to a security dealer for the purpose of financing inventory.

dealer market   A market in which securities are bought and sold through a network of dealers who buy, sell, and take positions in various security issues. —See also AUCTION MARKET.

dealer paper   Commercial paper that is sold by original issuers through dealers who wholesale the paper to its ultimate buyers. Individual investors are normally excluded from trading in dealer paper because of the size of the investment required ($250,000 minimum). —See also DIRECT PAPER.

death tax   1. —See ESTATE TAX.   2. —See INHERITANCE TAX.

debenture   A corporate bond that is not secured by specific property. In the event that the issuer is liquidated, the holder of a debenture becomes a general creditor and therefore is less likely than the secured creditors to recover in full. Owing to the higher risk factor, debentures pay higher rates of interest than secured debt of the same issuer. —See also SUBORDINATED DEBENTURE.

debit   An accounting entry resulting in an increase in assets or a decrease in liabilities or owners' equity. —See also CREDIT 2.

debit balance   The amount owed in a brokerage margin account. A debit balance occurs when an investor purchases securities on margin or borrows money from the account by using securities as collateral. Brokerage firms typically charge an interest rate on the borrowed funds that varies with the size of the debit balance. —See also CALL LOAN; CREDIT BALANCE.

debit-balance theory   The technical theory that the level and change in brokerage account debit balances can be used to forecast market trends. A rise in debit balances is generally considered bullish because debit balances result from the purchase of securities on margin by sophisticated investors. —See also CREDIT-BALANCE THEORY.

debit card A plastic card that may be used for purchasing goods and services or obtaining cash advances in which payment is made from existing funds in a bank account. Since a debit card provides about the same float as a checking account (two to five days), it is a less desirable method of payment than a credit card. These cards are often part of the comprehensive all-in-one accounts offered by many brokers.

debit spread The simultaneous sale of one option and purchase of another option, resulting in a debit to the investor's account. Thus, more funds are required for the purchase than are received from the sale. An example is the purchase of a six-month call at a price of $500 and the simultaneous sale of a 3-month call at the same strike price for $300. This trade results in a debit of $200 plus commissions to the investor's account. —See also CREDIT SPREAD.

debt —See LIABILITY.

debt-based asset An investment in the debt of another party. Savings accounts, bonds, annuities, and certificates of deposit are all debt-based assets because they represent debt of the issuer. Debt-based assets are generally conservative investments that pay a fairly predictable rate of return.

debt financing The acquisition of funds by borrowing. For example, a business may use debt financing to raise funds for constructing a new factory. Corporations find debt financing attractive because the interest paid on borrowed funds is a tax-deductible expense. —See also EQUITY FINANCING.

debt limit The statutory maximum amount of debt that a municipality may have outstanding.

debt management The regulation of the size and handling of the structure of the public debt. Actions taken to manage the debt have significant effects on the financial markets since government securities compete with private securities for limited funds in the capital market.

debt management ratio A measure of the extent to which a firm uses borrowed funds to finance its operations. Owners and creditors are interested in debt management ratios because the ratios indicate the riskiness of the firm's position. —See also DEBT RATIO; DEBT-TO-EQUITY RATIO; FINANCIAL LEVERAGE; FIXED-CHARGE COVERAGE; INTEREST COVERAGE.

debtor An individual or organization owing a debt or having an obligation to another party. —See also CREDITOR.

debt ratio The proportion of a firm's total assets being financed with borrowed funds. The debt ratio is calculated by dividing total assets into total long-term and short-term liabilities. Assets and liabilities are found on a company's balance sheet. For example, a firm with assets of $1,000,000, $150,000 in short-term debts, and $300,000 in long-term debts has a debt ratio of $450,000/$1,000,000 or 45%. A low debt ratio indicates conservative financing with an opportunity to borrow in the future at no significant risk. —See also BOND RATIO.

debt restructuring An exchange of one or more new debt issues for outstanding debt issues when the new issues have interest rates and/or maturities that are different from the outstanding issues. For example, a firm might offer holders of 9% coupon bonds with 5 years to maturity a new bond with a higher-coupon rate and a 25-year maturity. Creditors having difficulty making interest and/or principal payments often restructure their debt to reduce the size of the interest payments and extend debt maturity. —Also called *restructuring; troubled debt restructuring.*

debt security A security representing borrowed funds that must be repaid. Examples of debt securities include bonds, certificates of deposit, commercial paper, and debentures.

debt service Funds required to meet interest expenses, principal payments, and sinking fund requirements during a specific time period. A firm's ability to service its debt is estimated by comparing cash flow with debt service.

debt-to-equity ratio The relationship between long-term funds provided by creditors and funds provided by owners. A high debt-to-equity ratio, which indicates very aggressive financing or a history of large losses, results in very volatile earnings. A low debt-to-equity ratio indicates conservative financing and low risk, with reduced possibilities of large losses or large gains in earnings. A firm's debt-to-equity ratio is calculated by dividing owners' equity into long-term debt. Both items are shown on the balance sheet. —See also FINANCIAL LEVERAGE.

declaration date The date on which a firm's directors meet and announce the date and amount of the next dividend. Following the declaration, dividends become a legal liability of the firm. —See also EX-DIVIDEND DATE; INTEREST DATES; RECORD DATE.

declare To authorize a dividend formally.

declared dividend A dividend authorized by a firm's board of directors. At the time a dividend is declared, the firm creates a liability for the dividend's payment.

dedication —See PORTFOLIO DEDICATION.

deduction An expenditure permitted to be used in order to reduce an individual's income-tax liability. Potential deductions of particular interest to investors are expenditures for subscriptions to financial publications, a lock box for storing securities, and computer software for investment-related activities. These deductions, combined with employee business expenses and miscellaneous deductions, are deductible only to the extent that they exceed 2% of the taxpayer's adjusted gross income. Interest paid on loans used to finance investments is deductible only to the extent of investment income. —Also called *itemized deduction; tax deduction.* —See also CHARITABLE CONTRIBUTION DEDUCTION.

What are some investor-tailored deductions not to be missed?
• •

Here are some good deductions:
1. IRA fees: Pay them by separate check in order to get the deduction. If the trustee pays fees by withdrawing funds directly from your account, they are not deductible.
2. Investment management fees
3. Broker custodial fees
4. Subscription costs for investment publications and newsletters
5. Mutual fund pass through of expenses (effective in 1987 and beyond)
6. Safe deposit box fees

Note: All of the above deductions are subject to the 2% adjusted gross income floor.

Brokerage commissions increase an investor's basis and reduce the taxable gain.

Michele R. Bourgerie, CPA
Arthur Young, New York, NY

---

deep-discount bond 1. A long-term debt security that, because of a low coupon rate of interest compared with current rates of interest, sells at a substantial discount from face value. These bonds, if not original issue discounts, are preferred by some investors because they are unlikely to be called before maturity. —See also MUNICIPAL CONVERTIBLE; ZERO-COUPON BOND. 2. —See ORIGINAL-ISSUE DISCOUNT BOND.

deep-in-the-money —Used to describe a call (put) option that has a strike price considerably below (above) the market price of the underlying stock. A deep-in-the-money option is almost certain to be exercised on or before its expiration. —See also IN-THE-MONEY.

deep market A market for a security in which there are numerous, sizable bids and offers. A deep market for a security provides an investor in that security with more liquidity. —See also DEPTH; THIN MARKET; TIGHT MARKET.

deep-out-of-the-money —Used to describe a call option with a strike price significantly above the market price of the underlying asset or a put option with a strike price significantly below the market price of the underlying asset. A deep-out-of-the-money option sells at a low price because in all likelihood it will expire without value.

default Failure to live up to the terms of a contract. Generally, *default* is used to indicate the inability of a borrower to pay interest or principal on a debt when it is due.

default risk The possibility that a borrower will be unable to meet interest and/or principal repayment obligations on a loan agreement when due. Default risk has a significant effect on the value of a bond: if a borrower's ability to repay debt is impaired, default risk is higher and the value of the bond will decline.

defeasance The extinguishment of debt. While defeasance technically refers to extinguishment by any method (e.g., by payment to the creditor), in practice it is generally used to mean discharging debt by presenting a portfolio of securities (normally, Treasury obligations) to a trustee who will use the cash flow to service the old debt. This procedure permits the firm to wipe the debt off its financial statements and show extra income equal to the difference between the old debt and the smaller, new debt. —Also called *in-substance debt defeasance*.

defensive acquisition A firm or an asset purchased by a potential target of a takeover in order to make itself less desirable to raiders. For example, a target company might purchase another firm engaged in the same business as the raider in order to create an antitrust problem for the raider. —See also RAIDER; TARGET COMPANY.

defensive stock A stock that tends to resist general stock market declines. Stocks of electric utilities, gold and silver producers, and some consumer goods companies are considered defensive. While defensive stocks resist downturns, they generally move up more slowly than other stocks during bull markets.

When should I consider purchasing defensive stocks?

Consider purchase of defensive stocks when the market looks rough. The stocks should generally have:
1. a high quality balance sheet;
2. consistent earnings in good and bad markets/economies;
3. strong yields, but not enough to tie in to interest rates;
4. strong cash flow;
5. strong brand name recognition.

Food stocks and tobaccos are good examples.

Ray Ozyjowski, Regional Sales Coordinator
PaineWebber Incorporated, New York, NY

---

deferment period The period of time after issue, in which a security cannot be called by the issuer. —Also called *deferred call period; period of call protection.* —See also CALL PROTECTION.

deferred annuity An annuity that is not scheduled to begin payments until a given date in the future. These annuities may be purchased with a single payment, or, as is more often the case, with a series of periodic payments. Deferred annuities are most commonly purchased by people who wish to make periodic payments during their working lives in order to receive monthly or annual income payments from the annuities later, during their retirement. —See also IMMEDIATE ANNUITY; PERIODIC PUR-CHASE DEFERRED CONTRACT; SINGLE-PREMIUM DEFERRED ANNUITY.

deferred call period —See DEFERMENT PERIOD.

deferred compensation Currently earned compensation that is not tax-able until it is actually received at a later date. Deferred compensation includes various plans, some being pensions, profit-sharing, and stock options.

deferred contracts Futures contracts that settle in months beyond the closest current trading month.

deferred income tax A liability created by income recognized for ac-counting purposes but not for tax purposes. The liability recognizes future taxes due when already earned income is later reported for tax purposes. Use of accelerated depreciation for financial reporting to the Internal Revenue Service and straight-line depreciation for reporting to stockholders is one of the major reasons a firm includes deferred income taxes as a liability on its balance sheet.

deferred investment tax credit An investment tax credit that is allocated over a period of years (generally over the life of the asset that brought about the credit) subsequent to the purchase of the asset. For example, a company entitled to an investment tax credit of $10,000 because it had purchased a $100,000 asset with a 10-year estimated life, may use $1,000 of the credit each year for 10 years. Deferral is the more conservative method of accounting for the investment tax credit. —See also FLOW-THROUGH METHOD.

deferred liability A liability that normally should have been paid but is now past due.

deferred sales charge A fee levied by some open-end investment com-panies on shareholder redemptions and by many insurance companies on annuities. The charge of up to 5% of the value of the shares being redeemed frequently varies inversely with the period of time the shares have been owned. A deferred sales charge is indicated in mutual fund transaction tables in newspapers by the symbol *r*. —Also called *back-end load; exit fee; redemption charge.*

deficiency **1.** The amount by which an individual's or an organization's tax liability as computed by the Internal Revenue Service exceeds the tax liability reported by the taxpayer. **2.** The amount by which a firm's liabilities exceed assets.

deficiency letter A letter from the Securities and Exchange Commission expressing disapproval with one or more aspects of a security issuer's registration statement.

deficit **1.** A negative retained earnings balance. A deficit is the result of accumulated losses and dividend payments exceeding earnings sub-sequent to the date a business commenced operations. **2.** —See OPER-ATING LOSS.

deficit financing   The sale of debt securities in order to finance expenditures that are in excess of income. Generally, deficit financing is used to apply to government finance so that income is represented by tax revenues. Deficit financing puts upward pressure on interest rates because government debt securities compete with private securities for limited capital. —See also MONETIZE THE DEBT.

deficit net worth   —See NEGATIVE NET WORTH.

deficit spending   Expenditures in excess of revenues during a given period of time. Deficit spending is generally applied to governmental units but the concept is equally applicable to private businesses.

defined-benefit pension plan   A pension plan in which retirement benefits rather than contributions into the plan are specified. Thus, a retired employee who has reached a certain age with a given number of years of service and who has earned certain income is entitled to a specific monthly pension payment.

defined-contribution pension plan   A pension plan in which an employer's periodic payments into the plan, rather than eventual retirement benefits to employees, are specified. For example, a defined-contribution pension plan may require an employer to contribute 5% of its employees' gross pay into a fund with contributions earmarked for each employee upon retirement.

deflation   A reduction in consumer or wholesale prices. The term generally applies to more than just a temporary decline. —See also DISINFLATION; INFLATION.

What types of stocks do well in periods of deflation?

In general, deflation (or, rather *disinflation*, because deflation is likely only in severe recessions) is good for stock prices as we observed in the early 1980s. Among stock groups, however, the best ones in such periods should be those whose earnings growth rates will be least reduced by lesser inflation. For the longer term, these are usually either stocks of companies whose unit sales growth is expected to be high and which have been little affected by inflation in the past (e.g., computer hardware and software or biomedical companies) or stocks of companies with unique niches enabling them to determine the prices at which they sell (e.g., newspapers and specialty retailers). For the shorter term, however, they may also include stocks of companies which can, and have, cut expenses sharply, such as selected companies in most industry sectors.

J. Kendrick Noble, Jr., First Vice President
PaineWebber Incorporated, New York, NY

deindustrialization The shift in an economy from producing goods to producing services. Such a shift is most likely to occur in mature economies such as that of the United States. This shift has considerable impact on investors' view of the attractiveness of various industries.

delayed convertible A security with a conversion feature that does not come into effect until a specified future date.

delayed delivery Delivery of a certificate after the day on which regular-way delivery would occur. Normally, regular-way delivery is five business days following the transaction date; therefore, delivery beyond five days would be classified as delayed. Delayed delivery is sometimes specified by the seller when the order to sell is entered. —See also SELLER'S OPTION CONTRACT.

delayed opening An intentional delay in the opening transaction of a particular security. Generally, the delay occurs when unexpected developments before the opening make it difficult for the specialist to match buy and sell orders.

delayed settlement Transfer of a security or cash at a date beyond the normal settlement date. A seller may prefer delayed settlement in order to be listed on a firm's books on the record date for a dividend.

delist To drop a security from trading on an organized exchange. Delisting may occur for a number of reasons, among them being failure to meet an exchange's standards or having a new listing on another exchange. —See also LIST.

deliver To relinquish possession of a security for transfer to another party.

delivering short Delivering borrowed shares in order to fulfill the requirements of an option that has been exercised.

deliver versus payment (DVP) A settlement procedure in which a customer instructs that he or she will make immediate payment upon delivery of the purchased security. —Also called *cash on delivery*. —See also RECEIVE VERSUS PAYMENT.

delivery 1. The transfer of a security to an investor's broker in order to satisfy an executed sell order. Delivery is required by the settlement date. 2. The transfer of a specified commodity in order to meet the requirements of a commodity contract that has been sold.

delivery day In futures trading, the day on which delivery of the asset is to be made according to the quantity, quality, and location specified in the contract.

delivery instructions A customer's directions to a broker as to the disposition of funds and securities in the customer's account. For example, a customer must instruct the broker whether securities placed in the account should be sent to the customer or kept in street name in the account.

delivery notice In futures trading, a notice that the party having sold (short) a contract intends to make delivery of the commodity in settlement of its terms. The quantity, quality, and point of delivery are designated by the exchange. —Also called *transfer notice.*

delivery point The specified location at which a commodity may be delivered to satisfy a futures contract. The points and procedures for delivery are established by the exchange on which the contract trades.

delta The change in the price of an option for a one-point change in the price of the underlying stock. For example, a delta of .5 indicates that the option will rise in price by one-half point (50¢) for each one-point ($1) rise in the price of the underlying stock. Call options have positive deltas; put options have negative deltas. —See also HEDGE RATIO.

demand deposit A checking account balance held at a financial institution. Since demand deposits constitute one of the most important segments of the nation's money supply, the financial community closely monitors their size. —See also M1; TIME DEPOSIT.

demand loan A loan due at any time the lender decides to request payment.

denomination The face value of a security. For bonds, it is normally $1,000 ($5,000 for municipals) or multiples thereof, and for stock it is the par value.

dependent variable A variable affected by another variable or by a certain event. For example, because a stock's price is affected by dividend payments, earnings projections, interest rates, and many other things, stock price is a dependent variable. —See also INDEPENDENT VARIABLE.

depletion The periodic cost assigned for a reduction in the quantity and indicated value of a natural resource such as a mineral deposit or timber. Thus, depletion indicates an activity such as harvesting or mining a natural resource. —See also COST DEPLETION; DEPRECIATION; PERCENTAGE DEPLETION.

depository —See SECURITY DEPOSITORY.

Depository Trust Company (DTC) A national depository for security certificates that records, maintains, and transfers securities for member firms. The DTC seeks to reduce the movement of certificates by arranging for computerized transfers. —See also BOOK-ENTRY SECURITY.

depreciable Pertaining to a long-term tangible asset subject to depreciation.

depreciate To reduce the value of a long-term tangible asset.

depreciated cost —See BOOK VALUE 1.

depreciation The periodic cost assigned for the reduction in usefulness and value of a long-term tangible asset. Since firms can use several types of depreciation, the amount of depreciation recorded on corporate financial statements may or may not be a good indication of an asset's reduction in value. Depreciation not only affects the asset's value as stated on the balance sheet; it also affects the amount of reported earnings. —See also ACCELERATED COST RECOVERY SYSTEM; ACCELERATED DEPRECIATION; AC-CUMULATED DEPRECIATION; DEPLETION; RECAPTURE OF DEPRECIATION; STRAIGHT-LINE DEPRECIATION.

depreciation recapture —See RECAPTURE OF DEPRECIATION.

depreciation reserve —See ACCUMULATED DEPRECIATION.

depth —Used to refer to a security market's ability to absorb large security purchases or sales without significant price changes. A market's depth is an important consideration in selecting securities to trade and markets in which to trade. —See also DEEP MARKET.

deregulate To reduce or eliminate control. One of the major forces in the financial markets in the 1970s and 1980s has been the federal government's decision to deregulate interest rates. The commissions charged to investors on security trades were deregulated in 1975.

deregulation The act of removing controls from some sector of the economy. In nearly all cases, deregulation of a given industry has both positive and negative implications for investors. Typically, firms in a strong financial position benefit from deregulation while firms in a weak financial position suffer.

derivative instrument A security that derives its value from another security. For example, an option is a derivative instrument that obtains value from the security that can be purchased with the option. —See also UNDERLYING ASSET 2.

derivative suit —See STOCKHOLDER DERIVATIVE SUIT.

descending tops In technical analysis, a chart formation made by a security achieving successively lower highs during a period of up-and-down price movements. For technical analysts, a series of descending tops indicates lower prices in the future.

descending triangle In technical analysis, a triangle-shaped chart formation in which the left side is nearly vertical, the bottom is nearly horizontal, and the third side slopes downward to the right. A descending triangle is a bearish indicator in which a sell signal is confirmed if the price breaks downward through the bottom side. —See also ASCENDING TRIANGLE; TRIANGLE.

Designated Order Turnaround (DOT) An electronic system on the New York Stock Exchange that channels smaller orders directly from a member firm to the specialist post on the Exchange floor. The system speeds the execution of orders and allows increased volume on the floor through bypassing commission brokers.

detachable warrant A warrant issued in conjunction with another security (nearly always a bond) that can trade or be exercised separately following the issue date.

detailed audit A thorough and complete examination of all or a selected portion of an organization's books. In a detailed audit, as opposed to a normal audit, systems of internal control, the details of all the transactions, books of account, subsidiary records, and supporting documentation may be examined with a view to accuracy, the utilization of generally accepted accounting principles, total accountability, and legality.

devaluation A reduction in the value of one currency in relation to other currencies. For example, if Mexico devalues the peso, more pesos will be required to obtain a given amount of a foreign currency. Devaluation is generally undertaken by a government in order to make its country's products more competitive in world markets. Devaluation can significantly reduce the value of investments held by foreign investors in the devaluing country. In the case of the peso devaluation, U.S. investors holding high-interest peso accounts in Mexican banks will find their account balances worth very little in terms of U.S. dollars. —See also EXCHANGE RATE; FIXED EXCHANGE RATE.

Please explain how devaluation of a foreign currency can affect investors with positions in foreign securities.
• •

Investors caught by a devaluation—those with assets in a foreign currency when its value in dollars is knocked down—usually find that something has proved too good to be true. Savings accounts or other investments in foreign currencies may offer interest rates far higher than those available in U.S. dollars at home. Some investors jump in. Others wonder why, or how, such high interest rates could be. Usually it is because the foreign currency suffers high inflation and the apparently rich rates partially compensate investors for the losses in real value caused by inflation. When one currency is inflating away, the balloon of apparent values can burst suddenly in a devaluation. If investing in a foreign currency looks too good to be true, look at the currency. It may be inflating, leading to an investment in hot air, not cold cash.

David M. Blitzer, Vice President & Chief Economist
Standard & Poor's Corporation, New York, NY

---

developmental oil and gas partnership —See OIL AND GAS DRILLING LIMITED PARTNERSHIP.

diagonal spread Any spread with different strike prices in which the purchased options have a longer maturity than the written options.

differential 1. In commodities trading, the premium or discount in the futures contract price caused by delivering a commodity that does not exactly meet the standards fixed by the exchange. Allowances for these differentials are included in the contract specifications. 2. —See ODD-LOT DIFFERENTIAL.

digits deleted —Used on the consolidated tape service to indicate that only the last digits and fractions of stock prices will be reported until further notice. Thus, what would ordinarily be reported as XON 5s52½ will be listed as XON 5s2½. Deleting digits is the first step in speeding the reporting process when the tape falls behind because of heavy volume. —See also LATE TAPE; VOLUME DELETED.

dilution A decrease in the equity position of a share of stock because of the issuance of additional shares. Dilution is normally detrimental to the position of existing shareholders because it weakens their proportional claim on earnings and assets. —See also POTENTIAL DILUTION.

dip A small, short decline in a variable such as the price of a security or interest rates. A broker may advise a customer to accumulate a particular stock on dips. When the security begins declining in price it is difficult to know if the decline is just a dip or if it is the initial step in a more substantial price reduction.

direct cost A cost that can be directly related to producing specific goods or performing a specific service. For example, the wages of an employee engaged in producing a product can be attributed directly to the cost of manufacturing that product. Certain other costs such as depreciation and administrative expenses are more difficult to assign and are not considered direct costs. —See also INDIRECT COST.

directed sale The sale of a large block of stock to a single buyer as part of a new issue. Shares for a directed sale are withheld by the lead underwriter from members of the underwriting syndicate.

direct (federal) government obligation A debt that is backed by the full taxing power of the U.S. government. Direct obligations include Treasury bills, Treasury bonds, and U.S. savings bonds. These investments are generally considered to be of the very highest quality. —See also FEDERAL AGENCY SECURITY.

direct financing The raising of funds without using an intermediary. For example, a firm may decide to save an underwriter's fee by offering new securities directly to investors.

director A member of a firm's board of directors. A director also may hold a management position within the firm. —See also CHAIRMAN; INSIDE DIRECTOR; OUTSIDE DIRECTOR.

⚠$ Outside corporate directors once had more perks than headaches: short working hours, minimal decision-making responsibilities, and relatively high compensation, given the amount of work actually done. For that reason, it was fiscally advantageous to serve on not just one but a number of boards. Today, however, the scenario has radically changed. Although their compensation remains relatively high, directors now end up having to earn it. They must spend substantial amounts of time—sometimes on weekends—evaluating corporate matters, reviewing future company plans, and making strategic decisions for which they will be held accountable. In addition, the directors more often than not can become targets of lawsuits by activist shareholders. In fact, the litigation problem has become so acute that many firms now have difficulty obtaining liability insurance for their directors, a factor having negative impact on the acquisition of good directors. As a result of the insurance problem in particular, nominees for directorships investigate very carefully the firms trying to acquire them before accepting seats on the boards, and incumbent directors are expected to exercise more diligence in overseeing a firm's operations. Clearly, the good old days of snoozing over *The Wall Street Journal* during canned presentations and making rubber-stamp decisions are over. The shareholders' attorneys and the shareholders themselves have put through an unmistakable wake-up call.

directors' and officers' liability insurance Insurance to protect a firm's directors and officers against lawsuits—mainly those instituted by unhappy shareholders of the firm. Directors' and officers' liability insurance has become more expensive and more difficult to obtain in recent years as the number of lawsuits has increased dramatically. Companies find it very difficult to recruit outside directors unless the candidates are supplied with liability insurance. —Also called *D&O Coverage.*

direct paper Commercial paper that is sold directly by issuers to individual investors without the use of an intermediary. This method is most often utilized by finance companies such as General Motors Acceptance Corporation. —See also DEALER PAPER.

direct participation program An investment program in which tax consequences and cash flows pass directly from the investment to the investors. The purpose of a direct investment program is to permit investors to enjoy certain benefits (e.g., depreciation deductions) normally available to a corporation.

direct placement The sale of a new security issue to a limited number of large buyers rather than to the general public. Direct placement generally involves less expense to the issuer although the buyer may be able to negotiate a more favorable price.

direct play The stock of a firm that concentrates its operations in a specific industry. An investor expecting favorable opportunities from a particular line of business may seek a direct play in the business itself rather than by investing in the stock of a company engaged not only in that business but also in a variety of other businesses. Although a direct play has good profit potential, it is generally more risky than a security in a widely diversified company. —Also called *play.*

direct stock purchase plan A plan initiated by some firms that permits investors to purchase stock directly from the issuer (thereby avoiding brokerage commissions). Although generally open only to employees and current shareholders, a few companies do allow customers to make direct purchases.

direct tax A tax paid by the individual or organization on which it is levied. For example, the personal income tax is levied on individuals who end up bearing the entire burden of the tax. A direct tax cannot be shifted from the entity on which it is levied. —See also INDIRECT TAX.

disabilities Restrictions or special handling requirements placed on an individual's brokerage account. For example, an employee of a financial institution involved in the securities business must have special permission from the employer in order to have a margin account.

disbursement   A payment in cash or by check.

disclaimer of opinion   The statement of a Certified Public Accountant that an audit opinion cannot be rendered because of limitations on the extent of the examinations. —See also ADVERSE OPINION; CLEAN OPINION; QUALIFIED OPINION; SUBJECT TO OPINION.

disclosure   Revelation of facts and details concerning a situation or business operation. In general, security exchanges and the Securities and Exchange Commission require firms to disclose to the investment community facts concerning issues that will affect the firms' stock prices. Disclosure is also required when firms file for public offerings. —See also FULL DISCLOSURE.

discontinued operation   A segment of business that has been abandoned or sold or for which plans have been approved for such. —See also CONTINUING OPERATION.

discount   The amount by which a bond sells below face value. —See also BELOW PAR; DISCOUNT BOND.

discount   To deduct the charge for making a loan from the loan's principal before distributing funds to the borrower.

discount basis   —See BANK DISCOUNT BASIS.

discount bond   A bond selling at a price that is less than its par value. In addition to semiannual interest payments, a discount bond offers investors additional appreciation if the security is held until maturity.

discount brokerage firm   A brokerage firm that discounts commissions for individuals to trade securities. Most discount brokerage firms offer limited advice but reduce their fees by 50% or more, compared with full-service brokerage firms. —See also FULL-SERVICE BROKERAGE FIRM; MAY DAY; NEGOTIATED COMMISSION.

discounted cash flow   A sophisticated method of estimating an investment's current value based on the discounting of projected future revenues and costs. The answer derived from the technique is only as accurate as the estimates used, which, in many cases, are far from certain.

discount rate   1. The interest rate charged by the Federal Reserve on loans to its member banks. A change in this rate is viewed as a strong indicator of Fed policy with respect to future changes in the money supply and market interest rates. Generally, a rise in the discount rate signals increasing interest rates in the money and capital markets. 2. The rate at which an investment's revenues and costs are discounted in order to calculate its present value.

discount security   1. Any security that is issued at less than face value. —See also ORIGINAL-ISSUE DISCOUNT. 2. A money market security, such as a Treasury bill or commercial paper, that is issued at a discount but that matures at face value. The only income received by the investor is the difference between the price paid and the proceeds received at maturity or the sale of the security. —See also BANK DISCOUNT BASIS.

discount window The lending facility of the Federal Reserve through which commercial banks borrow reserves. Federal Reserve policy toward supplying banks with reserves has a major effect on credit conditions and interest rates.

discount yield —See BANK DISCOUNT BASIS.

discretionary account A brokerage account in which the customer permits the broker to act on the customer's behalf in buying and selling securities. The broker has discretion as to the choice of securities, prices, and timing—subject to any limitations specified in the agreement. Since a discretionary account can be quite risky, it should be avoided unless the customer has a great deal of confidence in the broker. —Also called *controlled account.* —See also ADVISORY ACCOUNT; LIMITED DISCRETION.

discretionary income Individual income that is not allocated to necessary expenditures for items such as food and shelter. Increasing amounts of discretionary income are especially favorable for the prospects of firms that sell luxury or leisure items and services.

discretionary order A customer order to a broker giving the broker discretion in buying and selling securities. Depending on the customer's instructions, the amount of discretion may vary from very limited (i.e., price only) to nearly complete.

disinflation A slowdown in the rate of inflation. A drop in the inflation rate from 9% in one year to 5% in the next year is an example of disinflation. On an overall basis, disinflation is good for security prices but it can be painful for individual companies that have made investment and borrowing decisions on the basis that a high rate of inflation would continue. —See also DEFLATION; INFLATION.

disinflation stock Stock that tends to benefit from a slowdown in the rate of inflation. Disinflation stock includes, among others, utility stock and the stock of savings and loans, which are hurt by high inflation and rising interest rates.

disintermediation The withdrawal of funds from financial intermediaries such as banks, thrifts, and life insurance companies in order to invest directly with ultimate users. Disintermediation was more of a problem when financial intermediaries were limited in the returns they could pay to savers. Deregulation of financial intermediaries was intended to dampen the periodic swings toward disintermediation. —See also INTERMEDIATION.

disinvestment Divestiture, liquidation, or sale of a segment of a firm. Disinvestment may occur for a number of reasons including a poor outlook for a particular line of business or a firm's need to raise additional capital for other more promising segments of its business.

disposable income Aftertax income, calculated quarterly, that consumers have available for spending or saving. Economists view changes in disposable income as an important indicator of the present and future health of the economy. —See also PERSONAL INCOME.

dissident director   A director who wishes to change a firm's policies and generally acts in opposition to the wishes of the other directors.

dissident shareholders   Shareholders who oppose a firm's management or management policy. For example, dissident shareholders of Shell Oil opposed Royal Dutch Petroleum's squeeze-out of the Shell minority shareholders at $58 per share.

distribute   To sell a relatively large amount of stock in a firm over a period of time. For example, a mutual fund may liquidate a position in a security over a period of days or weeks so as not to drive down the market price of the security. —See also ACCUMULATE.

distribution   —See PUBLIC OFFERING.

distribution area   In technical analysis, a rectangular-shaped chart formation occurring when stock is being sold by insiders and other knowledgeable investors in anticipation of a major price decline. A distribution area is generally characterized by relatively small price movements and heavy volume. —See also ACCUMULATION AREA; RECTANGLE; REVERSAL PATTERN.

distribution stock   A relatively large block of stock sold over a period of time in either the primary or the secondary markets.

diversifiable risk   —See UNSYSTEMATIC RISK.

diversification   The acquisition of a group of assets in which returns on the assets are not directly related over time. An investor seeking diversification for a securities portfolio would purchase securities of firms that are not similarly affected by the same variables. For example, an investor would not want to combine large investment positions in airlines, trucking, and automobile manufacturing because each industry is significantly affected by oil prices and interest rates. Proper investment diversification, requiring a sufficient number of different assets, is intended to reduce the risk inherent in particular securities. Diversification is just as important to companies as it is to investors. —See also UNSYSTEMATIC RISK.

diversified company   A company engaged in varied business operations not directly related to one another. A diversified company is less likely to suffer either a collapse or a spectacular gain in earnings compared with a firm concentrating its operations in a single business. Likewise, the stock of a diversified company is unlikely to bring extraordinarily large gains or losses to its shareholders.

diversified management company   An investment company with a minimum of 75% of its assets being cash, government securities, securities of other investment companies, and other securities subject to a limitation of no more than 5% of the diversified management company's assets or 10% of the voting securities of the issuing company. Most investment companies (including mutual funds and closed-end investment companies) are diversified management companies. —See also NONDIVERSIFIED MANAGEMENT COMPANY.

diversify   To acquire a variety of assets that do not tend to change in value together. To diversify a securities portfolio is to purchase different types of securities in different companies in unrelated industries.

divestiture   The sale, liquidation, or spinoff of a division or subsidiary. For example, a firm may decide to divest itself of a division in order to concentrate its managerial efforts on more promising segments of its business.

> ⚠$ Divestitures occur for a variety of reasons. For one thing, management may decide that some of its operations simply do not fit its charter or its strategic goals. In another case, a firm may divest itself of a business in which losses have occurred or in which the level of profitability has been unacceptable. In still other instances, companies must resort to divestitures in order to raise funds for reducing debt—a situation that became increasingly prevalent during the takeover frenzy of the 1980s when firms used borrowed money to make acquisitions or to buy back their own shares. In August of 1986, Beatrice Companies, Inc. agreed to sell its International Playtex Division for $1.25 billion as part of an ongoing divestiture program. Beatrice, a diversified company engaged primarily in food and food-related products and services, had recently acquired Esmark and, in the process, had incurred a large amount of new debt. The sale of Playtex was contracted to reduce the firm's debt and to focus its future on food products. Beatrice, a company enjoying $13 billion in sales, had earlier agreed to sell its soft drink bottling operations and its Avis Rental Car unit.

dividend   A share of a company's net profits distributed by the company to a class of its stockholders. The dividend is paid in a fixed amount for each share of stock held. Although most companies make quarterly payments in cash (checks), dividends also may be in the form of property, scrip, or stock. Unlike interest on a debt, dividends must be voted on by the company's directors before each payment. A number of financial publications, including *Moody's Dividend Record*, provide investors with information on the amounts and dates of past and current dividend payments. —See also BOND DIVIDEND; CAPITAL DIVIDEND; CASH DIVIDEND; CONSENT DIVIDEND; CONSTRUCTIVE DIVIDEND; DECLARATION DATE; DECLARED DIVIDEND; EX-DIVIDEND DATE; FINAL DIVIDEND; INTEREST DATES; INTERIM DIVIDEND; LIABILITY DIVIDEND; LIQUIDATING DIVIDEND; OPTIONAL DIVIDEND; RECORD DATE; STOCK DIVIDEND.

dividend adjustment   Extra proceeds to an investor submitting convertible preferred stock for conversion to account for dividends accrued since the last date of record for a dividend payment. The dividend adjustment is an unusual practice designed to compensate holders of convertible preferred stock for dividends lost between the time of the last dividend and the time of conversion. —Also called *adjustment*. —See also INTEREST ADJUSTMENT.

dividend capture   Trading of a stock primarily in order to be the holder of record for dividend payment purposes. Once the right to receive the dividend payment has been earned, the stock is sold. Dividend capture is practiced chiefly by corporations because they are permitted to exclude from their taxable income 80% of dividends received. Certain specific tax rules apply to dividend capture.

dividend coverage The extent to which a firm's net income supports the company's total dividend payments. For example, a utility earning $5.00 per share and paying a dividend of $4.79 per share has relatively weak dividend coverage. Poor coverage permits a firm's management to enjoy less flexibility to raise dividends or keep them at the same level in the event that earnings decline. —See also COVERAGE RATIO; PAYOUT RATIO; PREFERRED DIVIDEND COVERAGE.

dividend discount model A model for determining the price at which a security should sell based on the discounted value of estimated future dividend payments. Dividend discount models are used to determine if a security is a good buy (i.e., one selling at a lower current price than the model says it should sell) or a bad buy (i.e., one selling at a higher current price than the model says it should sell).

dividend exclusion For corporate stockholders, the 80% of dividends received that are exempt from taxation. Thus, if Company A owns stock in Company B and receives $100,000 in dividends paid by Company B, only 20%, or $20,000, need be reported as income by Company A. If one company owns over 80% of the common stock of another company, none of the dividends received are taxable. The dividend exclusion of $100 annually for individual stockholders was eliminated in 1987.

dividend payment date The date on which an issuer's paying agent will send dividend payments to stockholders. —See also EX-DIVIDEND DATE; PAYMENT DATE.

dividend payout ratio —See PAYOUT RATIO.

dividend reinvestment plan (DRIP) A plan whereby stockholders may automatically reinvest dividend payments in additional shares of the company's stock. Instead of receiving the normal dividend checks, participating stockholders will receive quarterly notification of shares purchased and shares held in their accounts. Dividend reinvestment is normally an inexpensive way of purchasing additional shares of stock since the fees are low or are completely absorbed by the company. In addition, some companies offer stock at a discount from the existing market price. Normally, these dividends are fully taxable even though no cash is received by the stockholder. —Also called *automatic dividend reinvestment; reinvestment plan.*

dividend requirement Total annual preferred dividends to be paid by a company.

dividends in arrears Dividend payments on cumulative preferred stock that have been passed by a firm's directors. These dividends must be brought up to date before any payments are made to common stockholders. Any payments of dividends in arrears go to the current holders of the preferred stock regardless of who held the stock when the divi-

dend was passed. —Also called *accumulated dividend.* —See also CUMU-
LATIVE.

dividend test A provision in some borrowing agreements that restricts
the borrower's ability to pay dividends to stockholders. This provision
is supposed to protect the position of creditors against a drawdown on
assets by dividend payments.

dividend yield The annual dividends from a common or preferred stock
divided by its market price per share. If Exxon common stock trades at
a price of $50 per share, its $3.40 dividend provides a dividend yield of
$3.40/$50, or 6.8%. This figure measures the current return on a particular
common stock, but does not take into account potential gains and losses
in the security's value.

divider —See EUROPEAN CURRENCY QUOTATION.

DJA —See DOW JONES AVERAGES®.

DJIA —See DOW JONES INDUSTRIAL AVERAGE℠.

DK —See DON'T KNOW.

dollar bond A bond that is traded and quoted on the basis of its dollar
price rather than on its yield. Dollar quotations are fairly unusual except
in the case of municipal revenue bonds. Price quotes may or may not
include any dealer fees; therefore, it is important for an investor to
determine which is the case.

What types of investors should use dollar-cost averaging?
• •

When asked what the market was going to do, J. P. Morgan
reportedly said, "It will fluctuate." Morgan was right! This concept refers to putting a fixed amount of money into securities
periodically. In so doing one's average price per share is lower
than the mean average price during the holding period. This is
basic math: $100 buys 10 shares of a stock at $10, only 5
shares at $20 when the market is higher. The mean average
price was $15. But the investor owns 15 shares and paid just
$200 for an average price per share of just $13.33. TIP: A good
approach for smaller investors just getting started, and also for
IRAs. It works particularly well with diversified mutual funds.

Thomas J. McAllister, CFP
McAllister Financial Planning, Indianapolis, IN

---

dollar-cost averaging Investment of an equal amount of money at regular intervals, usually each month. This process results in the purchase
of extra shares during market downturns and fewer shares during market
upturns. Dollar-cost averaging is based on the belief that the market or

a particular stock will rise in price over the long term and that it is not worthwhile (or even possible) to identify intermediate highs and lows. —Also called *averaging*.

dome In technical analysis, an upside-down U-shaped chart formation indicating a market top. A dome is an example of a reversal pattern. —Also called *inverted saucer; rounded top*.

domestic corporation A firm incorporated under the laws of the country or state in which it does business. For example, a firm incorporated in the United States is considered a domestic corporation in the United States but a foreign corporation elsewhere. —See also FOREIGN CORPORATION.

donated capital Funds or property given as a gift to a corporation. The donation may be from individuals or organizations not affiliated with the corporation. —See also CONTRIBUTED CAPITAL.

do not reduce An addition to a limit order to buy or a stop order to sell stock, directing that the price not be automatically reduced when the stock goes ex-dividend. Without this instruction, the price is reduced by the amount of the dividend to be paid.

don't know (DK) A broker-dealer response to a transaction report when the facts of the trade are in doubt or are unknown.

DOT —See DESIGNATED ORDER TURNAROUND.

double-barreled municipal bond A municipal obligation that is a general obligation of the issuer and is also secured by a particular revenue source outside the general fund.

double bottom In technical analysis, a chart formation in which a stock's price drops to a low level, recovers, and declines a second time to the previous low price. If the stock price recovers a second time, the low price reached at the two bottoms becomes a level of support for the stock. It is a bearish sign if the stock subsequently falls through this level. —See also DOUBLE TOP.

double-declining-balance depreciation A depreciation method that records large depreciation expenses in the early years of an asset's life and reduced depreciation expenses in the later years of an asset's life. The acceleration of depreciation is designed to reduce taxable income and tax payments so that extra cash will be available for reinvestment. Double-declining-balance depreciation is calculated by multiplying twice the straight-line depreciation rate times the asset's book value each year. —See also SUM-OF-THE-YEARS' DIGITS DEPRECIATION.

double-exempt fund A mutual fund that limits its investments to tax-free bonds of issuers from a single state. Thus, a double-exempt fund pays investors residing in the same state as the issuers of the bonds with income free of federal and state income taxes. Double-exempt funds have been particularly popular in the populous, high-tax states of California and New York. If an investor lives in a city with an income tax, these funds are exempt from three taxes. —Also called *single state mu-*

nicipal bond fund. —See also MUNICIPAL BOND FUND; TAX-EXEMPT MONEY MARKET FUND; TRIPLE TAX EXEMPT.

double option   A commodity option traded in Europe that gives its owner the right either to call (buy) or to put (sell) the underlying asset, but not both. When one side of the option is exercised, the opposite side is automatically terminated.

double taxation   Taxation of the same income twice by the same taxing authority. It is generally used to refer to the taxation of dividends which are taxed once at the corporate level (as income before dividends are declared) and again at the personal level (when the dividends are received).

double top   In technical analysis, a chart formation traced by a stock price reaching a single high price on two different occasions. The price level represented by the double top becomes a resistance level through which the stock will later have difficulty breaking. —See also DOUBLE BOTTOM.

doubling option   A provision in some indentures that allows the borrower, at its option, to retire twice as many bonds as stipulated under a sinking fund requirement. The additional retirements take place at or near par, so that the option is utilized during periods of low interest rates. Thus, the provision operates to the disadvantage of investors. —See also CALL PROVISION; SINKING FUND PROVISION.

Dow   —See DOW JONES INDUSTRIAL AVERAGE℠.

dower   A widow's portion of her husband's assets that were acquired during the course of their marriage. The dower, normally amounting to one third, applies even if the deceased husband wills her a portion less than this. —See also CURTESY.

Dow Jones & Company, Inc.   A major publisher of financial data and business news. Although best-known as the publisher of *The Wall Street Journal* and compiler of the Dow Jones Averages, Dow Jones also publishes books, sells computer software, produces a radio show, and provides an electronic news service to the financial community.

Dow Jones Averages® (DJA)   A trademark for an index of the relative prices of selected industrial, transportation, and utility stocks based on a formula developed and periodically revised by Dow Jones & Company, Inc.

Dow Jones Industrial Average℠ **(DJIA)**   A trademark for one of the oldest and most widely quoted measures of stock market price movements. The Average is calculated by adding the share prices of 30 large, seasoned industrial firms such as IBM, Exxon, AT&T, Westinghouse, and GM and dividing the sum by a figure that is adjusted for such things as stock splits and substitutions. Also called *the Dow*.

Dow Jones Transportation Average℠   A trademark for a stock average that uses the share prices of 20 large companies in an effort to show overall price movements in the stocks of transportation-related firms.

This Average, which used to be limited to the stocks of railroads, now includes those of airlines and trucking companies.

Dow Jones Utility Average® A trademark for a stock average of 15 large electric and gas utility companies that attempts to show overall price movements of utility stocks. The direction that this Average takes is heavily influenced by changes in long-term interest rates.

down and out option A call option that expires with the underlying stock trading at a price under the option's exercise price.

downgrading Reduction in the quality rating of a security issue, generally a bond. A downgrading may occur for various reasons including a period of losses, or increased debt service required by restructuring a firm's capital to include more debt and less equity. For example, takeover targets that engage in stock buybacks to prop up the price of their shares are subject to debt issue downgrading by the rating agencies. —See also UPGRADING 1.

> ⚠️💲 In mid-1986 Standard & Poor's Corporation (S&P) downgraded Coca-Cola Company's long-term debt rating from AAA to AA-plus. S&P said that the reduced rating resulted from Coca-Cola's more aggressive financial and strategic policies. In recent years Coca-Cola had borrowed funds to an increasing extent for the purpose of making acquisitions and enhancing the price of its common stock. The effect of the S&P downgrading was that the firm had to pay a higher interest rate on its new long-term debt than would have been the case had the rating remained as AAA. Because the downgrading applied to bonds already outstanding, existing holders of Coca-Cola's long-term debt were adversely affected by the decision.

downside risk Potential losses that may occur if a particular investment position is taken. For example, the downside risk from holding Treasury bills is quite small. —See also UPSIDE POTENTIAL.

downstream Pertaining to earnings or operations at a firm that are near or at the final stage of consumption. For example, marketing and transportation are downstream operations for a large, integrated oil company. —See also UPSTREAM.

downstream merger The merger of a parent firm into one of its subsidiaries.

downtick A downward price movement for a security transaction compared with the preceding transaction of the same security. —Also called *minus tick.* —See also UPTICK.

downtrend A series of price declines in a security or the general market. Many analysts feel that investors should avoid securities in a downtrend until the pattern is broken. —See also UPTREND.

downturn Declining security prices or economic activity following a period of rising or stable prices or activity. Even strong bull markets are subject to occasional downturns.

Dow theory A technical trading theory of forecasting stock market price trends based on price movements of the Dow Jones Averages (industrials and transportation). The theory classifies price movements into individual components of primary, secondary, and daily. Only when both Averages reach new highs or lows (one Average confirms the other) is a major trend in progress.

draft   A written order by one party for a second party to make payment to a third party. A check is an example of a draft drawn by a depositor (first party) on a financial institution (second party) and payable to an individual or organization (third party). —See also OVERDRAFT; SIGHT DRAFT; TIME DRAFT.

drawback   A rebate for tariffs paid by a firm on imported goods that are processed for reexport. Thus, if a business in the United States importing television sets from Korea adds on sophisticated microprocessing units that turn the sets into "smart televisions" and then exports the redesigned televisions to Europe, the U.S. firm would receive all or part of the tariffs paid at the time the sets were brought into the United States from Korea.

DRIP   —See DIVIDEND REINVESTMENT PLAN.

droplock bond   A floating-rate bond that automatically converts to a fixed-rate bond if the interest rate used to peg the floating rate falls to a predetermined level. The new fixed rate stays in place until the droplock bond reaches maturity.

DTC   —See DEPOSITORY TRUST COMPANY.

dual-currency bond   A bond denominated in one currency (normally, the currency of the country in which the bond is issued) but redeemed in a different currency. The investor in a dual-currency bond benefits if the currency used for redemption appreciates in relation to the currency used in the investor's home country.

> ⚠️ IBM Credit Corporation sold $106 million worth of franc-denominated notes in Switzerland in the early part of 1986. The bonds pay semiannual interest in francs, but are to be redeemed in U.S. dollars at maturity in 1994. Each 5,000 franc bond is to be redeemed for $3,000. Swiss investors in the bonds would benefit if the U.S. dollar appreciated in relation to the Swiss franc before maturity because the principal received in dollars could be exchanged for a greater number of Swiss francs. Investors expecting the dollar to decline in value relative to the franc would avoid the dual-currency issue.

dual fund   —See DUAL PURPOSE FUND.

dual listing   The listing of a security on more than one exchange. Many stocks are traded on the New York or the American stock exchanges and on one or more of the regional exchanges. For example, the common stock of Occidental Petroleum is listed on the New York Stock Exchange but it also enjoys a large amount of activity on the Pacific Stock Exchange. Although dual listing theoretically should improve the liquidity of a stock thereby benefiting investors, most dual listed securities trade chiefly on one exchange.

dual presentation   The presentation of a firm's earnings per share on a primary and a fully diluted basis. Dual presentation of earnings per share is required only for firms with complex capital structures.

dual purpose fund   A special-purpose, unusual type of closed-end investment company offering two classes of stock in approximately equal amounts. One class (income shares) is entitled to all the portfolio's income (i.e., dividends from investments), while the second (capital shares) is entitled to appreciation in investments in the firm's portfolio. At the time a dual purpose fund is established, a date is set on which the fund will be liquidated. At that time, income shareholders receive preference up to the par value of their shares and capital shareholders receive any excess. —Also called *dual fund; leveraged investment company.* —See also CAPITAL SHARES; INCOME SHARES.

Please provide some additional information about dual purpose funds.
• •

A dual purpose fund is a closed-end mutual fund with two classes of shares that are listed on a stock exchange. One class, which has the objective of seeking income, entitles shareholders to receive all dividends and interest income received by the fund. The second class, which has the objective of seeking long-term growth of capital, gives its shareholders the capital appreciation from the fund's assets. One of the primary characteristics of dual purpose funds is that both classes of shares represent leveraged investments. Although each shareholder class supplies only a portion of the fund's total capital at its inception, in return, both have more assets working for their respective goals than they have contributed.

Merrill Lynch Asset Management, Inc., Princeton, NJ

---

due   Pertaining to an obligation or receivable that is outstanding and payable.

due bill   A statement of a liability by one party to another party following a transaction. In the case of a security transaction, a due bill reflects money or securities owed by one broker to the other broker. For example, stock purchased on the ex-dividend date gives the seller rather than the buyer the right to receive the subsequent dividend. However, because the actual payment date of the dividend may follow the ex-dividend date by as much as a month, the buyer will be required to sign a due bill indicating that the dividend belongs to the selling party. —Also called *bill.*

due-diligence meeting   A meeting between officials of the organization that will be issuing securities and members of the syndicate that will be distributing the securities. A due-diligence meeting is held for the purpose of discussing the terms of the issue, preparing a final prospectus, and negotiating a final agreement between the issuer and syndicate members.

dummy director   The director of a firm who acts and votes according to the wishes of another party who is not a member of the board.

dummy stockholder   An individual or firm holding stock in its own name when the stock is really owned by another party.

dumping   **1.** The selling of large amounts of a stock or stocks in general at whatever market prices are in effect. For example, investors might dump stocks upon hearing of an outbreak of fighting in some part of the world. **2.** The selling of a product in one market at an abnormally low price while selling the same product at a significantly higher price in another market. For example, a firm may sell a product in its home market at a price covering all costs and then sell the product in a foreign market at a significantly lower price covering only variable costs.

durable goods   Goods, such as appliances and automobiles, that have a useful life over a number of periods. Firms that produce durable goods are often subject to wide fluctuations in sales and profits.

duration   The number of years required to receive the present value of future payments, both interest and principal, from a bond. Duration is determined by calculating the present value of the principal and each coupon, and then multiplying each result by the period of time before payment is to occur. The concept of duration is used to relate the sensitivity of bond price changes to changes in interest rates. —Also called *mean term*.

Dutch auction   An auction in which the seller reduces the offering price until a level can be found that clears the market. This is the price at which all sales will take place. The auction for Treasury bills is similar to this except for the fact that the Treasury accepts the highest bids first and then works through progressively lower bids until an issue is completely sold. Thus, in a Treasury bill auction, various prices are accepted.

> ⚠️$ Whittaker Corporation announced plans in 1986 to sell several of its business units and use the proceeds to repurchase a significant proportion of its own outstanding stock. The stock buyback was to occur through a process by which Whittaker's shareholders could submit offers for varying numbers of shares at various prices. A shareholder might submit an offer to sell 500 shares at $35; 500 shares at $34; and 500 shares at $33, for example. Depending on the number of available shares and the prices offered by the shareholders, Whittaker would then set a price at which it would purchase the stock. Thus, if Whittaker set a price of $34.75, the shareholder would sell 1,000 shares (those offered at $34.75 or less) at a price of $34.75 each. Whittaker undertook the Dutch auction to determine the lowest price at which it could buy back the desired number of shares.

duty   —See TARIFF.

DVP   —See DELIVER VERSUS PAYMENT.

E

e —Used in the dividend column of stock transaction tables in newspapers to indicate the dividend that was declared and paid in the preceding 12 months: *1.75e.*

early exercise The exercise of an option before it expires. Although somewhat unusual, an option holder may decide to exercise early in order to receive an upcoming dividend (in the case of a stock option) or in order to satisfy another commitment.

earned income Individual income (as commissions, salaries, and bonuses) derived as compensation for personal services. —See also UNEARNED INCOME.

earned surplus —See RETAINED EARNINGS.

earning power **1.** The earnings that an asset could produce under optimal conditions. For example, AT&T may currently be earning $2.50 per share; however, under optimal conditions each share could have earnings of $3.75. **2.** The expected yield on a security.

earnings Income of a business. *Earnings* usually refers to aftertax income but may occasionally be used synonymously with *before-tax income* or even *revenues.*

earnings before interest and taxes (EBIT) —See OPERATING INCOME.

earnings capitalization rate —See EARNINGS-PRICE RATIO.

earnings multiple —See PRICE-EARNINGS RATIO.

earnings per share (EPS) Net income for a period, divided by the average number of common shares outstanding during that period. EPS is the amount of reported income, on a per-share basis, that a firm has available to pay dividends or reinvest in itself. As with other financial measures, EPS is subject to various accounting techniques; therefore, reported EPS may give a very misleading signal as to how the firm is really doing. —Also called *income per share.* —See also FULLY DILUTED EARNINGS PER SHARE; PRIMARY EARNINGS PER SHARE.

earnings-price ratio (E/P) The rate at which investors are capitalizing a firm's expected earnings in the coming period. This ratio is calculated by dividing the current market price of the stock into projected earnings per share. A relatively low E/P ratio anticipates higher-than-average growth in earnings. Earnings-price ratio is the inverse of the price-earnings ratio. —Also called *earnings capitalization rate; earnings yield.*

earnings quality The extent to which a firm's reported earnings accurately reflect income for that period. Firms using conservative accounting practices tend to penalize current earnings and are said to have high earnings quality. At least over the short run, the earnings reported by a firm are as much a function of its accounting methods as they are a measure of its business success. —Also called *quality of earnings.* —See also INVENTORY PROFIT.

How do you go about measuring earnings quality?
• •

Earnings quality essentially refers to the reliability or dependability of earnings to fund corporate operations and dividend payments. For example, average earnings quality has improved in recent years because of disinflation. With inflation, the prices of raw materials rose appreciably while they were being processed by corporations, producing inventory profits on their sale. But such profits were of poor quality; new raw materials might cost even more, making it difficult for the company to stay in business. Likewise, earnings produced largely by nonrecurring events, such as the sales of productive assets, or by changes to less conservative accounting rules, are deemed of poor quality because they are not considered to reflect the true health of the reporting company.

J. Kendrick Noble, Jr., First Vice President
PaineWebber Incorporated, New York, NY

---

earnings report —See INCOME STATEMENT.

earnings statement —See INCOME STATEMENT.

earnings variability Fluctuations in a corporation's net income or earnings per share (EPS) over a given period of time. Past earnings variability is generally considered undesirable because it makes investors less certain of future EPS and dividends. As such, a history of earnings variability may be expected to penalize a firm's stock with a lower-than-average price-earnings ratio.

earnings yield —See EARNINGS-PRICE RATIO.

easy money A condition of the money supply in which the Federal Reserve permits substantial funds to accrue in the banking system, thereby cutting interest rates and facilitating the acquisition of loans. In the resultant period when borrowing is relatively easy and inexpensive, security prices may be initially stimulated. But an extended period of easy money eventually may depress security values as investors begin to fear inflation. —Also called *cheap money.* —See also TIGHT MONEY.

EBIT —See EARNINGS BEFORE INTEREST AND TAXES.

economic activity The production and distribution of goods and services at all levels. Economic activity and expected future levels of it have an important influence on security prices because of the interrelationship between economic activity and corporate profits, inflation, interest rates, and other variables. One frequently used measure of economic activity is the gross national product.

economic growth   Increased production levels of goods and services. If measured in monetary terms, the increases must occur after adjustments for inflation have been made.

economic life   The period of time during which a fixed asset competitively produces a good or service of value. The economic life of an asset may be particularly short in a rapidly changing field such as electronics where new developments often render an asset obsolete shortly after the asset is purchased. Companies sometimes continue to carry assets with expired economic lives on their balance sheets because they do not wish to penalize their earnings by writing off the assets. —See also PHYSICAL LIFE.

Economic Recovery Tax Act of 1981 (ERTA)   Sweeping legislation of the Reagan administration that lowered corporate and individual income-tax rates and liberalized the depreciation of assets. The Act was greatly modified in 1982 and 1984. —See also ACCELERATED COST RECOVERY SYSTEM.

ECU   —See EUROPEAN CURRENCY UNIT.

Edge Act corporation   A corporation established under the 1919 Edge Act to undertake activities in international banking and investing. The Act gives firms more flexibility in competing effectively with foreign competitors. Corporations established under the Edge Act are often organized in order to finance foreign trade or to own foreign securities.

EEC   —See EUROPEAN ECONOMIC COMMUNITY.

effective date   The date on which a new offering registered with the Securities and Exchange Commission may be sold by underwriters. There is normally a 20-day period between the filing of a registration and the effective date. —See also COOLING-OFF PERIOD.

effective rate of interest   The rate of interest that incorporates compounding in determining the amount of interest to be credited to an account. For amounts invested during an entire year, the annual effective rate of interest times the principal will equal the amount of interest that will be earned.

effective sale   The trade that determines the price for an odd-lot order. For odd-lot market orders, the effective sale is the first trade following the specialist's receipt of the odd-lot order. For an odd-lot limit order, the effective sale is the trade that permits an odd-lot differential. —See also ELECTING SALE.

efficient market   A market in which security prices reflect all available information and adjust instantly to any new information. If the security markets are truly efficient, it is not possible for an investor consistently to outperform stock market averages such as the Standard & Poor's 500 except by acquiring more risky securities. Significant evidence supports the premise that the security markets are very efficient. —Also called *market efficiency*. —See also RANDOM-WALK HYPOTHESIS.

efficient portfolio   A combination of investments offering the highest possible yield at a given risk level or the minimal possible risk at a given yield level. Although the concept of an efficient portfolio is important to understand, in practice it is more academic than practical.

EFT —See ELECTRONIC FUNDS TRANSFER.

eighth One eighth of a point. With stock quotes, an eighth represents 12.5¢; therefore, a stock quote of 10⅜ indicates a price of $10.375. With bond quotes, an eighth represents one eighth of a percent. For example, a quote of 90⅛ indicates 90⅛% of par, or normally, $901.25 per bond.

8–K A report filed by a firm with the Securities and Exchange Commission (SEC) providing information on a material event that affects the company's financial condition. The report must be filed by any firm with shares traded on a national exchange or in the over-the-counter market. The SEC makes 8–Ks available to the public. —Also called *form 8–K*.

elastic Pertaining to the demand for a good or service when quantity purchased varies significantly in response to price changes in the good or service. For example, the demand for a product with many close substitutes is elastic because a small price rise will cause consumers to switch to competing brands. —See also INELASTIC.

elasticity The responsiveness of the quantity purchased of an item to changes in the item's price. If the quantity purchased changes proportionately more than the price, the demand is elastic. If the quantity purchased changes proportionately less than the price, the demand is inelastic. For example, price increases by cigarette manufacturers have a relatively small effect on cigarette consumption, which means smokers are not influenced much by price; thus, the demand is inelastic. Producers of products and services facing inelastic demand curves have an easier time passing on price increases.

elect To convert a stop limit order or a stop order to a limit order or a market order.

electing sale The round-lot transaction that activates an odd-lot or round lot stop order. The first transaction after the electing sale is the effective sale for determining the price of the odd-lot order. An electing sale can take place only when the price of a security is at or through the price specified on the order. For example, if a customer enters an order to buy at 15 stop, the electing sale will be the first sale at which the stock trades at a price of $15 or more.

election cycle —See PRESIDENTIAL ELECTION CYCLE.

electronic funds transfer (EFT) The transfer of funds, as from one account to another or from buyer to seller, by telephone or computer. The use of EFT results in instantaneous movement of money. The additional time that the funds are available to earn income can more than offest the fees charged by institutions for this service. —Also called *wire transfer*.

eligible margin Collateral specified by a firm or an exchange as acceptable for satisfying margin requirements. For example, certain low-priced stocks may not be acceptable as margin.

embezzle   To take illegally something of value being held in custody for someone else.

emerging growth stock   The common stock of a relatively young firm operating in an industry with very good growth prospects. Although this kind of stock offers unusually large returns, it is very risky because the expected growth may not occur or the firm may be swamped by the competition.

Keys to spotting a good emerging growth stock.

Keep these points in mind:

1. High percentage of management ownership. If management has a vested interest, its commitment to succeed will be all the stronger.
2. What stage is the overall industry in?
3. More important, where is the target stock focusing its efforts within the industry?
4. What will be the industry leader's reaction to another player?

Richard Mazur, Vice President, Research Marketing
Steven Flagg, Research Coordinator
PaineWebber Incorporated, New York, NY

Employee Retirement Income Security Act (ERISA)   A 1974 act that protects the retirement income of pension fund participants by setting standards for eligibility, performance, investment selection, funding, and vesting. The Act was designed to ensure that retirement funds would actually be available at the time of the workers' retirement through curbing of abuses by pension fund managers.

employee stock option   —See INCENTIVE STOCK OPTION.

Employee Stock Ownership Plan (ESOP)   A qualified retirement plan in which employees receive shares of the common stock of the company for which they work and the company receives an investment tax credit. The purpose of the plan is to give employees a vested interest in the company, thereby providing them with an additional incentive toward greater productivity.

encumbrance   **1.** A liability on real property. For example, a mortgage encumbers title to real estate because the lender has an interest in the property. —See also UNENCUMBERED.   **2.** A commitment within an organization to use funds for a specific purpose. Thus, a college may encumber funds for later payment to cover expenses associated with a faculty member's trip to recruit new professors.

ending inventory   Goods available for sale at the end of an accounting period. —See also BEGINNING INVENTORY.

endorse   To sign a negotiable instrument in order to transfer it to another party. For example, investors holding securities must endorse the certificates before delivery to the broker.

endorsement   The owner's signature transferring the legal rights to a negotiable certificate to another party.

endorsement in blank   An endorsement of a security by the owner without any transferee being named. Such an endorsement is risky because anyone coming into possession of the security may become its new owner.

endowment life insurance   A life insurance policy that provides benefits for a specified period (say, 20 years or until age 65) and that may be redeemed at face value if the insured is still alive at the end of the specified period. Thus, payment is made regardless of whether the insured lives or dies, although the cost of the policy is quite high compared with other types of life insurance.

energy stock   The stock of a company engaged in an energy-related business such as coal mining, oil refining, or electric power generation. Because of the diverse nature of this industry, the stocks do not always move together.

entrepreneur   A risk-taker with the skills and initiative to establish a business.

E/P ratio   —See EARNINGS-PRICE RATIO.

EPS   —See EARNINGS PER SHARE.

equalizing dividend   A dividend payment intended to compensate for a change in regular dividend dates. For example, a firm may move back its dividend payment dates by one month and compensate its shareholders with a one-time equalizing dividend to account for the four-month, as opposed to the normal three-month, interval before the first payment under the new schedule.

equipment   Fixed assets acquired as additions or supplements to more permanent assets. Equipment includes lighting fixtures in a building, for example. Equipment, unlike real estate, is generally moveable.

equipment leasing limited partnership   A partnership in which investors' funds are used to acquire equipment that is leased to businesses. Lease payments are passed through to partners with much of the income sheltered from taxation by depreciation and interest expense. At the termination of a lease, the equipment is sold and a cash distribution is made to the partners.

equipment trust certificate   An intermediate- to long-term security that pays a fixed return based on payments received from the lease of equipment. These certificates are frequently used by railroads and airlines to finance rolling stock and aircraft, respectively.

⚠️$ Aircraft and railroad cars make particularly good collateral for a loan because they are easily interchangeable among firms. Thus, if an airline is unable to make payments on a loan for which planes have been pledged as collateral, creditors will have a relatively easy time locating buyers and recovering the loan's unpaid principal. In April of 1986 People Express Airlines announced that it would sell $115 million of 10-year equipment trust certificates. The certificates, carrying a 14⅜% interest rate, were secured by 21 of the firm's used aircraft. Proceeds from the sale were then used for repaying existing debt and for general corporate purposes. Unfortunately, this financing was unable to help the firm very long. Later in the year People Express was deeply in debt, was suffering huge losses, and was on the verge of bankruptcy before Texas Air made an offer to take it over.

equity **1.** In a brokerage account, the market value of securities less the amount borrowed. Equity is particularly important for margin accounts, for which minimum standards must be met. **2.** Stock—both common and preferred. For example, an investor may prefer investing in equities as opposed to bonds. —Also called *equity security.* **3.** In accounting, funds contributed by stockholders through direct payment and through retained earnings. —See also OWNERS' EQUITY.

equity arbitrage —See RISK ARBITRAGE.

equity commitment note Corporate debt that eventually will be repaid by issuing stock.

equity financing Acquisition of funds by issuing shares of common or preferred stock. Firms normally use equity financing when they are unable to raise sufficient funds through retained earnings or when they have to raise additional equity capital to offset debt. —See also DEBT FINANCING.

equity kicker An addition to a fixed-income security that permits the investor to participate in increases in the value of equity ownership. Two common types of equity kickers are a convertible feature on some bonds that allows the bonds to be exchanged for shares of stock, and warrants to purchase stock that are sold in combination with a new bond issue. —See also REAL ESTATE CERTIFICATE OF DEPOSIT.

equity method A method of accounting for an investment in another company in which the book value of the investment reflects a share of the acquired firm's increases in retained earnings. Thus, if Firm A purchases 20% of Firm B's stock and Firm B earns $3 million after taxes during the next year, Firm A will increase the carrying value of its investment by 20% of $3 million, or $600,000. If Firm B pays half its earnings in dividends, Firm A will increase its investment by $300,000.

equity note Intermediate-term debt that is automatically converted into common stock at maturity.

equity option An option for which the underlying asset is stock. —See also NONEQUITY OPTION.

equity participation loan A loan in which the lender obtains or has the right to obtain an ownership interest in the project being financed.

equity REIT A real estate investment trust that purchases property with investors' money. Investors in an equity REIT earn dividend income from rental income earned by the REIT on property it owns. The investors also participate in increases in value of the owned real estate. —See also MORTGAGE REIT.

equity security —See EQUITY 2.

equivalent bond yield The annual yield on a short-term security that is normally quoted on a bank discount basis to make the yield comparable with quotations on other interest-bearing debt.

equivalent taxable yield The taxable return that must be achieved in order to equal, on an aftertax basis, a given tax-exempt return. Equivalent taxable yield is calculated by dividing the available tax-exempt yield by 1 minus the investor's marginal tax rate. For example, a tax-exempt return of 9% for an investor in a 40% marginal tax bracket would require a taxable return of .09/.6, or 15%, to produce the same aftertax equivalent.

Does the purchase of tax-free securities make sense?

When determining whether tax-free securities make tax sense, one needs to compare their tax-free yield with their taxable equivalent. The formula used to determine the taxable equivalent is:

$$\frac{\text{Tax-free Yield}}{1 - \text{Marginal Tax Rate}}$$

Assuming the risk factors of the investments are similar, one can ascertain whether taxable investments are yielding a comparable return. If not, the tax-free investment is preferred. For example: Assume that an investor is in a combined federal and state 40% tax bracket. Assume further that 10-year municipal bonds are yielding 6%. Using the above formula, the taxable equivalent of this investment equals 10%. It is unlikely that the investor will be able to find a taxable investment of similar risk level yielding 10% in today's investment climate.

Michele R. Bourgerie, CPA
Arthur Young, New York, NY

ERISA —See EMPLOYEE RETIREMENT INCOME SECURITY ACT.

ERR —Used on the consolidated tape to indicate that an error has been made when reporting a transaction in the indicated security: *ERR.LAST.IBM.* The previous report, therefore, should be disregarded.

ERTA —See ECONOMIC RECOVERY TAX ACT OF 1981.

escheat The right of the state to claim a deceased person's property when there are no individuals legally qualified to inherit it or make a claim to it. This occurrence is fairly unusual even when the deceased leaves no will.

escrow The holding of assets (i.e., securities) by a third party.

ESOP —See EMPLOYEE STOCK OWNERSHIP PLAN.

essential function bond A bond issued by a municipality when funds from the bond issue are used for traditional government purposes such as government office buildings, libraries, parks, prisons, roads, and schools. Interest on municipal essential function bonds is exempt from federal income taxation and is not subject to the alternative minimum tax. —Also called *traditional governmental purpose bond.* —See also MUNICIPAL BOND; PRIVATE ACTIVITY BOND.

estate tax A tax on the estate of the deceased before any distribution is made to the heirs. A federal unified gift and estate tax provides an exemption of $600,000 before any tax is paid. Although some states also levy an estate tax, it is generally at a much lower rate than the federal tax, which begins at 37%. —Also called *death tax.* —See also INHERITANCE TAX.

estimated tax The estimated tax liability on income not subject to withholding. Individuals with even moderate investment income are generally expected to file a declaration of estimated tax and to pay quarterly installments on the estimated tax liability.

ethical fund A mutual fund that limits investment alternatives to securities of firms meeting certain social standards. For example, an ethical fund might exclude securities of companies that are known to practice discrimination, that operate in certain countries, or that produce specific products (e.g., those having to do with nuclear weapons or nuclear power plants). Ethical funds include the Dreyfus Third Century Fund, the New Alternatives Funds, and the Working Assets Fund, among others. —See also SOCIAL INVESTING.

ethical investing —See SOCIAL INVESTING.

Eurobond A bond issued and traded in countries other than the one in which the bond is denominated. A dollar-denominated bond sold in Europe by a U.S. firm is a Eurobond. —See also FOREIGN BOND.

Euro CD A certificate of deposit issued primarily in London by a foreign bank or a foreign branch of a U.S. bank.

Eurocurrency Funds deposited in a bank when those funds are denominated in a currency differing from the bank's own domestic currency. Eurocurrency applies to any currency and to banks in any country. Thus, if a Japanese company deposits yen in a Canadian bank, the yen will be considered Eurocurrency.

Eurodollar bond A dollar-denominated bond sold to investors outside the United States. These securities allow buyers to benefit (or lose) from variations in currency exchange rates. A Eurodollar bond is an example of a Eurobond.

Eurodollars Dollar-denominated deposits in foreign banks or foreign branches of U.S. banks. Depositors sometimes transfer their funds to European banks in order to take advantage of higher interest rates. The Eurodollar is one type of Eurocurrency.

European currency quotation In foreign exchange trading, the value of a dollar in terms of a foreign currency. For example, if the West German mark is worth 40¢, the European currency quotation would be expressed as 2.500, meaning that there are 2.5 marks to the dollar. —Also called *divider.* —See also AMERICAN CURRENCY QUOTATION.

European Currency Unit (ECU) A weighted index of 10 European Economic Community currencies. For bonds denominated in ECUs, U.S. investors risk not only the possibility of interest-rate increases but also the chance that the dollar will rise relative to the ECU (i.e., one ECU will buy fewer dollars). On the plus side, these securities provide investors with the opportunity of overseas diversification without reliance on the currency of a single country.

European Economic Community (EEC) A group of Western European countries joined together to promote trade and economic and political cooperation. Essentially, the EEC represents an attempt to combine a group of countries into a single economic unit. —Also called *Common Market.*

European option An option that can be exercised only on its expiration date, in contrast to the more normal option available in the United States whereby the owner may exercise any time up to and including the expiration date.

evaluator An expert who appraises and assigns a worth to assets for which it is difficult to determine market value.

even lot —See ROUND LOT.

even up To buy or sell a security in a quantity that offsets an existing position in that security.

ex —Used in combination to refer to a security that trades without something, such as a dividend, warrant, or some other distribution. For example, when a stock trades ex-dividend, it trades without the right to receive the next dividend payment. —See also EX-DISTRIBUTION; EX-DIVIDEND DATE; EX-RIGHTS; EX-WARRANTS.

exception An auditor's qualification of a financial report indicating disagreement with an item in the report or limitations to the extent of the audit.

excessive trading The act of churning.

excess margin The dollar amount of equity in an investor's brokerage margin account in excess of what is necessary for meeting either initial margin or maintenance margin requirements. An investor with $30,000 of unmargined securities has an excess initial margin of $15,000 (with

Regulation T margin of 50%) and an excess maintenance margin of $22,500 (if the maintenance requirement is 25%). Excess margin may be withdrawn or used to purchase more securities. —See also SPECIAL MISCELLANEOUS ACCOUNT.

excess reserves   Reserves held by banks and thrifts that are in excess of what is required by the Federal Reserve. Large excess reserves indicate a potential for credit expansion and reduced interest rates that could prove beneficial to the security markets. Conversely, small excess reserves indicate reduced possibilities for credit expansion and a relatively tight monetary policy by the Federal Reserve. —See also REQUIRED RESERVES.

excess return   The return on an asset or a portfolio in excess of the risk-free return. If short-term corporate debt provides a return of 9½% while U.S. Treasury bills are yielding 7½%, excess return on the corporate debt is 2%. Excess return is normally correlated with the riskiness of an investment.

exchange   —See SECURITIES EXCHANGE.

exchange   —See SWAP.

exchangeable bond   A special type of convertible security permitting the holder to exchange the bond for shares of a company in which the issuer has an ownership position. An exchangeable bond differs from an ordinary convertible bond in that a convertible permits the holder to convert it into shares of stock of the issuer.

exchange acquisition   The filling of a large buy order on the floor of an exchange in which a member solicits numerous sellers whose orders are then lumped together. This group of transactions is reported as a single transaction. —See also EXCHANGE DISTRIBUTION; SPECIAL BID.

exchange distribution   The sale of a large block of stock on the floor of an exchange in which a member solicits numerous buyers, each of whom takes a portion of the block. All the buy orders are combined, are crossed with the orders to sell, and are reported as a single trade. An exchange distribution is facilitated by the fact that buyers normally do not have to pay a commission. —See also EXCHANGE ACQUISITION.

exchange fund   An open-end investment company that swaps its own shares for an equal value of securities owned by an individual investor. Although the exchange is tax-free, the fund assumes the stockholder's basis on the securities it obtains. Thus, exchange funds ordinarily have large potential capital gains liabilities. Because of a 1967 Internal Revenue Service ruling, shares of these funds are no longer offered.

exchange offer   An offer by a firm to exchange its own securities for those of another firm or for a different series of the same firm's securities. For example, a firm may offer a new bond issue in exchange for an older series currently outstanding. Depending on the type of securities included in the offer, the exchange may result in a taxable event to the security holder.

⚠️$ In 1980 Eastern Air Lines presented an exchange offer to the holders of two outstanding series of its bonds. Eastern offered $575 principal amount of a new convertible debenture due in the year 2005 for each $1,000 principal amount of a 5% convertible debenture due in 1992 and a 4¾% convertible debenture due in 1993. The new bond, having a more favorable conversion price to common stock, generated more current income from its interest payments. However, it significantly extended the period to maturity, the point at which Eastern would have to repay the principal. Eastern undertook the exchange offer so as to defer repayment of its debt and to increase the likelihood that the holders would convert to common stock, in which case no repayment of the principal would be required at all. For a number of reasons, not the least of which was the huge amount of debt outstanding, the firm encountered significant financial difficulties and, in 1986, was acquired by Texas Air.

exchange privilege The right to exchange shares in one mutual fund for shares in another fund managed by the same firm. The rate at which shares are exchanged is determined by differences in relative values. There is normally a nominal charge for each transfer. This privilege is designed to allow investors to move their money among funds without incurring additional sales fees as their investment goals change. —Also called *conversion privilege*.

exchange rate The price of one currency in terms of another currency. For example, if the U.S. dollar buys 1.40 Canadian dollars, the exchange rate is 1.40 to 1. Changes in exchange rates have significant effects on the profits of multinational corporations. Exchange rate changes also affect the value of foreign investments held by individual investors. For a U.S. investor owning Japanese securities, a strengthening of the U.S. dollar relative to the yen tends to reduce the value of the Japanese securities because the yen value of the securities is worth fewer dollars. —Also called *foreign exchange rate*. —See also DEVALUATION; FIXED EXCHANGE RATE; FLOATING EXCHANGE RATE; FOREIGN EXCHANGE RISK.

exchange-traded security —See LISTED SECURITY.

excise tax A tax on the manufacture, purchase, or sale of a good or service. The tax may be based on the number of units or on value. —See also CONSUMPTION TAX.

exclusionary tender offer An offer to purchase shares of a firm's stock on a pro-rata basis while excluding the offer from one or more specific shareholders. The Securities and Exchange Commission has prohibited exclusionary tender offers. —See also ALL-HOLDERS RULE.

ex-distribution Pertaining to a stock, such as a spinoff of a subsidiary's stock, that no longer carries the right to a specific distribution. A mutual fund trading on an ex-distribution basis is indicated in transaction tables in newspapers by the symbol *d*.

ex-distribution date The first day of trading when the seller, rather than the buyer, of a stock will be entitled to a recently announced distribution of an asset. The price of the stock can be expected to fall by approximately the value of the distribution on this date since the stock no longer carries the right to the distribution.

ex-dividend —Used to refer to a stock no longer carrying the right to the next dividend payment because the settlement date occurs after the record date determining the holders who will receive the dividend. If GenCorp common stock goes ex-dividend on May 31, an investor purchasing the stock on or after that date will not receive the next dividend check. A stock trading ex-dividend is indicated in stock transaction tables by the symbol x in the volume column. —See also CUM DIVIDEND.

ex-dividend date The first day of trading when the seller, rather than the buyer, of a stock will be entitled to the most recently announced dividend payment. The length of time ensuing between the ex-dividend date and the date of actual payment may be up to a month. —See also DIVIDEND PAYMENT DATE.

execution Consummation of a security trade.

exemption An annual deduction permitted a taxpayer and each dependent for use in computing taxable income. An extra exemption is allowed for being blind or for being 65 years of age or older. The size of the annual exemption is altered each year according to the level of inflation.

exempt security A security exempt from registration under the Security Act of 1933 or margin requirements of the Securities Exchange Act of 1934. Examples of exempt securities are small issues, intrastate issues, and direct placements.

exercise To require the delivery (e.g., a call option) or to force the purchase (e.g., a put option) of the option's underlying asset. Many options expire without being exercised because the strike price stated in the option is unfavorable to the holder.

exercise limit The maximum number of option contracts that a holder can exercise during a specified period. This limit is established by the exchange on which the option trades.

exercise notice A notice sent by an option holder to the Options Clearing Corporation, calling for fulfillment of the option's terms. The Options Clearing Corporation will then assign fulfillment to someone short the same option.

exercise price The dollar price at which the owner of a warrant or an option can force the writer to sell an asset (in the case of a call option or warrant) or buy an asset (in the case of a put option). The exercise price is set at the time the option is issued and, except for unusual instances including warrants, remains constant until the option expires. A market price of an asset above or expected to be above an option's exercise price gives the option value. —See also AGGREGATE EXERCISE PRICE; STEP-UP; STRIKE PRICE.

exhaustion gap In technical analysis, a gap in a charted price range that occurs when a stock declines following a rapid rise. The exhaustion gap normally occurs on relatively low volume as demand, at least temporarily, falls off. Technical analysts generally believe that an exhaustion gap eventually will be filled when the stock resumes its upward push. —See also BREAKAWAY GAP; RUNAWAY GAP.

exit fee —See DEFERRED SALES CHARGE.

ex-legal Pertaining to a municipal bond that is traded without the legal opinion of a bond counsel. The trading of ex-legal municipal bonds is permitted as long as the buyers are informed about the lack of legal opinion.

expected rate of return The rate of return expected on an asset or a portfolio. The expected rate of return on a single asset is equal to the sum of each possible rate of return times the respective probability of earning each return. For example, if a security has a 20% probability of providing a 10% rate of return, a 50% probability of providing a 12% rate of return, and a 25% probability of providing a 14% rate of return, the expected rate of return is (.25)(10%) + (.50)(12%) + (.25)(14%), or 12%.

expense ratio The proportion of assets required to pay annual operating expenses and management fees of a mutual fund. If a fund charges an annual fee of 50¢ per $100 of net assets, the expense ratio will be .5%. Expense ratios range from .4% to 1.0%, depending on the size of the fund and on the degree of cost control employed by its managers. The expense ratio is independent of any sales fee.

expensive Pertaining to or being a security that sells at a market price above what is expected, given fundamental factors such as earnings, assets, and management ability. Whether or not a security is expensive is a subjective judgment. —See also CHEAP.

expiration Relinquishment of the rights of an options contract by permitting the contract to terminate on the expiration date. —Also called *abandonment*.

expiration cycle The three-month interval between successive option expiration dates. For example, Exxon options on the Chicago Board Options Exchange have an expiration cycle of February, May, August, and November. Only the most current three options trade at any time. When the current option expires, a new option expiring in nine months begins trading.

expiration date The last day on which an option holder may exercise an option. This date is stated in the contract at the time the option is written.

expiration effect The effect on securities, options, and futures prices and volume as traders unwind their positions shortly before expiration of the options and futures contracts. Trading near the expiration dates often produces a flurry of activity and large price changes. —See also TRIPLE WITCHING HOUR.

What should individual investors know about expiration effect?

Investors can cushion themselves from the expiration effect by adjusting their stock trading strategies to accommodate the volatility that occurs on quarterly expiration days. The major market moves triggered by program trading on these days make it unwise to enter an order at the open or close. This is especially true when buying or selling the blue chip stocks that make up the major indices and therefore reflect the most volatility. Limit orders can help investors protect themselves—and even profit from—expiration day volatility. A limit order indicates the maximum price at which an investor will buy a stock or the minimum price at which he or she will sell it.

That order will be executed only if the stock reaches the specified price. An investor who expects the stock price to fall on expiration day could enter a limit order to buy the stock at a lower price. An investor who expects the stock price to rise on expiration day could enter a limit order to sell the stock if it moves higher than its original price. If the stock reaches the limit order price, the broker will execute the order. If the stock doesn't reach the price set by the investor, the limit order won't be executed and the investor will retain his or her original position.

Henry Nothnagel, First Vice President—Retail Marketing
Chicago Board Options Exchange, Chicago, IL

expiration Friday The Friday once each quarter when stock index futures, index options, and stock options simultaneously expire. Investors tend to close out positions in futures, options, and stocks on expiration Friday with the result being extremely volatile prices on this day. —See also TRIPLE WITCHING HOUR.

expiration series A group of options or futures expiring on the same monthly cycles.

ex-pit transaction A commodity trade off the exchange floor.

exploration cost The cost of exploring and drilling exploratory gas and oil wells.

exploratory oil and gas partnership —See OIL AND GAS DRILLING LIMITED PARTNERSHIP.

export A good or service produced in one country and then sold to and consumed in another country. Since many companies are heavily dependent on exports for sales, any factors such as government policies or exchange rates that affect exports, can have significant impact on corporate profits. —See also BALANCE OF TRADE; IMPORT.

ex-rights —Used to describe a stock that trades without giving the stockholder the privilege to receive rights to buy shares of a new stock issue. Because new shares are sold at below market price to rights holders, the rights have value. Thus, a stock trading ex-rights is worth less than the same stock with rights attached. A stock trading ex-rights is indicated in stock transaction tables in newspapers by the symbol *x* near the volume column. —Also called *rights off*. —See also RIGHTS OFFERING; RIGHTS ON.

ex-rights date The first day of trading on which new buyers of a firm's stock will not be entitled to receive recently declared rights to buy shares in a new security issue.

extendable bond A long-term debt security permitting the owner to extend the maturity such that interest payments continue and the principal repayment is delayed beyond the original date. This relatively rare type of bond works to the advantage of investors during periods of declining interest rates.

extension swap Exchanging a bond or note for another virtually identical security with a longer maturity.

external audit An examination of a company's records and reports by an outside party. —Also called *independent audit; outside audit*. —See also INTERNAL AUDIT.

external funds Funds raised from sources outside a firm. Monies received from the sale of stock and bonds are external funds. Firms seek external funds when they are unable to finance expenditures with money generated from operations. External funds are particularly important for a young, fast-growing company with capital requirements that greatly outstrip its ability to generate funds internally. —See also INTERNAL FUNDS.

extra dividend A nonrecurring additional payment to stockholders that is brought about by special circumstances. An extra dividend may be issued when a firm in a cyclical industry has an especially profitable period and wishes to distribute some extra funds to its stockholders. —Also called *extra; special dividend*.

extraordinary call The repurchase of revenue bonds by an issuer because the facilities or instruments providing revenue to pay principal and interest on the bonds have been eliminated. Extraordinary calls are most frequently used to retire single-family mortgage revenue bonds but are possible for nearly any type of revenue bond. Extraordinary calls generally occur in the first few years after bonds are issued but are possible at any time. Extraordinary calls, generally made at par, are disadvantageous to the investor. —Also called *special call*. —See also CALL 3; CALL PRICE; OPTIONAL CALL; SINKING FUND CALL.

extraordinary gain Income from an unusual, infrequently occurring event or transaction. For example, a firm might sell a subsidiary at a price significantly higher than the value at which that subsidiary's assets are carried on the firm's balance sheet. An extraordinary gain is reported separately from regular income to emphasize the fact that it is nonre-curring.

extraordinary item   An infrequently occurring transaction or event that, if material, is reported separately from continuing operations.

extraordinary loss   A loss caused by an unusual, infrequently occurring event or transaction. For example, a firm might sell a money-losing business at a price lower than the value at which the business is carried on its balance sheet.

ex-warrants   —Used to refer to a stock that no longer carries the right to a distribution of declared warrants. The buyer of a stock trading ex-warrants therefore will not receive the warrants. A stock trading ex-warrants is indicated in stock transaction tables by the symbol *xw*. —See also WITH WARRANTS.

F

f   **1.** —Used in bond transaction tables in newspapers to indicate a bond that trades flat: *LTV 5s88f*.   **2.** —Used in mutual fund transaction tables in newspapers to indicate that the price quotation is derived from the previous day's trading: *Gro Inc f*.

F   —Used in earnings reports in newspapers to identify the primary market of a firm's common stock as being outside the United States and Canada.

face-amount certificate   Debt issued by a face amount certificate company obligating the issuer to redeem the certificate at face value at maturity. The buyer makes installment payments that earn interest over the life of the certificate.

face value   —See PAR VALUE 1.

factor   A firm that purchases accounts receivable from another firm at a discount. The purchasing firm then attempts to collect the receivables.

factor   To sell accounts receivable to another party at a discount from face value. Thus, a firm in need of cash to pay down short-term debt may decide to factor its accounts receivable to another firm.

FAF   —See FINANCIAL ANALYSTS FEDERATION.

fail   Designating a trade in which the seller does not deliver securities or the buyer does not deliver funds in the prescribed manner at the prescribed time, normally on the settlement date. —See also CLEAR; FAIL FLOAT.

fail float   Funds available for short-term investing beyond the normal settlement date when securities are not delivered within five business days of a transaction. —See also CLEAR; FAIL; FLOAT 1.

fail to deliver —Used to refer to the nondelivery of securities from a selling broker to a buying broker by the settlement date.

fail to receive —Used to refer to the failure of a buying broker to receive delivery of securities by the settlement date. As a result, the buying broker does not have to make payment until the securities have been delivered.

fair market value The price at which a buyer and a seller willingly consummate a trade.

fairness opinion An independent opinion characterizing the fair value of a firm's stock. A fairness opinion is frequently obtained by a majority owner of a company that is attempting to buy out the interests of minority shareholders. For example, Royal Dutch Petroleum, the 70% owner of Shell Oil, sought a fairness opinion from Morgan Stanley in an attempt to set a price on the the shares it wished to purchase from Shell's minority stockholders. —See also SQUEEZE-OUT.

fair price amendment An addition to a company's bylaws that prevents an acquiring firm or investor from offering different prices for the shares held by different stockholders during a takeover attempt. The amendment tends to discourage takeover attempts by making them more expensive. —See also GREENMAIL; TWO-TIER TENDER OFFER.

fallen angel A once-popular security that has lost investor favor and has declined in value. For example, a high-growth company may hit a period of heavy competition or saturated markets such that its stock declines in price and becomes a fallen angel.

What are the advantages of buying into a family of funds?

Dealing with a family of funds is very much like going into a supermarket. The selection is very broad and, generally, there is a fund for every investor's specific investment objective(s). Should objectives change, companies offering a family of funds make it easy to switch from one fund to another; this usually can be done over the phone and goes into effect immediately. In addition, recordkeeping is made simpler since all transactions are kept under one roof.

Neal Litvack, Marketing Manager
Fidelity Investments, Boston, MA

---

family of funds A group of mutual funds operated by the same investment management company. Investors are often able to transfer money between mutual funds within a particular family of funds at only a nominal charge. Thus, an investor with shares in a growth fund could move funds out of the growth fund and into a money market fund or a bond fund without paying a new sales charge if each of these funds is managed by a single investment firm. Investing money with a company permitting this flexibility is advantageous to the investor. —Also called *fund group; group of funds.* —See also FUND SWITCHING.

family trust A trust for the purpose of passing assets to children or other heirs rather than to a surviving spouse. —See also SPRINKLING TRUST.

Fannie Mae 1. —See FEDERAL NATIONAL MORTGAGE ASSOCIATION. **2.** A security issued by the Federal National Mortgage Association that is backed by insured and conventional mortgages. Monthly returns to holders of Fannie Maes consist of interest and principal payments made by homeowners on their mortgages.

farther in Pertaining to an option contract with an earlier expiration date than a contract currently owned or being considered.

farther out Pertaining to an option contract with a later expiration date than a contract currently owned or being considered. For example, a contract with a May expiration date is farther out than a contract with a February expiration date of the same year.

FASB —See FINANCIAL ACCOUNTING STANDARDS BOARD.

FASB Statement A standard set by the Financial Accounting Standards Board as to a financial accounting and reporting method. Essentially, FASB Statements determine the acceptable accounting practices that Certified Public Accountants use in reporting corporate financial information to stockholders, the Securities and Exchange Commission, and the general public. —See also APB OPINION.

favorite fifty —See NIFTY FIFTY.

F/C —See FIRST COUPON.

FCM —See FUTURES COMMISSION MERCHANT.

FDIC —See FEDERAL DEPOSIT INSURANCE CORPORATION.

Fed —See FEDERAL RESERVE SYSTEM.

federal agency security The debt obligation of a government-owned agency such as the Export-Import Bank and Government National Mortgage Association. Federal agency securities offer higher yields than direct Treasury obligations even though, with the exception of Postal Service and Tennessee Valley Authority issues, they are guaranteed by the U.S. government. Certain issues are exempt from state and local taxes. —Also called *indirect government obligation.* —See also FEDERALLY-SPONSORED CORPORATE SECURITY.

Federal Deposit Insurance Corporation (FDIC) The federal agency that insures deposits at commerical banks to a limit of $100,00 per depositor or combination of depositors at each insured bank. This insurance also applies to certificates of deposit sold through retail brokerage houses. The insurance fund is financed by a small fee paid by the banks, based on the amount of their insured deposits.

Federal Farm Credit Bank A federally-sponsored financing organization intended to consolidate operations of the Banks for Cooperatives, the Federal Intermediate Credit Banks, and the Federal Land Banks. The Federal Farm Credit Bank issues short-term securities that trade in the secondary market.

federal funds Reserve balances above those required that are maintained by commercial banks in the Federal Reserve System. These excess reserves are available for lending to other banks in need of reserves. Although the loans are normally made on a single-day basis, they may be renewed. The availability of and the rate paid for federal funds are important indicators of Federal Reserve policy; hence, both are watched closely by financial analysts in order to forecast changes in the credit markets. —Also called *fed funds*. —See also FORWARD FEDERAL FUNDS.

federal funds rate The rate of interest on overnight loans of excess reserves among commerical banks. Because the Federal Reserve has significant control over the availability of federal funds, the rate is considered an important indicator of Federal Reserve monetary policy and the future direction of other interest rates. A declining federal funds rate may indicate that the Federal Reserve has decided to stimulate the economy by releasing reserves into the banking system. Care is needed in using this indicator, however, because a declining rate may simply mean that the banks have weak demand for commercial loans and little need for borrowing reserves.

Federal Home Loan Bank Board (FHLB) The federally chartered agency that supervises and is owned by member savings and loan associations. The agency raises funds for loans to member institutions by selling bonds to the public. Although the bonds issued by the FHLB are of high quality, they are not guaranteed by the U.S. government. Interest on the securities is exempt from state and local, but not federal, taxation.

Federal Home Loan Mortgage Corporation (FHLMC) A government organization established in 1970 to create a secondary market in conventional mortgages. The FHLMC purchases mortgages from federally insured financial institutions and resells them in the form of mortgage-backed, pass-through certificates. All income on securities issued by the FHLMC is subject to federal, state, and local taxation. —See also PASS-THROUGH SECURITY.

Federal Housing Administration (FHA) A government-sponsored organization insuring mortgage loans made by private lenders.

Federal Intermediate Credit Banks Privately owned, government-sponsored organizations that provide short-term loans to the agricultural sector. Federal Intermediate Credit Banks obtain funds from debt issues of the Federal Farm Credit Bank.

Federal Land Banks Privately owned, government-sponsored organizations that make funds available for farm-related activities. Federal Land Banks secure funds from the Federal Farm Credit Bank, which issues debt securities.

federally-sponsored corporate security A security issued by a privately owned, government-sponsored firm such as the Federal National Mortgage Association or the Federal Land Banks. These securities, primarily debt obligations, are not guaranteed by the U.S. government, but they are generally considered relatively safe. —See also FEDERAL AGENCY SECURITY.

Federal National Mortgage Association (FNMA) A privately owned profit seeking corporation that adds liquidity to the mortgage market by purchasing loans from lenders. It finances the purchases by issuing its own bonds or by selling mortgages it already owns to financial institutions. —Also called *Fannie Mae*. —See also QUASI-PUBLIC CORPORATION.

Federal Open Market Committee (FOMC) An important policy-making committee within the Federal Reserve that has the responsibility of establishing and carrying out open-market operations. Policies and decisions of the Committee have a substantial impact on interest rates and the securities markets. The FOMC is composed of the 7 members of the Board of Governors of the Federal Reserve System and presidents from 5 of the 12 Federal Reserve Banks.

Federal Reserve Board The 7 governing members of the Federal Reserve System who are appointed by the President for 14-year terms. Board members play an important role in determining the country's monetary policy which, in turn, strongly influences economic activity.

Federal Reserve System The independent central bank that influences the United States's supply of money and credit through its control of bank reserves. Federal Reserve actions have great impact on security prices. For example, restriction of bank reserves and lending ability in an attempt to restrain inflation tends to drive up interest rates and drive down security prices over the short run. —Also called *Fed*. —See also FEDERAL OPEN MARKET COMMITTEE.

Federal Savings and Loan Insurance Corporation (FSLIC) A federal agency that insures deposits at participating savings and loan associations to a maximum of $100,000 per depositor or combination of depositors at each insured savings and loan. FSLIC is to savings and loans what the Federal Deposit Insurance Corporation (FDIC) is to commercial banks.

Federal Trade Commission (FTC) A federal agency whose job it is to maintain the competitive markets, thereby discouraging restraint of trade and monopoly. The clout and aggressiveness of the FTC vary greatly depending on its membership and the incumbent Presidential administration.

Federal Trade Commission Act of 1914 The federal law establishing the Federal Trade Commission and providing the Commission with limited power to investigate corporate conduct, hold hearings, and issue cease-and-desist orders. In a 1938 amendment, the FTC was given expanded powers in halting merger activities. —See also ANTITRUST LAWS; CLAYTON ACT; SHERMAN ANTITRUST ACT.

fed funds —See FEDERAL FUNDS.

fed wire A high-speed communications system for transferring funds and ownership of book-entry securities between banks. The fed wire is used to move bank reserves and to make credit available without delay.

felines —See ANIMALS.

FGIC —See FINANCIAL GUARANTY INSURANCE CORPORATION.

FHA —See FEDERAL HOUSING ADMINISTRATION.

FHLB —See FEDERAL HOME LOAN BANK BOARD.

FHLMC —See FEDERAL HOME LOAN MORTGAGE CORPORATION.

fictitious credit The dollar amount credited to an investor's brokerage account following a short sale. The credit, which represents both the proceeds of the sale and the margin required under Regulation T, is used as collateral for the borrowed shares and may not be withdrawn by the investor.

fidelity bond —See BLANKET FIDELITY BOND.

fiduciary A person (e.g., an investment manager or the executor of an estate) or an organization (e.g., a bank) that is entrusted with the property of another party, in whose best interests the fiduciary is expected to act when holding, investing, or otherwise utilizing that party's property.

FIFO —See FIRST-IN, FIRST-OUT.

Should you fight the tape or go with the flow?

Crowd mentality may be an oxymoron—a contradiction in terms. Sudden swings in market action—the "tape" showing a preponderance of up or down moves—are generally followed in quick order by a correction. If you have invested your time before you invest your money, you may find this to be a time of opportunity. First, if you have pre-established overall investment goals and specific objectives for each purchase, the emotion of the moment will not interfere with what you set out to do. Stick to your guns on upside objectives rather than getting greedy for the fractions of a point. And set realistic downside cut points that are sufficiently off the market so that you don't get whipsawed in market skirmishes. Stay flexible enough with liquid assets so that you can bargain hunt as stocks come down within your buying range. Overall, the time to decide whether to fight the tape or go with the flow is *not* when the current is racing ahead of you or against you.

Kathleen Hegenbart, Vice President, Financial Consultant
Shearson Lehman Brothers, Newton Centre, MA

fight the tape To trade securities against the trend. A trader fights the tape if he or she continues to buy stock in a declining market or sell stock in a rising market. One of the old axioms of stock market trading is to not fight the tape. Of course, the premise is that a trader is actually able to determine what the tape is really saying.

FIGS —See MUNICIPAL CONVERTIBLE.

fill To complete a customer's order to buy or sell a security. —See also PARTIAL EXECUTION.

fill-or-kill order An order sent to the floor of an exchange, demanding that it be filled immediately and in full or that it be canceled.

filter rule A technical trading rule in which an investor buys and sells stocks if their price movement reverses direction by a minimally acceptable percentage. For example, a technician may decide on a filter of 10%. If a stock being followed by the technician subsequently reverses a downtrend and rises by 10% from its low price, the filter rule indicates that the stock should be bought. A 10% decline from a high price indicates that a stock should be sold or sold short. The size of the filter is determined by the technician. The filter rule is supposed to permit an investor to participate in a security's major price trends without being misled by small fluctuations.

final dividend **1.** The final dividend payment from a firm that is liquidating. —See also LIQUIDATING DIVIDEND. **2.** The last dividend of a firm's fiscal year. The final dividend is declared when management is able to estimate rather accurately the firm's earnings and its dividend-paying ability. —Also called *year-end dividend.* —See also INTERIM DIVIDEND.

Financial Accounting Standards Board (FASB) The independent accounting organization that determines the standards for financial accounting and reporting. The rules set by FASB play a large role in determining the numbers that companies show the financial analysts and stockholders. —See also FASB STATEMENT.

financial analyst A person with expertise in evaluating financial investments. Financial analysts, who serve as investment advisers and portfolio managers, use their training and experience to investigate risk and return characteristics of securities. —Also called *analyst.* —See also CHARTERED FINANCIAL ANALYST; FINANCIAL ANALYSTS FEDERATION.

Financial Analysts Federation (FAF) A professional organization of investment managers and securities analysts. FAF holds seminars, publishes a widely read journal, and enforces a code of ethics and professional standards among its members. —See also INSTITUTE OF CHARTERED FINANCIAL ANALYSTS.

Financial and Operational Combined Uniform Single Report —See FOCUS REPORT.

financial asset A certificate evidencing a claim on the issuer. Bonds and common stocks are examples of financial assets.

financial condition —See FINANCIAL POSITION.

financial futures Obligations to buy or sell particular positions in fixed-income securities or security classes. Their features are identical to those of any futures contract except that the asset for delivery is of a financial nature. Financial futures are traded on certificates of deposit, commercial paper, GNMA certificates, Treasury bills, and Treasury bonds. —See also FUTURES MARKET.

Financial Guaranty Insurance Corporation (FGIC) A private insurer of interest and principal payments on municipal bond issues. As with other insurers, the issuer (municipality) pays the required premium to FGIC in order to obtain a higher rating on the bond issue. In this way, the bonds can be sold at a lower interest rate.

financial highlights The section of a corporate report providing investors with an overview of the firm's performance during the period covered by the report. For example, a report's highlights may note a major acquisition made by the firm during the period and it may discuss the implications of the acquisition relative to future sales and corporate earnings.

financial intermediary A financial institution such as a commercial bank or thrift that facilitates the flow of funds from savers to borrowers. Financial intermediaries profit from the spread between the amount they pay for the funds and the rate they charge for the funds. —Also called *intermediary.* —See also DISINTERMEDIATION; INTERMEDIATION.

financial lease —See CAPITAL LEASE.

financial leverage The extent to which interest on debt magnifies changes in operating income into even larger proportionate changes in earnings after taxes. Financial leverage magnifies increases in earnings per share during periods of rising operating income but adds significant risks for stockholders and creditors because of added interest obligations. —See also DEBT MANAGEMENT RATIO; DEBT-TO-EQUITY RATIO; OPERATING LEVERAGE.

financial planner A person who counsels individuals and corporations with respect to evaluating financial status, identifying goals, and determining ways in which the goals can be met. Although many people call themselves financial planners, a large number are primarily interested in selling a limited number of products they represent. A full-time professional planner, including a certified financial planner, an investment manager, or a tax attorney, may be better able to provide unbiased advice to the investor. —See also CERTIFIED FINANCIAL PLANNER; CHARTERED FINANCIAL CONSULTANT.

financial position The state of and the relationships among the various financial data found on a firm's balance sheet. For example, a company with fairly valued and relatively liquid assets, combined with a small amount of debt compared to owner's equity, is generally described as being in a strong financial position. —Also called *financial condition.*

financial ratio —See RATIO.

financial risk The risk that a firm will be unable to meet its financial obligations. This risk is primarily a function of the relative amount of debt that the firm uses to finance its assets. A higher proportion of debt increases the likelihood that at some point the firm will be unable to make the required interest and principal payments.

financial statement A report providing financial statistics relative to a given part of an organization's operations or status. The two most common financial statements are the balance sheet and the income statement. —See also COMPARATIVE FINANCIAL STATEMENTS.

finder A person who puts deals together. A finder may locate funds for a corporation seeking capital, bring together firms for a merger, or find a takeover target for a company seeking an acquisition.

finder's fee The charge levied by a person or firm for putting together a deal. For example, a finder may receive a fee equal to 3% of the principal amount paid for a corporate acquisition.

fineness A measure of the purity of gold. Fineness is quoted in parts per 1,000 with 1,000 fine being equivalent to 24-karat gold, and 583.3 fine being equivalent to 14-karat gold.

fingerprint In technical analysis, the unique way that a particular stock trades. Technical analysts believe that an understanding of a security's fingerprint allows the investor to detect unusual variations in volume or changes in price signaling a buying or selling opportunity.

firm commitment In securities offerings, a commitment by the underwriter to purchase securities from the issuer for resale to the public. Thus, the sale is guaranteed by a firm commitment to the issuer. With a firm commitment, the risk of being unable to sell an entire issue at the offering price is transferred from the issuer to the underwriter. —Also called *bought deal.*

firm order **1.** An investor's order to buy or sell that is not conditional on any additional instruction. **2.** An order placed on behalf of a broker-dealer firm rather than on behalf of the firm's client.

firm quote A quotation from a market maker to buy and sell a security at firm bid and ask prices. —See also NOMINAL QUOTE.

first call date The earliest date on which a security may be redeemed by the issuer. This date is particularly important to an investor who holds a security that is selling above or near its call price. The first call date is likely to be either five years or ten years after the date of issue; however, the timing varies by bond issue. Information regarding the first call date may be found on the bond certificate or it may be obtained from the brokerage firm holding the security. —See also YIELD TO CALL.

first coupon (F/C) The date on which a bond's initial interest payment will be made by the issuer.

first-in, first-out (FIFO) An accounting procedure for identifying the order in which items are used or sold. With FIFO, the oldest remaining items are assumed to have been sold first. During a period of inflation this procedure tends to keep costs low for accounting purposes; it results in higher reported profits and a greater tax liability, however. —See also AVERAGE-COST METHOD; INVENTORY PROFIT; INVENTORY VALUATION; LAST-IN, FIRST-OUT.

first mortgage A real estate loan with the right to payment in full before payments to other lenders are made. First mortgages are generally considered low risk investments although the quality of real estate pledged as collateral is of crucial importance in determining the riskiness of the mortgage.

first position day The initial day on which the investor who is short a commodity futures contract may notify the clearing corporation of an intention to deliver the commodity. The first position day occurs two business days before the first date on which delivery may be made. —See also POSITION DAY.

first section The section in each of Japan's three largest securities exchanges where more seasoned securities are traded.

fiscal agent The organization responsible for paying the interest and principal of another oganization's debt. For example, Valdosta State Bank may be fiscal agent for, and make interest and principal payments on, debt incurred by Scott Motors Corporation.

fiscal period The period of time covered by financial reports. For example, an annual report covers a fiscal period of one year, but a quarterly report includes accounting data for three months. —Also called *accounting period.*

fiscal policy Government spending and tax policy. Fiscal policy directly affects economic variables, such as tax rates, interest rates, and government programs, that influence security prices. —See also MONETARY POLICY.

fiscal year (FY) The 12-month accounting period for an organization. Since many firms end their accounting year on a date other than December 31, the fiscal year often differs from the calendar year.

fit A condition in which a security fulfills an investor's portfolio needs. For example, an investor may select a new municipal bond because that bond's maturity makes it a good fit in the investor's portfolio.

Fitch Investors Service A financial services company best known for the bond ratings it provides investors.

Fitch Sheets A relatively expensive investment aid of Fitch Investors Service that lists the daily sequence of price movements of all listed stocks. This service is of special interest to serious chartists.

501(c)(3) bond A bond issued by a nonprofit college or hospital that pays tax-exempt interest not subject to the alternative minimum tax. Interest from municipal bonds used to finance private activity are either fully taxable or are subject to the alternative minimum tax. —See also HOSPITAL REVENUE BOND.

five-hundred-dollar rule The Securities and Exchange Commission provision prohibiting brokers from instituting punitive measures against an investor's margin-deficit account if the amount of the deficiency is under $500. The five-hundred-dollar rule is intended to preclude brokers from having to sell part of a client's investment position because of a relatively small cash deficiency in the client's account.

five-percent rule A National Association of Securities Dealers rule requiring its members to use ethical and fair standards in setting commissions and in establishing quotation spreads. While members may set markups and markdowns in excess of 5%, they must be able to justify the commissions and spreads if complaints are filed. —See also RISKLESS TRANSACTION.

fix To set the price of a commodity. For example, commodity traders in London fix the price of gold on a daily basis. —See also GOLD FIX.

fixed annuity A stream of unchanging payments for a specific period or for an individual's lifetime, depending on the terms of the annuity contract. Fixed annuities are sold by insurance companies to people who desire a fixed income. —Also called *guaranteed-dollar annuity.* —See also HYBRID ANNUITY; VARIABLE ANNUITY.

fixed asset An asset not readily convertible to cash that is used in the normal course of business. Examples of fixed assets include machinery, buildings, and fixtures. A firm whose total assets are made up primarily of fixed assets is in a less liquid financial position, thus entailing greater risk of a big tumble in profits if its revenues fall.

fixed asset turnover A financial ratio that indicates a firm's ability to generate sales based on its long-term assets. Fixed asset turnover is calculated by dividing the dollar amount of fixed assets into annual sales. A high fixed asset turnover indicates effective management utilization of the firm's fixed assets. —See also ACTIVITY RATIO; TOTAL ASSET TURNOVER.

fixed-charge coverage The number of times that a firm's operating income exceeds its fixed payments. Fixed-charge coverage is a measure of the firm's ability to meet contractually fixed payments, with high coverage indicating significant flexibility for making payments in the event that business conditions deteriorate and earnings decline. Expenses used in calculating fixed-charge coverage normally include interest, lease payments, preferred dividends, and principal payments on debt. —Also called *times fixed charges.* —See also COVERAGE RATIO; INTEREST COVERAGE; PREFERRED DIVIDEND COVERAGE.

fixed cost A cost that remains unchanged even with variations in output. An airline with 20 airplanes has the fixed costs of depreciation and interest (if the planes are partially financed with debt), regardless of the number of times that the planes fly or the number of seats that are filled on each flight. Firms with high fixed costs tend to engage in price wars and cutthroat competition because extra revenues incur little extra expense. These firms tend to experience wide swings in profits. —See also AVERAGE COST; MARGINAL COST; VARIABLE COST.

fixed exchange rate An exchange rate between currencies that is set by the governments involved rather than being allowed to fluctuate freely with market forces. In order to keep currencies trading at the prescribed levels, government monetary authorities actively enter the currency markets to buy and sell according to variations in supply and demand. —See also DEVALUATION; FLOATING EXCHANGE RATE.

fixed-income security A security, such as a bond or preferred stock, that pays a constant income each period. Price changes in a fixed-income security are caused primarily by changes in long-term interest rates.

fixed price —See OFFERING PRICE.

fixed trust —See UNIT INVESTMENT TRUST.

flag —See TRIANGLE.

flash price The price of a selected security reported out-of-order on the consolidated tape when market volume becomes so heavy that the tape runs six or more minutes late. Flash prices are intended to provide traders and investors with up-to-date information on widely-held stocks. —See also LATE TAPE.

flat **1.** Designating a market maker's inventory position that is neither long nor short, i.e., the inventory is zero. **2.** Designating a bond that trades without accrued interest. For example, bonds of a company in bankruptcy proceedings trade flat. A bond trading flat is indicated in bond transaction tables by the symbol f.

flat loan A loan without interest to the lender. A firm lending securities for a short sale is often compensated by the borrowing firm with a flat loan. Thus, the lending firm has use of the funds without charge.

flat market A securities market in which there has been no tendency either to rise or to fall significantly. —Also called *sideways market*.

flat scale A municipal bond offering in which similar yields are available at all the various maturities.

flat tax An income tax involving a single rate of taxation. For example, a taxing authority may levy a flat tax of 3% against gross income. —See also GRADUATED FLAT TAX; PROGRESSIVE TAX; REGRESSIVE TAX.

flat yield curve At a particular time, similar yields on bonds of similar risk at all maturity lengths. During a period of a flat yield curve an investor would receive approximately the same yield on a long-term bond as would be the case on a short-term bond, although the former would be subject to greater price fluctuations. —See also NEGATIVE YIELD CURVE; POSITIVE YIELD CURVE; YIELD CURVE.

flexible exchange rate —See FLOATING EXCHANGE RATE.

flight to quality A movement by investors to purchase higher quality securities. For example, an investor might sell bonds rated lower than BBB and invest the proceeds in bonds rated AA or AAA. A flight to quality occurs when investors expect a deterioration in political stability or in economic activity.

flip-over pill   An entitlement granted by a firm's management to its stockholders giving them the right to purchase shares of an acquiring company's stock at a bargain price in the event of a merger. The flip-over pill is a variation of the poison pill. The difference between the two is that a poison pill allows stockholders to purchase additional shares of the target firm's stock rather than shares of the acquiring firm's stock.

flipper   A trader who attempts to make a small profit by very quick in-and-out buying and selling. For example, a flipper might try to take advantage of a hot market for new issues by purchasing a new issue at the offering and then selling it on the first day of trading.

float   **1.** Funds that are on deposit at two institutions at the same time because of inefficiencies in the collection system. This situation permits a person or firm to earn extra income since the two institutions are paying interest on the same funds. As an example, a person writes a check on a money market fund in order to make a deposit in a local financial institution. Until that check gets back to the bank on which it was written (a transit often entailing two or three days), the investor receives interest on his or her funds from both institutions. —See also FAIL FLOAT. **2.** The number of shares in public hands and available for trading. Institutional investors require that a security have a large float before they will take a position in it. The large float guards against a substantial price change in the security while the institution is buying. —Also called *floating supply.*

float   To permit a country's currency to change freely in value against foreign currencies.

float an issue   To sell a security issue in the primary market. For example, a firm may decide that it needs to expand its manufacturing facilities and float a new issue of common stock to pay for the expansion. Issuers generally employ an investment banker to assist in floating an issue.

floater   —See FLOATING-RATE NOTE.

floating debt   Short-term debt subject to continual refunding by the issuer.

floating exchange rate   An exchange rate between two currencies that is allowed to fluctuate with the market forces of supply and demand. Floating exchange rates tend to result in uncertainty as to the future rate at which currencies will exchange. This uncertainty is responsible for the increased popularity of forward, futures, and option contracts on foreign currencies. —Also called *flexible exchange rate.* —See also FIXED EXCHANGE RATE.

floating-rate note   An unsecured debt issue with an interest rate that is reset at specified intervals (normally every six months) according to a predetermined formula. Floating-rate notes usually can be redeemed at face value on certain dates at the holder's option. Floating-rate notes pay short-term interest and generally sell in the secondary market at nearly par value. Floating-rate notes are indicated in bond transaction tables in newspapers by the symbol *t*. —Also called *floater; variable-rate note*. —See also CONVERTIBLE FLOATING-RATE NOTE; DROPLOCK BOND; YIELD CURVE NOTE.

floating-rate preferred stock   A special and unusual type of preferred stock with a dividend that is reset at specified intervals according to a predetermined formula. Floating-rate preferred stock contrasts with most preferred stock issues that pay a fixed quarterly dividend. Floating-rate preferred stock issues do not generally fluctuate much in price because the dividend is automatically adjusted to keep the shares selling near to par. —Also called *adjustable-rate preferred stock*.

floating supply   —See FLOAT 2.

floor   The area of an organized exchange where securities are traded. Customer orders are transferred to the floor where they are executed by members of the exchange.

floor broker   A member of a securities exchange who executes orders on the exchange floor. For example, commission brokers and two-dollar brokers are floor brokers.

floor give-up   Announcement of the names of the principal organizations represented by participants after a transaction has taken place on the floor of a securities exchange. Thus, when a transaction has been completed, exchange members must inform one another which firms they are representing.

floor official   An exchange member or employee who mediates disputes among members on the floor of the exchange. For example, two floor brokers may disagree as to which one of them has priority on an order. The floor official would then umpire the dispute.

floor ticket   A ticket that summarizes a customer order ticket, used by a floor broker in executing the customer's order at the trading post on the exchange floor.

floor trader   An independent trader on a securities exchange who trades primarily for his or her own account. Floor traders generally attempt to profit from short-term price swings. They tend to add liquidity to the market and are required to make at least 75% of their trades against the last price change in the security traded. Thus, the majority of a floor trader's purchases must occur when the last price change in the security is a downtick. —Also called *competitive trader; registered competitive market maker 2; registered competitive trader; registered equity market maker; registered trader*.

flotation cost   The expense involved in selling a new security issue. This expense includes items such as registration of the issue and payment to the investment banker. Flotation costs depend on the size and riskiness of an issue as well as on the type of security to be sold. —See also GROSS SPREAD.

flower bond One of a limited series of U.S. government bonds that may be used at par to pay federal estate taxes. The bond is unique because there is no minimum time for which it must be held; further, its holder does not have to wait until maturity to use it at par for paying the tax. The supply of flower bonds, which have not been issued since 1971, has now become small as the existing bonds mature or are used to pay estate taxes.

flow of funds statement 1. For municipal bond issues, a listing of priorities for municipal revenues including the relative position of debt service and sinking fund requirements. 2. —See STATEMENT OF CHANGES IN FINANCIAL POSITION.

flow-through method A method of accounting for tax benefits from the investment tax credit in which these credits are utilized to increase net income at the earliest possible time—generally the year during which the asset is purchased. The flow-through method is considered a liberal accounting technique in that benefits are taken as soon as possible. —See also DEFERRED INVESTMENT TAX CREDIT.

FNMA —See FEDERAL NATIONAL MORTGAGE ASSOCIATION.

FOB —See FREE ON BOARD.

FOCUS Report A monthly and quarterly report on net capital position submitted by members of the New York Stock Exchange to the Exchange. —Also called *Financial and Operational Combined Uniform Single Report*.

FOMC —See FEDERAL OPEN MARKET COMMITTEE.

footnote A detailed explanation of an item in a financial statement. Footnotes are nearly always located at the end of a statement. For example, a company is likely to attach footnotes to its annual report to expand on the depreciation and inventory valuation methods used by its accountants. Many financial analysts consider footnotes the most important information in an annual report. —Also called *note*.

Forbes 500 The annual listing of the 500 largest publicly traded firms published by *Forbes* magazine. The Forbes 500, a compilation of separate lists categorized by assets, market value of shares, profits, and sales, is constructed somewhat differently from the Fortune 500, which lists firms on the basis of industry segment and amount of assets owned.

forced conversion The call for redemption of a convertible security at a price lower than the market value of the underlying asset into which the convertible may be exchanged. The investor finds it more favorable to exchange the convertible for the underlying asset than to give up the security for cash at the call price. For instance, suppose a $1,000 principal bond with a call price of $1,080 is converted into 20 shares of stock selling at $70 each. The bond is worth $1,400 in underlying stock. If the issuer calls the bond, the investor will be forced to convert before the call becomes effective.

⚠$ In 1986 Beatrice Companies called for redemption all the shares of an issue of its convertible preferred stock. The shares had a call price of $52.00, with the holders receiving a quarterly dividend of 84.5¢. Thus, the total value per share was $52.845. At their option, owners of the preferred stock could convert each share into .744 share of a different preferred issue plus $74.40 in cash. Because the convertible preferred stock was so much more valuable upon conversion compared with the amount the holders would receive from surrendering their shares at the call price, the calling of the stock effectively resulted in a forced conversion. Consequently, Beatrice advised its preferred holders to consider strongly the conversion of their shares in lieu of accepting the redemption price.

foreign bond A debt security issued by a borrower from outside the country in whose currency the bond is denominated and in which the bond is sold. A bond denominated in U.S. dollars that is issued in the United States by the goverment of Canada is a foreign bond. A foreign bond allows an investor a measure of international diversification without subjection to the risk of changes in relative currency values. —See also EUROBOND.

foreign corporation A firm conducting business in states or countries other than the state or country in which it is incorporated. For example, a firm incorporated in Canada but conducting business all over North America is considered a foreign corporation in the United States. —See also DOMESTIC CORPORATION.

Foreign Corrupt Practices Act A 1977 amendment to the Securities Exchange Act penalizing those engaging in bribery of foreign government officials or foreign personnel, and requiring adequate records and internal controls in all publicly held companies.

foreign crowd Members of the New York Stock Exchange trading foreign bonds on the Exchange floor. —See also CROWD.

foreign currency translation —See TRANSLATION.

foreign exchange controls Restrictions imposed by a nation on the free exchange and convertibility of its own currency. Foreign exchange controls are most often instituted by countries whose currencies are weak and whose citizens prefer to hold and use the currencies of other nations. Institution of foreign exchange controls hinders foreign investors in extricating their funds.

foreign exchange rate —See EXCHANGE RATE.

foreign exchange risk The risk that the exchange rate on a foreign currency will move against the position held by an investor such that the value of the investment is reduced. For example, if an investor residing in the United States purchases a bond denominated in Japanese yen, a deterioration in the rate at which the yen exchanges for dollars (i.e., a depreciation of the yen) will reduce the investor's rate of return, since he or she must exchange the yen for dollars.

foreign tax credit The reduction in a U.S. tax liability because of taxes accrued or paid to a foreign government during the same taxable year.

form F–1   A Securities and Exchange Commission form for foreign issuers of securities to be offered in the United States.

form F–6   A Securities and Exchange Commission form for registering depository securities represented by American Depository Receipts.

form FR–1   A National Association of Securities Dealers (NASD) form that requires foreign securities dealers purchasing new issues for resale to comply with NASD rules for hot issues. The form helps to ensure that foreign broker-dealers will not sell a stock intended for public offering above the offering price or to individuals associated with those broker-dealers. —Also called *blanket certification form.*

form N–1A   A Securities and Exchange Commission form for registering mutual funds.

form N–2   A Securities and Exchange Commission form for registering closed-end investment companies.

form PD 4632   The Federal Reserve form that investors must complete in order to buy Treasury bills at auction from a Federal Reserve bank. The form may be submitted by mail or in person to any of the 12 Federal Reserve banks or any of the 25 branch banks. The form has three categories, depending on whether a 13-week, 26-week, or 52-week bill is desired.

form PD 4633–1   The Federal Reserve form that investors must complete in order to roll over a matured Treasury bill into a newly issued Treasury bill. This form must be in the hands of the Federal Reserve 20 business days before the maturity of currently-held bills.

form S–1   A statement that must be filed by a firm with the Securities and Exchange Commission before the firm's securities can be listed for trading on a national securities exchange. The form S–1 contains information on the firm's business, financing, and directors. It also includes a description of the securities listed.

form S–2   A simplified registration form filed with the Securities and Exchange Commission for firms that have already reported under the Securities and Exchange Act of 1934.

form S–4   A Securities and Exchange Commission form for registering securities to be issued in connection with business combinations.

form S–6   A Securities and Exchange Commission form for registering securities to be issued by unit investment trusts.

form S–11   A Securities and Exchange Commission form for registering securities to be issued by real estate investment trusts.

form S–18   A Securities and Exchange Commission registration form for issuers of securities having a market value of $7.5 million or less.

form X17–A5   An audited financial statement filed annually with the Securities and Exchange Commission by brokers and dealers.

form 3   A Securities and Exchange Commission form that directors and officers, and holders of 10% or more of a firm's stock are required to file.

Form 3 requires disclosure of all shares and all securities convertible into shares that are directly or beneficially owned by these people.

form 4 A Securities and Exchange Commission (SEC) form for reporting changes in the holdings of a firm's common stock or stock equivalents. A reporting of changes is required of holders of over 10% of a firm's stock and of all directors and officers. Form 4 must be filed with the SEC within 10 days of the end of the month in which the change took place.

form 8–K —See 8–K.

form 10–K —See 10–K.

form 10–Q —See 10–Q.

form 13–F A quarterly report of security holdings with the Securities and Exchange Commission by large institutional investors.

form 6781 An Internal Revenue Service tax form on which an investor discloses open option positions showing gains and calculates the unrecognized gain in each open position.

formation —See CHART FORMATION.

formula plan Buying and/or selling securities according to a predetermined formula, with the purpose being to eliminate the investor's emotions and instead rely on a mechanical set of rules. A huge number of formula plans have been developed over the years.

Fortune 500® A trademark for a well-known, widely quoted annual listing by *Fortune* magazine of the largest industrial corporations in the United States. Firms are listed along with assets, sales, and profits. Subsequent issues include the largest retailers, utilities, financial institutions, transportation companies, foreign corporations, and the second 500 largest industrial firms.

for valuation only (FVO) —See FOR YOUR INFORMATION.

forward contract An agreement between two parties to the sale and purchase of a particular commodity at a specific future time. Although forward contracts are similar to futures, they are not easily transferred or canceled. Thus, they are not liquid.

forward federal funds Federal funds traded for delivery at a future date.

forward pricing The pricing of mutual fund shares on the basis of the next net asset valuation following receipt of a customer's order to buy or sell. While the price is based on net asset value, this value is adjusted for any applicable redemption or sales fee. Forward pricing is required by the Securities and Exchange Commission.

forward rate **1.** The expected yield on a given fixed-income security at a particular time in the future. For example, if the yield on 6-month Treasury bills is expected to be 10.5% in one year, this yield is the forward rate on 6-month bills. **2.** The rate at which a particular currency or commodity may be purchased on a forward contract.

for your information (FYI) Pertaining to a market maker's quotation for trading purposes when the price is not firm. For example, a market maker might supply an FYI quote for valuation purposes. —Also called *for valuation only; throwaway.*

four horsemen   The four regional investment banking firms that became well-known for bringing new issues of common stock to market. These firms are: Alex Brown & Sons; Hambrecht & Quist; Robertson, Colman & Stephens; and L.F. Rothschild, Unterberg, Tobin.

401(K) plan   —See SALARY REDUCTION PLAN.

403(b) plan   —See TAX-SHELTERED ANNUITY.

fourth market   The market for securities in which large investors bypass exchanges and dealers in order to trade directly among themselves. —See also AUTEX; INSTINET®; SECONDARY MARKET; THIRD MARKET.

fractional discretion order   A customer's order to buy or sell a security, giving the broker limited discretion as to price. For example, an order to sell 200 shares of GY at 75, ⅜ of a point discretion, informs the broker that the customer would like a price of $75 per share but will accept a price as low as $74⅝ per share.

fractional share   Less than one share of stock, i.e., one-third or one-half a share. Fractional shares are generally created from dividend reinvestment plans or stock dividends. For example, if a firm's directors declare a 2% stock dividend, an owner of 70 shares would be entitled to 1.4 additional shares. Because corporations do not issue certificates including fractional shares, the stockholder would receive one share and the cash equivalent for the fractional share. Fractional shares are credited to dividend reinvestment plans.

franchise   **1.** An agreement between a firm and another party in which the firm provides the other party with the right to use the firm's name and sell or rent its products. Selling franchise rights is a method of expanding a business quickly with a minimum of capital. —See also FRANCHISEE; FRANCHISOR.   **2.** A right granted to another party by a government to engage in certain types of business. For example, a firm may obtain a government franchise to supply certain public services within a limited geographic region.

franchisee   An individual or a company that has the right to sell or rent another firm's products and use its name. —See also FRANCHISOR.

franchise tax   A tax on the right of a firm to do business within a certain geographic region.

franchisor   A firm that sells to others the right to sell or rent its products and to use its name. —See also FRANCHISEE.

fraud   Deception with the purpose of achieving personal gain while causing injury to another party. For example, selling a new security issue while intentionally concealing important facts related to the issue is fraud.

Freddie Mac   A security issued by the Federal Home Loan Mortgage Corporation that is secured by pools of conventional home mortgages.

Holders of Freddie Macs receive a share of the interest and principal payments made by the homeowners.

free box   The physical location in brokerage firms of securities that are fully owned by customers. Securities in the free box are free of encumbrances. —See also BOX; OPEN BOX.

free credit balance   Cash held in a brokerage account that may be withdrawn or used to acquire additional securities. Free credit balances generally originate from dividends, interest payments, and security sales. Many firms automatically send balances to customers on the first day of each month. Investors may also request placement of the funds in a money market mutual fund. —See also CREDIT BALANCE; DEBIT BALANCE.

freed up   Having members of an underwriting syndicate released from selling a security only at the fixed issue price.

free on board (FOB)   —In commodities contracts, used to indicate the location to which the price includes delivery. From this point the buyer is responsible for all risks and delivery costs. The FOB point is only important to someone who sells or buys a futures contract with the intention of making or taking delivery of the specific commodity.

freeriding   1. A syndicate member's withholding of a portion of a new security issue from sale in anticipation of reselling the withheld securities at a higher price later. Freeriding is prohibited by the Securities and Exchange Commission.   2. The purchase and sale of a security in a short period of time without putting up any money. Freeriding by investors is prohibited by Federal Reserve Board Regulation T. —See also FROZEN ACCOUNT.

free right of exchange   The ability of an investor to transfer a security from one form to another without charge. For example, free right of exchange permits a security owner to transfer a certificate from registered to bearer form or from street name to registration in the investor's name without paying a charge.

free supply   In commodities trading, the amount of a commodity that is available for trading.

frequency of compounding   The number of times that interest is calculated and added to principal plus any previous interest during a period of time (nearly always one year). More frequent compounding results in a more rapid buildup of funds. For example, $1,000 deposited at 12% compounded twice a year equals $1,000(1.06)(1.06), or $1,123.60 at the end of 1 year, while compounding 4 times a year results in $1,000(1.03)(1.03)(1.03)(1.03) or $1,125.51.

friendly takeover   The acquisition of a firm with approval of the acquired firm's board of directors. —See also UNFRIENDLY TAKEOVER.

front-end load   —See LOAD.

front running   Entering into an option trade with advance knowledge of an impending block transaction that is likely to affect the price of the underlying security and the option.

frozen account   A brokerage account in which a customer must pay in full before securities are bought, and must deliver certificates before securities are sold. An account is frozen when a customer fails to maintain the proper margin required by Regulation T. —See also FREERIDING 2.

frozen asset   An asset that may not be liquidated.

frozen collateral   Collateral that the lender is unable to seize in order to satisfy repayment of a debt. For example, a lender may find that there is a legal question as to who actually owns the asset pledged as collateral.

FSLIC   —See FEDERAL SAVINGS AND LOAN INSURANCE CORPORATION.

FSLIC-insured municipal bonds   Bonds issued by tax-exempt agencies with proceeds being used to purchase certificates of deposit at financial institutions insured by the Federal Savings and Loan Insurance Corporation. The financial insitution uses the funds to finance a specific project such as a low-income housing development. These high-grade bonds were very popular until their issuance was stopped by the federal government in 1984.

FTC   —See FEDERAL TRADE COMMISSION.

full coupon   —See CURRENT COUPON.

full disclosure   The disclosure of all relevant financial and operating information. For example, the Securities and Exchange Commission requires public corporations to make full disclosure when they issue securities.

full-faith-and-credit bond   —See GENERAL OBLIGATION BOND.

full-faith-and-credit pledge   In a municipal obligation, a pledge of the full financial resources and taxing power of the issuer. A full-faith-and-credit pledge is an important element of general obligation bonds. —See also SPECIAL ASSESSMENT BOND.

A full-service brokerage firm is best for which kinds of investors?

Full-service brokerage firms invest millions analyzing and determining what the most compelling opportunities in changing market environments are. An individual seeking advice, both short- and long-term, is probably best suited for a full-service firm.

*Katherine L. Robinson, Assistant Vice President
Kidder, Peabody & Co., Boston, MA*

full price   Fair price as applied to a security or an acquisition. For example, if a firm's stock is selling at close to full price the firm is less likely to be a candidate for a takeover.

full-service brokerage firm   A brokerage firm that provides a wide range of services and products to its customers, including research and advice. Merrill Lynch, Shearson, PaineWebber, and Dean Witter are examples of nationally known full-service firms, although many other good regional and local full-service firms also exist. —See also DISCOUNT BROKERAGE FIRM.

fully diluted earnings per share   Net income for a period divided by the average number of shares of common stock that would be outstanding if all convertible securites were converted into shares of common stock. Fully diluted earnings per share is a particularly effective method of presenting earnings-per-share data for companies with complex capital structures. —See also DUAL PRESENTATION; PRIMARY EARNINGS PER SHARE.

fully distributed   Pertaining to a new issue of securities that is sold out.

fully invested   Having committed nearly all available funds to assets other than short-term investments such as savings and money market accounts. —Generally used in reference to institutional investors (mutual funds or trust departments). It indicates that these investors are very bullish.

fully valued   Pertaining to a stock selling at a price most analysts believe fully reflects the company's asset values and earnings potential. If a stock is in fact fully valued, it generally has limited appreciation potential.

fundamental analysis   Analysis of security values grounded in basic factors such as earnings, balance sheet variables, and management quality. Fundamental analysis attempts to determine the true value of a security, and, if the market price of the stock deviates from this value, to take advantage of the difference by acquiring or selling the stock. Fundamental analysis may involve investigating a firm's financial statements, visiting its managers, or examining how a particular industry is affected by changes in the economy. —See also TECHNICAL ANALYSIS.

fundamentalist   An investor who buys and sells securities on the basis of fundamental analysis. Some investors use fundamental and technical analysis. Fundamental analysis is utilized for security selection; and technical analysis, for timing purchases and sales. —See also TECHNICIAN.

fundamentals   Basic economic, financial, and operating factors influencing the success of a business and the price of its securities. Fundamentals of a security include the price-earnings ratio, dividend payout, earnings-per-share growth, and numerous other variables.

funded debt   Long-term interest-bearing debt, such as bonds and debentures.

fund group   —See FAMILY OF FUNDS.

fund of funds   An open-end investment company that invests only in the shares of other open-end investment companies. This type of mutual fund was popular during the 1960s but subsequently fell into disfavor with investors. Many analysts consider it more of a gimmick than a useful investment vehicle.

fund switching Selling shares in one mutual fund and reinvesting the proceeds in another mutual fund. Fund switching results from an investor's changed perception of investment opportunties. For example, an individual may become bearish and switch money from a growth fund to a money market fund. Because of the high sales charges involved in purchasing some funds, fund switching is practical only if no-load funds are used or if the investor switches within a family of funds.

Please explain how to decide when to switch funds.

The ability to switch from one fund to another is a feature of several family of funds companies designed to maximize investors' flexibility and control over investment dollars. Fund switching should take place if investment objectives change or if market conditions warrant. For instance, when the recognizable trend of the stock market is up, an investor may want his or her investment dollars working in an aggressive mutual fund to take best advantage of the movement upward. If the recognizable trend of the market turns down, the investor may want to move those dollars into a liquid, high-yielding money fund. Generally, companies offer the privilege of fund switching by phone, and charges vary.

Neal Litvack, Marketing Manager
Fidelity Investments, Boston, MA

---

funds statement —See STATEMENT OF CHANGES IN FINANCIAL POSITION.

fungible Pertaining to assets of identical quality that are interchangeable. Commodities, options, and securities are fungible assets. For example, an investor's shares of Xerox left in custody at a brokerage firm are freely mixed with other customers' Xerox shares. Likewise, stock options are freely interchangeable among investors just as wheat stored in a grain elevator is not specifically identified as to its ownership.

funnel sinking fund A special type of bond retirement system in which an issuer has the option to make all its outstanding bonds subject to one annual sinking fund requirement. Thus, the issuer may take the annual sinking fund requirements for all outstanding issues and concentrate them into retiring an unusually large amount of a high-coupon issue. A funnel sinking fund generally operates to the disadvantage of bondholders and to the advantage of the issuer.

furtherest out In futures and options trading, the contract month with the most distant delivery or expiration. —See also NEARBY.

futures commission merchant (FCM) A firm that carries out futures transactions for another party. Essentially, futures commission merchants are to futures trading what ordinary brokerage firms are to stock and bond trading. Some futures commission merchants are full-line brokerage firms in which futures trades make up only a small part of their business. —Also called *commodity brokerage firm; futures commission firm.*

futures contract An agreement to take (i.e., by the buyer) or make (i.e., by the seller) delivery of a specific commodity on a particular date. The commodities and contracts are standardized in order that an active resale (secondary) market will exist. Futures contracts are available for a variety of items including grains, metals, and foreign currencies. —See also SECTION 1256 CONTRACTS.

futures market A market in which futures contracts are bought and sold. The various organized futures exchanges specialize in certain types of contracts. For example, corn, oats, soybeans, and wheat are traded on the Chicago Board of Trade, while the Commodity Exchange in New York handles trades in aluminum, copper, gold, and silver. Other futures markets include the Chicago Mercantile Exchange, the Chicago Rice and Cotton Exchange, the Coffee, Sugar and Cocoa Exchange, the International Monetary Market, the Kansas City Board of Trade, the MidAmerica Commodity Exchange, the Minneapolis Grain Exchange, the New York Futures Exchange, the New York Mercantile Exchange, and the Philadelphia Board of Trade.

futures option A put or call option on a futures contract. Because of the price volatility of futures contracts, options on these contracts are high-risk investments. —See also SECTION 1256 CONTRACTS.

future value The amount to which a specific sum or series of sums will grow on a given date in the future. The sums are assumed to earn an annual return that is related to the market rate of interest. For example, $1,000 has a future value of $1,120 in one year, assuming an annual return of 12%. —See also PRESENT VALUE.

FVO —See FOR VALUATION ONLY.

FY —See FISCAL YEAR.

FYI —See FOR YOUR INFORMATION.

G

g —Used immediately following the stock name in stock transaction tables of newspapers to indicate that dividends and earnings are in Canadian currency but that the stock price is in U.S. dollars: *Dome g .12.*

GAAP —See GENERALLY ACCEPTED ACCOUNTING PRINCIPLES.

GAAS —See GENERALLY ACCEPTED AUDITING STANDARDS.

gain The excess of the amount received as opposed to the amount expended in a transaction. For example, receipt of $4,500 from the sale of an asset with a book value of $3,000 results in a gain of $1,500. —See also LOSS.

gainer A security that has risen in price during a specified time period. —See also LOSER.

GAINS® A trademark for a security that combines the features of a zero-coupon bond with those of interest-bearing bonds. —See also MUNICIPAL CONVERTIBLE.

gap A price range in which no shares are traded. A gap on a chart is created when the lowest price at which a security trades on one day is above the highest price at which the same security was traded on the previous day. Thus, if a stock trades between a low of 51 and a high of 52½ on Monday and between 53½ and 54 on the following day, a gap from 52½ to 53½ is created on a chartist's graph. A gap may have varying degrees of significance, depending on the general formation and the volume at the time the gap occurs. —Also called *price gap*. —See also BREAKAWAY GAP; EXHAUSTION GAP; RUNAWAY GAP.

Garage An annex floor to the main trading floor of the New York Stock Exchange.

GATT —See GENERAL AGREEMENT ON TARIFFS AND TRADE.

general account —See MARGIN ACCOUNT.

General Agreement on Tariffs and Trade (GATT) A 1947 multilateral trade agreement designed to establish rules, reduce tariffs, and provide a setting for a solution to international trade problems. GATT agreements are of particular importance to industries and firms heavily involved in international trade. Changes or even discussion of changes in these agreements can have a significant effect on the prices of the securities of affected companies.

general creditor A lender with an uncollateralized loan, such as the owner of a debenture. In the event that a borrower goes bankrupt, its general creditors are likely to recover a smaller proportion of what is owed them than secured creditors will.

generally accepted accounting principles (GAAP) Guidelines and rules for use by accountants in preparing financial statements. These principles, which evolved over a period of years, are designed to help ensure that financial data are presented fairly and are comparable from firm to firm and from industry to industry. In expressing an opinion on financial statements, Certified Public Accountants are required to stipulate whether or not their statements have been prepared according to generally accepted accounting principles.

generally acccepted auditing standards (GAAS) Guidelines established by the American Institute of Certified Public Accountants to guide public acccountants in conducting external audits of financial statements. —See also AUDITED STATEMENT; UNAUDITED STATEMENT.

general obligation bond (GO) A municipal debt obligation on which interest and principal are guaranteed by the full financial resources and taxing power of the issuer. This broad promise makes a general obligation bond of higher quality than issues secured by a particular project or a more limited guarantee. It also results in lower returns to bondholders. —Also called *full-faith-and-credit bond.* —See also REVENUE BOND.

Choosing among general obligation bonds: which are the best?

• •

The type of political entity which backs a GO bond is generally more important than its rating. For example, state GOs, because they are backed by a wide range of taxing power, are the strongest GOs on the market, and state GOs rated A or Baa are excellent buys. So too are school district GOs which are backed by state aid or special state funds as in New York, Pennsylvania, Michigan, and Texas, to name a few.

Steven J. Hueglin, Executive Vice President
Gabriele, Hueglin & Cashman, New York, NY

---

general partnership A partnership in which each of the partners is liable for all of the firm's debts and the actions of one partner are binding on each of the other partners. —See also LIMITED PARTNERSHIP.

general price level accounting —See INFLATION ACCOUNTING.

General Securities Registered Representative Examination —See SERIES 7.

General Utilities Doctrine An Internal Revenue Service provision permitting a firm to liquidate its assets at more than book value and pass the proceeds of the liquidation through to stockholders without making the firm pay income taxes on the gains. Rather, stockholders receiving the distribution are required to report the gain (but not the entire liquidation) as income. The General Utilities Doctrine was repealed in 1986 tax reform. As a result of the repeal, any gain from liquidation is taxed twice: once to the liquidating firm, and again to the stockholders.

ghost stock Stock that has been sold short but that has not been borrowed and therefore cannot be delivered to the buyer.

gift tax A federal tax imposed on the giver, and determined on the basis of a unified gift and estate tax schedule. Annual gifts of more than $10,000 per recipient are deducted from a lifetime exemption of $600,000 which applies jointly to accumulated gifts and the taxable estate left at death. In general, only relatively large gifts incur a tax. —See also UNIFIED CREDIT.

Gilded Age The years between the Civil War and World War I when institutions undertook financial manipulations that went virtually unchecked by government. This era produced many infamous actions in the security markets.

gilt-edged security 1. A bond issued through the United Kingdom Treasury and guaranteed by the British government. The market for gilt-edged securities is similar to the market for U.S. Treasury securities, with a high degree of safety, liquidity, and maturity selection. —Also called *gilt.* 2. Any high quality security in which the chance of default or failure is quite slim.

Ginnie Mae 1. —See GOVERNMENT NATIONAL MORTGAGE ASSOCIATION. 2. —See GINNIE MAE PASS THROUGH.

Ginnie Mae mutual fund A mutual fund that invests exclusively in Ginnie Mae certificates and passes through the interest payments to owners of the fund's shares. Since the fund continually invests in new certificates, the yield on the fund varies over time. In addition, the value of a fund will change as long-term interest rates change. The primary advantage of buying a fund over buying Ginnie Mae certificates directly is that the fund is sold to investors in smaller denominations. Furthermore, a fund's investments are spread over a large number of certificates so that prepayment of principal is not as much of a problem. The main disadvantage of a fund is that it may entail a sales fee from 4% to 6% of the amount invested and will charge an annual investment fee. (Some Ginnie Mae funds do not charge a sales fee.)

Ginnie Mae pass through A security backed by the Federal Housing Administration (FHA), Veterans Administration (VA), and the Farmers Home Administration (FHA) mortgages that are guaranteed by the Government National Mortgage Association (GNMA). The issuers of the securities service the mortgages and pass through interest and principal payments to the security holders. During periods of declining interest rates, holders of Ginnie Mae pass throughs are likely to receive extra principal payments as mortgages are refinanced and paid off early. —Also called *Ginnie Mae.* —See also ADJUSTED EXERCISE PRICE; CURRENT PRODUCTION RATE; NOMINAL EXERCISE PRICE; PASS-THROUGH SECURITY.

Ginnie Mae trust A unit trust that invests in Ginnie Mae certificates and passes through interest and principal repayments to the trust's owners. Ginnie Mae trusts differ from Ginnie Mae mutual funds in that the trusts do not continually invest in new certificates. As principal is returned, the trust's owner will receive progressively smaller interest payments. Essentially, owning a Ginnie Mae trust is much like owning a certificate itself. A sales fee is charged, but, unlike Ginnie Mae funds, a trust charges no managment fee because no management is involved once the trust has been set up and has become operative.

Ginnie Mae pass through: high quality and yield with changing cash flows.
• •

Ginnie Maes offer the highest degree of safety with timely payments of interest and principal guaranteed by the U.S. government. The investor receives monthly a cash flow of both interest and principal, which can provide greater reinvestment flexibility and more spendable income. Ginnie Maes make for an excellent long-term investment. There is also an active secondary market, so that sales can be easily effected.

Cash flow, however, is uneven and difficult to estimate precisely, as mortgage prepayments inevitably occur. And, since prepayments usually increase when interest rates decline, there will be more principal to reinvest when returns are lower. Ginnie Maes have more limited price appreciation potential when compared with equivalent Treasury bonds, as investors are reluctant to pay a large premium beyond the principal coming back to them.

Irwin H. Metzger, Vice President
Merrill Lynch, Pierce, Fenner & Smith Inc., New York, NY

---

giveback The relinquishment by employees of certain existing benefits or contract provisions. For example, many companies engaged in manufacturing have asked for employee givebacks on the premise that lower costs are needed in order for the companies to be more competitive with foreign competitors. Givebacks are good news for investors because they result in higher profits or smaller losses for the company obtaining the concessions.

give-up 1. A now prohibited practice in which a large investor directs that a portion of the commission charged in a security trade be handed over to another broker. Give-ups were popular when commission rates were fixed and when large trades produced artificially high commissions transferrable to other firms providing the investor with valuable services such as research information. 2. The reduction in yield when a bond position is swapped for bonds with a lower coupon.

glamor stock A widely-held stock receiving much favorable publicity in the financial press. Glamor stocks typically represent firms with strong earnings growth and bright futures. Glamor stocks, which tend to sell at relatively high price-earnings ratios, are found in most institutional portfolios.

Glass-Steagall Act A 1933 act prohibiting commercial banks from undertaking investment banking activities such as underwriting the securities of private corporations. The legislation was passed to keep banks from entering into nonfinancial businesses (e.g., owning corporate stock) and more risky activities. Although the law is still in effect, many bankers feel that the need for such regulation has long since passed. —Also called *Banking Act of 1933*.

global fund A mutual fund that includes at least 25% foreign securities in its portfolio. The value of the fund depends on the health of foreign economies and exchange rate movements. A global fund permits an investor to diversify internationally. —See also INTERNATIONAL FUND.

GNMA —See GOVERNMENT NATIONAL MORTGAGE ASSOCIATION.

GNP —See GROSS NATIONAL PRODUCT.

GNP deflator A price index used to adjust gross national product for changes in prices of goods and services included in the GNP. The GNP deflator is a more broadly based and, many economists argue, a better measure of inflation than the consumer price index or the producer price index. —Also called *gross national product deflator*.

GO —See GENERAL OBLIGATION BOND.

go-go fund An investment company that concentrates on short-term investment performance through frequent trading of highly speculative securities. The funds were very popular during the late 1960s but lost favor following the market decline of the early 1970s that produced large price drops in the types of stocks held by the go-go funds. —Also called *performance fund*.

go-go thrift A savings and loan association using its government-insured deposit base to make risky, high-yield investments. For example, a go-go thrift may lend funds for a corporate takeover attempt.

going away The purchase by institutional investors of large amounts of a serial bond issue in a particular maturity.

going concern A business expected to continue operating in the foreseeable future. A going concern is valued differently from a firm for which liquidation is expected.

going lines —See CONTINUING OPERATIONS.

going private The process by which a publicly held company has its outstanding shares purchased by an individual or by a small group of individuals in order to obtain complete ownership and control. The group wishing to take the firm private may feel that the market is undervaluing the shares. In addition, the purchaser(s) may not wish to meet the various requirements imposed on a publicly held company. —Also called *management buyout*.

> In September of 1986 a group of Viacom International managers and outsiders proposed that the company go private. The proposal took the form of an offer to the stockholders of $37 in cash and preferred stock valued at $3.50 for each share of Viacom's common stock. The deal resulted in a total payment of $2.16 billion for an equivalent of slightly over 53 million shares of stock. Viacom, which had been the subject of takeover rumors for a number of months, had repurchased earlier in the year 17% of its outstanding stock from Carl Icahn after having fended off his takeover attempt.

going public The process by which a privately held company sells a portion of its ownership to the general public through a stock offering. Owners generally take their firms public because they need additional large sums of equity funding that they are unable or unwilling to contribute themselves.

going south —Used to describe a security or the general market during a period of declining prices.

gold bond —See COMMODITY-BACKED BOND.

gold bug An individual who thinks that investors should keep all or part of their assets in the form of gold. The tendency to recommend gold nearly always stems from the gold bug's expectation of rapid or uncontrolled growth of the money supply accompanied by high rates of inflation. Some gold bugs also predict economic collapse with gold becoming the standard of payment.

gold certificate Receipt of ownership for a stated quantity of gold. A certificate, normally issued by a major bank, allows an investor to own gold without actually taking possession of the metal. A commission is generally charged at the time of purchase.

golden handcuffs A lucrative incentive offered to a firm's executive in order to keep him or her from moving to a job at another company or to buy the executive's longer-range cooperation after departure.

golden parachute An employment agreement that provides a firm's key executives with lucrative severance benefits in the event that control of the firm changes hands, and shifts in management subsequently occur. A golden parachute benefits management more than the stockholders. —Also called *golden umbrella.*

> 🪙 Two executives of Manville Corporation, a firm emerging from a Chapter 11 bankruptcy, received severance compensation of nearly $1.8 million upon leaving the firm in 1986. The two golden parachutes included payments over two years of $1.3 million to the retiring chairman and a payment of $530,000 to the firm's president who had already resigned in a dispute with a group involved in the bankruptcy proceedings. The golden parachutes, which were approved by the bankruptcy judge, went unopposed by a committee of plaintiffs in the proceedings.

golden umbrella —See GOLDEN PARACHUTE.

gold fix The setting of the price of gold by dealers for valuing gold bullion, gold products, and gold-related products. The price of gold is fixed twice a day in each of the world's gold centers. —See also FIX.

gold fund An investment company with all or a major part of its assets in gold or gold-related securities. A gold fund's price—closely related to the value of gold—frequently moves opposite the prices of other securities and stock market indices.

gold standard A monetary system under which a country's money is defined in terms of gold and convertible into a fixed quantity of gold. A gold standard effectively takes monetary policy out of the hands of government policymakers. While use of the gold standard reduces the likelihood of inflation, the accompanying inability to pursue other economic goals, such as full employment or reduced interest rates, has resulted in the gold standard's falling from favor.

good delivery Delivery of a security that meets all the standards required to transfer title to the buyer. Thus, a certificate must be delivered on time with proper denomination, endorsements, and endorsement guarantee. —See also BAD DELIVERY.

good faith deposit 1. A sum of money required of an investor placing an order when the investor is not known to the brokerage firm. A good faith deposit ensures that the customer will follow through with proper payment for a buy order or delivery of securities for a sell order. 2. A sum of money deposited by competing underwriters of a new municipal bond issue. The deposit is a relatively small proportion (usually under 5%) of the value of the issue being underwritten.

goods in process —See WORK IN PROGRESS.

good-this-month order —See MONTH ORDER.

good-till-canceled order (GTC) An order either to buy or to sell a security which remains in effect until it is canceled by the customer or until it is executed by the broker. —Also called *open order*.

What are the dangers inherent in entering good-till-canceled orders?
• •

The biggest danger when entering good-till-canceled orders is that you can forget they were originally entered and then buy or sell twice. Good-till-canceled has also been called good-till-close, which suggests that people change their minds as the price they are waiting for is approached. Still another danger is that if the market moves precipitously, it's possible that you'll have an order executed when you are unprepared.

Bonnie Briskin, Stockbroker
Tucker, Anthony & R. L. Day, Inc., Boston, MA

---

goodwill The discounted value of a larger-than-normal return on tangible assets. A business may build goodwill over time as customers become loyal to the firm's products. Goodwill does not appear on a company's financial statements unless another business is purchased at a price greater than book value.

Government National Mortgage Association (GNMA) A government-owned corporation that acquires, packages, and resells mortgages and mortgage purchase commitments in the form of mortgage-backed securities. —Also called *Ginnie Mae*. —See also GINNIE MAE PASS THROUGH; MOBILE HOME CERTIFICATE.

governments All bonds issued by the U.S. Treasury or other agencies of the U.S. government. —Also called *United States government securities*. —See also FEDERAL AGENCY SECURITY; SAVINGS BOND; TREASURIES.

graduated flat tax An income tax with a minimal number of progressively higher rates. For example, a taxing authority may levy a tax of 10% on all income up to $15,000, 15% on income from $15,000 to $25,000, and 20% on all income above $25,000. The graduated flat tax is a compromise between a flat tax and a progressive tax.

grandfathering Alteration of the rules that apply to a certain investment or investment technique while stipulating that investment actions taken before a certain date remain subject to the old rules. For example, Congress may change the law by stipulating that certain types of municipal bonds no longer pay tax-free interest while at the same time grandfathering the municipal bonds issued before the date on which the new law is to take effect.

graph —See CHART.

gray market trade An open-market transaction in a when-issued security through brokers outside the selling syndicate.

Great Crash The major declines in economic activity and stock prices that occurred in 1929 and the early 1930s.

greater fool theory The theory that no matter what price an investor pays for a security, someone else with less sense will be willing to buy it later. The greater fool theory reaches its height of popularity near the end of a bull market when speculation is high.

greenmail An antitakeover maneuver in which the target firm purchases the raider's stock at a price above that available to other stockholders. The funds for the purchase are often borrowed; other stockholders are ordinarily excluded from the transaction. —See also ANTIGREENMAIL PROVISION; FAIR PRICE AMENDMENT.

⚠️ In 1984 Walt Disney Productions fought to avoid being taken over by Saul Steinberg's Reliance Group Holdings Inc. At first, Disney diluted its stock by consenting to acquire a real estate development company and a greeting card company for $525 million in newly issued shares. Then, when these tactics failed, Disney's management paid Steinberg $325.5 million for his 11% stock holdings in the Disney company. Ordinary stockholders were excluded from the deal, and within one week of the buyback, their stock had dropped by 31% in value to a level well below what Steinberg had been paid. Disney management subsequently decided not to acquire the greeting card company and in 1987 sold the real estate subsidiary at a profit. Disney stock soared in 1985 and 1986, during which time the common was split 4 for 1. Thus, while stockholders suffered short-term losses because of the greenmail, the longer-term consequences were quite favorable.

green shoe An underwriting agreement provision permitting syndicate members to buy additional shares at the original price.

gross income 1. For a business, total revenues exclusive of any expenses. 2. For an individual, all income except as specifically exempted by the Internal Revenue Code. For example, an inheritance is specifically excluded from gross income.

gross lease A lease in which costs of maintaining the leased asset including insurance and taxes are paid by the lessor (owner). —See also NET LEASE.

gross margin —See GROSS PROFIT MARGIN.

gross national product (GNP) The dollar output of final goods and services in the economy during a period of time (usually a year). GNP, one measure of the economic vitality of a country, provides some indication of the health of near-term corporate income. —See also ECONOMIC ACTIVITY.

gross national product deflator —See GNP DEFLATOR.

gross per broker The amount of commissions produced by a broker during a period of time. The productivity of a registered representative and a brokerage office is often measured by the gross commissions per broker. Registered representatives are generally allowed to keep about one third of their gross commissions.

gross profit Total revenue of a business less cost of goods sold. Gross profit does not include income from incidental sources. It also excludes selling and administrative expenses. —See also NET INCOME.

gross profit margin Gross profit divided by net sales. Gross profit margin is a measure of a firm's ability to turn a dollar of sales into profit after the cost of goods sold has been accounted for. —Also called *gross margin; margin of profit.* —See also NET PROFIT MARGIN; RETURN ON SALES.

gross sales Total sales for a period before discounts, returns, and freight expenses have been deducted. —See also NET SALES.

gross spread The difference in the price that an investor pays for a new security issue and the price paid the issuer by the lead underwriter. The gross spread is a function of a number of variables including the size of the issue and the riskiness, or price volatility, of the security. —Also called *underwriting spread.* —See also CONCESSION; FLOTATION COST.

> In the fall 1984 Cracker Barrel Old Country Store, the owner and operator of "country store" restaurants in the southeastern United States, issued 750,000 new shares of its common stock. The stock, already being traded publicly in the over-the-counter market, had recently ranged in price from a low of $6⅛ in late 1982 to a high of $27⅝ in mid-1983. The new shares were sold to the public at the existing market price of $17¼. Of this amount, Cracker Barrel received $16¼. The difference provided a gross spread of $1 per share, or $750,000 ($1 × 750,000 shares), to a team of underwriters headed by J.C. Bradford, Alex Brown, and Montgomery Securities. Thus, nearly 6% of the offering price went to the underwriters.

gross working capital —See CURRENT ASSET.

group of funds —See FAMILY OF FUNDS.

group sales Sales of a new security offering to institutional investors. Group sales are prorated among syndicate members in proportion to the part of the original issue that each agreed to take.

growth fund An investment company whose major objective is long-term capital growth. Growth funds offer substantial potential gains over time but vary significantly in price during bull and bear markets. This type of fund is most appropriate for someone who will not need to withdraw funds anytime soon.

What factors should I keep in mind when selecting a growth fund?

These are funds whose primary objective is to make investment dollars grow over time as opposed to dividend yield or income. While these funds share the same primary objective, their strategies for reaching this goal may vary considerably. For instance, some funds may choose to invest in companies whose earnings are accelerating; another may choose to concentrate its holdings in smaller, emerging companies. In choosing a growth fund, investors should assess which types of stocks have the greatest growth potential, and match this conviction to a growth fund which will pursue this type of investment strategy. Investors should also be careful to study a fund's performance over time and under different market conditions, as well as understand the level of risk inherent in the fund. Other factors to be considered include the size of the fund, the background and track record of the portfolio manager, and the fund's load and/or expense ratio.

George Domolky, Portfolio Manager
Fidelity Investments, Boston, MA

growth rate The annual rate at which a variable, such as gross national product or a firm's earnings, has been or is expected to grow. One common method of estimating future growth rate is simply to measure a variable's past growth rate and then project a continuation of the trend.

growth recession An economy in which the output of goods and services slowly expands but unemployment remains high or even grows.

growth stock The stock of a firm that is expected to have above-average increases in revenues and earnings. These firms normally retain most earnings for reinvestment and therefore pay small dividends. The stocks, often selling at relatively high price-earnings ratios, are subject to wide swings in price. Examples include Du Pont, General Electric, and IBM.

GTC —See GOOD-TILL-CANCELED ORDER.

guaranteed account   A brokerage account with margin requirements or losses guaranteed by the assets of another account.

guaranteed bond   A bond issued by one firm that is guaranteed as to interest and principal by one or more other firms. Such bonds, often resulting from joint ventures, are particularly common among railroads that lease tracks to and from one another.

guaranteed-dollar annuity   —See FIXED ANNUITY.

guaranteed mortgage certificate   A pass through issued by the Federal Home Loan Mortgage Corporation (FHLMC) in which conventional mortgages purchased by FHLMC are resold to investors in $100,000, $500,000, and $1,000,000 principal amounts. Interest is paid semiannually and principal repayments are made each year. —See also PASS-THROUGH SECURITY.

guaranteed stock   Preferred stock issued by one compnany and guaranteed as to dividends by one or more other companies. Guaranteed stock issues, like guaranteed bonds, are most prevalent among railroads.

guarantee letter   A letter issued by a commercial bank guaranteeing that an investor who is writing a put option will pay the required sum in the event that the put is exercised against the investor.

gun jumping   1. Trading a security before inside information has been released to the public.   2. Solicitation of orders for a new security underwriting before the Securities and Exchange Commission has approved the registration statement.

H

h —Used in over-the-counter stock transaction tables in newspapers to indicate the size of the dividend in the previous year and to indicate that the most recent dividend has been omitted: *NarcoIntl .05h*.

H —Used in stock transaction tables in newspapers to indicate the fact that during the day's activity the stock traded at a new 52-week high price.

haircut   A deduction in the market value of securities being held by brokerage and investment banking firms as part of net worth for calculating their net capital. The size of a haircut varies with the particular type of security held.

half   One half of a point. For stock quotes, a half represents one half of $1, or 50¢. For bond quotes, one half represents one half of 1% of par, or $5. For option quotes, a half represents $50.

half-life   The length of time before half the principal on a debt is expected to be repaid through amortization or sinking fund payments. For example, a 25-year bond issue may require the issuer to retire 5% of the beginning principal commencing 5 years after the issue date. Thus, the bond issue has a half-life of 5 years plus the number of years required to retire half the issue, or 15 years. Mortgage-backed securities often have a relatively short half-life because many homeowners pay off or refinance their mortgages early. —Also called *average life.*

handle The whole dollar price of a bid or offer. A bid of 91½ and an ask of 91⅝ would have a handle of 91.

hard asset —See TANGIBLE ASSET.

hard dollars Cash payment to a brokerage firm for goods or services provided by the firm. Thus, individual investors are normally required to pay cash for a market letter. —See also SOFT DOLLARS.

head-and-shoulders In technical analysis, a chart formation in which a security price reaches a peak and declines, rises above its former peak and again declines, and rises again but not to its second peak and then again declines. The first and third peaks are shoulders while the second peak is the formation's head. Technical analysts generally consider a head-and-shoulders formation to be a very bearish indicator if the second shoulder declines below a line connecting the bottom points of the two intermediate declines between the shoulders and head. An upside-down formation is said to be an inverted head-and-shoulders formation; it is a bullish indicator. —See also NECKLINE; REVERSAL PATTERN.

heart bond A bond issued by a private nonprofit corporation such as a church, hospital, or school. —So called because the sales pitch often appeals more to buyers' hearts than to their pocketbooks.

hedge A security transaction that reduces the risk on an already existing investment position. An example is the purchase of a put option in order to offset at least partially the potential losses from owned stock. While hedges reduce potential losses, they also tend to reduce potential profits. —See also PERFECT HEDGE; RISK HEDGE; SHORT HEDGE; SPECIAL ARBITRAGE ACCOUNT.

hedge clause A statement in an advertisement, a market letter, or a security report indicating that the information therein is believed to be accurate and that it has been obtained from normally reliable sources, with nothing, however, guaranteed. Essentially, a hedge clause indicates to readers that the writer believes the information is accurate and that reasonable care has been taken to ensure its accuracy.

hedged tender An investor's tender of securities accompanied by the short sale of a portion of the securities tendered. The short sale hedges the possibility that not all the tendered securities will be accepted by the buyer and that the value of those securities not accepted will be less than the tender price.

hedge fund A very specialized, volatile open-end investment company that permits the manager to use a variety of investment techniques normally prohibited in other types of funds. These techniques include borrowing money, selling short, and utilizing options. Hedge funds offer investors the possibility of extraordinary gains with above-average risk.

hedge margin   In commodities trading, a special low margin rate for hedgers such as manufacturers and dealers. The hedge margin is lower because of offsetting positions.

hedge ratio   The number of options required to offset the change in value due to a price change in 100 shares of common stock. For example, if two options are needed to offset value changes for 100 shares of stock, the hedge ratio is 2. —See also DELTA.

hemline theory   The theory that stock prices tend to move in the same direction as the length of hemlines on dresses. Thus, rising hemlines are a bullish sign and falling hemlines are a bearish sign.

hidden assets   Items of value owned by a firm but not appearing on its balance sheet. For example, a trademark or patent may be a firm's most valuable owned asset; yet, it would not appear as such on the balance sheet.

hidden reserve   The amount by which a firm's net worth is understated. For example, overdepreciation results in assets and net worth being carried on the firm's financial statements at less than market value.

high flyer   A heavily-traded stock that sells at a high price-earnings ratio. High flyers go through a period of rapidly rising prices as something about the firms or the industries in which they operate catches the investing public's fancy. Unfortunately, however, most high flyers eventually come to earth with plunging prices when investors' expectations and dreams are shattered.

high-grade   Designating a bond with little risk of default on the part of the issuer. High-grade is usually reserved for bonds rated AAA or AA by the rating services. —See also INVESTMENT-GRADE.

high-low index   A cumulative tabulation of the number of stocks reaching new highs less the number of stocks reaching new lows. Technical analysts use the high-low index to measure the strength of the market's movement. In general, movement of the high-low index in the same direction as the market confirms the market's movement and indicates that this movement is likely to continue in the same direction.

highs   The number of stocks exceeding the highest price reached by each stock during the most recent 52-week period. Technicians consider an increasing number of highs to be a bullish sign, especially if accompanied by other favorable indicators. Conversely, record highs by market averages not accompanied by an increasing number of individual highs would be suspect. —See also LOWS.

high-technology stock   The stock of a company involved in sophisticated technology such as electronics, computer software, robotics, life sciences, and so forth. High-technology stocks often offer large potential gains but tend to be quite risky because of intense competition and uncertain success.

high-yield financing —See JUNK FINANCING.

historical cost The amount of money that was originally used to pay for an asset. A company records assets on a balance sheet at historical cost, which often bears little relation to the market value of the assets after they have been owned several years. —Also called *original cost.*

historical trading range The highest and lowest prices at which a security has traded since going public.

historical yield The yield that a money market mutual fund has provided during a specified time period. Investors frequently compare historical yields among firms when trying to select a fund to purchase. Historical yields are more useful when comparing funds than when estimating future yields.

hit 1. To sell a security at a bid price quoted by a dealer. For example, a trader will hit a bid. **2.** To lose money on a trade. For example, a dealer may take a hit on the holdings of Moore's Fried Foods common stock.

holder The owner of a security.

holder of record A security holder listed in a firm's books as having ownership of the security on the record date. This list is used in determining who will receive dividends, interest, proxies, financial reports, and so on. —Also called *owner of record; stockholder of record.* —See also RECORD DATE.

holding company A company that exists primarily to exercise control over other firms. The control is exercised through ownership of a majority of the controlled firm's shares. Earnings of the holding company are derived from earnings of the controlled firms, which pay dividends on the shares. —See also OPERATING UNIT; PARENT COMPANY; SUBSIDIARY.

⑤ American Electric Power, a large utility holding company, is the sole owner of eight operating companies and associated subsidiaries in the Midwest. American Electric Power neither generates electricity nor mines coal, but it owns the operating units that do the mining and generating. Common stock in the operating units is not publicly traded because all the stock is owned by the holding company. Thus, an investor who purchases shares in American Electric Power indirectly becomes an owner of each of the operating units. While only the holding company issues publicly traded shares of ownership, the bonds and preferred stock are issued by each of American Electric Power's operating companies. For example, as of December 31, 1985, Indiana and Michigan Electric Company, an operating unit of AEP, had 14 separate bond issues and 11 issues of preferred stock outstanding.

holding period The length of time during which a security is held.

holding period return (HPR) The return achieved on an investment including current income and any change in value during an investor's holding period. This measure proves useful in comparing expected returns on different investments. —Also called *holding period yield.*

holding the market —See PEG 1.

horizon —See TIME HORIZON.

horizontal analysis Comparison of financial statements or specific items in a financial statement over two or more periods. —See also RATIO ANALYSIS; VERTICAL ANALYSIS.

horizontal count A measure of the horizontal width of a congestion area on a point-and-figure chart. Technical analysts use the horizontal count to determine a price target for a stock once it breaks out of the congestion area.

horizontal merger A merger between firms with similar products or services. Merging one steel manufacturer into another steel manufacturer is an example of a horizontal merger. Horizontal mergers permit the surviving firm to control a greater share of the market and, it is hoped, gain economies of scale. —See also VERTICAL MERGER.

horizontal price movement Movement of the price of a security or the market in a narrow range day after day. On a chart this price movement appears as a horizontal line or a horizontal bar across the page.

horizontal security exchange The exchange of one security for a like security (i.e., stock for stock, debt for debt). Exchange offers involving horizontal exchanges are generally tax-free, although a taxable event will occur if and when the new securities are sold.

horizontal spread —See CALENDAR SPREAD.

hospital revenue bond Tax-exempt debt issued by a city, county, state, or hospital authority with debt service guaranteed by hospital revenues. While the facility that the bond issue is used to finance may be leased or sold to the hospital, it is the financial strength of the hospital, not the issuer, that backs the debt. Hospital bonds are generally more risky than general obligation or water and sewer bonds since the hospital has no taxing power. —See also 501(C)(3) BOND.

hostile leveraged buyout The purchase of a firm, against the wishes of the acquired firm's managers, in which a small group of investors finance the purchase primarily by borrowing. While leveraged buyouts have become quite frequent, hostile leveraged buyouts are unusual because lenders financing takeovers generally prefer that the acquired firms' managements remain, albeit under new ownership.

hostile takeover —See UNFRIENDLY TAKEOVER.

hostile tender offer An offer to purchase shares from a firm's stockholders when directors of the target firm have recommended that stockholders not sell their stock. Hostile tender offers sometimes cause the directors of the target company to seek a better offer from another party. —See also TENDER OFFER; UNFRIENDLY TAKEOVER; WHITE KNIGHT.

hot issue A new security issue for which investor demand exceeds securities available in the issue. National Association of Securities Dealers rules forbid members from taking advantage of the likelihood that these securities will rise in price immediately after issue. —See also BLOWOUT;

FORM FR-1; INVESTMENT HISTORY; NORMAL INVESTMENT PRACTICE; UNDER-WRITE.

Are hospital revenue bonds so risky that my portfolio and I will land in traction?
● ●

Before you buy a hospital revenue bond, you need to review carefully the financial and demographic characteristics of the issuing hospital and have some understanding of how it might be influenced by competition from other health care providers in its market. Although many hospitals represent reasonable credit risks, they are certainly not all alike and the group should not be painted with a broad brush in the same manner that municipal bond investors sometimes paint other types of bonds (i.e., water and sewer revenue bonds or school district bonds). Many hospitals are struggling as a result of numerous factors, several of which are overbuilding of capacity relative to community needs, tightening reimbursement policies on the part of Medicare and other insurers, rising costs as hospitals are forced to update equipment to keep up with leaps in health care technology, and heightened competition, including that from nonmedical facilities. Of course, these industry problems have been compounded by cuts in federal aid to states and municipalities. Although these problems are greater for the not-for-profit hospitals, the for-profit hospitals are clearly not immune to them. In reviewing a hospital to determine its relative creditworthiness, financial analysts focus on institutional characteristics and market position, management factors, medical staff characteristics, financial indicators, and legal covenants. Because of the greater risks often associated with hospital revenue bonds, most bonds of this type are issued with some kind of credit enhancement, usually in the form of insurance, but sometimes via letter-of-credit facilities.

Stephanie R. Goldsborough, Treasury Officer
Maryland National Bank, Baltimore, MD

hot money Funds controlled by investors seeking high short-term yields that are likely to be reinvested somewhere else at any time. Some financial institutions attract hot money by offering above-average yields on certificates of deposit. However, if the rate is lowered, the funds are likely to be lost to another institution or investment.

hot stock A stock having large price movements on very heavy volume. Hot stocks often run in cycles depending on the investing public's interest in particular industries or particular concepts. Hot stocks are normally quite risky and are suitable for speculators involved in short-term trading.

house maintenance requirement The minimum equity that must be kept in a customer's margin account as determined by the firm holding the account. A house maintenance requirement is imposed when a brokerage firm desires a more strict maintenance margin requirement than the one required by an exchange or by the National Association of Securities Dealers.

house of issue —See LEAD UNDERWRITER.

house rules A brokerage firm's regulations regarding customer accounts and practices. For example, the firm must establish rules concerning margin requirements, the handling of customers' checks, and good faith deposits on new accounts, among others. House rules must be at least as strict as industry regulations require.

housing bond —See MORTGAGE-BACKED REVENUE BOND.

HPR —See HOLDING PERIOD RETURN.

hybrid annuity A single annuity in which a part of an investor's payments purchase units of a variable annuity and the remaining funds purchase units of a fixed annuity.

hybrid security A security with features characteristic of two or more other securities. A convertible bond, for example, is a hybrid security in that it has the features (interest, maturity, and principal) of an ordinary bond; however, it is heavily influenced by the price movements of the stock into which it is convertible.

hyperinflation A very high level of inflation that tends to result in a breakdown of the monetary system, the hoarding of goods, and difficulty in achieving real economic growth. The classic case of hyperinflation occurred in Germany during the 1920s. Hyperinflation, which tends to motivate people to own real goods, adversely affects security prices.

hypothecate To pledge securities as collateral for a loan without giving up ownership of the securities. —See also REHYPOTHECATE.

hypothecation agreement A written agreement between a customer opening a margin account and a brokerage firm that pledges stock in the account as collateral for margin loans. The brokerage firm is permitted to sell the stock in the event that equity in the account falls below a stipulated level.

I

i —Used in the dividend column of stock transaction tables to indicate that the dividend was paid after a stock dividend or split: *Lehigh s.20i.*

ICAA —See INVESTMENT COUNSEL ASSOCIATION OF AMERICA.

ICFA —See INSTITUTE OF CHARTERED FINANCIAL ANALYSTS.

idle funds Money, as the funds in a checking account, that is not invested and therefore earns no income. Investors wishing to increase their income try to keep idle funds to a minimum.

illiquid **1.** Pertaining to an asset that is difficult to buy or sell in a short period of time without its price being affected. For example, a large block of stock or a small amount of an infrequently traded stock is likely to be difficult to sell without a reduced price being offered to potential buyers. —See also LIQUID 1. **2.** Designating an investment position in which a low proportion of assets is in cash or near-cash, thereby creating difficulty for the investor who is trying to raise funds for another purpose.

imbalance of orders —See ORDER IMBALANCE.

IMF —See INTERNATIONAL MONETARY FUND.

IMM —See INTERNATIONAL MONEY MARKET.

immaterial Of such small importance or little relevance as to have no significant impact on an outcome. For example, a firm may be involved in a lawsuit involving such an insignificant amount of money that the lawsuit's outcome will not appreciably affect the firm. Thus, the lawsuit and its potential results are immaterial in preparing the firm's financial statements. —See also MATERIAL.

immediate annuity An annuity that is purchased with a lump sum and that begins making payments one period after the purchase. Immediate annuities are most commonly purchased by people who have accumulated a sum of money and are ready for retirement. —See also DEFERRED ANNUITY.

immediate family Close relatives by birth or marriage including siblings, parents, children, in-laws, and any financial dependents. The National Association of Securities Dealers restricts financial transactions between a broker-dealer and his or her immediate family.

immediate-or-cancel order A customer order that not only specifies a price but also requires the broker to fill immediately as much of the order as possible and cancel any part remaining. This type of order differs from a fill-or-kill order, which disallows a partial fill.

immunization A technique of investing in bonds such that the portfolio's target return is protected against interest rate fluctuations. Changes in returns at which cash flows can be reinvested are offset by changes in the value of the securities in the portfolio. —See also BULLET IMMUNIZATION.

impairment Reduction in a firm's capital as a result of distributions or losses.

import A good or service brought into a country from another country and offered for sale. While some imported items originate in foreign subsidiaries of domestic companies, large increases in imports tend to hurt sales and profits of many firms located in the importing country. —See also BALANCE OF TRADE; EXPORT; QUOTA.

improvement An increase in the value of real estate achieved by changing its configuration or by adding to it. —Also called *land improvement*.

imputed interest Interest on an investment that is assumed for certain purposes to be paid even though no interest payment is physically received by the investor. For example, the Internal Revenue Service considers annual accretion on a zero-coupon corporate or a zero-coupon Treasury bond to be imputed interest for tax purposes even though investors holding these bonds receive no annual interest payments from the issuers.

imputed interest rate A minimum market rate of interest assumed by the government for tax purposes regardless of the actual rate charged on a loan. The imputing of interest was included as part of the 1984 tax act in order to stop tax avoidance by people making loans at artificially low interest rates.

inactive account A brokerage account in which few transactions take place. Some brokerage firms levy a fee on accounts in which securities are deposited but no activity occurs during a specified time.

inactive bond crowd —See CABINET CROWD.

inactive post The location on the floor of an exchange where inactive securities are traded. —See also POST 30 STOCK.

inactive security A security with relatively low trading volume. A particularly inactive security may not trade for days or weeks at a time, although bid and ask quotations for it are generally available. Inactive securities are often difficult to buy or sell in any significant quantity without affecting the price.

in-and-out The purchase and sale of an investment over a short period of time.

incentive stock option An option permitting an employee to purchase shares of the employer's stock at a predetermined price. No tax is due on any gain until the time of sale if the sale date is at least one year subsequent to the date on which the option was granted. —Also called *employee stock option; option*.

income averaging A technique for the calculation of personal income taxes permitting an individual with large variations in annual taxable income to average income over a specified period. Income averaging was eliminated by 1986 tax reform.

income bond A long-term debt security in which the issuer is required to pay interest only when it is earned. This rare security, issued principally as part of a corporate reorganization, offers an investor a relatively weak promise of payment. Some issues require that unpaid interest be accumulated and made up in periods that earnings permit. —Also called *adjustment bond*.

income dividend A distribution of dividends, interest, and short-term capital gains by an investment company to its shareholders. This type of dividend is taxed at the recipient's marginal rate. —See also CAPITAL GAINS DISTRIBUTION.

income fund An investment company, the main objective of which is to achieve current income for its owners. Thus, it tends to select securities such as bonds, preferred stocks, and common stocks that pay relatively high current returns. This type of fund is most appropriate for someone seeking high current income rather than growth of principal.

income per share —See EARNINGS PER SHARE.

income property Real estate producing current income, typically from rental payments. Apartments, office buildings, and rental homes are considered income property.

income shares One of the two types of stock issued by a dual purpose fund in which the owner is entitled to all the income earned by the portfolio plus the return of the stock's par value (if sufficient funds remain) at the time the fund dissolves. These shares appeal mainly to investors seeking high current income since the chance for capital gain is negligible. —See also CAPITAL SHARES.

income statement A business financial statement that lists revenues, expenses, and net income during a period of time. Because of the various methods used to record transactions, the dollar values shown on an income statement often can be misleading. —Also called *earnings report; earnings statement; operating statement; P&L; profit and loss statement.* —See also CONSOLIDATED INCOME STATEMENT.

Do income statements tell the truth, the whole truth, and nothing but the truth? How to spot the buts.

Income statements vary in detail; the best are usually the audited statements in annual reports. Investors should recognize that a variety of accounting techniques are acceptable. Therefore, footnotes, balance sheets, and statements of changes in financial position (flow of funds statements) should also be considered and are found in annual reports. But, ultimately, the trustworthiness of management is the key, unstated factor.

J. Kendrick Noble, Jr., First Vice President
PaineWebber Incorporated, New York, NY

Look for income from sources other than basic business; this can be a real telltale sign of trouble.

Ray Ozyjowski, Regional Sales Coordinator
PaineWebber Incorporated, New York, NY

---

income stock A stock with a relatively high dividend yield. The stock's issuer is typically a firm having stable earnings and dividends and operating in a mature industry. The price of an income stock is heavily influenced by changes in interest rates.

income tax A tax levied on the annual earnings of an individual or a corporation. Income taxes are levied by the federal government and by a number of state and local governments. One set of rules applies to individual income and another to corporate income. The size and structure of an income tax greatly influence security prices and investor decisions.

incorporate To obtain a state charter establishing a corporation. Owners of proprietorships and partnerships incorporate in order to obtain limited liability for themselves and for potential investors. The limited liablity makes it easier for the firm to raise additional equity capital. —See also CORPORATION.

incremental cost —See MARGINAL COST.

indenture A legal contract between a bond issuer and its lenders that specifies the terms of the issue. Typical provisions are the amount and dates of interest payments, the name of the trustee, the maturity date, collateral, restrictions on dividends or other borrowing, and the specifics of a sinking fund or potential calls. It is the trustee's job to ensure that the terms of the indenture are fulfilled. —Also called *trust deed*. —See also COVENANT.

indenture qualification statement A statement presented to the Securities and Exchange Commission by the issuer of debt securities detailing the terms of the borrowing arrangement. An indenture qualification statement is required of debt securities exempt from the Securities Act of 1933 but subject to the Trust Indenture Act of 1939.

independent audit —See EXTERNAL AUDIT.

independent broker —See TWO-DOLLAR BROKER.

independent variable A variable not affected by any other variables with which it is compared. For example, in comparing the price of an electric utility stock with interest rates, the interest rates are an independent variable because they are not affected by utility stock prices. —See also DEPENDENT VARIABLE.

index The relative value of a variable in comparison with itself on a different date. Many security price indicators such as the Standard & Poor's series and the New York Stock Exchange series are constructed as indices. —Also called *stock index*. —See also AVERAGES; BASE YEAR.

index To adjust a variable by a selected measure of relative value. For example, it has been proposed that an investor's basis on a security be indexed for changes in consumer prices so that only real increases in value will be taxed. —Also called *tax indexing*.

Index and Option Market (IOM) A subsidiary of the Chicago Mercantile Exchange that in 1982 commenced trading futures contracts on the Standard & Poor's 500 Stock Index.

index-based offer An offer either to buy or to sell a security at a price based on an index. For example, in 1985 Exxon Pipeline Company offered to purchase up to $100,000,000 principal amount of two of its bond issues at a price that would provide a yield to maturity of 170 points less than the *Bond Buyer*'s 40-Bond Index.

index fund A mutual fund that keeps a portfolio of securities designed to match the performance of the market as a whole. The market is represented by a market index such as the Standard & Poor's 500. An index fund has low administrative expenses; it appeals to investors who believe it is difficult or impossible for investment managers to beat the market. —Also called *market fund.*

index of industrial production —See INDUSTRIAL PRODUCTION.

index of leading economic indicators An index compiled by the Department of Commerce that indicates the future direction of economic activity. A rising index signals that economic activity can be expected to increase in the near future. While variations in this index are of interest to stock analysts, stock market price movements are also considered as a separate leading indicator; therefore, the series is not particularly useful in forecasting stock price changes.

index option A call option or put option with a specific index as the underlying asset. For example, a call option on the Standard & Poor's 500 Index gives the option buyer the right to purchase the value of the index at a fixed price until a predetermined date. Index options provide a means to leverage a bet on the future direction of the market or a particular industry segment without purchasing all the individual securities. Use of the option can entail considerable risk for an investor.

indication 1. An estimate of the bid and ask when a security begins trading. Brokers, dealers, or investors may seek an indication before a security begins trading to help them establish a trading strategy in that security. 2. A nominal quote disseminated by a stock exchange that gives the range in which a stock will open or reopen. —Also called *preopening indication.*

indication of interest An investor's expression of interest in purchasing part of a new security issue before the issue comes to market. Brokers frequently seek indications of interest from clients even though the indications are not firm commitments to purchase the security. —See also CIRCLE; UNDERBOOKED.

indicator A variable used to forecast the value or change in the value of another variable. For example, changes in the producer price index are used to forecast subsequent changes in the consumer price index. Likewise, some financial analysts believe a change in the money supply is an indicator of the direction of the stock market. —See also TECHNICAL INDICATOR.

indirect convertible A convertible security that may be exchanged into another convertible. The market price of the indirect convertible is actually a function of the value of the shares underlying the second convertible. As an example, a bond may be convertible into ten shares of a convertible preferred stock, each of which may be exchanged for five shares of common stock. Thus, the bond trades indirectly on the basis of the value of 50 shares of common stock.

indirect cost   A cost that is not directly related to the production of a specific good or service, but that is indirectly related to a variety of goods or services. For example, the cost of administering a large company is an indirect cost that must be spread over a number of products or services. —Also called *overhead*. —See also DIRECT COST.

indirect government obligation   —See FEDERAL AGENCY SECURITY.

indirect tax   A tax paid by an individual other than the one on which it is levied. For example, a retail sales tax is collected and remitted to the government by a business even though the tax is ultimately paid by the consumers. —See also DIRECT TAX.

individual account   A brokerage account opened in the name of one person. —See also INSTITUTIONAL ACCOUNT; JOINT ACCOUNT; PARTNERSHIP ACCOUNT.

individual retirement account   —See IRA.

industrial   Pertaining to companies engaged in the manufacture of products. The word also can refer to firms engaged in distribution. For example, Sears is classified as an industrial company for purposes of calculating the Dow Jones Averages but it is included as a retailer rather than an industrial in *Fortune* magazine's annual survey of America's largest firms.

industrial bond   A long-term debt security issued by a corporation engaged in manufacturing, refining, and so on.

industrial development bond   A special type of municipal revenue bond in which interest and principal payments are secured by the credit of a private firm rather than by the municipality. —Also called *industrial revenue bond*. —See also PRIVATE ACTIVITY BOND.

industrial production   A measure of the country's economic health judged by its output from manufacturing, mining, and utility industries. Industrial production is calculated by the Federal Reserve, which publishes a monthly index of industrial production. Rising industrial production is generally more favorable for stockholders than for bondholders because it can signal rising inflationary pressures and higher interest rates. —Also called *index of industrial production*.

industrial revenue bond   —See INDUSTRIAL DEVELOPMENT BOND.

industry life cycle   The stages of evolution through which an industry progresses as it moves from its initial conception to stabilization and stagnation. The stage in which a particular industry (and thus, a firm within the industry) currently exists plays a major role in the way investors view its future.

industry segment   An identifiable component of a business. The segment may be identified by product line, geographic region, division, or other divisible part of the company. Firms often evaluate performance on a segment basis. Segments also may be sold as the firm reevaluates its product lines or territories. —See also SEGMENT REPORTING.

inelastic Pertaining to the demand for a good or service when quantity purchased varies little in response to price changes in the good or service. For example, the demand for medicines and medical services is generally inelastic because the quantity purchased by consumers is unresponsive to price changes. —See also ELASTIC; ELASTICITY.

inflation A general increase in the price level of goods and services. Unexpected inflation tends to be detrimental to security prices, primarily because it forces interest rates higher. A point to keep in mind is that a certain amount of inflation is already embodied in security prices. —See also CONSUMER PRICE INDEX; DEFLATION; DISINFLATION; GNP DEFLATOR; HYPERINFLATION; PRODUCER PRICE INDEX; PURCHASING POWER RISK.

inflation accounting Alteration of a firm's financial statements to account for changes in the purchasing power of money. With inflation accounting, gains and losses from holding monetary items during periods of changing prices are recognized. Likewise, long-term assets and liabilities are adjusted for changing price levels. Inflation accounting is used to supplement regular financial statements in order to illustrate how changing price levels have impact on a firm. —Also called *general price level accounting*.

inflationary psychology Consumers' belief that prices will inevitably rise—a belief driving them to speed up purchases especially of real assets (i.e., gold, diamonds, and real estate) and avoid investment in financial assets (i.e., stocks and bonds). As a result, the consumers themselves can cause the inflation that they fear will occur.

inflation hedge An investment with a value directly related to the level of general price changes. Among securities, the common stocks of natural resource companies (gold, timber, oil, etc.) are often considered as inflation hedges since the value of the companies' assets should rise during a period of inflation.

inflation premium The portion of an investment's return that compensates for expected increases in the general price level of goods and services. The expectation of rising inflation results in higher long-term interest rates as lenders and borrowers build in an increased inflation premium.

inheritance tax A state tax levied on the recipient of an estate rather than on the estate itself. The tax varies by state, and its severity in a given state usually depends on the kinship between the deceased and the heir. Some states levy a tax on the estate instead of a tax on the amount inherited. —Also called *death tax*. —See also ESTATE TAX.

initial margin requirement The minimum portion of a new security purchase that an investor must pay for in cash. For example, with an initial margin requirement of 60%, the most an investor can borrow is $2,000 on a $5,000 purchase. This requirement is determined by the

Federal Reserve Board. —Also called *margin requirement.* —See also MAIN-
TENANCE MARGIN REQUIREMENT.

initial public offering (IPO)   A company's first sale of stock to the public.
Securities offered in an IPO are often but not always those of young,
small companies seeking outside equity capital and a public market for
their stock. Investors purchasing stock in IPOs generally assume very
large risks for the possiblity of large gains.

> ⟨$⟩ Morgan Stanley, one of the country's top investment banking con-
> cerns, made its own stock available to the public in the spring of 1986.
> The initial public offering (IPO) was priced at $56.50 in a $292 million
> sale that transferred 21% of the firm's ownership to the public. The
> stock price rose substantially during its initial day of trading on the
> New York Stock Exchange and closed at $71.25. Certain employees of
> the firm were permitted to buy a total of 10% of the IPO at a small
> discount from the offering price. Morgan Stanley sold the stock to raise
> capital for financing its growth.

in play   Pertaining to a company that has been, or is widely rumored to
be, the target of a takeover attempt. After a firm is in play, additional
offers may be forthcoming. —See also TARGET COMPANY.

inside buildup   Cash value increases in a life insurance policy. Inside
buildup is free of income taxation during the period of buildup, thus
making cash-value insurance a more desirable investment vehicle for
people in high income-tax brackets.

inside director   A member of a firm's board of directors who is also
employed in another capacity by that firm. An example is a chief executive officer who also sits on the board. —See also OUTSIDE DIRECTOR.

inside information   Details relating to a company's affairs known by its
directors and officers but not yet released to the public. For example,
initial data on a large oil strike that has not been publicized is inside
information.

inside market   A market involving price quotes for a security trade
between dealers. Price quotes between dealers normally entail a higher
bid and a lower ask than quotes on the same security made to individual
investors. —See also RETAIL MARKET; WHOLESALE.

insider   **1.** A person who, because of his or her position within a firm,
has access to proprietary information unavailable to the general public.
Although the term *insider* obviously includes corporate officers, it also
may extend to relatives of these officers or to employees of other firms
having a special relationship with the firm in question. **2.** Officially, an
officer, a director, or the owner of 10% or more of a firm's securities.
—See also FORM 3.

insider trading   The illegal buying or selling of securities on the basis of
information that is generally unavailable to the public. An example is
the purchase by a director of shares of his or her firm's stock just before
the release of surprisingly good earnings information.

⚠️$ In what the Securities and Exchange Commission (SEC) described as the largest insider-trading operation ever uncovered, the SEC in 1986 charged Dennis Levine with using confidential information to make nearly $13 million in trading profits over a 6-year period. Levine, who was employed as a merger-and-acquisitions specialist by Drexel Burnham Lambert, was alleged by the SEC to have traded through secret accounts opened in 1980 at a Swiss bank subsidiary in the Bahamas. A bank employee allegedly undertook Levine's trades through the bank's brokerage accounts in the United States. All told, the SEC charged Levine with trading in the stocks and options of 54 companies. In a more unusual example, the SEC alleged in 1986 that a psychiatrist had engaged in insider trading based on information he had supposedly obtained from a patient during treatment.

insolvent   Unable to meet debts or discharge liabilities.

installment   A partial payment on a financial obligation. For example, an annual or monthly payment to the seller of a farm (or any other asset) on a long-term contract is an installment. Installments are composed partly of principal and partly of interest. If all the installments are of equal size, each subsequent payment incorporates an increasing amount of principal and a decreasing amount of interest.

installment method   The accounting method of treating revenue from the sale of an asset on installments such that profits are recognized in proportion to the percentage of the sale price collected in a given accounting period. For example, if an asset with a book value of $12,000 is sold for $15,000 and payment is to occur in 5 equal installments of $3,000 each, the seller would record annual profits of ($15,000 − $12,000)/5, or $600. The installment method is a conservative way of treating an installment sale because profit is not recognized until receipt of payment.

installment sale   A sale in which the buyer is scheduled to make a series of payments over a period of time. An installment sale can offer certain tax advantages; however, the seller may have a lengthy wait before receiving the entire proceeds. Virtually any asset, including securities, may be disposed of through an installment sale.

Instinet®   A trademark for leasing computer equipment in connection with a communications network providing access time to a computer database which provides subscribers with trading information concerning stocks, etc. Instinet permits its subscribers to bypass brokers and trade directly among themselves. Instinet is a property of Institutional Networks Corporation.

Institute of Chartered Financial Analysts (ICFA)   An affiliate of the Financial Analysts Federation that administers examinations and awards the professional designation of Chartered Financial Analyst to successful applicants.

institutional account   A brokerage account of an investment management organization. —See also INDIVIDUAL ACCOUNT; JOINT ACCOUNT.

institutional broker   A broker specializing in security trades for institutions such as banks and pension funds. Institutions normally trade in large blocks that require special handling.

institutional favorites   —See NIFTY FIFTY.

How to track the pawprints of the big investors: where are they going, what are they buying, what are they selling?

While institutional investors leave rather impressive pawprints in the marketplace, individuals will have to do some investigative work to uncover timely and useful information. For mutual funds, one of the best places to start is with the fund's quarterly or annual report. Newsletters on mutual funds, such as the *United Mutual Fund Selector*, a bimonthly issue, highlight specific funds as well as monitor performance. The *Spectrum* publications contain quarterly reports on the holdings of mutual funds and other institutional investors. Much of this information is taken from required filings with the Securities and Exchange Commission. Publications such as *Barron's* and the *Wall Street Transcript* focus on institutional investors and regularly interview money managers. *Value Line* lists insider and institutional transactions on each company in its investment service. Most of these publications can be found in a good business library. Other newsletters feature what well-known investors or corporate insiders are buying or selling. Don't forget to follow the daily trading volume of companies—a major shift can indicate that institutions are buying or selling. SEC filings can be an excellent source of information. Large investors are required to file with the SEC for a variety of reasons. For example, mutual funds must file their portfolios quarterly, and any acquisition of more than 5% of a company's stock must also be reported. Recently, a number of on-line computer services that provide this information to the individual investor have been announced. Of course, the various business shows on TV often feature institutional managers discussing recent purchases and sales. By using a number of these sources, individual investors can glean what the institutions are doing. Will this necessarily make you a better investor? That is a much tougher question to answer!

Barry Allen, Senior Investment Consultant
Massachusetts Mutual Life Insurance Company, Springfield, MA

---

institutional investor   An entity such as an insurance company, an investment company, a pension fund, or a trust department that invests large sums in the securities markets. Institutional investing has had an increasing impact on securities trading: as the institutions buy and sell huge blocks of the same securities during short periods of time, large security fluctuations ensue.

Institutional Networks Corporation —See INSTINET®.

instrument A legal document, such as a check, a security, or a will.

in-substance debt defeasance —See DEFEASANCE.

insubstantial quantity The limited amount of stock or bonds from a new security issue that may be allocated to certain people involved in or related to other people involved in the distribution of the security issue.

intangible asset An asset such as a patent, goodwill, or a mining claim, that has no physical properties. Since intangible assets are often difficult to value accurately, such assets when included on a corporate balance sheet may have a true value significantly different from the dollar amounts indicated there. —See also TANGIBLE ASSET.

intangible drilling costs Expenses incurred while exploring for gas, geothermal, and oil reserves. These items may be expensed in the year incurred or they may be capitalized and deducted over a period of years. Intangible drilling costs are an effective means of reducing taxes because they can be used to offset income in a single year even though the costs were incurred in order to produce or develop a capital asset (energy reserves) that will in turn generate income over a period of years. Costs for fuel, preparation of a site, and wages are examples of intangible drilling costs.

intangible tax A tax imposed by some states or local governments on the value of intangible assets such as stocks, bonds, money market funds, and bank account balances.

integrated market making —See SIDE-BY-SIDE TRADING.

intercommodity spread An investment position in which an investor purchases one commodity and sells short a related but different commodity. An example of an intercommodity spread would be the purchase of a futures contract in silver and the sale of a contract in gold.

interest 1. Payment for the use of borrowed money. 2. An investor's equity in a business.

interest adjustment Extra proceeds going to an investor who submits a convertible bond for conversion to account for interest accrued since the last date of record for an interest payment. —Also called *adjustment.* —See also CONVERTIBLE SECURITY; DIVIDEND ADJUSTMENT.

interest coverage A measure of a firm's ability to meet required interest obligations. A high coverage ratio indicates enhanced ability to make timely interest payments. Interest coverage is calculated by dividing the firm's required interest payments into its operating income. —Also called *times interest earned.* —See also BOND RATING; COVERAGE RATIO; DEBT MANAGEMENT RATIO; FIXED-CHARGE COVERAGE.

interest dates The dates on which interest is paid to bondholders, nearly always involving two payments per year on either the first or the fifteenth of the month. Interest dates are set at the time of issue and remain unchanged throughout the life of the bond. —See also PAYMENT DATE.

interest equalization tax   A tax, no longer in effect, that was levied on income received from foreign securities owned by U.S. residents. By discouraging investment in foreign securities, the tax was intended to prevent an outflow of U.S. dollars.

How can one use interest rate futures to hedge risk?

Interest rate futures such as U.S. Treasury bond, Treasury note, Treasury bill, and GNMA futures contracts can be used to hedge the current and expected future inventories of interest-rate sensitive assets such as government securities, corporate bonds, and mortgage-related instruments against adverse interest rate changes. When interest rates are expected to increase (thus decreasing bond prices), a Treasury bond dealer can, for example, establish a short hedge to protect the value of his inventory by selling Treasury bond futures. When interest rates rise as expected, the gain from the Treasury bond futures transaction would approximately offset the loss incurred in the cash market trade. When interest rates are expected to decrease, on the other hand, a portfolio manager who is anticipating an additional fund to invest in GNMA certificates can establish a long hedge to lock in today's high yield level for his anticipated investment by buying GNMA futures now. When interest rates decrease as expected, the gain from the GNMA futures transaction would approximately offset the implicit loss from having to purchase GNMA certificates at a price higher than was offered earlier by the market. Through the use of arbitrages, intermonth spreads, intercommodity spreads and either long or short hedges, fixed-income dealers, savings and loan associations, insurance companies, pension fund and portfolio managers, investment banks, corporate financial executives, and state and local governments can effectively manage the risk inherent in holding and trading interest-rate sensitive assets.

Jin Wook Choi, Ph.D., Advisory Economist
Chicago Board of Trade, Chicago, IL

---

interest rate future   A contract on the future delivery of interest-bearing securities—primarily U.S. Treasury bills (on the International Money Market) or Treasury bonds (on the Chicago Board of Trade), although contracts on certificates of deposit, GNMAs, and Treasury notes are also available. As with other futures contracts, interest rate futures permit a buyer and a seller to lock in the price of an asset (in this case, a specified package of securities) for future delivery. The contracts are large in amount ($1,000,000 for bills and $100,000 for bonds) and lend themselves to sophisticated analysis. Amateurs beware!

interest rate risk   The risk that interest rates will rise and reduce the market value of an investment. Long-term fixed-income securities, such as bonds and preferred stock, subject their owners to the greatest amount of interest rate risk. Short-term securities, such as Treasury bills, are influenced much less by interest rate movments. Common stock prices are also affected by changes in interest rates although the linkage is less clear than is the case with debt securities and preferred stock.

interest-sensitive stock   A stock that tends to move in the opposite direction from that of interest rates. Interest-sensitive stocks include nearly all preferred stocks, and the common stocks of industries such as electric utilities and savings and loans. A common stock may be interest-sensitive either because its dividend is relatively fixed (as with an electric utility) or because the firm raises a large portion of its funds through borrowing (as with a savings and loan or an electric utility).

interim dividend   A dividend declared before a firm's annual earnings and dividend-paying ability are accurately known by its management. An interim dividend is ordinarily paid in each of the first three quarters of the fiscal year. These payments are followed by a final dividend at the time that earnings can be accurately determined.

interim report   A financial statement as of any date other than the end of a fiscal year. Interim reports, generally unaudited, are intended to indicate the level of a firm's performance usually during quarterly intervals of the fiscal year.

interlocking directorates   Boards of directors of different firms having one or more of the same people serving as directors. Interlocking directorates are illegal among competing firms.

intermarket spread swap   The sale of one bond combined with the purchase of another bond having entirely different features in order to improve the investor's position.

Intermarket Surveillance Information System   A system for storing options and equity trade information from eight national securities exchanges (including the New York Stock Exchange) and the National Association of Securities Dealers. Included in the System is information on trades, the places where they occurred, the firms involved, and the brokers making the trades.

intermarket trading   Trading between two or more markets. For example, an individual might engage in arbitrage by purchasing stock index futures on one exchange and then selling options on the same futures on another exchange.

Intermarket Trading System (ITS)   An interconnection of security trading floors that allows brokers and market makers to trade securities in additional markets. The system is intended to allow customers to obtain the most favorable price available on any of the participating exchanges. —See also NATIONAL SECURITIES TRADING SYSTEM.

intermediary —See FINANCIAL INTERMEDIARY.

intermediate bond A debt security with a holding period ranging from 7 to 15 years to maturity. —Also called *medium-term bond.* —See also LONG BOND; SHORT BOND.

intermediate-term Pertaining to an investment with an expected holding period somewhere between short-term and long-term. For bonds, collectibles, and real estate, *intermediate-term* normally refers to a holding period ranging between one and seven years. For stocks, *intermediate-term* indicates a somewhat shorter period of six months to several years. For futures and options contracts, *intermediate-term* ranges from one to several months.

intermediation The flow of funds through financial intermediaries (banks, thrifts, etc.) on the way to the ultimate borrowers. Money deposited at financial institutions that make the money available to corporate borrowers is an example of intermediation. This process tends to facilitate saving and investing in sophisticated financial systems. —See also DISINTERMEDIATION.

internal audit Examination of a company's records and reports by its employees. Internal audits are normally intended to prevent fraud and ensure that board directives and management policies are being complied with. In contrast, the financial statements presented to stockholders are typically prepared by outside parties to ensure absolute objectivity. —See also EXTERNAL AUDIT.

internal funds Funds raised within a firm. For example, income after taxes and noncash expenses, such as depreciation, provide a firm with funds to use in acquisition of investments. Companies that are able to finance expenditures with internal funds are not required to rely on borrowing or the sale of additional shares of stock. —See also EXTERNAL FUNDS.

internal rate of return (IRR) The rate of discount on an investment that equates the present value of the investment's cash outflows with the present value of the investment's cash inflows. Internal rate of return is analogous to yield to maturity for a bond.

Internal Revenue Code The tax law of the United States.

Internal Revenue Service (IRS) The agency of the U.S. Treasury Department that administers the federal tax law.

international fund A mutual fund that invests only outside the country in which it is located. —See also GLOBAL FUND.

International Monetary Fund (IMF) An international financial agency affiliated with the United Nations, established in 1944, with goals of stabilizing foreign exchange rates, lowering trade barriers, and correcting trade imbalances among countries. The IMF works with countries much as a credit counselor works with individuals having financial difficulties.

International Money Market (IMM)   An organized exchange for the trading of standardized financial futures contracts. The IMM was organized in 1972 as a division of the Chicago Mercantile Exchange.

interpositioning   The involvement of a third party between a broker-dealer and the best available market price when the practice results in the customer paying a bigger markup or markdown than would have been the case without the presence of the third party. For example, Dealer A satisfies a customer order to buy a security by purchasing the security through Dealer B who in turn purchases the security from the market maker. Dealer B marks up the security to Dealer A, who then marks up the security again when selling it to the customer. Interpositioning is considered unethical by the National Association of Securities Dealers.

inter vivos trust   —See LIVING TRUST.

intestate   Relating to or being an individual who has died without leaving a valid will. In such a case, the deceased person's estate is distributed according to the laws of the state in which he or she resided.

in-the-money   —Used to describe a call (put) option that has a strike price less (more) than the price of the underlying asset. If Westinghouse common stock is trading at $40 per share, a call option on Westinghouse with a strike price of $35 is in-the-money. —See also DEEP-IN-THE-MONEY.

in the tank   —Used to describe a security or a securities market during or following a period of large price declines.

intraday   During a day. For example, during trading on February 20, 1985, American Telephone & Telegraph common stock reached an intraday low of 21⅛ before closing at 21¼.

intrastate offering   A security offering in which the issue is offered and sold only to persons within the state in which the issuer is incorporated. Intrastate offerings are exempt from registration under the Securities Act of 1933.

intrinsic value   The value of a security, justified by factors such as assets, dividends, earnings, and management quality. Intrinsic value is at the core of fundamental analysis since it is used in an attempt to calculate the value for an individual stock and then compare it with the market price. Since analysts view facts differently, there is often a wide disparity in estimates of a particular stock's intrinsic value.

invasion powers   A provision in a trust permitting the trustee to use the principal of the trust if its income is insufficient to fulfill the requirements of the beneficiary. Trustees are normally prohibited from exercising this power without prior authorization, however.

inventory   The amount of raw materials, work in progress, and finished goods being held for sale at a given time. Diamonds held by a jeweler, engines owned by General Motors, and coal stored by Republic Steel are examples of inventory. Inventory is generally the least liquid item listed by a firm in the current asset account of its balance sheet. —See also BEGINNING INVENTORY; ENDING INVENTORY.

inventory profit   Profit derived from the fact that assets in inventory increase in value during the time that they are being held. Inventory profit, ordinarily due to general inflation, is not considered to be of high quality because it is incidental to the firm's main business. —See also EARNINGS QUALITY; FIRST-IN, FIRST-OUT; LAST-IN, FIRST-OUT.

inventory turnover   The measure of the number of times a firm sells and replaces its inventory during a given period. A relatively low inventory turnover may indicate ineffective inventory management (i.e., carrying too large an inventory) or carrying out-of-date inventory to avoid writing off inventory losses against income. A high inventory turnover is generally desirable. Inventory turnover is calculated by dividing average inventory level into cost of goods sold. —See also ACTIVITY RATIO.

inventory valuation   The cost assigned to inventory for the purpose of establishing the inventory's current value. Inventory valuation is determined by the basis on which a firm assumes inventory units are sold. If the first units acquired are assumed to be the first units sold (first-in, first-out), costs of the last units purchased are used for valuing inventory remaining in stock. Conversely, if the last units acquired are assumed to be the first units sold (last-in, first-out), the costs of the first units purchased are used for valuing the inventory remaining in stock. —See also AVERAGE-COST METHOD; LOWER OF COST OR MARKET.

inverted formation   In technical analysis, a chart pattern upside-down from its normal configuration. For example, a saucer pattern is a U-shaped curve indicating a market bottom. An inverted saucer is an upside-down U-shaped formation indicating a market top. A chart formation, when inverted, indicates the opposite future stock movement of the basic formation. Thus, while a head-and-shoulders formation is a bearish indicator, an inverted head-and-shoulders formation is a bullish indicator.

inverted market   In futures or options trading, a market with nearby contracts having a price higher than more distant contracts. This unusual situation may occur when the underlying asset is heavily in demand. —Also called *backwardation.* —See also CONTANGO.

inverted saucer   —See DOME.

inverted scale   An issue of serial bonds with yields on short-term securities exceeding yields on long-term securities. An inverted scale is generally caused when investors judge interest rates to be abnormally high and expect them to fall.

inverted yield curve   —See NEGATIVE YIELD CURVE.

investment   1. Property acquired for the purpose of producing income for its owner. Just as plants and equipment are investments for manufacturers, stocks and bonds are investments for individuals. 2. Expenditures for income-producing assets.

investment adviser   A person who offers professional investment advice. Investment advisers are required to register with the Securities and Exchange Commission.

Investment Advisers Act of 1940   A federal act that defines investment advisers, requires them to register with the Securities and Exchange Commission, and sets standards for advertising, disclosure, fees, liability, and recordkeeping. The Act was passed to protect investors. —Also called *Advisers Act*.

investment banker   A firm that acts as a middleman between organizations needing additional funds and individuals and organizations with surplus funds to invest. An investment banker, an expert in the financial markets, sells its expertise to organizations wishing to raise funds. —See also PRIMARY DISTRIBUTION; STANDBY UNDERWRITING; UNDERWRITER.

> ⒮ Investment bankers are paid to advise corporations on various matters related to new security issues. Because the investment bankers are in the business of keeping abreast of developments in the financial markets, they are able to advise companies on matters of timing, pricing, issue size, and other things relating to new stock issues. However, on occasion even the most respected investment banker can misjudge a market. One such instance occurred in May of 1986 when Home Shopping Network, a Florida merchandiser that sells items on live television call-in shows, sold two million shares of stock in an initial public offering. The shares, offered at $18 each, quickly rose in price during trading on the American Stock Exchange, and closed the day at $42⅝. Home Shopping Network's investment banker must have smarted because, had the shares been priced initially at the level investors proved they were actually willing to pay, the issuer could have raised the same $36 million while selling less than half of the 2 million shares.

investment boutique   A relatively small, specialized brokerage company. —Also called *boutique*.

investment club   A group of people who meet regularly and pool their funds to invest in securities. In many instances, a club is formed as much for social and educational reasons as for making profits. Since most investment clubs are formed as partnerships, dividends, realized capital gains, and losses are passed through for tax reporting by the individual members.

investment company   A firm in which investors pool their funds for the sake of diversification and professional management. Since individual firms often specialize in particular types of investments, potential returns and risks do vary considerably among the firms. Charges to investors— both to acquire shares in a firm and to pay management for operating the company—vary significantly from investment company to investment company. —Also called *management company*. —See also CLOSED-END INVESTMENT COMPANY; CONDUIT THEORY; MANAGEMENT FEE; MUTUAL FUND; PERFORMANCE FEE; REGULATED INVESTMENT COMPANY.

Investment Company Act   A 1940 act that regulates the management of investment companies in relation to items such as financial statements, stated investment goals, personnel, debt issuance, and directors. The goal of the Act was to provide adequate disclosure and to curb the management abuses prevalent during the 1920s and 1930s.

Investment Company Amendments Act of 1970 An act that regulates sales charges and penalties on withdrawals from mutual fund accumulation plans. This Act sets the maximum load fee that may be charged and determines how the fees may be set in accumulation plans.

Investment Counsel Association of America (ICAA) An organization of investment counselors that establishes membership and practice standards for independent investment counseling firms (i.e., those unaffiliated with banks and securities firms).

investment-grade Designating a bond suitable for purchase by institutions under the prudent man rule. Investment-grade is restricted to those bonds graded BBB and above by the rating agencies. —Also called *bank grade.* —See also HIGH-GRADE.

investment history The past relationship between a broker-dealer and an investor. Rules of the National Association of Securities Dealers require a consideration of investment history in making certain judgments as to the adequacy of an underwriter's performance in issuing securities. For example, sale of a hot issue to certain accounts generally must conform to the investment history of those accounts.

investment letter A letter from the buyer of a private placement stating that the securities are for investment purposes and not for resale within two years. An investment letter is supposed to assure the Securities and Exchange Commission that the issue is not the first stage of a regular public offering subject to normal registration requirements. —See also RESTRICTED SECURITY.

investment tax credit (ITC) A deduction against owed income taxes, permitted when a firm invests in certain assets. The purpose of the investment tax credit was to encourage business investment and thereby provide for economic expansion. The investment tax credit was eliminated by tax reform passed in 1986. —See also DEFERRED INVESTMENT TAX CREDIT; FLOW-THROUGH METHOD.

investment vehicle A specific investment with attributes intended to accomplish certain goals. Examples of investment vehicles include common stock, preferred stock, bonds, options, futures, annuities, and collectibles.

investor A person who purchases income-producing assets. An investor—as opposed to a speculator—normally considers safety of principal to be of primary importance. On the other hand, a speculator is willing to sacrifice safety of principal for the possiblility of relatively large gains. In addition, investors frequently purchase assets with the expectation of holding the assets for a longer period of time than speculators.

involuntary bankruptcy Bankruptcy that is forced by creditors instead of being initiated by the bankrupt firm or individual. —See also CHAPTER 7; CHAPTER 11; VOLUNTARY BANKRUPTCY.

IOM —See INDEX AND OPTION MARKET.

IPO —See INITIAL PUBLIC OFFERING.

IRA A custodial account or trust in which individuals may set aside earned income in a tax-deferred retirement plan. For individuals who earn under $40,000 per year or who are not in an employer-sponsored retirement plan, contributions to an IRA (subject to an annual maximum) are deferred along with any income the contributions earn. Withdrawals at retirement are fully taxable. For individuals in an employer-sponsored plan and having an adjusted gross income above a specified amount, all or part of the contribution may be taxable although any income earned in the IRA is tax deferred. Rules governing IRAs were significantly altered in the 1986 tax reform. IRA investment opportunities include certificates of deposit, mutual funds, and securities purchased through brokerage accounts. —Also called *individual retirement account.* —See also KEOGH PLAN; SELF-DIRECTED IRA; SIMPLIFIED EMPLOYEE PENSION PLAN; TERMINATION FEE.

IRA rollover Reinvestment of a lump-sum distribution from an IRA when physical receipt of funds has been taken by the investor. The lump-sum distribution must be deposited in an IRA rollover account within 60 days of receipt to escape taxation. —See also IRA TRANSFER; PENSION ROLLOVER.

IRA transfer The direct transfer of assets in an individual retirement account from one trustee to another. With an IRA transfer, the investor does not take physical possession of the IRA assets; thus, there are no tax consequences to the movement of the funds. A direct transfer may result in some lost income to the investor as the funds could remain in transit for a number of days. —See also IRA ROLLOVER.

IRR —See INTERNAL RATE OF RETURN.

irrevocable trust A trust in which the grantor gives up any right to amendments or termination. Income from an irrevocable trust is taxable to the beneficiary if disbursed or to the trust if not disbursed. —See also REVOCABLE TRUST.

IRS —See INTERNAL REVENUE SERVICE.

issue A particular grouping of an organization's securities. For example, General Motors has a number of different issues of preferred stock listed on the New York Stock Exchange.

issue To sell securities in the primary market. For example, in 1984, Cracker Barrel Old Country Stores issued 750,000 additional shares of common stock.

issued capital stock Capital stock that has been authorized and issued but may have been reacquired in part. Issued capital stock reacquired as treasury stock or stock that has been retired is not included in earnings-per-share calculations. —See also AUTHORIZED CAPITAL STOCK; OUTSTANDING CAPITAL STOCK.

issuer An organization that is selling or has sold its securities to the public.

ITC —See INVESTMENT TAX CREDIT.

itemized deduction —See DEDUCTION.

ITS —See INTERMARKET TRADING SYSTEM.

J

j —Used in the dividend column of stock transaction tables to indicate that the listed dividend was paid earlier in the year but that the latest board meeting voted an omitted or a deferred dividend or decided to take no action on the dividend: *FinCpA .05j.*

January effect The tendency of stocks to perform better in January than at any other time of the year. Some analysts speculate that the stock market tends to become oversold in December when investors sell to establish losses for tax purposes or to obtain money for holiday spending.

January indicator The tendency of stock market movement in January to set the market trend for the entire year. Thus, if a market average is higher at the end of January than it is at the beginning of January, chances are that the year will produce a rising market.

job lot In commodities trading, the quantity of a commodity that is smaller than what is specified in a standard contract.

joint account A brokerage account in which two or more individuals hold joint interests. Joint accounts may be established in a number of different forms that produce very different results. —See also INDIVIDUAL ACCOUNT; INSTITUTIONAL ACCOUNT; PARTNERSHIP ACCOUNT.

Is a joint account preferable for investing couples?

A joint brokerage account is more beneficial from a legal point of view. In terms of an individual account, if the person dies all the assets are frozen until the deceased's estate has been settled. In a joint account, the other partner has full use of the funds without having to wait for the deceased partner's estate to be settled.

Bonnie Briskin, Stockbroker
Tucker, Anthony & R.L. Day, Inc., Boston, MA

joint account agreement   The form required to open a brokerage account or bank account in the names of two or more individuals.

joint and survivor annuity   An annuity that pays a lifetime income to the annuitant and to another person, generally a spouse. The payments may be scheduled to decrease at the death of either recipient.

jointly and severally   Pertaining to a securities offering in which the underwriter is responsible for its own allocation and, in addition, for a proportionate share of any securities that remain unsold. Thus, a syndicate member allocated 10% of the securities to be sold would also be responsible for 10% of any unsold securities. —Also called *severally and jointly.* —See also SEVERALLY BUT NOT JOINTLY.

joint ownership   Ownership of an asset such as property by two or more parties. Joint ownership of property has advantages and disadvantages, compared with individual ownership. For example, the property automatically passes to the co-owners upon the death of one of the other owners. Also, with one type of joint ownership, one owner can sell the property without the permission of the other owners. —See also JOINT TENANCY WITH RIGHT OF SURVIVORSHIP; TENANCY BY THE ENTIRETY; TENANCY IN COMMON.

joint return   One income-tax return filed jointly by husband and wife. Essentially, a joint return results in a tax liability calculated on the premise that each spouse has contributed equally to the reported income. A joint return is especially advantageous for couples in which one spouse has considerably more taxable income than the other spouse. —See also SEPARATE RETURN.

joint-stock company   A rare type of business organization characterized by some features of a partnership and some features of a corporation. Shares are transferrable and the firm is taxed according to corporate tax rates. However, the liability of each owner is unlimited. Joint-stock companies are established primarily because of the ease with which they are formed.

joint tenancy with right of survivorship (JTWROS)   Asset ownership for two or more persons in which each owner holds an equal share and may give away or sell that share without the permission of the other owner(s). In the event of death, an owner's share is divided equally among the surviving co-owners. —Also called *right of survivorship.* —See also TENANCY BY THE ENTIRETY; TENANCY IN COMMON.

joint venture   A business undertaking by two or more individuals or companies, used to share risk and utilize differences in expertise. For example, oil companies often enter into joint ventures on particularly expensive projects carrying a high risk of failure. —See also CONSORTIUM.

JTWROS   —See JOINT TENANCY WITH RIGHT OF SURVIVORSHIP.

jumbo certificate of deposit   A certificate of deposit with a denomination of $100,000 or more. Jumbo certificates of deposit are negotiable and ordinarily carry slightly higher interest rates than smaller certificates.

junior debt   A class of debt that is subordinate to another class of debt issued by the same party. Junior debt is more risky for an investor to own but it pays a higher rate of interest than debt with greater security. Debentures are junior debt. —See also SENIOR DEBT.

junior security   A security having a subordinate claim to assets and income with respect to another class of security. For example, preferred stock is a junior security compared with a debenture, and a debenture is a junior security compared with a mortgage bond. In general, a junior security entails greater risk but offers higher potential yields than securities with greater seniority.

junk bond   A high-risk, high-yield debt security that, if rated at all, is graded less than BBB. These securities are most appropriate for risk-oriented investors.

> ⚠💲 When LTV Corporation filed for bankruptcy in the summer of 1986, it listed liabilities of nearly $4.25 billion including $2.2 billion in long-term debt. LTV had been a major issuer of debentures qualifying as junk bonds. These high-yielding debentures suffered very large price declines immediately before and after the firm's bankruptcy filing. For example, its 5% subordinated debentures due in 1988 declined from a price near $700 on July 16 to $350 two days later. By October the debenture sold for only $200. Other LTV debentures suffered similar large losses. In addition to sustaining the loss in market value, the owners of the securities received no interest income during the reorganization. The LTV junk bonds offered investors a high yield only for as long as the firm remained able to pay interest on the securities.

junk financing   The raising of funds by issuing unsecured high-yield securities, e.g., during takeover attempts in which the acquiring firm has little cash and must issue unsecured debt to finance the acquisition. —Also called *high-yield financing*.

junk muni-bond fund   A mutual fund or unit trust that invests in relatively low-grade tax-exempt bonds in order to earn a higher return. Bonds purchased for the fund are rated below investment grade (i.e., lower than BBB) or they are not rated at all. —See also MUNICIPAL BOND FUND.

K

k   —Used in the dividend column of stock transaction tables of newspapers to indicate dividends that have been paid so far during the year on an issue of preferred stock with dividends in arrears: *pf 1.75k*.

K   —Used frequently in the financial literature as a symbol for 1,000.

Kansas City Board of Trade   A commodities exchange that provides facilities for trading futures contracts in wheat and the Value Line stock index.

karat　A measure of the purity of gold. Pure gold is indicated by the label 24 karat. —See also FINENESS.

Keogh plan　A federally approved retirement program that permits self-employed people to set aside for savings up to $30,000 (or up to 25% of their income). All contributions and income earned by the account are tax deferred until withdrawals are made during retirement. Investment opportunities include certificates of deposit, mutual funds, and self-directed brokerage accounts.

kickers　—See BELLS AND WHISTLES.

kill　To halt a trade before sending a confirmation of it.

killer bee　An individual or organization that assists a firm in repelling a takeover attempt, especially by devising defensive strategies.

know-your-customer rule　A requirement that brokers understand the financial needs and circumstances of a customer before providing investment advice.

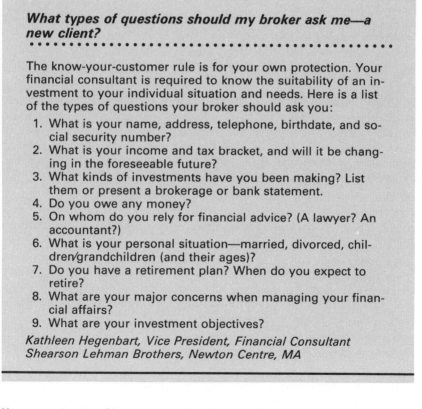

What types of questions should my broker ask me—a new client?

The know-your-customer rule is for your own protection. Your financial consultant is required to know the suitability of an investment to your individual situation and needs. Here is a list of the types of questions your broker should ask you:

1. What is your name, address, telephone, birthdate, and social security number?
2. What is your income and tax bracket, and will it be changing in the foreseeable future?
3. What kinds of investments have you been making? List them or present a brokerage or bank statement.
4. Do you owe any money?
5. On whom do you rely for financial advice? (A lawyer? An accountant?)
6. What is your personal situation—married, divorced, children/grandchildren (and their ages)?
7. Do you have a retirement plan? When do you expect to retire?
8. What are your major concerns when managing your financial affairs?
9. What are your investment objectives?

Kathleen Hegenbart, Vice President, Financial Consultant
Shearson Lehman Brothers, Newton Centre, MA

Krugerrand　A gold coin minted in South Africa.

L

L —Used in stock transaction tables in newspapers to indicate the fact that during the day's activity the stock traded at a new 52-week low: *L53½.*

lagging economic indicator An economic or a financial variable, the movements of which tend to follow the movement in overall economic activity. Thus, a lagging economic indicator would reach a peak after a peak in economic activity; it would hit bottom after a bottom in economic activity. —See also LEADING ECONOMIC INDICATOR.

laissez-faire Pertaining to or being an economy devoid of government interference.

land A firm's dollar investment in real estate.

land improvement —See IMPROVEMENT.

lapsed option An option remaining unexercised after its expiration. A lapsed option has no value.

large-capitalization stock The stock of a big corporation that has considerable retained earnings and a large amount of common stock outstanding. Large-capitalization stocks, which are generally well-known, include the ones listed in the Dow Jones Averages.

last —See CLOSE 2.

last-in, first-out (LIFO) An accounting method for identifying the order in which items are used or sold. With last-in, first-out, the most recently acquired items are assumed to be sold first. During a period of inflation, last-in, first-out accounting tends to result in high costs that reduce reported profits. The reduced profits result in a lower income-tax liability. —See also AVERAGE-COST METHOD; FIRST-IN, FIRST-OUT; INVENTORY PROFIT; INVENTORY VALUATION.

last sale The most recent transaction in a particular security.

last sale rule The National Association of Securities Dealers rule permitting investors to obtain information on an actual trade other than just the bid and ask.

last trading day 1. The day on which a trader must liquidate a futures position or else be required to receive (if long) or make delivery (if short). Following this day, the particular contract will cease trading. 2. The last day on which a particular option is traded. Currently, this day is the third Friday of the expiration month.

late tape Delayed reporting of stock transactions because of unusually heavy volume. —See also DIGITS DELETED; FLASH PRICE; VOLUME DELETED.

layoff The allocation of unsold shares to syndicate members from a new issue rights offering by the managing underwriter.

LBO —See LEVERAGED BUYOUT.

LCE —See LONDON COMMODITY EXCHANGE.

LDC —See LESS DEVELOPED COUNTRY.

leader An active stock that tends to lead the general market in price movements. For example, strength and activity may have made a stock a leader in a recent upward market movement.

leadership —See MARKET LEADERSHIP.

leading economic indicator An economic or a financial variable that tends to move ahead of and in the same direction as general economic activity. —See also INDEX OF LEADING ECONOMIC INDICATORS; LAGGING ECONOMIC INDICATOR.

lead month —See NEARBY.

lead underwriter The main underwriter of a new security issue. The lead underwriter forms a distribution system to sell the security issue and is generally responsible for the largest part of the offering. —Also called *house of issue; managing underwriter.*

lease An agreement permitting one party (the lessee) to use property owned by another party (the lessor). The lease, which may be written either for a short term or for a long term, often results in tax benefits to both parties. —See also CAPITAL LEASE; GROSS LEASE; LEVERAGED LEASE; NET LEASE; OPERATING LEASE.

leaseback —See SALE AND LEASEBACK.

lease fund An investment company that invests the shareholders' money in lease obligations. A lease fund is very similar to a bond fund except that the maturities of its investments are shorter. Since leases do not have an active secondary market, the fund manager must secure outside agreements to buy the leases in case the shareholders redeem their shares.

leasehold improvement An improvement of a leased asset that increases the asset's value. The expense of a leasehold improvement is carried as an asset that declines in value over time as the value is depreciated over the life of the lease or the improvement.

lease-rental bond A long-term state or municipal obligation, the proceeds of which are used to finance public-purpose projects such as police stations and public office buildings. Debt service, along with maintenance and operational expenses, is covered by rental or lease payments from the facilities although some bonds are also general obligations of the respective issuers.

leg One side of a combination option. —See also LEG LIFTING; LEG ON; LONG LEG; SHORT LEG.

legal —See LEGAL INVESTMENT.

LEGAL A New York Stock Exchange data bank of enforcement actions, investor complaints, and member audits.

legal capital Capital that by law or resolution must remain within a firm and that is restricted for purposes of dividends or other distributions. Legal capital is generally equal to the par or stated value of all outstanding stock. —Also called *stated capital.*

legal investment An investment eligible for purchase by a fiduciary. —Also called *legal; statutory investment.*

legal list The list of securities designated eligible as investments by institutions such as life insurance companies, restricted trust funds, and commercial banks. Such lists are generally limited to relatively high-grade securities of issuers exhibiting little chance of default. —Also called *approved list.* —See also PRUDENT MAN RULE.

legal list state A state with laws restricting investment of certain funds only to securities included in a legal list.

legal opinion Statement of a bond counsel that a municipal bond issue is legal under the laws and restrictions of the issuing jurisdiction and whether interest on the bonds is exempt from federal income taxes. A legal opinion is generally necessary to bring an issue to market. —See also EX-LEGAL.

legal transfer Transfer of a registered security when more than an endorsed bond or stock power is required for legal change of ownership. For example, transfer of securities registered to a deceased person normally requires submission of a death certificate.

leg lifting Selling one part of a combination option while continuing to hold the remaining part. For example, an owner of a straddle may sell one part (either the put or the call) when the premium is sufficient to make the entire investment profitable. —Also called *lifting a leg; taking off a leg.*

leg on Putting together a combination option (i.e., a straddle or a spread) one side at a time.

lending at a premium Imposition of an extra fee when securities are lent by one broker to another to cover a customer's short sale. Although lending at a premium is fairly unusual, it may occur when a particular security is difficult to borrow.

lending at a rate Payment of interest by a broker-dealer on a customer's credit balance from a short sale. When the investor sells short, the broker holds the proceeds from the sale in escrow to secure the securities borrowed for the short sale. In certain instances the broker may pay the customer interest on this balance.

less developed country (LDC) A country with relatively low per capita income and little industrialization. Less developed countries have been major borrowers from a number of banks worldwide. Analysts have questioned the countries' ability to service this debt.

lessee A party using under lease an asset owned by another party. —See also LESSOR.

lessor The owner of an asset who permits another party to use the asset under a lease. —See also LESSEE.

letter bond —See RESTRICTED SECURITY.

letter of credit (LOC) A promise of payment in the event that certain requirements are met. A letter of credit essentially substitutes the credit of a third party (usually a large bank) for that of a borrower. In the case of municipal bonds, an LOC generally permits a trustee to draw six months' interest and sufficient funds to retire outstanding bonds at par in the event of default.

letter of guarantee A letter from a bank stating that a customer owns a particular security and that the bank will guarantee delivery of the security. A letter of guarantee is used by an investor who is writing call options when the underlying stock is not in his or her brokerage account.

letter of intent An agreement by a mutual fund shareholder to invest a specific sum over a defined period in order to qualify for reduced sales fees. The reduced fee may apply to an individual fund or to all the funds operated by an investment management group. —See also BREAKPOINT; LOAD; RIGHT OF ACCUMULATION.

letter ruling —See REVENUE RULING.

letter security —See RESTRICTED SECURITY.

letter stock —See RESTRICTED SECURITY.

Level 1 A user level of the National Association of Securities Dealers Automated Quotation System (NASDAQ) that provides only a single median quote for each over-the-counter (OTC) stock carried on the System. This Level is intended for securities firms not actively engaged in trading OTC stocks for themselves or for their customers.

Level 2 A NASDAQ user level that provides current bid and offer quotes by all market makers in each security carried on the System. This Level is intended for firms trading significant amounts of OTC stocks for themselves or for their customers.

Level 3 The most extensive NASDAQ user level that permits customers to enter the System with their own quotes as well as to obtain complete bid and offer quotations on all other securities in the System. Level 3 is of primary interest to institutions making markets in OTC securities.

leverage Use of fixed costs in an attempt to increase the rate of return from an investment. One example of leverage is buying securities on margin. While leverage can operate to increase rates of return, it also increases the amount of risk inherent in an investment. —See also FINANCIAL LEVERAGE; OPERATING LEVERAGE.

leveraged Being or referring to an investment situation in which borrowed funds are used for the investment. A highly leveraged investor or firm is in a relatively risky position if interest rates rise or if the investment yields are disappointingly low.

leveraged buyout (LBO) Use of a target company's asset value in order to finance most or all of the debt incurred in acquiring the company.

This strategy enables a takeover using little capital; however, it can result in considerably more risk to owners and creditors. —See also HOSTILE LEVERAGED BUYOUT.

⚠️ Leveraged buyouts (LBOs) became popular in the 1980s when firms such as Beatrice Companies, Swift, ARA Services, Levi Strauss, Jack Eckerd, and Denny's were acquired and then were taken private. With an LBO, a firm's management often borrows funds using the firm's assets as collateral. The borrowed money is used to purchase all the firm's outstanding stock. As a result, a small group of individuals are able to take control of the firm without using any or much of their own money. Following the buyout the new owners frequently attempt to cut costs and sell assets in order to make the increased debt more manageable. Because the group initiating the LBO must pay a premium for the stock over the market price, an LBO nearly always benefits the stockholders of the firm to be acquired. However, investors holding bonds of the acquired company are likely to see their relative position deteriorate because of the increased debt taken on by the company. For example, the leveraged buyout of R. H. Macy & Company produced a $16 jump in the price of its common stock at the same time the price of its debt securities fell. Most bondholders have no recourse to the increased risks they face because of the greater resultant debt.

leveraged company A company that uses borrowed money to help finance its assets. Leveraged companies often have more volatile earnings than firms that rely solely on equity financing. This volatility is offset, however, by the possiblity of a higher return to stockholders if the firm is able to earn more on its assets than the cost of the money used to finance those assets.

leveraged investment company 1. An investment company that uses borrowed money to acquire securities. Leveraged investment companies produce more volatile returns for their shareholders than do investment companies not employing debt financing. 2. —See DUAL PURPOSE FUND.

leveraged lease A long-term lease in which a major part of the purchase price of the to-be-leased asset is financed by a third party. Thus, the lessor uses a combination of its own funds and borrowed money in order to purchase the asset that is then leased to another party.

leverage up To increase the portion of debt in a firm's capital structure by issuing debt and using the proceeds to repurchase stock or by financing any new expansion through debt. In the mid-1980s, firms decided to leverage up in an attempt to improve the market price of their stock, thereby fending off takeover attempts.

liability An obligation to pay an amount in money, goods, or services to another party. The balance sheet lists the liabilities. —Also called *debt*. —See also ASSET; CONTINGENT LIABILITY; CURRENT LIABILITY.

liability dividend A dividend paid with a type of debt, such as a bond. Liability dividends are normally paid when a firm is short of cash. —See also BOND DIVIDEND; SCRIP DIVIDEND.

LIBOR —See LONDON INTERBANK OFFERED RATE.

lien The legal right of a creditor to sell mortgaged assets when the debtor is unable or unwilling to meet requirements of a loan agreement. A lien makes a bondholder's claim more secure.

life annuity A stream of payments intended to continue during the annuitant's lifetime and to cease automatically at the annuitant's death.

life of contract In futures or options trading, the period of time in which trading can occur before the expiration or settlement. In general, a longer life makes an option more valuable.

life tenant A person who is entitled to the use of or the income from an asset during his or her lifetime. As an example, a person may stipulate in a will that all his or her assets are to go to a charity but that the surviving spouse, designated as life tenant, is to have the use or the income from the deceased's estate for his or her lifetime following which the remainder of the assets in the estate are to pass to the charity.

LIFO —See LAST-IN, FIRST-OUT.

lifting a leg —See LEG LIFTING.

lighten up To reduce, but not eliminate, a particular security position when the investor feels that the security constitutes too much of the portfolio's total value, or when the investor is feeling less bullish on the security. In either case, a residual position in the security is maintained.

limited company (Ltd.) A firm registered in such a way as to give its owners limited liability. Limited companies are most often associated with British registration, much as incorporated firms are associated with U.S. registration.

When should you give your broker limited discretion?

By giving limited discretion to your broker, you are asking the broker to use discretion on *your* behalf in specific, agreed-upon instances, which may include increased work load, travel, extended vacation, or ill health. Limited discretion does not mean carte blanche authority. Further, your objectives must be clearly understood and the broker in question should have demonstrated a working understanding of those objectives. Once the foundation of trust is in place, you may want to grant limited discretion when necessity or circumstances dictate that it is more practical to have someone else make decisions for you on a limited basis. But under no circumstances should you give away the store to someone whom you don't implicitly trust. Granting discretion to someone to invest on your behalf must be considered a serious matter. Make sure that you are able to review all actions taken on your behalf.

Kathleen Hegenbart, Vice President, Financial Consultant
Shearson Lehman Brothers, Newton Centre, MA

limited discretion   A broker's ability to make certain investment decisions for an investor without first getting in touch with the investor. The investor must sign a written agreement providing the broker with limited discretion. —Also called *limited trading authorization.* —See also DISCRETIONARY ACCOUNT.

limited liability   The liability of a firm's owners for no more capital than they have invested in the business. Essentially, the legal separation of ownership and liability means that a stockholder can lose no more than he or she has paid for the shares of ownership regardless of the firm's financial obligations. Limited liability is one of the major advantages of organizing a business as a corporation. —See also UNLIMITED LIABILITY.

limited partnership   A partnership in which some of the partners have a limited liability to the firm's creditors. —See also GENERAL PARTNERSHIP; MASTER LIMITED PARTNERSHIP.

limited-tax general obligation bond   A municipal bond that is secured by some limited taxing power of the issuer. For example, a bond may be secured by a municipality's property tax subject to a maximum rate at which the tax may be levied. Although a limited-tax general obligation bond is considered a general obligation of the issuer, because of the limited taxing power this bond is somewhat more risky than a general obligation bond secured by full taxing power.

limited trading authorization   —See LIMITED DISCRETION.

limited-voting stock   A class of stock that provides its holders with smaller than proportionate voting rights in comparison with another class of stock issued by the same firm. Limited-voting shares allow another class of stock effectively to control the election of a firm's directors even though the limited-voting shareholders may have contributed a majority of the firm's equity capital. —See also SUPERVOTING STOCK.

limit move   The maximum price change in a commodity futures contract permitted during a single trading session.

limit order   An order to execute a transaction only at a specified price (the limit) or better. A limit order to buy would be at the limit or lower and a limit order to sell would be at the limit or higher. Limit orders are used by investors who have decided on the price at which they are willing to trade. —See also ELECT; MARKET ORDER; OR BETTER; STOP ORDER 1.

Limit Order Information System   A proposed electronic system that would list specialists' price and size quotes for exchange-listed securities. The Limit Order Information System would be used by specialists and other subscribers to find the best market for making a trade.

limit price   The price specified by an investor for a limit order. With a limit order to buy, the price represents the highest price the investor will pay. The price of a limit order to sell represents the lowest price the investor will accept.

line   In technical analysis, a horizontal line on a price chart indicating a period during which supply and demand for a security are relatively equal. Technical analysts generally look for the price to break away from the line, at which time they are likely to take a position in the direction of the movement. —See also MAKING A LINE.

line chart   A graph displaying successive variable stock values over time. For example, a line chart of a stock would display the stock's closing prices over a period of time, connected by a line. Line charts for graphing stock prices are useful if an analyst is interested only in a single value each time. But if high, low, and closing prices all are required, a bar chart is used. —See also BAR CHART; POINT-AND-FIGURE CHART; 200-DAY MOVING AVERAGE.

line-of-business reporting   —See SEGMENT REPORTING.

line of credit   A credit arrangement in which a financial institution agrees to lend money to a customer up to a specified limit. A line of credit, generally arranged before the funds are actually required, provides flexibility for the customer in that it ensures the ability to meet short-term cash needs as they arise. —Also called *bank line; credit line; revolver; revolving credit agreement*.

LIONS   —See COUPON STRIPPING.

liquid   **1.** Being or designating an asset that may be bought or sold in a short period of time with relatively small price changes engendered by the transaction. A U.S. Treasury bill is an example of a very liquid asset. (Many issues of municipal bonds are not very liquid.) —See also ILLIQUID 1.   **2.** Being or pertaining to an investment position in which most of the assets are in money or near money. This kind of position generally earns a relatively low return but allows the investor to take advantage of other investment opportunities.

liquid asset fund   —See MONEY MARKET FUND.

liquidate a position   To sell all the stock or debt securities of a particular type. For example, a portfolio manager might decide to liquidate a position in a stock by selling all the shares of that stock held in the portfolio. A variety of reasons may induce the investor to do this, but the most common one is simply a belief that the security price will fall.

liquidating dividend   A pro rata distribution of cash or property to stockholders as part of the dissolution of a business. For example, a firm may be liquidated because the officers feel that its stock price does not adequately reflect the value of its assets. All debts and other obligations normally must be satisfied before issuance of a final liquidating dividend. A stock paying a liquidating dividend is indicated in stock transaction tables in newspapers by the symbol *C*, next to the dividend column. —See also FINAL DIVIDEND 1; GENERAL UTILITIES DOCTRINE.

liquidating value   The estimated value of a firm in the event that its assets are sold and its debts paid. This value is often stated on a per-share basis so as to indicate some kind of minimum value for a given share of the stock. Liquidation value above the stock's market price indicates that the firm is worth more dead than alive.

liquidation **1.** Conversion of assets into cash. Just as a company may liquidate an entire subsidiary by selling it to another firm, so too may an investor liquidate by selling a particular type of security. **2.** The paying of a debt. **3.** The selling of assets and the paying of liabilities in anticipation of going out of business.

⚠️ Occasionally a company will decide to liquidate its entire operation. Case in point: in 1986 the directors of Uniroyal, Inc. voted to liquidate the firm by selling its businesses, settling its obligations, and distributing the remaining funds to the stockholders. The firm estimated that it would need $840 million to pay its debts, $100 million to provide for employee retirement benefits, and $87 million for payments to its preferred stockholders. Uniroyal, which had already reached agreements to sell three of its operations for a total of $1.11 billion, was in the process of seeking a buyer for Uniroyal Plastics. A firm may liquidate for a number of reasons including protection from a corporate raider. Whatever the reason for liquidation, however, management must feel that the firm's stock price does not reflect the value of its underlying assets. Thus, stockholders should be better off with funds received from the liquidated assets than from continued possession of the common stock.

liquidity A large position in cash or in assets easily convertible to cash. High liquidity produces flexibility for a firm or an investor in a low-risk position; however, it also tends to decrease profitability.

liquidity diversification Spreading of the maturities of bonds held in a portfolio so as to hedge against potential changes in interest rates. If interest rates rise, the investor is partially protected by the ability to reinvest interest payments and principal payments from maturing bonds at higher rates. Interest from long-term bonds will cushion the investor against a decline in income from falling interest rates.

liquidity ratio **1.** Comparison of financial variables that serves as a measure of a company's ability to meet its short-term obligations as they become due. —See also CURRENT RATIO; QUICK RATIO; WORKING CAPITAL. **2.** The value of trading in a stock required to change the stock's price by 1%. A high ratio indicates that the stock has considerable liquidity. A stock's liquidity ratio is of primary importance to institutions and traders that deal in large volume and that wish to avoid securities with a lack of liquidity.

liquidity risk The risk of having difficulty in liquidating an investment position without taking a significant discount from current market value. Liquidity risk can be a significant problem with certain lightly-traded securities such as unlisted options and municipal bonds that were part of small issues. —Also called *marketability risk.*

list To admit a security for trading on an organized exchange. In order to be listed, the security and the issuer must meet certain minimal standards established by the exchange. These standards may relate to assets, earnings, market value, and stock voting rights. —See also DELIST; FORM S–1.

listed security A security traded on any of the national or regional securities exchanges. Listed securities are generally more liquid than securities that trade only in the over-the-counter market. —Also called *exchange-traded security.* —See also UNLISTED SECURITY.

listing department —See STOCK LIST.

listing requirements Requirements that are made of a firm and the firm's security before the security can be listed for trading on an exchange. Each exchange has its own listing requirements, covering things such as the minimum shares outstanding, the number of shareholders, the earnings history, and so forth.

living trust A trust created for the trustor and administered by another party during the trustor's lifetime. The living trust may be formed because the trustor is incapable of managing, or unwilling to manage, his or her assets. The trust can be revocable or irrevocable, depending on the trustor's wishes. —Also called *inter vivos trust.*

LME —See LONDON METAL EXCHANGE.

load The sales fee that the buyer pays in order to acquire an asset. This fee varies according to the type of asset and the way it is sold. Many mutual funds impose a sales charge. As a result of the load, only a portion of the investor's funds go into the investment itself. —Also called *front-end load; sales load.* —See also RIGHT OF ACCUMULATION.

load fund A mutual fund with shares sold at a price including a sales charge—typically 4% to 9.3% of the net amount invested. Thus, load funds are sold at a price exceeding net asset value, but they are redeemed at net asset value. There is no reason to expect an investment company with a sales charge to outperform one without a sales charge. —See also LOAD; LOW-LOAD FUND; NO-LOAD FUND.

load spread option The allocation of sales charges on mutual fund shares purchased on a contractual plan over a period of years. Sales charges may amount to as much as 20% of any single year's payments during the first 4 years, provided the total charges for the 4 years do not exceed 64% of any single year's payments. Also, the total sales charge cannot exceed 9% of contributions of the total value of the contract.

loan portfolio Loans that have been made or bought and are being held for repayment. Loan portfolios are the major asset of banks, thrifts, and other lending institutions. The value of a loan portfolio depends not only on the interest rates earned on the loans, but also on the quality or likelihood that interest and principal will be paid.

loan value The maximum amount that may be borrowed, using a security as collateral. If the Federal Reserve specifies an initial margin requirement of 50% under Regulation T, $5,000 in securities would have a loan value of $2,500.

LOC —See LETTER OF CREDIT.

Load funds: reasons for and against buying into them.

Several studies have shown that load funds do not outperform no-load or low-load funds. So why is it that the lion's share of all fund sales go to load funds? There are various reasons— some good, some bad. Here's a list of the most common ones:

- "My broker advised me to buy it." Okay, if you need the prodding and/or guidance. Not okay, if you can do your own investment evaluations.
- "My broker advises me when to be in or out of the market." Okay, if your broker is experienced *and good* at timing and doesn't try for the very bottom or top of the market. Not okay, if you have the knowledge *and discipline* to time the market yourself.
- "I didn't (or don't) know what fund to buy." This means you need to educate yourself. Stay liquid, perhaps in a money market fund, until you do so. In the meantime, read everything you can on mutual funds.
- "Load funds have better investment results." This is the most common misconception. Sure, there are plenty of excellent load funds, and you may have a particular one in mind. Check it out against no-loads and low-loads. If you still feel the load offers more value to you, go for it.

RECAP: Buy a load fund only if doing so *adds* an appreciable advantage to your overall financial plan.

Rudolph D. Watz, CLU, ChFC
Vice President, Director, Retirement Plans
Value Line Securities, Inc., New York, NY

---

locked in   Having a large paper, or unrealized, profit in a security position, with the result being that sale of the security would engender substantial taxation.

locked market   A somewhat unusual occurrence in which the bid price and ask price for a security are equal.

lock in   To guarantee, as a return or cost. For example, an investor who purchases a noncallable 10% coupon Treasury bond at par locks in a return of 10% annually until the bond matures. The Treasury also locks in a 10% cost for the funds raised through the sale of this bond issue.

lockup agreement   A contractual offer of valuable assets or stock made by a takeover target to the suitor deemed most acceptable to management. A lockup agreement tends to discourage unwanted suitors but it may penalize the target firm's stockholders because it eliminates counteroffers. —Also called *crown jewel lockup agreement*.

London Commodity Exchange (LCE)   A trading floor in London that offers facilities to five different commodity exchanges. The LCE is similar in concept to New York's Commodity Exchange Corporation.

London interbank offered rate (LIBOR)   The basic short-term rate of interest in the Eurodollar market and the rate to which many Eurodollar loans and deposits are tied. It is similar in concept to the prime rate in the U.S. except that it is less subject to individual bank management.

London Metal Exchange (LME)   An exchange, established in 1876, for trading spot and forward contracts in metals.

long   —See LONG POSITION.

long bond   A debt security with a relatively long period remaining until maturity. —Also called *long coupon.* —See also INTERMEDIATE BOND; SHORT BOND.

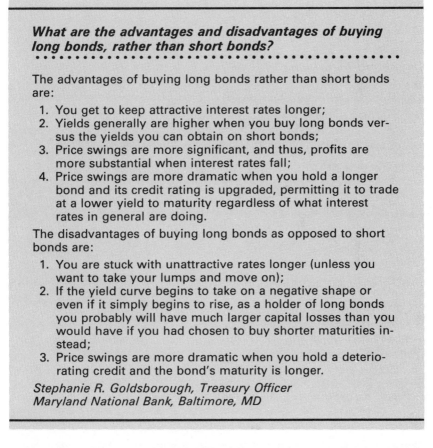

What are the advantages and disadvantages of buying long bonds, rather than short bonds?

The advantages of buying long bonds rather than short bonds are:

1. You get to keep attractive interest rates longer;
2. Yields generally are higher when you buy long bonds versus the yields you can obtain on short bonds;
3. Price swings are more significant, and thus, profits are more substantial when interest rates fall;
4. Price swings are more dramatic when you hold a longer bond and its credit rating is upgraded, permitting it to trade at a lower yield to maturity regardless of what interest rates in general are doing.

The disadvantages of buying long bonds as opposed to short bonds are:

1. You are stuck with unattractive rates longer (unless you want to take your lumps and move on);
2. If the yield curve begins to take on a negative shape or even if it simply begins to rise, as a holder of long bonds you probably will have much larger capital losses than you would have if you had chosen to buy shorter maturities instead;
3. Price swings are more dramatic when you hold a deteriorating credit and the bond's maturity is longer.

Stephanie R. Goldsborough, Treasury Officer
Maryland National Bank, Baltimore, MD

long hedge   The purchase of a call option or futures contract on fixed-income securities to protect against a decline in interest rates. The long hedge allows the investor to lock in a specific yield.

long leg   The side of an option spread (i.e., one option bought long and one option sold short) that an investor is long. With a spread that involves owning a June 20 put and being short a March 20 put, the June 20 put represents the long leg. —See also SHORT LEG.

long position   The net ownership position in a particular security. If an investor owns 500 shares of General Motors common stock, that person is said to be long 500 shares of GM. Likewise, the more unusual situation of owning 1,000 shares of a particular stock at a time when 300 shares of the same stock have been sold short produces a long position of 700 shares. Being long indicates an expectation of rising share prices. —Also called *long*. —See also SHORT POSITION 1.

long-term   **1.** Designating a gain or loss in the value of a security that has been held over a specific length of time. —See also HOLDING PERIOD; SHORT-TERM 1.   **2.** Describing a liability for which a long period of time (usually one year) remains until payment of the face amount comes due. A long-term bond is a long-term liability.

look   A price and size quotation for a security. For example, a floor broker may ask for a look at GM.

lookback call option   A specialized commodity option that gives its owner the right to purchase the underlying asset at the lowest price at which it traded between the effective date and the expiration date of the option. The added advantage of being able to look back makes this option command a relatively high premium.

lookback put option   A specialized commodity option that gives its owner the right to sell the underlying asset at the highest price at which it traded between the effective date and the expiration date of the option.

loser   A security that has fallen in price during a specified time period. —See also GAINER.

loss   The deficiency of the amount received as opposed to the amount invested in a transaction. —See also GAIN; NET LOSS.

lot   —See ODD LOT; ROUND LOT.

lowball   Pertaining to or being an unrealistically low bid. —See also PRICEY.

lower of cost or market   A method of determining an asset's value such that either the original cost or the current replacement cost, whichever is lowest, is used for financial reporting purposes. For example, an inventory item originally purchased for $50 that has a current market value of $30 would appear on the firm's balance sheet at $30. The use of lower of cost or market is considered a conservative method of valuing assets. —See also AVERAGE-COST METHOD; INVENTORY VALUATION.

low-load fund   An open-end investment company with a sales charge ranging from 1% to 3% of the net amount invested by a shareholder, as opposed to charges of up to 9.3% on regular load funds and no charges on no-load funds. Low-load funds gained popularity in the mid-1980s, a period which witnessed renewed public interest in investment companies of all types.

lows The number of stocks dropping below the lowest price reached by each stock during the most recent 52-week period. Falling stock market averages accompanied by a large number of new lows tend to confirm that a bear market is in progress. Technicians consider an increasing number of lows to be a bearish sign, especially if accompanied by other bearish indicators. Conversely, record lows by market averages not accompanied by an increasing number of individual lows would be suspect. —See also HIGHS.

Ltd. —See LIMITED COMPANY.

lump-sum distribution With retirement plans, the disbursement of an individual's benefits in a single payment. A lump-sum distribution has important income tax implications; hence, the individual must investigate this option thoroughly before choosing a single payment.

When is lump-sum distribution desirable? To whom?

When available, a lump-sum distribution is almost always preferred over an annuitized payment, for such payments cease at the death of the annuitant(s). There is no guarantee that anyone will live to his or her statistical life expectancy, as used in the calculation of the annuity. By taking a lump sum, on the other hand, the recipient immediately receives the full value of the benefit to which he or she is entitled. Further, the time value of money supports this position: a dollar today is worth more than a dollar tomorrow. However, in taking a lump-sum distribution, an individual will be required to deal with the appropriate investment of those funds. If unable to deal with the investment responsibility, the individual might be better off electing an annuity.

Michele R. Bourgerie, CPA
Arthur Young, New York, NY

M

m —Used in bond transaction tables in newspapers to indicate a bond that has matured and is no longer drawing interest: *Cuba 4½ 77m.*

M1 The most restrictive measure of the domestic money supply that incorporates only money that is ordinarily used for spending on goods and services. M1 includes currency, checking account balances (including

NOW accounts and credit union share draft accounts), and travelers' checks. This money measure is closely watched by financial observers because it is a key indicator of past and future Federal Reserve actions.

M2   A measure of the money supply that includes M1 plus savings and time deposits, overnight repurchase agreements, and personal balances in money market accounts. Basically, M2 includes money that can be used for spending (M1) plus items that can be quickly converted to M1.

M3   A very broad measure of the money supply that includes M2 plus large time deposits and money market fund balances held by institutions.

MAC   —See MUNICIPAL ASSISTANCE CORPORATION FOR THE CITY OF NEW YORK.

maintenance and replacement call   A special provision of some bond indentures (especially those of utilities) that permits the borrower to pay off the issue (normally at par) before maturity if the collateral is replaced or disposed of.

maintenance call   A call to an investor for additional funds when the market value of securities in the investor's margin account has fallen to the point that the investor's equity (i.e., the value of the securities less the amount owed) does not meet an established minimum. If the investor does not supply the required money or securities, the firm will sell a certain number of securities sufficient to bring the account into conformity. A maintenance call is a type of margin call.

maintenance fee   The fee charged by a financial institution to keep an investor's account. For example, some brokerage firms levy a maintenance fee on accounts that have been inactive during a year. Nearly all firms offering sweep accounts charge an annual maintenance fee.

maintenance margin requirement   The minimum equity in an account as a percentage of the value of the account. For example, if the maintenance requirement is 25%, the account equity (the market value of the securities less the amount owed) must at least equal one-quarter the value of the securities in the account. The maintenace margin requirement becomes important when securities purchased on margin fall in price. —Also called *margin requirement; minimum maintenance.* —See also HOUSE MAINTENANCE REQUIREMENT; INITIAL MARGIN REQUIREMENT.

major bracket   The listing of the primary underwriters in a securities offering. The major bracket appears immediately under the names of the issue's comanagers. —See also BRACKETING; MEZZANINE BRACKET; TOMBSTONE.

majority-owned subsidiary   A firm in which over 50% of outstanding voting stock is owned by the parent company.

majority stockholder   A single stockholder or a group of stockholders working in concert who control over 50% of a corporation's voting stock. —See also WORKING CONTROL.

majority voting   A type of voting right in which stockholders are granted one vote for each director's position for each share held. Thus, the holder of 100 shares would have the right to cast 100 votes for each position for which an election is held. Under this system, any stockholder or group holding 51% of the shares voting is able to control every position up for election. —Also called *statutory voting*. —See also CUMULATIVE VOTING.

Major Market Index An index of 20 bellwether stocks that closely tracks changes in the Dow Jones Industrial Average. Nineteen of the stocks in the Major Market Index are also included in the Dow Jones Industrial Average. The Major Market Index is used primarily by program traders who take a long or short position in the stocks included in the Index and the opposite position in a futures contract on the Index. The Major Market Index was developed in 1983 by the American Stock Exchange.

major turn A significant change in an intermediate- or long-term trend. For example, an analyst may look for a major turn in stock prices following an extended bull market.

make a market To quote a bid price at which a security will be purchased and an ask price at which the security will be sold. An individual makes a market by quoting the prices at which he or she will buy and sell. —See also MARKET MAKER 1.

making a line In technical analysis, movement of a stock price in such a way that it traces a relatively thick line across a graph. The thickness of the line is determined by the size of the upward and downward price movements. A breakout from the line in an upward direction is bullish and a breakout in a downward direction is bearish.

Maloney Act A 1935 act providing for the self-regulation of security brokers and dealers in the over-the-counter market. The only organization currently registered under the Act is the National Association of Securities Dealers with slightly under 3,000 members. As an incentive to join, members receive discounts on securities traded among themselves.

managed account An investment account managed by a broker or other professional. Managed accounts are designed for investors lacking the time or expertise to make their own decisions.

management audit A detailed audit concentrating on analysis and evaluation of management procedures and the overall performance of an organization. A management audit is undertaken to discover weaknesses and to institute improvements within the organization. —Also called *operational audit; performance audit.*

management buyout —See GOING PRIVATE.

management company —See INVESTMENT COMPANY.

management fee The money paid to the managers of an investment company. The fee is generally based on a percentage of the net asset value of the fund with the percentage becoming smaller as the fund's assets grow larger. Fees vary considerably among firms but average about ½ of 1% of assets. A fund's management fee must be listed in its prospectus and can be found in a number of publications including the *Forbes* annual issue on mutual funds (appearing in early August).

managing underwriter —See LEAD UNDERWRITER.

manipulate To cause a security to sell at an artificial price. Although investment bankers are permitted to manipulate temporarily the stock that they underwrite, most other forms of manipulation are illegal.

maple leaf A gold coin minted in Canada.

margin 1. The amount of funds that must be deposited when purchasing securities. —See also INITIAL MARGIN REQUIREMENT. 2. The equity in an investor's account. —See also MAINTENANCE MARGIN REQUIREMENT.

margin account A brokerage account that permits an investor to purchase securities on credit and to borrow on securities already in the account. Buying on credit and borrowing are subject to standards established by the Federal Reserve and/or by the firm carrying the account. Interest is charged on any borrowed funds and only for the period of time that the loan is outstanding. —Also called *general account.* —See also CASH ACCOUNT; INITIAL MARGIN REQUIREMENT; MAINTENANCE MARGIN REQUIREMENT.

margin agreement The written document that describes the functioning of a margin account and that permits a customer's broker to pledge securities in the account as collateral for loans. A customer must sign a margin agreement before undertaking trades on credit in an account. —See also CUSTOMER'S LOAN AGREEMENT.

marginal cost The additional cost of producing or purchasing one more unit of a good or service. For example, if a firm can produce 150 units of a product at a total cost of $5,000 and 151 units for $5,100, the marginal cost of the 151st unit is $100. Industries with sharply declining marginal costs tend to be made up of firms that engage in price wars to gain market share. For example, the airlines often discount fares to fill empty seats with customers from competing airlines. —Also called *incremental cost.* —See also AVERAGE COST; FIXED COST; MARGINAL REVENUE; VARIABLE COST.

marginal revenue The extra revenue generated by selling one extra unit of a good or service. For example, if a firm can sell 10 units of a product at a price of $25 per unit, total revenue is $250. If, in order to sell 11 units, it must reduce the price to $24, total revenue rises to 11 × $24, or $264. Thus, the marginal revenue of the 11th unit is $264 − $250, or $14. —See also MARGINAL COST.

marginal tax rate The percentage of extra income received that must be paid in taxes. It is crucial for an investor to know his or her marginal tax rate in order to make intelligent investment decisions. For example, a decision whether or not to purchase municipal bonds is primarily a function of the investor's marginal tax rate. —Also called *tax bracket.* —See also PROGRESSIVE TAX.

margin call A call for additional funds or securities in a margin account either because the value of equity in the account has fallen below a required minimum (also termed a *maintenance call*) or because additional securities have been purchased (or sold short).

How to calculate your marginal tax rate and how to use that rate in making sound investment decisions.
• •

Your marginal tax rate is the rate at which your next dollar of income will be taxed. If you are married and are filing a joint return, your marginal rates are based on the amount of taxable income you have:

1987		1988 and beyond	
0–$3,000	11%	0–$29,750	15%
$3,000–28,000	15%	$29,750–71,900	28%
$28,000–45,000	28%	$71,900–149,250	33%
$45,000–90,000	35%	over $149,250	28%
over $90,000	38.5%		

When looking at any investment alternative, you must understand the impact that taxes will have on the projected return. In order to compare investments, you need to look at their after-tax yields. By knowing your marginal tax rate, you will be able to make this evaluation. Further, those of you who live in states with high income-tax rates should calculate your combined federal and state marginal rate. The formula is as follows:

$$[(State\ MTB) \times (1 - Federal\ MTB)] + Federal\ MTB$$
$$MTB = Marginal\ Tax\ Bracket$$

Michele R. Bourgerie, CPA
Arthur Young, New York, NY

---

margin department   The section of a brokerage firm's back office operation that is responsible for overseeing customer credit accounts. The margin department ensures that investors meet the margin standards determined by the Federal Reserve, the various exchanges, and the brokerage firm itself. —Also called *credit department*.

margin of profit   —See GROSS PROFIT MARGIN.

margin requirement   —See INITIAL MARGIN REQUIREMENT; MAINTENANCE MARGIN REQUIREMENT.

margin stock   A stock with qualifications such that it is considered to have loan value in a margin account. This kind of stock normally includes all listed stocks and selected over-the-counter stocks meeting Federal Reserve criteria. Stocks not on the margin list must be paid for in full. —Also called *OTC margin stock*.

margin trading   The buying and selling of securities in an account in which money is owed to the brokerage firm.

marital deduction   The deduction for tax purposes of property transferred between spouses. For estate and gift purposes, all transfers between spouses are free of federal taxation.

marital-deduction trust   A trust designed to pass assets to a spouse. The trust is used instead of leaving the assets to the spouse directly. The beneficiary receives income from the trust until his or her death, at which time the trust's assets are distributed or the trust is included in the deceased's estate. —See also QTIP TRUST.

markdown   **1.** A decrease in a security price made by a dealer because of changing market conditions. For example, a bond trader may take a markdown in long-term bonds held in inventory when market interest rates rise. —See also MARKUP 1.   **2.** The difference between the price paid by a dealer to a retail customer and the price at which the dealer can sell the same security to a market maker. —See also MARKUP 3.

marketability   The ease with which an investment may be bought and sold in the secondary market. Poor marketability tends to reduce the value of a security.

marketability risk   —See LIQUIDITY RISK.

marketable security   A security that may be resold by one investor to another. Most securities are marketable; they develop secondary markets for trading. —Also called *negotiable security.*

market averages   —See AVERAGES.

market bottom   The low point of stock prices measured by one or more of the stock averages or indices. —See also MARKET TOP.

market breadth   —See BREADTH OF MARKET.

market capitalization   The total value of all of a firm's outstanding shares, calculated by multiplying the market price per share times the total number of shares outstanding. For example, at a current price of $50 for each of its 20 million shares of outstanding stock, GenCorp has a market capitalization of $50 times 20 million, or $1 billion. —Also called *market value.*

market efficiency   —See EFFICIENT MARKET.

market fund   —See INDEX FUND.

market if touched (MIT)   An order to buy or sell that becomes a market order as soon as a specified price has been reached. Execution does not have to occur at the specified price but at the first available price once the specified price has been touched. Market if touched orders are most frequently used in commodities trading.

market index   —See AVERAGES.

market leadership   The stocks that tend to dominate trading volume during a given period of time. Some people believe the quality of market leadership indicates future trends for market movement. For example, poor quality leadership (i.e., leadership exhibited by low-priced, speculative stocks) may indicate excessive speculation and forecast a major decline in stock prices. —Also called *leadership.*

Can the quality of market leadership be used to forecast accurately security prices?
• •

Remember what was included in *Reminiscences of a Stock Operation* by Edwin LeFevre: "Be advised that a bull market, or a leg of a bull market, is ending when the stocks that had been the leaders of the market dropped a few points and for the first time in many months did not return to those prices or higher highs. Watch for the rest of the market to advance under new standard bearers."

Ray Ozyjowski, Regional Sales Coordinator
PaineWebber Incorporated, New York, NY

---

market letter   A newsletter containing information on topics such as market trends, security recommendations, economic forecasts, and virtually anything else having impact on security prices and investor profits. Market letters are provided by most full-service brokerage companies, often for a fee, and by individual investment advisers registered with the Securities and Exchange Commission.

market line   —See CAPITAL MARKET LINE.

market maker   1. One (as a person or firm) that, on a continuous basis, buys and sells a security for one's own account. Market makers normally try to profit from a rapid turnover in security positions rather than from holding those positions in anticipation of gradual price movements. Specialists on the organized exchanges and dealers in the over-the-counter market are market makers. —See also MAKE A MARKET.   2. A dealer in options on the floor of an options exchange who makes a market in one or more options. The Chicago Board Options Exchange and the Pacific Stock Exchange use market makers.

market multiple   —See PRICE-EARNINGS RATIO.

market not held order   —See NOT HELD.

market order   A customer order for immediate execution at the best price available when the order reaches the marketplace. This, the most common type of order, has the advantage of nearly always being filled since no price is specified. —See also ELECT; LIMIT ORDER; STOP ORDER 1.

market price   The price at which a security trades in the secondary market.

market risk   1. The risk that because general market pressures will cause the value of an investment to fluctuate, it may be necessary to liquidate a position during a down period in the cycle. Market risk is highest for securities with above-average price volatility and lowest for stable securities such as Treasury bills. Market risk is of little consequence to a person who purchases securities with the intention of holding them for long periods of time. **2.** —See SYSTEMATIC RISK.

market segmentation theory The theory that certain groups of investors are interested in certain types of investments to the exclusion of all others. For example, some investors purchase only short-term debt securities while others are interested only in long-term bonds. Likewise, certain individuals or institutions may limit their investments to common stocks.

market sentiment The intuitive feeling of the investment community regarding the expected movement of the stock market. For example, if market sentiment is bullish, then most investors expect an upward move in the stock market.

market share The proportion of industry sales of a good or service controlled by a firm. Some investors prefer companies with relatively large market shares since they are generally less likely to be squeezed by competitors.

market technician —See TECHNICIAN.

market timing The purchase and sale of securities based on short-term price patterns as well as on asset values. Some analysts use fundamental analysis to select the securities to purchase or sell; then they rely on market timing to decide when to trade those securities.

market to book A ratio comparing the market price of a firm's common stock with the stock's book value per share. Essentially, the market to book ratio relates what the investors believe a firm is worth to what the firm's accountants say it is worth according to accepted accounting principles. A low ratio indicates investors' belief that the firm's assets have been overvalued on its financial statements. —Also called *price-to-book-value ratio*.

market tone The condition of a securities market with respect to trading activity and strength of prices. An active market with steady or strong prices has a good tone.

market top The high point of stock prices measured by one or more of the stock averages or indices. —See also MARKET BOTTOM.

market value **1.** The price at which a security currently can be sold. **2.** —See MARKET CAPITALIZATION.

market value weighted average A measure of security prices adjusted according to the market value of each security included in the average. The greater a firm's number of shares outstanding and the higher the price of the shares, the greater the weight of that security in a market value weighted average. The Standard & Poor's 500 is a market value weighted average. —See also PRICE WEIGHTED AVERAGE.

mark to the market The adjustment of an account to reflect gains and losses at the end of a trading period. This adjustment is especially relevant in accounts trading commodity futures because it is used daily in determining whether or not the appropriate margin is being maintained. —See also TAX STRADDLE.

markup **1.** An upward revaluation of a security by a dealer because of a rise in the security's market price. For example, a dealer may decide that a markup on a security issue held in inventory is in order because of a rising stock market. —See also MARKDOWN 1. **2.** —See also SPREAD 3. **3.** The difference between the price charged by a dealer to a retail customer and the prevailing price at which the same security is being offered by market makers. —See also MARKDOWN 2.

married put and stock A put and stock that are purchased at the same time so that a hedge position can be established. This purchase provides the investor with unlimited upside potential with the put acting as insurance against losses from a declining stock price.

marry a stock To hold a stock for long periods of time regardless of other investment opportunities or indications that the security should be sold. Most investment advisers consider it unwise to marry a stock since the investor's needs and the desirability of a particular stock will change over time.

master limited partnership (MLP) A limited partnership that provides an investor with a direct interest in a group of assets (generally, oil and gas properties). Master limited partnership units trade publicly like stock and thus provide the investor significantly more liquidity than ordinary limited partnerships do. —See also ROLL-UP.

matched and lost A report to a customer from a broker that an order was not executed because it lost out to another broker with an order of equal priority. When two or more orders are considered equal, the brokers must match to determine which one is executed.

matched book The position of a broker-dealer when funds borrowed are equal to funds lent to customers.

matched orders **1.** The purchase and sale of the same security by an individual or organized group of individuals to give the impression of unusual trading activity in the security. Matching orders is intended to get other investors interested in a particular security, but it is illegal. **2.** A balance of buy orders and sell orders before the opening of trading in a security.

matching —See PORTFOLIO DEDICATION.

material Of sufficient importance or relevance as to have possible significant impact on an outcome. For example, the possibility that a firm might lose its right to operate a number of television stations because competitors have filed with the Federal Communications Commission for those licenses would be a material fact in preparing the firm's financial statements. —See also IMMATERIAL.

matrix trading Swapping bonds of different classes or risk levels to take advantage of unusual differences in yield. For example, during a period when the difference between yields on AAA and AA bonds is especially small, an investor swaps AA bonds for AAA bonds to pick up added safety at a small sacrifice in yield. When the difference in yields widens, the investor then swaps back to the higher risk, higher yielding AA-rated bonds.

mature industry An industry in which future growth is so limited that firms in it must grow by taking sales from competitors or by diversifying. Stocks of firms in mature industries often have high dividend yields and sell at low price-earnings ratios. Owing to their limited growth prospects, these stocks are most appropriate for conservative investors seeking high current income. The automotive, petroleum, and tobacco industries are examples of mature businesses.

maturing liability A debt to be paid within a short period of time.

maturity The date on which payment of a financial obligation is due. In the case of a bond, the maturity date is the one on which the issuer must retire the bond by paying the face value of the bond to its owners. Shares of stock do not have specific maturity dates.

maturity basis In calculating yield, the premise that a bond will be held to maturity. —See also YIELD TO MATURITY.

maturity value The amount to be paid to the holder of a financial obligation at the obligation's maturity. In the case of a bond, the maturity value is the principal amount (i.e., of the bond) to be paid by the issuer to the owner at maturity.

May Day May 1, 1975, the day on which brokerage commissions on securities became negotiable. May Day ushered in discount brokerage firms that charge investors reduced fees. —See also NEGOTIATED COMMISSION.

MBIA —See MUNICIPAL BOND INSURANCE ASSOCIATION.

MCE —See MIDAMERICA COMMODITY EXCHANGE.

mean term —See DURATION.

medium-term bond —See INTERMEDIATE BOND.

member One that owns a seat on a commodities or securities exchange. —See also ALLIED MEMBER.

member firm A securities firm with officers or partners who are members of an organized securities exchange. National brokerage firms are generally members of a number of organized exchanges. Organized exchanges have established standards of conduct and financial conditions required of members. —See also ABC AGREEMENT.

member short sale ratio The ratio of shares sold short by New York Stock Exchange (NYSE) members compared with total short sales. Because NYSE members are thought to be knowledgeable about market conditions and trends, a high member short sale ratio is considered bearish and a low member short sale ratio is considered bullish.

Merc —See CHICAGO MERCANTILE EXCHANGE.

merger A combination of two or more companies in which the assets and liabilities of the selling firm(s) are absorbed by the buying firm. Although the buying firm may be a considerably different organization after the merger, it retains its original identity. —See also CONSOLIDATION; DOWNSTREAM MERGER; SYNERGY.

mezzanine bracket The list of underwriters playing a moderately important role in a securities offering. —See also BRACKETING; MAJOR BRACKET; TOMBSTONE.

MGIC Indemnity Corporation A subsidiary of MGIC Investment Corporation that insures the tax-exempt portfolios of mutual funds and unit investment trusts as to payment of interest and principal. —See also AMERICAN MUNICIPAL BOND ASSURANCE CORPORATION; MUNICIPAL BOND INSURANCE ASSOCIATION.

MidAmerica Commodity Exchange (MCE) A Chicago exchange that provides facilities for the trading of commodity and financial futures contracts. Of special interest on this Exchange are the downsized versions of contracts traded on other exchanges.

Midwest Stock Exchange (MSE) The most active of the regional securities exchanges, providing facilities in Chicago for trading stocks and bonds. Unique regional securities as well as national-interest stocks listed on other exchanges are traded on it.

MIG —See MOODY'S INVESTMENT GRADE.

minicoupon bond A bond with a coupon lower than the market rate of interest at the time of issue, resulting in sale of the bond at a discount from face value at issuance. A zero-coupon bond is a special type of minicoupon bond. —See also DEEP-DISCOUNT BOND; ORIGINAL-ISSUE DISCOUNT BOND.

mini manipulation Manipulation of a security underlying an option so as to influence the market value of the option. Because stock price changes often produce magnified changes in the value of options, mini manipulation, while illegal, can produce enhanced profits for the manipulators.

minimum maintenance —See MAINTENANCE MARGIN REQUIREMENT.

minimum tax —See ALTERNATIVE MINIMUM TAX.

minimum tick The smallest possible price movement of a security or contract. For example, equity options with a premium of 3 points and greater are traded in eighths of a point while equity options with premiums under 3 points may be quoted at $\frac{1}{16}$-of-a-point intervals. —Also called *trading variation.*

minority interest 1. From an accounting viewpoint, ownership by the parent company of less than 100% of an affiliated firm. 2. From a financial standpoint, proportional ownership of a firm insufficient to constitute control. Generally, minority interest is viewed as ownership of under 50% of the voting shares.

minus (−) **1.** —Used in the net change column of security transaction tables to indicate a closing price lower than the closing price on the last previous day that the security was traded. **2.** —Used in reporting closed-end investment company share prices to indicate the percentage amount by which net asset value exceeds market price. —See also PLUS 2.

minus tick —See DOWNTICK.

missing the market Failing to execute a customer's order at an available price that was favorable to the customer. For example, through oversight on the part of the broker, a customer's limit order to purchase stock at $20 might not be executed even though the stock traded at less than $20 after the order was entered. The broker who misses the market is generally responsible for making good on the order.

MIT —See MARKET IF TOUCHED.

mixed account A brokerage account with long and short security positions.

MLP —See MASTER LIMITED PARTNERSHIP.

Mo —Used in earnings reports in newspapers to identify the Montreal Stock Exchange as the primary market of a firm's common stock.

mobile home certificate A security issued by the Government National Mortgage Association that is secured by mortgages on mobile homes. Mobile home certificates pass through interest payments and principal repayments to investors.

model An abstraction of reality, generally referring in investments to a mathematical formula designed to determine security values. Economists also use models to project trends in economic variables such as interest rates, economic activity, and inflation rates.

modern portfolio theory —See PORTFOLIO THEORY.

momentum The tendency of a security to continue movement in a single direction. Momentum is the underlying factor behind trend analysis of stock prices.

monetarism An economic theory, the proponents of which argue that economic variations, such as changes in prices and output, are primarily the result of changes in the money supply. (Thus, the Federal Reserve Board is the most important economic policymaker in the country.) Proponents of monetarism believe that changes in the money supply precede changes in other economic variables including stock prices and that a rational policy calls for moderate, steady increases in the money supply. —See also MONEY SUPPLY.

monetarist A proponent, usually an economist, of monetarism. Milton Friedman is probably America's best-known monetarist.

monetary gain The gain in purchasing power derived from holding monetary assets and/or monetary liabilities during a period of changing prices. An increase in prices tends to devalue monetary assets and monetary liabilities. Thus, if a firm's monetary liabilities exceeded its monetary assets, inflation would tend to produce monetary gains.

monetary items Assets on a firm's balance sheet that are fixed in dollar amount. Cash, short-term loans, and long-term bonds are monetary items.

monetary policy Federal Reserve actions to influence the availability and cost of money. Specific policy includes changing the discount rate, altering bank reserve requirements, and open-market operations. In general, a policy to restrict monetary growth results in tightened credit conditions and, at least temporarily, higher rates of interest. This situation can be expected to have a negative impact on the security markets in the short run, although the long-run effects may be positive because of reduced inflationary pressures. —See also ACCOMMODATIVE MONETARY POLICY; FISCAL POLICY.

monetize the debt To convert government debt from interest-bearing securities into money. Although both the securities and the money are considered government debt, the latter can be used for purchasing goods and services. Thus, monetizing the debt is considered an inflationary process and, although it may temporarily depress interest rates, it is likely to result in higher interest rates and lower bond prices over the long run. —See also ACCOMMODATIVE MONETARY POLICY; DEFICIT FINANCING.

money A generally accepted medium for the exchange of goods and services, for measuring value, or for making payments. Many economists consider the amount of money and growth in the amount of money in an economy very influential in determining interest rates, inflation, and the level of economic activity. There is some disagreement among economists as to what types of things actually should be classified as money; e.g., should balances in money market funds be included? —See also MONEY SUPPLY.

money manager —See PORTFOLIO MANAGER.

money market The market for trading short-term, low-risk securities such as commercial paper, U.S. Treasury bills, bankers' acceptances, and negotiable certificates of deposit. The market is made up of dealers in these securities who are linked by electronic communications.

money market center bank A big commercial bank located in a large metropolitan center. Money market center banks play a leading role in trading financial instruments, determining market interest rates, and providing leadership to commercial banks located outside the money centers.

money-market deposit account A savings account at a commercial bank or thrift institution that pays a return competitive with money market funds. The number of transactions that may take place each month is limited. Institutions offering the accounts may require a minimum balance in order to receive money market yields. Because of their liquidity and adequate returns, these accounts are ideal temporary repositories for funds awaiting more permanent investment.

money market fund A mutual fund that sells shares of ownership and uses the proceeds to purchase short-term, high quality securities such as Treasury bills, negotiable certificates of deposit, and commercial paper. Income earned by shareholders is received in the form of additional shares of stock in the fund (normally priced at $1 each). Although no fees are generally charged to purchase or redeem shares in a money market fund, an annual management charge is levied by the fund's advisors. This investment pays a return that varies with short-term interest rates. It is relatively liquid and safe, but yields and features vary. —Also called *liquid asset fund*.

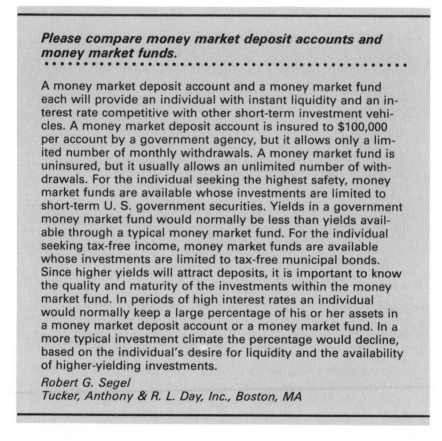

Please compare money market deposit accounts and money market funds.

A money market deposit account and a money market fund each will provide an individual with instant liquidity and an interest rate competitive with other short-term investment vehicles. A money market deposit account is insured to $100,000 per account by a government agency, but it allows only a limited number of monthly withdrawals. A money market fund is uninsured, but it usually allows an unlimited number of withdrawals. For the individual seeking the highest safety, money market funds are available whose investments are limited to short-term U. S. government securities. Yields in a government money market fund would normally be less than yields available through a typical money market fund. For the individual seeking tax-free income, money market funds are available whose investments are limited to tax-free municipal bonds. Since higher yields will attract deposits, it is important to know the quality and maturity of the investments within the money market fund. In periods of high interest rates an individual would normally keep a large percentage of his or her assets in a money market deposit account or a money market fund. In a more typical investment climate the percentage would decline, based on the individual's desire for liquidity and the availability of higher-yielding investments.

Robert G. Segel
Tucker, Anthony & R. L. Day, Inc., Boston, MA

money spread In options trading, the combination of buying one option and selling another option identical to it except for the strike price. For example, purchasing a January call with a strike price of $30 and selling a January call with a strike price of $25 is a money spread. —Also called *price spread; strike spread; vertical spread*.

money supply The amount of money in the economy. Since the money supply is considered by many to be a critical element in determining economic activity, the financial markets attach great importance to Federal Reserve reports of changes in the supply. For example, consistently large increases in the money supply bring fears of future inflation. There are a variety of measures of the supply of money depending on how strictly it is defined. —Also called *money stock.* —See also M1; M2; M3; MONETARISM.

monopoly A business that is the sole supplier for a particular good or service. Regulated monopolies, such as electric utilities, are generally restricted as to the returns they are permitted to earn. Other monopolies such as firms with unique products or services derived from patents, copyrights, or geographic location may be able to earn very high returns. —See also OLIGOPOLY; OLIGOPSONY.

monopoly Pertaining to or being a market in which there is a single seller of a particular good or service. For example, electric utilities nearly always operate in monopoly markets. —See also MONOPSONY; OLIGOPOLY; OLIGOPSONY.

monopsony Pertaining to or being a market in which there is a single buyer of a particular good or service. Businesses selling in a market characterized by monopsony are likely to suffer below-average profitability because of the lack of alternative outlets for their products. —See also MONOPOLY; OLIGOPSONY.

month order A security order which, if it has not been executed, is automatically canceled at the end of the calendar month during which it is entered. Month orders are monitored by the brokerage firms handling the orders rather than by specialists on the floor of an exchange. —Also called *good-this-month order.*

Montreal Stock Exchange An organized securities exchange for trading stocks and bonds, located in Montreal, Canada.

Moody's® A trademark for issuance of ratings denoting the relative investment quality of corporate and municipal bonds and for various financial publications including *The Handbook of Common Stocks*, *Moody's Manuals*, *Moody's Bond Record*, and *Moody's Stock Survey.*

Moody's Investment Grade (MIG) A rating system used by Moody's Investors Service for municipal notes. The rating classifies notes into four grades with MIG 1, meaning best quality; MIG 2, meaning high quality; MIG 3, meaning favorable quality; and MIG 4, meaning adequate quality.

moral obligation debt Government or municipal debt that carries an implied pledge of support but that is not explicitly guaranteed by the full faith and credit of the guarantor organization. Moral obligation debt is generally issued in order to circumvent legal restrictions on borrowing. The securities are rated lower and carry higher yields than general obligation bonds of the same issuer do.

mortgage A pledge of specific property as security for a loan. —See also FIRST MORTGAGE; REVERSE ANNUITY MORTGAGE; SECOND MORTGAGE.

mortgage-backed revenue bond A municipal bond, the proceeds of which are used to provide funds to financial institutions for making mortgage loans at relatively low interest rates. Interest and principal on the bond are backed by borrower payments on the mortgages. As with other revenue bonds, the quality varies significantly among different issues of these securities. —Also called *housing bond.*

mortgage banker An organization making real estate loans that are then resold by the mortgage banker to another party. The mortgage banker's income derives from the fees it charges to originate and service the mortgages. Sale of the mortgages gives the mortgage banker more funds to use in making additional loans.

mortgage bond A long-term debt security secured by a lien on specific assets—normally fixed assets such as real estate. —See also CLOSED-END MORTGAGE; OPEN-END MORTGAGE.

mortgage participation certificate A pass-through security that represents ownership in a pool of conventional mortgages put together by the Federal Home Loan Mortgage Corporation (FHLMC). Principal and interest on the certificates are guaranteed by FHLMC and the income is subject to federal, state, and local taxation. —See also PASS-THROUGH SECURITY.

mortgage pool A combination of similar mortgages used as collateral for loans or participations sold to investors. —Also called *pool.*

mortgage purchase bond A housing revenue bond, the proceeds of which have been used to purchase mortgages from lending institutions. Interest and principal payments are derived from payments on the mortgages underlying the bond issue.

mortgage REIT A real estate investment trust that combines investors' funds with other borrowed money to make loans on real estate. The return earned by the investors depends on the spread between the interest rates charged on the loans made and the interest rates paid on the loans taken out. Earnings on a mortgage REIT are subject to wide fluctuations if the REIT makes short-term loans and takes out long-term loans. —See also EQUITY REIT.

most-active list The list of the most-active securities in a specific market during a defined period of time. The most-active list is viewed with interest by analysts because it includes unusually active stocks frequently accompanied by large price movements.

most-active stocks Stocks with trading volume high enough to warrant inclusion on the most-active list. Some widely-held stocks with many shares outstanding (i.e., AT&T and IBM) routinely make the list. Other stocks make the list because of special circumstances such as a tender offer or an unexpected news item about the issuer.

moving average A series of successive averages of a defined number of variables. As each new variable is included in calculating the average, the last variable of the series is deleted. Suppose a stock's price at the end of each of the last 6 months is $40, $44, $50, $48, $50, and $52. The

4-month moving average in the fifth month is: ($44 + $50 + $48 + $50)/ 4, or $48. At the end of the sixth month, the 4-month moving average is ($50 + $48 + $50 + $52)/4, or $50. Technical analysts frequently use moving averages to discover trends in stock prices. —See also 200-DAY MOVING AVERAGE.

MSB —See MUTUAL SAVINGS BANK.

MSE —See MIDWEST STOCK EXCHANGE.

MSRB —See MUNICIPAL SECURITIES RULEMAKING BOARD.

multimaturity bond —See PUT BOND.

multinational Pertaining to or being a company with subsidiaries or other operations in a number of countries. The diversity of operations of such companies subjects them to unique risks (e.g., exchange rate changes or government nationalization) but at the same time offers them unique profit opportunities closed to domestic companies.

multiple —See PRICE-EARNINGS RATIO.

multiple management Apportionment of a large portfolio's assets among several managers, a process that permits the managers more flexibility, allows for closer monitoring of investments, and creates a competitive atmosphere among the managers. The major disadvantages are higher cost and the potential for lack of coordination in meeting the fund's overall investment goals.

multiple option strategy The use of more than a single option on the same underlying security at the same time. For example, an investor might buy a call on IBM at 135 with a May expiration and sell a call on IBM at the same strike price with an August expiration. A multiple option strategy may be as simple as buying a call and a put at the same time or it may be as complex as the investor desires (or can comprehend).

multiple round lots Stock transactions of 200 shares and over in units of 100 shares.

multiplier —See AMERICAN CURRENCY QUOTATION.

muni —See MUNICIPAL BOND.

municipal —See MUNICIPAL BOND.

Municipal Assistance Corporation for the City of New York (MAC) A public benefit corporation established in 1975 to provide assistance in financing New York City. MAC was authorized to issue its own debt securities backed by revenues from the sales tax, stock transfer tax, and per capita aid from the state. —See also BIG MAC.

municipal bond The debt issue of a city, county, state, or other political entity. Interest paid by most municipal bonds is exempt from federal income taxes and often from state and local taxes as well. The tax exemption stems from the use to which the funds from a bond issue have been devoted. Municipal bonds with tax-exempt interest appeal mainly to investors with significant amounts of other taxable income. —Also called *muni; municipal; tax-exempt bond.* —See also BOND BUYER'S INDEX;

ESSENTIAL FUNCTION BOND; EX-LEGAL; 501(C)(3) BOND; PRIVATE ACTIVITY BOND; TAXABLE MUNICIPAL BOND.

municipal bond fund A mutual fund that invests in tax-exempt securities and passes through tax-free current income to its shareholders. Some municipal bond funds purchase long-term securities providing a relatively high current yield but varying substantially in price with changes in interest rates. Other funds choose short-term securities having lower yields but fluctuating little in value. Municipal bond funds differ from municipal bond unit trusts in that the funds manage the bond portfolios and charge an annual management fee. —See also DOUBLE-EXEMPT FUND; JUNK MUNI-BOND FUND; TAX-EXEMPT MONEY MARKET FUND.

municipal bond insurance A guarantee from a third party that principal and interest will be paid to a bondholder. Municipal bond insurance is written by private corporations for a fee paid by issuers hoping to obtain higher ratings and lower interest costs. Investors purchasing insured bonds or insured trusts obtain increased safety at the cost of lower yields.

Municipal Bond Insurance Association (MBIA) A consortium of five private casualty insurance companies formed in 1974 to guarantee interest and principal payments on issues of municipal debt. The issuers pay a fee and, in return, the issues receive a higher rating and carry a lower interest rate. Aetna Casualty, Aetna Insurance, Continental, Fireman's Fund, and Travelers make up the consortium. —See also AMERICAN MUNICIPAL BOND ASSURANCE CORPORATION; MGIC INDEMNITY CORPORATION.

municipal bond unit trust An unmanaged portfolio of municipal securities that is put together at the time the units are initially sold. Tax-free interest and repayments of principal are passed through to the owners who are charged a fee of around 4% to acquire the units. This investment allows individuals to have a diversified portfolio of municipal bonds without investing large sums of money. —See also UNIT INVESTMENT TRUST.

municipal convertible A unique municipal bond that is issued at a large discount from face value because it pays no interest until a specified date, at which time interest payments begin and continue until maturity. For example, a bond issued in 1988 and due in 2015 might begin paying interest in 1998. Essentially, a municipal convertible is a combination of a zero-coupon bond and an ordinary interest-paying bond. Municipal convertibles are traded under a variety of acronyms including BIGS, CCAB, FIGS, GAINS®, PACS℠, STAIRS®, and TEDIS, depending on the underwriter of the particular issue.

Municipal Securities Rulemaking Board (MSRB) A 15-member self-regulatory board that sets and oversees the standards and practices of the municipal securities industry. The Board is of particular importance since the issuing and trading of municipal securities are not subject to much of the federal regulation affecting other security transactions.

mutilated security A stock or bond certificate that, because of damage or improper printing, cannot be transferred. The owner of a mutilated security must obtain a guarantee to ownership from the transfer agent before delivering the security to a buyer.

mutual company A company owned by its customers rather than by a separate group of stockholders. Many thrifts and insurance companies (e.g., Metropolitan and Prudential) are mutual companies. —See also STOCK COMPANY.

mutual fund An investment company that continually offers new shares and stands ready to redeem existing shares from the owners. Since the shares are purchased directly from and are sold directly to the mutual fund, there is no secondary market in these companies' stock. Individual mutual funds vary substantially in terms of the types of investments, the sales charges (many have none), and the management fees. —Also called *open-end investment company.* —See also CLONE FUND; CLOSED-END INVESTMENT COMPANY; FAMILY OF FUNDS; LOAD FUND; MUTUAL FUND CUSTODIAN; REGULATED INVESTMENT COMPANY; REINVESTMENT PRIVILEGE.

Finding socially responsible mutual funds: Is performance sacrificed on the altar of ideology?
• •

Sometimes yes, sometimes no. The issue facing the "socially responsible investor" is not performance per se, but diversification and opportunity cost. In some periods, investing in nuclear utilities or in South African gold mines or defense stocks has made a lot of money for investors versus the broad market; in other periods, these industries have lagged major benchmarks. By imposing a social responsibility test the investor limits opportunity and increases potential risk; however, the outcome in terms of "return" is not forecastable and only time will tell if the markets agree with the investor with a conscience.

Allan R. Emkin, Vice President
Wilshire Associates, Santa Monica, CA

---

mutual fund cash-to-assets ratio The proportion of total assets held in cash by mutual funds. Because cash indicates liquidity and potential buying power on the part of mutual funds, a high ratio is generally considered bullish and a low ratio is considered bearish. —See also SENTIMENT INDEX.

mutual fund custodian An organization that holds in custody the securities owned by a mutual fund. —See also CUSTODIAN.

mutual savings bank (MSB) A deposit-gathering thrift institution that makes chiefly mortgage loans. Mutual savings banks, typically located in the northeastern states, are organized much like savings and loan associations. MSBs are technically not depositor-owned although all are state-chartered. —Also called *savings bank.*

N

n —Used in stock transaction tables in newspapers to indicate a new stock that has been listed within the last 52 weeks. The high and low prices are for a period of less than a year: *WeinR n.*

N —Used in earnings reports in newspapers to identify the New York Stock Exchange as the primary market of a firm's common stock.

na —Used in bond transaction tables in newspapers to indicate a bond that trades on a nonaccrual basis (that is, on the basis of no obligation to repay any back interest owed).

naked option An opening transaction in an option when the underlying asset is not owned. An investor writing a call option on 100 shares of IBM without owning the stock is writing a naked option. If the stock is called by the option holder, the writer must purchase shares in the market for delivery and is therefore caught naked. —Also called *uncovered option.* —See also COVERED OPTION.

naked position A security position, either long or short, that is not hedged. For example, an investor short 500 shares of IBM with no other position in IBM stock (such as ownership of calls) has a naked position in that security. Since a naked position subjects the investor to large potential gains or losses, it is an aggressive investment position.

naked writer The writer or seller of an option who does not also own the underlying security.

narrow basis A market condition in which only a small difference exists between a spot price and futures prices for the same type of contract. —See also WIDE BASIS.

narrow the spread To reduce the difference between the bid price and ask price for a security. Market makers will narrow the spread as trading in a particular security becomes more active and competition increases.

NASD —See NATIONAL ASSOCIATION OF SECURITIES DEALERS.

NASDAQ —See NATIONAL ASSOCIATION OF SECURITIES DEALERS AUTO-MATED QUOTATION SYSTEM.

NASDAQ National Market System A system for reporting transactions of active over-the-counter securities such that volume, high, low, and last price quotations are available. The increased information accessible to investors on this system is one of the major steps toward establishing a true national market system for securities.

NASDAQ OTC Composite Index An index that indicates price movements of securities in the over-the-counter market. It includes all domestic OTC common stocks in the NASDAQ System (approximately 2,400) and is weighted according to the market value of each listed issue. The Index was initiated in 1971 with a base of 100. Six specialized industry indices are also published.

National Association of Securities Dealers (NASD) An association of over-the-counter (OTC) brokers and dealers that establishes legal and ethical standards of conduct for its members. NASD was established in 1939 to regulate the OTC market in much the same manner as organized exchanges monitor actions of their members. One major advantage to membership is that members sell securities at wholesale to other members but at retail to nonmembers. —See also RULES OF FAIR PRACTICE; UNIFORM PRACTICE CODE.

National Association of Securities Dealers Automated Quotation System (NASDAQ) A computerized system for storing and displaying current price quotations on a large number of the more active securities traded in the over-the-counter (OTC) market. Dealers making markets in NASDAQ listed stocks constantly monitor and update their own quotations on the System. Since most OTC securities are less active and are not included on the System, brokers have to call individual dealers to obtain current quotations on these issues. The System provides three levels of service depending on the needs of its users. —See also CODE OF PROCEDURE; LEVEL 1; LEVEL 2; LEVEL 3.

National Clearing Corporation (NCC) A subsidiary of the National Association of Securities Dealers through which transactions in the over-the-counter market are compared by broker-dealers. The National Clearing Corporation is similar in concept to the Securities Industry Automation Corporation that is used for comparisons of exchange transactions.

National Futures Association (NFA) A futures industry self-regulatory body established in 1982. The NFA serves a variety of functions including making rules, registering brokers, and arbitrating disputes. The NFA is to the futures industry what the NASD is to the securities industry. —See also COMMODITY FUTURES TRADING COMMISSION.

nationalization A government takeover of private property or operations. The government may or may not compensate the property owners. Multinational companies with operations in Third World countries have frequently seen their assets nationalized.

national list Securities included in the national market system.

national market system (NMS) 1. A centralized system for reporting transactions and quotations from all qualified market makers. A national market system has been encouraged by the Securities and Exchange Commission as a trading system that would increase competition among exchanges and market makers, thus providing investors with more liquidity and better prices. Essentially, a national market system is envisioned as a single large market in which market makers are linked by telecommunications with information being freely available. Customer orders would be automatically filled at the best available prices. 2. —See NASDAQ NATIONAL MARKET SYSTEM.

National Quotation Bureau   A private organization that compiles and distributes dealer bid and ask prices for securities traded in the over-the-counter market. Corporate bond quotes are distributed on yellow sheets, while stock quotes appear on pink sheets.

National Securities Clearing Corporation (NSCC)   A jointly-owned firm of the New York Stock Exchange, the American Stock Exchange, and the National Association of Securities Dealers, that settles accounts among brokerage firms. NSCC nets trades among the firms and directs payments and security transfers appropriate to each participant. —See also CONTINUOUS NET SETTLEMENT.

National Securities Trading System (NSTS)   An automated centralized quotation system used by the Cincinnati Stock Exchange that permits brokers to enter orders for certain securities and expose them to other brokers and dealers around the country. This experiment in developing a national market for securities differs from the Intermarket Trading System in that the Intermarket Trading System connects only specialists on the organized exchanges.

natural corner   A corner in a security not caused by manipulation. If two groups are secretly attempting a takeover of a firm while speculators are shorting the stock, the raiders may achieve a corner without having intended to squeeze the short sellers. This maneuver differs from most corners in which the buyers lend stock to the short sellers with the intention of making the short sellers repurchase the shares at an artificially high price.

NAV   —See NET ASSET VALUE PER SHARE.

NC   —See NONCALLABLE.

NCC   —See NATIONAL CLEARING CORPORATION.

nearby   In futures and options trading, the contract month with the closest delivery or expiration. —Also called *lead month*. —See also FURTHEREST OUT.

near money   Assets that can be converted quickly and easily into cash with virtually no loss in value. Examples of near money are savings account balances and Treasury bills.

neckline   A line connecting the two bottom points on the intermediate declines of a head-and-shoulders chart formation. In an inverted head-and-shoulders formation, the neckline connects the two intermediate tops. If the second shoulder breaks through the neckline, it is an indication of a major price movement in the direction of the breakout.

negative carry   The net cost of an investment position when the cost of carrying the investment exceeds the current income from the investment. For example, buying a bond with a current yield of 10% and financing the purchase with money borrowed at 13% will result in a negative carry. —See also CARRYING CHARGES 1; POSITIVE CARRY.

negative covenant   A clause in a loan agreement that prohibits the borrower from an activity. For example, a negative covenant may restrict the payment of dividends or the issuance of new debt. —See also POSITIVE COVENANT.

negative net worth An excess of liabilities over assets. If the assets are fairly valued, a firm with negative net worth could sell all its assets and then be unable to pay all its outstanding loans. Thus, nothing would remain for the owners. —Also called *deficit net worth*.

negative pledge clause A restriction in a borrowing agreement that limits a borrower's ability to issue new debt having a priority claim on the firm's assets. A negative pledge clause, a part of some debenture agreements, protects the creditors against a dilution of security.

negative yield curve An unusual relationship between bond yields and maturity lengths that results from lower interest rates on long-term bonds than the interest rates on short-term bonds. The word *negative* refers to the downward slope of the curve that is drawn to depict this relationship. —Also called *inverted yield curve.* —See also FLAT YIELD CURVE; POSITIVE YIELD CURVE; YIELD CURVE.

What should investors do when short-term rates exceed long-term rates?
• •

By its very existence, a negative yield curve should be viewed as a market consensus or prediction that interest rates are going to fall, because the market in general has commanded a higher yield for short maturity periods than it has required to attract investment dollars for longer maturity periods. A negative yield curve is usually followed by a flattening and then by a positive yield curve. When this happens, yields on short maturities would probably fall substantially. This shift could occur for various reasons, e.g., as a result of the market coming to expect an easing of inflation; thus, yields on longer maturities would also be expected to decline. The longer the maturity, the greater the profit potential for a given decline in yields.

Stephanie R. Goldsborough, Treasury Officer
Maryland National Bank, Baltimore, MD

---

negotiable **1.** Pertaining to or being a price that is not firmly established. **2.** Describing an instrument that is easily transferable from one owner to another owner. With proper endorsement, most securities are negotiable.

negotiable certificate of deposit A large denomination ($100,000 and over) certificate of deposit that is issued in bearer form and that can be traded in the secondary market. Negotiable CDs appeal mainly to companies and institutional investors interested in low-risk investments with a high degree of liquidity. —See also MONEY MARKET.

negotiable order of withdrawal —See NOW ACCOUNT.

negotiable security —See MARKETABLE SECURITY.

negotiated commission A fee for trading securities that is subject to bargaining between the customer and the brokerage firm. Negotiated commissions became widespread in the United States beginning in 1975. —See also DISCOUNT BROKERAGE FIRM; MAY DAY.

Can individual investors negotiate commissions at a full-service brokerage firm? By how much in general?
● ●

The amount of commission in a full-service brokerage firm is dictated by the size and frequency of trades. In general, the percentage commission declines as volume increases. Discount brokerage does not mean that you will necessarily receive the cheapest execution. The amount of the discount can vary. It's not unlike discounting in the retail business. You can find loss leaders, designed to attract business, but overall the rates may not be in your favor. It's also good to remember that you get what you *should* get—that is, what you pay for. If a full-service brokerage firm charges you more than you could get else-where, you should also expect an increased level of service to include:

1. A personal portfolio review;
2. Availability of research;
3. Access to a cash management account, which can include check access to cash and/or credit lines;
4. Detailed monthly statements;
5. A year-end summary for tax preparation;
6. Call alerts on bonds;
7. Accessibility to one financial consultant for financial advice and counsel.

Kathleen Hegenbart, Vice President, Financial Consultant
Shearson Lehman Brothers, Newton Centre, MA

---

negotiated offering A method by which a securities issuer selects an investment banking firm to assist in or guarantee the sale of securities on the basis of discussions and factors including the best price. —See also COMPETITIVE BIDDING 1.

net 1. For the closing transaction in a security, the difference between net proceeds from the sale and the total outlay for the purchase. 2. —See NET INCOME.

net assets —See OWNERS' EQUITY.

net asset value per share (NAV) The market value of an investment company's assets less any liabilities divided by the number of shares outstanding. This factor illustrates the amount a shareholder would receive for each share owned if the fund sold all its assets (stocks, bonds, etc.) at their current market value, paid off any outstanding debts with the proceeds, and then distributed the remainder to the stockholders. In general, net asset value per share is the price an investor would receive when selling a fund's shares back to the fund. Net asset value per share is similar in concept to book value per share for other types of firms.

net capital requirement The minimal ratio of cash and assets readily convertible to cash as a proportion of total indebtedness that broker-dealers must maintain. The net capital requirement is set and monitored by the Securities and Exchange Commission. —See also RULE 15C3–1.

net change The points or dollars by which the closing price of a security or a security average has changed from the closing price on the last previous day it traded. For example, a net change of −½ indicates a 50¢-per-share decline from the last previous closing price to the present closing price. —Also called *change; price change.*

net current assets —See WORKING CAPITAL.

net income Income after all expenses and taxes have been deducted. Net income, the most frequently viewed figure in a firm's financial statements, is used in calculating various profitability and stock performance measures including price-earnings ratio, return on equity, earnings per share, and many others. —Also called *aftertax profit; bottom line; net; net profit; profit.* —See also GROSS PROFIT.

net lease A lease in which the costs of maintaining the asset including taxes and insurance are paid by the lessee. —See also GROSS LEASE.

net loss The operating result when expenses exceed revenues for a given period. —See also LOSS.

net margin —See NET PROFIT MARGIN.

net plant and equipment —See PLANT AND EQUIPMENT.

net present value The discounted value of an investment's cash inflows less the discounted value of its cash outflows. To be adequately profitable, an investment should have a net present value greater than zero. For investment in securities, the initial cost is normally the only outflow. —See also PRESENT VALUE.

net proceeds Revenues from the sale of an asset reduced by commissions or other expenses directly related to the sale. Net proceeds from a security's sale equal the security's price times the number of shares sold less the brokerage commission and any taxes or other fees derived from the sale. —See also PROCEEDS.

net profit —See NET INCOME.

net profit margin Aftertax net income divided by net sales, a measure of management's ability to carry a dollar of sales down to the bottom line for the stockholders. In other words, net profit margin refers to that which is left for the owners from a dollar of sales after all expenses and taxes have been paid. —Also called *net margin*. —See also GROSS PROFIT MARGIN; RETURN ON SALES.

net quick assets Current assets readily convertible into cash, less current liabilities. A large amount of net quick assets often characterizes a conservative firm with a very liquid financial position. —See also QUICK RATIO.

net realized capital gains per share For an investment company, the excess of realized long-term capital gains over realized long-term capital losses per share outstanding.

net sales Gross sales for a period after cash discounts, returns, and freight expenses have been deducted. —See also GROSS SALES.

net tangible assets per share Tangible assets less liabilities and the par value of preferred stock divided by the number of common shares outstanding. Net tangible assets per share is frequently used by investors and raiders seeking undervalued stocks.

net transaction A transaction in which no additional fees are paid. For example, securities that are part of a new issue are priced to include all fees.

Network A The reporting service of the consolidated tape that includes price and volume data for trades on the New York Stock Exchange (NYSE) and on regional exchanges and the over-the-counter market in NYSE-listed stocks. The service is carried in brokerage offices, on cable television, and by the reporting exchanges. —Also called *A-network*.

Network B The reporting service of the consolidated tape that includes price and volume data for round-lot trades on the American Stock Exchange (AMEX), on regional exchanges, and the over-the-counter market in AMEX-listed stocks. —Also called *B-network*.

net working capital —See WORKING CAPITAL.

net worth Total assets minus total liabilities. For an individual, total assets are recorded at current market value. For a company, net worth uses assets as recorded on the balance sheet at historical cost less any depreciation. —See also OWNERS' EQUITY.

neutral A security position that is neither bearish nor bullish.

neutral hedge ratio The number of options contracts necessary to offset exactly any changes in the price of a contract's underlying asset. This ratio varies depending on the time to expiration and the difference between the asset's market price and the option's strike price. It approaches 1 when the option is near maturity and is in-the-money.

new account report A form listing investment objectives, income, net worth, and other personal financial information that brokers must complete for each new customer. The information in a new account report is supposed to assist the broker in choosing the types of investments appropriate for a particular investor.

new issue A security that is being initially offered to the public. New stock issues are often quite risky; the securities may change significantly in price shortly after the initial sale has been completed. The greatest number of new issues generally appear near the end of an extended bull market. —See also OFFERING PRICE.

What to look for in new issues. Who should buy new issues?

Bear in mind that the offering usually reflects high prices for the kind of stock it is. All new issues are not necessarily attractive. Consider the prices of similar stocks and the investment banker's track record.

J. Kendrick Noble, Jr., First Vice President
PaineWebber Incorporated, New York, NY

---

new issue market —See PRIMARY MARKET.

new listing A security that has recently been added to an organized exchange's trading list. The security may have been moved from the over-the-counter market or from a different exchange, or it may be the stock of a firm that recently went public.

new money In corporate or U.S. Treasury debt refunding, the amount by which the par value of new securities exceeds the par value of the securities being refunded. The new money is the additional funds borrowed from the refunding operation.

new money preferred Preferred stock issued subsequent to October 1, 1942. Corporate owners of new money preferred are permitted to exclude 80% of the stock dividends from taxation.

New York Cotton Exchange (NYCE) An organized securities exchange located in New York City that provides facilities for trading futures and futures options in cotton, orange juice, and the consumer price index.

New York Futures Exchange (NYFE) A wholly-owned subsidiary of the New York Exchange formed in 1979 to provide facilities for trading futures and futures options contracts. Most trading on this Exchange is in NYSE composite stock index futures.

New York Mercantile Exchange (NYM) An organized exchange for the trading of futures contracts in potatoes, precious metals, and energy-related commodities such as oil and gasoline.

New York Stock Exchange (NYSE), Inc. The largest and oldest organized securities exchange in the United States. The NYSE, founded in 1792, currently trades about 85% of the nation's listed securities. Most large publicly traded firms' stock including all those listed in the Dow Jones Averages, list their stock on the NYSE. The NYSE operates as an auction market in which orders are brought to the trading floor for execution. Specialists at various locations on the floor are assigned stocks for trading. The specialists bring buyers and sellers together. They also buy and sell for their own accounts. The Exchange, which has 1,469 members, lists over 1,600 securities. —See also BOND ROOM; GARAGE; SECURITIES EXCHANGE.

New York Stock Exchange Index A composite index made up of all the stocks listed on the New York Stock Exchange and weighted according to the market value (stock price times shares outstanding) of each security. The base was set at 50 when the Index was established in 1966. Four specialized indices for industrial, transportation, finance, and utility issues are also computed and published.

next day Pertaining to a transaction requiring settlement one business day following the trade date. For example, options require next day settlement.

next-out In futures trading, the contract month immediately after the nearest available delivery.

NFA —See NATIONAL FUTURES ASSOCIATION.

nifty fifty Fifty large growth stocks that tend to be favorite holdings of institutional investors. These stocks typically have large numbers of shares outstanding and a history of consistently rising earnings and dividends. Examples include DuPont, General Electric, and Amoco. —Also called *favorite fifty; institutional favorites.*

nine bond rule A requirement of the New York Stock Exchange that members' customer orders for nine or fewer bonds be sent to the trading floor in an attempt to secure an execution. Although the rule does not guarantee execution, it at least permits small orders temporary exposure to the marketplace. —Also called *Rule 396.*

19c3 stock A stock that may be traded by an exchange member as well as on an exchange because it was listed after April 26, 1979. Prior to this date, exchange members were prohibited from making a market in exchange-listed securities. Thus, the change permits a member of an exchange to act as principal in making a market in a 19c3 stock as well as to act as an agent in trading on the floor. These stocks are named for Securities and Exchange Commission Rule 19c3 permitting off-board trading.

N.L. —Used in the offer price column of mutual fund transaction tables in newspapers to indicate the shares of a no-load fund: *Welsley 14.83 N.L. +.04.*

NMS —See NATIONAL MARKET SYSTEM 1.

no-action letter A response from the Securities and Exchange Commission staff to an individual inquiry, stating that the staff will recommend to the Commission that no action be taken on a specific transaction if the transaction is carried out in the fashion indicated.

no-load fund An open-end investment company, shares of which are sold without a sales charge. No-load funds sell directly to customers at net asset value with no intermediate salesperson charging a fee. No-load funds can be expected to perform on a par with other funds that do charge a sales fee. —See also LOAD FUND; LOW-LOAD FUND.

What factors should I keep in mind when considering no-load funds?

Base your decision to buy a no-load fund on sound educated thinking. During 1986, sixteen of 25 top performing mutual funds were no-load. Does that mean you can automatically invest in any no-load fund? Definitely not. Here are some things you should consider before investing:

- Does this fund meet my investment objective(s)? If you don't know the answer, carefully evaluate your financial needs to narrow down the type of fund best suited for the job.
- "I've narrowed down my choice to a particular fund type. What now?" Using sound reference sources, look for the funds that appear to parallel your investment style and degree of aggressiveness. Select the one, or ones, offering good (not necessarily spectacular) track records in up and down years.
- "Now what?" Now, look at what the fund(s) charge(s). All things being equal, if your list has a fund that has no front-end, contingent, or redemption/exit/back-end sales fees, consider it. Next look for funds with low or no 12b–1 charges. The funds with the lowest overall charges make it to the finals. Check their prospectuses, statements of additional information, and latest reports. Look for a fund in a family and opt for telephone switching privileges if available.

RECAP: Don't be a lemming. Make an intelligent investment choice based on your financial objectives, advantages and performance. The fund you select should do what you want at the lowest price.

Rudolph D. Watz, CLU, ChFC
Vice President, Director, Retirement Plans
Value Line Securities, Inc., New York, NY

---

nominal exercise price The price at which an option on a Government National Mortgage Association (GNMA) certificate can be exercised. The nominal exercise price is calculated by multiplying the adjusted exercise price of the option by the unpaid principal balance on the GNMA certificate. —See also GINNIE MAE PASS THROUGH.

nominal interest rate The stated rate of interest, exclusive of any compounding, that is paid on an investment. Annual interest of $80 on a

$1,000 investment is a nominal rate of 8% whether the interest is paid in $20 quarterly installments, in $40 semiannual installments, or in an $80 annual payment. Use of nominal rates can be misleading in comparing returns on different investments. —See also EFFECTIVE RATE OF INTEREST.

nominal quote   The approximate price of a security although no firm bid or ask price is implied. —Also called *subject quote.* —See also FIRM QUOTE.

nominal return   The rate of return on an investment without adjustment for inflation. While nominal return is useful in comparing the returns from different investments, it can be a very misleading indication of true investor earnings on an investment. —See also REAL RETURN.

nominee   A person or an organization in whose name a security is registered even though true ownership is held by another party.

nonassessable capital stock   Capital stock for which owners cannot be assessed additional funds to cover any liabilities of the firm. Thus, an owner of nonassessable capital stock can lose no more than his or her original investment. Nonassessable stock is the dominant kind issued in the United States.

noncallable (NC)   A provision of some bond and preferred stock issues that prohibits the issuer from redeeming the security before a certain date, or, in some cases, until maturity. A noncallable provision operates to the advantage of the investor. —See also CALL PROTECTION; NONREFUNDABLE.

nonclearing member   A member of a securities exchange that does not belong to the exchange's clearing facility. Rather, the nonclearing member pays another firm to provide the service.

noncompetitive bid   A method of purchasing U.S. Treasury bills at the weekly public auction without having to submit a price. With a noncompetitive bid, the investor agrees to purchase a given amount of securities (a minimum of $10,000 and a maximum of $500,000) at the average price set at the auction. Noncompetitive bids permit small investors to participate in the auction.

noncontributory pension plan   A pension plan in which the participating employees are not required to support the plan with contributions. —See also CONTRIBUTORY PENSION PLAN.

noncumulative   Designating a relatively unusual kind of preferred stock on which missed dividends do not have to be made up. —See also CUMULATIVE.

noncurrent asset   An asset that is not expected to be turned into cash within one year during the normal course of business. Noncurrent assets include buildings, land, equipment, and other assets held for relatively long periods. Noncurrent assets are generally more profitable than current assets, but they also entail more risk because they are more difficult to turn into cash and are likely to fluctuate in value more than current assets.

noncurrent liablity A liability not due to be paid within one year during the normal course of business. A long-term debt issue is a noncurrent liability.

nondiversifiable risk —See SYSTEMATIC RISK.

nondiversified management company An investment company that does not agree to be subject to the investment limitations required of a diversified management company. Many venture capital funds, not wishing to be subject to diversification requirements, are classed as nondiversified management companies. —See also DIVERSIFIED MANAGEMENT COMPANY.

nonequity option An option for which the underlying asset is anything other than stock. Nonequity options include commodity options, currency options, debt options, and stock index options. —See also EQUITY OPTION; SECTION 1256 CONTRACTS.

nonessential function bond —See PRIVATE ACTIVITY BOND.

nonmarketable security A security that may not be sold by one investor to another. This type of security is generally redeemable by the issuer, although within certain limitations. U.S. Treasury savings bonds and most certificates of deposit are nonmarketable securities. —Also called *nonnegotiable security.*

nonmember firm A firm that is not a member of an organized securities exchange. Nonmember firms must work through member firms to have their orders executed on the exchange floor.

nonnegotiable security —See NONMARKETABLE SECURITY.

nonoperating income Income from a source other than a firm's regular activities. For example, a firm may record as nonoperating income the profit gained from the sale of an asset other than inventory.

nonoperating unit A firm or a firm's subsidiary that operates no assets on its own but distributes income received from other firms that operate assets leased from the nonoperating company. For example, a railroad may lease its line and equipment to other railroads and merely distribute net income received from the lease payments to the nonoperating railroad's stockholders. —See also OPERATING UNIT.

nonparticipating Designating or being a class of preferred stock that does not have the right to participate with common stock in earnings growth through increases in dividends. Nearly all preferred stock issues are nonparticipating. —See also PARTICIPATING.

nonperforming asset An asset that produces no income. The term *nonperforming asset* is often used to describe a loan on which the borrower is not making payments. Firms often continue to include these assets, which are of questionable value, on their financial statements because they do not wish to show the losses entailed in writing them off. —Also called *nonperforming loan.* —See also UNDERPERFORMING ASSET.

$\boxed{\$}$ The major asset of a lending institution such as a bank or a savings and loan association is loans to that institution's customers. When a customer discontinues interest or interest and principal payments (with the exception of a loan that has been paid off), the loan becomes what is called a *nonperforming asset*. In its 1985 annual report, Financial Corporation of America, a large publicly owned California savings and loan, reported that loans with unpaid principal balances of over $1 billion were 90 days or more contractually delinquent or in the process of foreclosure. Such enormous nonperforming assets made it difficult for the institution to earn income even with a favorable spread between the interest rate it charged on loans and the interest rate it paid depositors.

nonperforming loan —See NONPERFORMING ASSET.

nonprice competition Competition among firms that choose to differentiate their products by nonprice means, e.g., by quality, style, delivery methods, locations, or special services. Nonprice competition is often practiced by firms desiring to differentiate virtually identical products. Companies producing cigarettes, over-the-counter medications, and food products spend large sums on nonprice competition.

nonprobate property An asset (as one held in joint tenancy) that does not have to pass through probate in order to be transferred.

nonpurpose loan A loan using securities as collateral for a purpose other than the purchase of securities on credit. A person may prefer a nonpurpose loan over a regular installment loan because of the lower interest rate. Nonpurpose loans are not subject to margin requirements as regular margin loans are. —See also PURPOSE LOAN.

nonqualifying annuity An annuity not approved by the Internal Revenue Service for tax-deferred pension contributions. A nonqualifying annuity permits the investor to defer taxes on income earned by the annuity but not to reduce taxable income for contributions made to the annuity. —See also QUALIFYING ANNUITY.

nonrecourse loan A loan in which the lender cannot claim more than the collateral as repayment in the event that payments on the loan are stopped. Thus, a group of investors may purchase an asset with a downpayment and the proceeds from a nonrecourse loan. In the event that the investment turns sour, the investors are not apt to lose more than the downpayment and payments already made on the loan. The unpaid balance on the loan will be absorbed by the lender. —See also RECOURSE LOAN.

nonrecurring charge An expense not expected to be encountered again in the foreseeable future.

nonrefundable (NR) A provision of some bond issues that prohibits the issuers from retiring the bonds before a specified date on which funds for the retirement will be raised externally (i.e., from outside the issuing firm). Essentially, this provision restricts a borrower from taking advantage of lower interest rates by replacing a bond issue carrying a high coupon rate of interest with a new bond issue carrying a reduced coupon rate of interest. Most bonds are nonrefundable for five to ten years from the date of issue. However, when the funds are raised internally, the bonds ordinarily may be called for some other reason such as a reorganization or merger. A nonrefundable feature works to the advantage of the investor since the bonds are normally not refunded unless interest rates have fallen below the coupon. —See also CALL PROTECTION; NONCALLABLE; PREREFUNDED BOND; REFUND.

nonsufficient funds An account in a financial institution lacking sufficient money to cover one or more checks written on the account. —See also NSF CHECK; OVERDRAFT.

nontaxable income Income items specifically exempted from taxation. On federal returns, interest from most municipal bonds, life insurance proceeds, gifts, and inheritances are generally nontaxable income.

nonvoting stock Stock in which the holder has no vote in the election of directors, the appointment of auditors, or other matters that may be brought up at the annual meeting. Corporations sometimes create a special class of nonvoting stock to restrict corporate control only to certain groups. (Most preferred stock is nonvoting.) —See also VOTING RIGHTS; VOTING STOCK.

no par Pertaining to a stock with no specific value assigned to it at the time of issue. Whether a stock has a par value or not is no longer of any consequence to investors.

normal investment practice The history of security purchases recorded in a customer account for purposes of allocating hot issues. The National Association of Securities Dealers prohibits underwriters from overallocating hot issues to customers based on the customers' normal investment practice.

normalized earnings Past or forecasted earnings that have been adjusted for cyclical variations. Earnings are generally normalized by using a moving average of earnings per share over a number of successive periods.

normal trading unit —See ROUND LOT.

note 1. A written promise to pay a specific sum of money on a certain date. —Also called *promissory note.* 2. —See FOOTNOTE.

note payable Debt owed to a lender and evidenced by a written promise of payment. Note payable, an entry on many corporate balance sheets, indicates that a certain dollar amount of liabilities will be repaid to the lenders at a future time.

note receivable Debt due from borrowers and evidenced by a written promise of payment. Note receivable, an entry on the asset side of many corporate balance sheets, indicates the dollar amount of loans due to be repaid by borrowers.

not held A customer instruction that permits an exchange member to use personal judgment in executing either a market or limit order with respect to the time and/or the price of execution. In theory, this instruction is designed to obtain a more favorable price since the floor broker may have a feel for whether prices are likely to rise or decline. Unlike a regular market order, however, a market not held order does not guarantee that the order will be filled. —Also called *market not held order*.

notice of intention day   In futures trading, the day on which the clearing firm matches the investor who has declared an intention to deliver on a contract with the investor who must accept delivery. This situation occurs one day after the person holding the short position has declared his or her intention to the clearing firm and one day before delivery is to occur. —See also DELIVERY DAY; FIRST POSITION DAY; POSITION DAY.

not rated (NR)   Pertaining to an issue of fixed-income securities that has not been rated by an agency such as Moody's or Standard & Poor's. The fact that an issue is not rated does not necessarily mean the securities are risky.

not reoffered (NRO)   Pertaining to an issue or a portion of an issue of securities that already has a buyer and is not being resold to the public by the underwriter.

novation   The substitution of one debt with another debt.

NOW account   An interest-bearing account on which checks may be written. Authorized on a national scale in 1981, these accounts pay a relatively small return. Therefore, the balances in NOW accounts should be kept at the minimum necessary to provide needed funds without incurring service charges. —Also called *negotiable order of withdrawal*. —See also SUPER NOW ACCOUNT.

NR   1. —See NONREFUNDABLE. 2. —See NOT RATED.

NRO   —See NOT REOFFERED.

NSCC   —See NATIONAL SECURITIES CLEARING CORPORATION.

NSF check   A check not honored by the bank on which it was written because of insufficient funds in the drawer's account. An NSF check is an overdraft.

NSTS   —See NATIONAL SECURITIES TRADING SYSTEM.

NYCE   —See NEW YORK COTTON EXCHANGE.

NYFE   —See NEW YORK FUTURES EXCHANGE.

NYM   —See NEW YORK MERCANTILE EXCHANGE.

NYSE   —See NEW YORK STOCK EXCHANGE.

O

o   —Used immediately following a security name in option transaction tables to indicate an option on other than 100 shares of stock. Such an option could be the result of a stock dividend or stock split: *Amoco o 60*.

O —Used in earnings reports in newspapers to identify the over-the-counter market as the primary market of a firm's common stock.

OARS —See OPENING AUTOMATED REPORTING SERVICE.

OB —See OR BETTER.

OCC —See OPTIONS CLEARING CORPORATION.

odd lot Less than 100 shares of stock or $25,000 face amount of bonds. —See also EFFECTIVE SALE; ON-THE-QUOTATION ORDER; ROUND LOT.

odd-lot dealer A member of an organized securities exchange that buys and sells in less than round lots. On most exchanges this dealer is the specialist in a particular stock.

odd-lot differential The extra markup on odd-lot purchases and mark-down on odd-lot sales to compensate the brokerage firm or specialist for dealing in less than round lot transactions. The differential (generally ⅛ of a point) normally does not apply to odd-lot executions on market opening or to odd lots submitted with round lot orders for the same security (i.e., 260 shares). —Also called *differential*. —See also BASIS PRICE 2; WITH OR WITHOUT.

odd-lot short sales The number of shares sold short in less than round lots. Because investors trading odd lots are viewed by many market analysts as unsophisticated, many odd-lot short sales are interpreted as bullish. The number of shares sold short in odd lots is sometimes used to construct an index to gauge small investor speculative activity. The index is calculated by dividing total odd-lot sales into odd-lot short sales. A rising index, indicative of increased speculation by less sophisticated investors, is a bearish sign.

odd-lotter An investor who buys and sells securities in less than the standard unit of trading. Odd-lotters are generally small investors lacking the financial resources to engage in larger trades.

odd-lot theory The technical theory holding that an investor should make investment decisions contrary to what the odd-lotters, on balance, are doing. For example, if odd-lot sales exceed odd-lot purchases, the odd-lot theory says that the smart investor should buy. Conversely, if odd-lot purchases exceed odd-lot sales, the theory says that the smart investor should sell. The odd-lot theory is based on the premise that small investors who trade in odd lots tend to make the wrong decisions.

off-balance-sheet financing Lease obligations to acquire assets such that neither the asset nor the liability appears on the firm's balance sheet. Off-balance-sheet financing was at one time a common method of acquiring additional assets for obligations that would not have to be entered on a balance sheet and thereby dilute a firm's financial ratios. Off-balance-sheet financing is now limited by accounting regulations.

off-board trade Purchase or sale of securities, particularly those that are listed on an exchange, without using an exchange. An example is trading 10,000 shares of General Motors common stock (listed on the New York

Stock Exchange) in the over-the-counter market. —See also RULE 19C3; THIRD MARKET.

offer —See ASK.

offering —See PUBLIC OFFERING.

offering circular An abbreviated prospectus describing a new securities issue.

offering date The date on which a new securities issue is to be sold.

offering price The price at which an investment is offered to buyers. This price, including any sales fee, is fixed by the underwriting syndicate. —Also called *fixed price.*

offering scale —See SCALE.

offer wanted (OW) A notice by a broker-dealer interested in purchasing a security in which there are no current offers.

off-floor order An order originating outside an exchange to trade a security. Orders entered by individual investors with brokers are off-board orders because they originate off the exchange. Off-floor orders have precedence over orders originating on the exchange floor. —See also ON-FLOOR ORDER.

official notice of sale An announcement by a municipality that it is accepting bids from underwriters for a proposed bond issue.

official rate In foreign exchange trading, the lawful rate at which an exchange rate is set.

official statement A disclosure of financial and operating information relevant to a municipal bond issue. This statement is similar to the registration statement filed by private issuers that municipalities are not required to publish.

offset The liquidation of a futures or option position by purchasing (for a short position) or selling (for a long position) an equal number of identical contracts so that no further obligation exists.

offshore Pertaining to a financial organization whose headquarters lies outside the United States. While offshore institutions must abide by U.S. regulations for operations carried on within the United States, other activities generally escape domestic regulation.

off-the-run issue A security issue that is not included in a dealer's list of offerings. —See also RUN 1.

OID —See ORIGINAL ISSUE DISCOUNT.

oil and gas drilling limited partnership A partnership in which investors' funds are used to look for new oil and gas sources. Developmental programs search in areas of proven reserves while more risky exploratory programs limit their activities to virgin areas. —Also called *developmental oil and gas partnership; exploratory oil and gas partnership.*

oil and gas income limited partnership A partnership in which investors' funds are used to buy oil and gas royalty interests or producing oil and gas properties. This partnership ordinarily provides investors with a stream of sheltered or partially sheltered income.

oligopoly A market in which a limited number of sellers follow the lead of a single major firm. For example, the domestic automobile market was long characterized as an oligopoly with American Motors, Chrysler, and Ford following the pricing lead of industry giant General Motors. —See also MONOPOLY; OLIGOPSONY.

oligopsony A market in which a limited number of buyers follow the leadership of a single large firm. For example, in a town or region a large bank may set rates on certificates of deposit that are then adopted by smaller banks and savings and loan associations on their own certificates of deposit. —See also MONOPOLY; MONOPSONY; OLIGOPOLY.

on-balance volume A measure of volume distinguished as to whether trades take place on rising prices or on falling prices. Technical analysts consider great volume on rising prices bullish because it indicates the possibility that large traders are accumulating investment positions in a security. Conversely, the technicians consider greater volume on falling prices bearish.

one-cancels-the-other order —See ALTERNATIVE ORDER.

one-decision stock A stock that can be bought and held indefinitely such that no second decision to sell is required. Selecting one-decision stocks was a popular investment philosophy during the 1970s when institutional investors concentrated their funds on a limited number of high-quality growth stocks such as IBM, Kodak, and Procter & Gamble. The essence of this investment philosophy is that, although temporary aberrations in the stocks' prices may occur, the stocks should outperform the market over an extended period of time.

one hundred percent statement —See COMMON-SIZE STATEMENT.

one-sided market The market for a security in which only a single side, either the bid or the ask, is quoted. —Also called *one-way market.* —See also TWO-SIDED MARKET; WITHOUT.

on-floor order An order to trade a security, originating from an exchange member on the exchange floor. On-floor orders are subordinated to off-floor orders. —See also OFF-FLOOR ORDER.

on-the-quotation order A customer odd-lot market order to sell instructing that the order be executed at the existing bid price of the security. An order to buy is at the prevailing ask price. An on-the-quotation order is unusual because most odd-lot orders are executed on the basis of the price of the next round-lot transaction.

on the sidelines Pertaining to investors who, having assessed the market, have decided to avoid committing their funds. These investors keep their money in short-term investments such as money market funds and wait for a more opportune time to invest.

When should an investor stay on the sidelines? Key danger signals to get off the playing field.
• •

When the action is wild and woolly;

During periods of rising interest rates;

When the probabilities say that cash equivalents will out-perform stocks.

Ray Ozyjowski, Regional Sales Coordinator
PaineWebber Incorporated, New York, NY

Investors vary in temperament and needs, and the best performance over time for most small investors comes from sticking with a consistent investment policy rather than constantly trading. Therefore, a small investor should sell whenever he or she cannot afford to lose the current value of his or her porfolio, and stay on the sidelines whenever he or she cannot afford to lose the money involved or is uncomfortable about a new investment and might therefore sell it at the wrong time. Professionals look at such things as the prospects for corporate profits, inflation, and interest rates; and the degree of speculative froth reflected in such things as the numbers and types of stock groups acting well; but the small investor may not have access to such information.

J. Kendrick Noble, Jr., First Vice President
PaineWebber Incorporated, New York, NY

OPD —Used on the consolidated tape to indicate an opening transaction that is being reported late: *GY.OPD 2s51½*.

open box The physical location within brokerage firms of securities that are available for use as collateral for loans. —Also called *active box.* —See also BOX; FREE BOX.

open-end investment company —See MUTUAL FUND.

open-end mortgage A mortgage that permits the issuer to sell additional bonds under the same lien. If the amount of additional bonds is restricted, the mortgage is termed *limited open-end.* —See also CLOSED-END MORTGAGE; MORTGAGE BOND.

opening 1. The beginning of a trading session. 2. The initial price at which a security trades for the day. —Also called *opening price.*

Opening Automated Reporting Service (OARS) A computerized system that determines imbalances between buy and sell orders for individual securities before the opening of the market. The Service is used by specialists to assist in fixing opening prices for the securities assigned to them.

opening balance The balance in an account at the beginning of a period.

opening price —See OPENING 2.

opening transaction **1.** The initial transaction during a trading day for a particular security. The price at which an opening transaction takes place is important to investors who have placed market orders before the market opens or who have placed at-the-opening orders, because the price at which the opening transaction takes place is the price that these investors will pay or receive for the security. —See also CLOSING TRANSACTION 1. **2.** An option order that establishes a new investment position or that increases the size of an existing investment position. —See also CLOSING TRANSACTION 2.

open interest The number of contracts for particular futures or an option which, at a given time, are outstanding. A large open interest indicates more activity and liquidity for the contract.

open-market operations The purchase and sale of government securities in the open market by the Federal Reserve in order to influence the money supply, credit conditions, and interest rates. For example, large purchases of securities will release funds into bank reserves which, in turn, will be used for lending. This action increases the supply of money, and, at least temporarily, pushes down interest rates. Open-market operations have significant effects on security prices. —See also FEDERAL OPEN MARKET COMMITTEE; PRIMARY DEALER; REPORTING DEALERS.

open-market purchase The buying of stocks and bonds in the securities markets. For example, in order to satisfy the sinking fund requirement of a bond indenture, the issuer may call securities from investors or make open-market purchases. Likewise, a firm wishing to reduce the number of its shares outstanding may make a tender offer to the firm's stockholders or purchase shares in the open market.

open on the print Pertaining to a block trade that has been completed by a block positioner and printed on the consolidated tape. The block positioner is left in a risky position because, depending on which side of the transaction he or she was on, the block positioner is either long or short the security.

open order —See GOOD-TILL-CANCELED ORDER.

open position An option or futures contract that has been bought or sold and that has not yet been offset or settled through delivery.

open repo A repurchase agreement without a fixed term.

operating company A business that engages in transactions with outsiders. —See also OPERATING UNIT.

operating expense An expense incurred in transacting normal business operations. Operating expenses include administrative and selling expenses but exclude interest, taxes, and cost of goods sold.

operating income The excess of revenues over expenses derived from normal business operations. Operating income, representing income from ordinary business activities, excludes expenses such as interest and taxes. Unusual, nonrecurring items such as gains from selling a subsidiary or losses from closing a plant are not included in the calculation of operating income. —Also called *earnings before interest and taxes; operating profit.* —See also OPERATING LOSS; OPERATING REVENUE.

⚠ What is and is not operating income is sometimes open to question, the definition above notwithstanding. In 1986, a large property and casualty insurance company restated its reported operating income for 1983 and 1984 downward by nearly $275 million. The firm's original reports described certain income from investments as operating income, when in fact the income should have been classified elsewhere in the interest of accuracy. For example, the insurer had been writing covered call options with strike prices below the market prices of the underlying stock, and had been classifying the premiums received as operating income. This situation resulted in sales of the stock below market price and erosion of the value of the firm's stock portfolio. (In effect, the insurer was transferring gains on investments to operating income.) The firm was also purchasing stock just before the record date for dividends with an agreement to resell the stock ex-dividend at a capital loss. The dividend was then credited to operating income through the movement of capital to income. Although the insurance company's outside auditor signed clean opinions on the company's 1983 and 1984 financial reports, it subsequently asked for the downward restatement and in 1986 re-signed as auditor.

operating lease   A short-term lease (as that of a telephone on a monthly basis) in which rental payments are made by the lessee and full ownership rights are kept by the lessor. An operating lease contrasts with a capital lease in which ownership of the asset effectively passes from the lessor to the lessee.

operating leverage   The extent to which fixed operating costs magnify changes in sales or revenues into even greater proportionate changes in operating income. For example, a company that substitutes robots or other machinery for laborers also substitutes fixed costs for variable costs and increases its operating leverage. High operating leverage tends to produce volatile earnings. —See also FINANCIAL LEVERAGE.

operating loss   The excess of operating expenses over revenue. As with operating income, operating losses exclude revenues and expenses from operations that are not considered a regular part of the business. —Also called *deficit.*

operating profit   —See OPERATING INCOME.

operating rate   The portion of capacity at which a business operates. For example, an operating rate of 80% indicates that the business is producing 80% of the output that could be produced at a maximum with existing resources. A low operating rate is generally accompanied by losses or small profits, although the opportunity for profit growth is still great. Conversely, a high operating rate is generally accompanied by high profits but limited opportunity for further profit improvement.

operating ratio   A financial ratio measuring the portion of revenue going to operating expenses.

operating revenue   Revenue from any regular source. Revenue from sales is adjusted for discounts and returns in calculating operating revenue. —See also OPERATING INCOME; OTHER REVENUE.

operating statement   —See INCOME STATEMENT.

operating unit   A business that engages in transactions with outsiders and that is owned by another business. For example, in 1985 the stockholders of Nabisco Brands approved a merger with R.J. Reynolds Industries whereupon Nabisco became an operating unit of Reynolds. —See also NONOPERATING UNIT; OPERATING COMPANY.

$\triangle$ Corporations, especially utilities, are frequently structured in such a way that a parent or holding company controls one or more units that actually do the manufacturing or selling. The parent company's primary responsibility is to provide management for the operating units, which in turn tend to the daily business of generating profit. Under this corporate structure, operating units pass earnings to the parent company in the form of intercorporate dividends. In general, these dividends are taxed at a very low rate or not at all. The dividends then may be paid to the parent company's stockholders. However, if an operating unit experiences problems and reduces or discontinues its payments to the parent, the parent's dividends to its stockholders are likely to be reduced or even discontinued. Middle South Utilities, a large utility holding company, omitted stockholder dividends after four of its operating units discontinued their own dividends to Middle South. These operating units had encountered problems with two large nuclear power plants, a financial squeeze causing them to eliminate their intercorporate dividend payments. As might be expected, ownership of the parent company was directly affected by the performance of the parent's operating units.

operational audit   —See MANAGEMENT AUDIT.

operations department   —See BACK OFFICE.

opinion   A Certified Public Accountant's written attestation as to the fairness of presentation of financial statements. Anything other than an opinion that the statements have been presented fairly is a matter of serious concern to investors. —Also called *accountant's opinion; auditor opinion.* —See also ADVERSE OPINION; CLEAN OPINION; DISCLAIMER OF OPINION; QUALIFIED OPINION; SUBJECT TO OPINION.

opinion shopping   Searching for an accounting firm that will provide the desired opinion for a financial statement. Firms sometimes opinion shop when their current auditors consider their accounting practices questionable or unacceptable. Investors should spend extra time investigating firms that have recently changed auditors.

opportunity cost   The best alternative that is foregone because a particular course of action is pursued. An example is the interest income that is given up when large balances are kept in a checking account. Likewise, purchasing a home means that less money is available for another investment.

option 1. A contract that permits the owner, depending on the type of option held, to purchase or sell an asset at a fixed price until a specific date. An option to purchase an asset is a *call* and an option to sell an asset is a *put*. Depending on how an investor uses options, the risks can be quite high. Investors in options must be correct on timing as well as on valuation of the underlying asset to be successful. —See also CALL 1; COMBINATION OPTION; CONVENTIONAL OPTION; EUROPEAN OPTION; EXERCISE PRICE; EXPIRATION DATE; LAPSED OPTION; PUT 1; RESTRICTED OPTION; STOCK OPTION. 2. —See INCENTIVE STOCK OPTION.

option agreement A formal written document that must be signed by an investor and put into the possession of the brokerage firm before the investor may trade options. The purpose of the agreement is to help assure that the investor has the financial resources and appropriate goals to qualify for trading options and that sufficient information in the form of an Options Clearing Corporation prospectus has been supplied so that the investor can understand the rules and risks.

optional call The call of a bond by an issuer who wishes to terminate a loan—generally because interest rates have declined since the time of issuance. Optional calls are frequently made at prices slightly higher than par value. Some bond issues are not subject to call; most issues provide a period of years after issuance during which optional calls are prohibited. —See also CALL 3; CALL PRICE; CALL PROTECTION; EXTRAORDINARY CALL.

optional dividend A dividend in which the shareholder may choose among two or more forms of payment. For example, a firm's directors may give the shareholders a choice between cash or an equal dollar amount of stock.

option exchange An organized securities exchange, the primary purpose of which is to provide a location and framework for trading standardized option contracts. An option exchange handles its trading much as a stock exchange handles its trading in stocks and bonds. Until 1973, with the opening of the Chicago Board Options Exchange, all options were traded through a limited number of firms specializing in them. Most of the options traded at that time were so unique that it was difficult or impossible to close a position in one before its expiration.

option-growth fund A mutual fund that invests at least 5% of its portfolio of securities in options.

option holder The owner of an option to purchase (call) or sell (put) an asset such as shares of common stock or a further contract. The option holder pays the premium and has the alternative of using the option or allowing it to expire. An option holder's loss is limited to the amount of the premium required to purchase it.

option premium —See PREMIUM 1.

option pricing model A mathematical formula for determining the price at which an option should trade. The model expresses the value of an option as a function of the value of the underlying asset, length of time until maturity, exercise price, yields on alternative investments, and risk. —See also BLACK AND SCHOLES MODEL.

Options Clearing Corporation (OCC) An organization established in 1972 to process and guarantee the transactions in options that take place on the organized exchanges. The OCC substitutes its own credit for that of the parties undertaking the options transactions.

option series All option contracts on a stock that have an identical expiration date and strike price. An example of a series is March options on IBM with a $130 strike price. —Also called *series*.

options-income fund A mutual fund that attempts to increase current income by writing covered options on securities held in the fund's portfolio.

option spread —See CALL SPREAD; PUT SPREAD.

option tender bond —See PUT BOND.

option writer The seller of a call option or a put option in an opening transaction. The option writer receives a premium and incurs an obligation to sell (if a call is sold) or to purchase (if a put is sold) the underlying asset at a stipulated price until a predetermined date. —See also WRITING.

or better (OB) —Used as a designation on a limit order ticket to indicate that the limit, in the case of a buy order, is higher than the market price; and in the case of a sell order is lower than the market price.

order A customer's instructions to buy or sell securities.

order imbalance An excess of buy or sell orders such that it is impossible to match one type of order with its opposite. Order imbalances normally occur after unexpected news causes a rush to buy or sell a security. In extreme cases, an order imbalance may cause suspension of trading in a security for a limited time. —Also called *imbalance of orders*.

orderly market A market in which bid and ask prices are continually provided and price changes between transactions are relatively small. It is the specialist's job to maintain an orderly market in assigned securities on the floor of an exchange.

order period The period of time during which syndicate members take orders for a new security issue.

order ticket A paper form on which a security order is written. —Also called *ticket*.

ordinary annuity An annuity that makes payments at the end of each period. —See also ANNUITY DUE.

ordinary income Income that does not qualify for special tax treatment. Ordinary income is taxed at the taxpayer's highest marginal tax rate. Wages, dividends, and interest are ordinary income.

organized securities exchange —See SECURITIES EXCHANGE.

original capital Funds contributed to a business by the owners of the business at the time the business is incorporated.

original cost —See HISTORICAL COST.

original-issue discount (OID) The amount by which a bond is sold below its par value at the time of issue. With the exception of normally tax-free securities (i.e., municipals), investors must report a certain portion of the discount as income for tax purposes each year.

original-issue discount bond A bond issued at a discount from par value. The discount occurs when the coupon on the bond is less than the market rate of interest for a bond of similar risk and maturity. —Also called *deep-discount bond.* —See also MINICOUPON BOND; ZERO-COUPON BOND.

original maturity The period between a security's maturity date and issue date. A bond issued 15 years ago that has an additional 10 years to maturity had an original maturity of 25 years. —See also CURRENT MATURITY.

originator A financial institution making loans that are then resold.

OTC —See OVER-THE-COUNTER MARKET.

OTC margin stock —See MARGIN STOCK.

other assets Assets of relatively small value. For financial reporting purposes, firms frequently combine small assets into a single category rather than listing each item separately.

other liabilities Small and relatively insignificant liabilities. For financial reporting purposes, firms often combine small liabilities into the single category, *other liabilities*, rather than listing each liability separately.

other revenue Revenue from sources other than regular ones. For example, a steel manufacturer would classify interest on customers' overdue accounts as other revenue. —See also OPERATING REVENUE.

out-of-the-money —Used to describe a call option with a strike price above the price of the underlying asset or a put option with a strike price below the price of the underlying asset. For example, a put option to sell 100 shares of GM stock at $50 per share is out-of-the-money if the stock currently trades at $70. Even though an out-of-the-money option has no intrinsic value it may well have market value.

outside audit —See EXTERNAL AUDIT.

outside director A member of a firm's board of directors who is not employed in another capacity by that firm. An example is the president of one firm who serves as a director of another firm. Some people believe that at least some outside directors are needed to give a board balance and to protect stockholders' interests. —See also INSIDE DIRECTOR.

outstanding capital stock The number of shares of capital stock that have been issued and that are in public hands. Outstanding stock excludes shares issued but subsequently repurchased by the issuer as treasury stock. Outstanding stock is used in the calculation of book value per share and earnings per share. —Also called *shares outstanding; stock outstanding*. —See also AUTHORIZED CAPITAL STOCK; ISSUED CAPITAL STOCK.

overbooked —See OVERSUBSCRIBED 1.

overbought Designating or being a stock market that has risen very rapidly in the recent past and is likely to suffer short-term price declines in the near future. Whether or not a market is overbought is difficult to determine and is subject to individual interpretation.

How to identify an overbought stock and an overbought market.
• •

Overbought is a technical term implying that, relative to normal performance, a stock or the market has moved upward for an unusually long time on unusually high volume. By definition, on average, such a stock or market is overdue for a correction—a move in the opposite direction. But bull markets often remain overbought for long periods as may certain stocks. Therefore, one need not sell simply on this signal.

J. Kendrick Noble, Jr., First Vice President
PaineWebber Incorporated, New York, NY

---

overdepreciation 1. Depreciation that is more than sufficient to allow for the eventual replacement of the asset being depreciated. —See also UNDERDEPRECIATION 1. 2. Depreciation that causes an asset to be carried on a firm's books at a lesser value than it is worth if it were sold. Overdepreciation produces understated earnings and assets on the financial statements. —See also UNDERDEPRECIATION 2.

overdraft A draft for more than the balance in the account on which the draft is drawn. A bank may honor an overdraft, depending on the importance of the customer and on prior arrangements (if any) to cover overdrafts. —See also NSF CHECK.

overgrowth Rapid growth in the sales of a mutual fund's shares to the extent that the fund has difficulty finding promising new investments or it must take such large positions in individual investments that its trading flexibility is reduced. In other words, a very successful fund may grow so large that the fund may have trouble sustaining its success.

overhanging supply A relatively large block of a security that may or will be sold under certain circumstances. For example, a large stockholder may announce a secondary offering of a security. Overhanging supply is of interest to technical analysts who consider a resistance level to be caused by unhappy investors determined to sell the security if it reaches a certain price. There is an overhanging supply of the security at the resistance level. Overhanging supply tends to be bearish for a security because investors feel the security will have difficulty rising in price.

overhead —See INDIRECT COST.

overhead resistance level —See RESISTANCE LEVEL.

overlapping debt Debt of a municipality that is shared with another political entity. For example, a city may share responsibility with the county in which the city is located for bonds issued by the county to finance a facility such as a public auditorium. —See also UNDERLYING DEBT.

overnight position A broker-dealer's net security position at the end of a trading day. A large overnight position leaves the broker-dealer vulnerable to events occurring before the market opens the next day.

overnight repo A repurchase agreement in which securities are sold provided that they will be repurchased on the following day. Financial institutions use overnight repos to raise short-term money for financing inventories.

overriding royalty interest A third-party interest in royalty income derived from oil and gas rights. —See also ROYALTY INTEREST.

oversold Designating or being a stock market that has declined rapidly and steeply in the recent past and is likely to exhibit short-term price increases in the near future. Whether or not a market is oversold is difficult to determine and is subject to individual interpretation.

How to identify an oversold stock and an oversold market.

Oversold, the reverse of *overbought* and another technical term, suggests that a reversal of some sort is overdue on average but should not be taken as a buy signal by itself. Bear markets can remain oversold for long periods of time. However, this may be taken as a signal to prepare to buy.

J. Kendrick Noble, Jr., First Vice President
PaineWebber Incorporated, New York, NY

oversubscribed **1.** Pertaining to or being a new security issue for which there are requests to purchase more securities than are available for sale. For example, brokers may take a sufficient number of preliminary orders for a new issue of stock for which there are insufficient shares available to satisfy the demand. —Also called *overbooked*. **2.** Pertaining to or being a buyback or takeover attempt in which more securities are offered than the purchaser has agreed to buy. In such a case the purchaser may decide to buy the additional securities or may buy the agreed-upon number on a pro rata basis.

oversubscription privilege The opportunity to purchase, on a pro rata basis, any remaining shares not already subscribed to in a new stock offering. In a typical new offering using stock rights, new shares are priced below the market price in order to ensure a successful sale. Generally, however, some stockholders will neither use nor sell their rights to buy the new shares, thus leaving some stock unsold even at the bargain price. The issuer therefore allows the stockholders to over-subscribe in anticipation of extra available shares. It is generally in the stockholder's interest to use the oversubscription privilege. —See also SUBSCRIPTION PRICE.

What to look for—good signals and bad—in over-the-counter stocks before buying them.

Do your homework before buying any stock. Develop an opinion by looking at the companies by means of fundamental analysis and technical analysis. The fundamentals of a company involve its financial position—earnings, income, debt, industry position, management, etc. Technically, the same company should be examined as to how it is received by the marketplace. Trading volume, price studies, and trends in the market are believed to foretell price movements. Armed with the fundamentals (financial position) and market trend (technical position), you'll find that the guesswork is diminished to a considerable degree. Traditionally, the OTC markets have represented emerging growth companies and low priced, more volatile situations. Information used to be sketchier on OTC issues than their exchange-listed counterparts. In 1982, we witnessed the start-up of NASDAQ National Market System trading with established qualification criteria for NASDAQ securities. Today, over half the NASDAQ securities have entered the National Market System (NMS). On these securities, the market information available and disseminated is the same as on board-listed issues. Executions are reported with full details within 90 seconds and are available throughout the trading day on NASDAQ terminals and on over 120,000 brokers' desktop terminals. Additionally, all issues trading in the NASDAQ National Market System are immediately eligible for margin. As a result, many highly capitalized issues that could meet New York Stock Exchange or American Stock Exchange criteria are choosing to stay on the OTC market. NASDAQ daily volume is gaining rapidly on the New York Stock Exchange and institutions are an increasing presence in the OTC marketplace.

*Kathleen Hegenbart, Vice President, Financial Consultant
Shearson Lehman Brothers, Newton Centre, MA*

over-the-counter market (OTC) A widespread aggregation of dealers who make markets in many different securities. Unlike an exchange on which trading takes place at one physical location, OTC trading occurs through telephone or computer negotiations between buyers and sellers. Although stocks traded over the counter are often more speculative than listed stocks, virtually all government and municipal bonds and most corporate bonds are traded in the OTC market. —See also NATIONAL QUOTATION BUREAU; THIRD MARKET.

over-the-counter stock A stock not listed on an exchange and trading only in the over-the-counter market.

overtrade 1. To purchase a client's securities at an above-the-market price in return for the client's purchase of part of a new issue. 2. —See CHURN.

overvalued Pertaining to or being a security that trades at a price higher than it logically should be. It is difficult, if not impossible, to determine whether or not a security is overvalued. —See also UNDERVALUED.

overwriting In options trading, the writing of more options than one expects to have exercised. Investors overwrite call options because they consider the underlying stock overvalued. Investors overwrite put options because they consider the underlying stock undervalued.

OW —See OFFER WANTED.

owner of record —See HOLDER OF RECORD.

owners' equity The owners' interest in the assets of a business. Owners' equity includes the amount invested by the owners plus the profits (or less the losses) in the enterprise. Owners' equity and liabilities are used to finance a firm's assets. —Also called *net assets; shareholders' equity; stockholders' equity.*

P

p —Used in over-the-counter stock transaction tables in newspapers to indicate that the stock has been granted temporary exemption from NASDAQ qualifications in order to remain listed in the NASDAQ System: *AmHomeShld p.*

P —Used in earnings reports in newspapers to identify the Philadelphia Stock Exchange as the primary market of a firm's common stock.

Pa —Used in earnings reports in newspapers to identify the Pacific Stock Exchange as the primary market of a firm's common stock.

Pacific Stock Exchange (PSE) A regional securities exchange that provides facilities for trading stocks, bonds, and options. The Exchange has trading floors in Los Angeles and San Francisco where securities of regional and national interest are listed. Most of the national stocks are also traded on the New York Stock Exchange or the American Stock Exchange but options and most regional stocks are unique to the Pacific Exchange. —Also called *P-Coast.* —See also SECURITIES COMMUNICATION ORDER ROUTING AND EXECUTION®.

Pac Man defense   A defensive antitakeover tactic in which the target firm attempts to take over the acquiring firm. The target hopes that the acquiring firm will call off the takeover attempt and look for easier pickings.

PACS⒮⒨   —See MUNICIPAL CONVERTIBLE.

paid-in capital   Funds and property contributed to a firm by its stockholders. Paid-in capital is generated when a firm issues stock in the primary market, not when the stock is traded in the secondary market. —See also ADDITIONAL PAID-IN CAPITAL; CONTRIBUTED CAPITAL.

paid-in surplus   —See ADDITIONAL PAID-IN CAPITAL.

painting the tape   1. Illegal trading of a security by manipulators among themselves in order to create the illusion of heavy trading activity, perhaps the kind generated by insiders. The increased trades are then reported on the consolidated tape, a situation that often lures unwary investors into the action. Once the market price of the security escalates, the manipulators expect to sell out at profit.   2. Breaking down larger orders into more numerous smaller orders to have more trades appear on the tape and attract investor interest.

paired shares   Shares of two firms under common management that are sold as a single unit. A single certificate may be issued to represent ownership in both firms. —Also called *stapled stock.*

P&L   —See INCOME STATEMENT.

panda   A gold coin minted in the People's Republic of China.

P & S department   —See PURCHASE AND SALES DEPARTMENT.

panic buying   A flurry of security purchases accompanied by high volume and sharp price increases. During a period of panic buying the buyers do not have time to evaluate fundamental or technical factors because their primary goal is to acquire securities before the prices rise even more. For example, panic buying occurred on the day following President Lyndon B. Johnson's announcement of his decision not to run for reelection.

panic selling   A flurry of selling in a particular security or in securities as a whole. Panic selling is accompanied by particularly heavy volume and sharp price declines as owners scramble to sell before prices drop even more. Panic selling is generally set off by an unexpected event viewed by traders as particularly negative. For example, uncertainty surrounding the outbreak of serious hostilities and a cutoff of oil supplies in the Middle East might be sufficient to cause panic selling.

paper   A short-term unsecured note. —Generally synonymous with *commercial paper.*

paper company A corporation formed in order to accomplish a specific financial task rather than to produce a good or service. Such a firm normally has few assets other than those of a financial nature.

paper gain —See UNREALIZED GAIN.

paper loss —See UNREALIZED LOSS.

paper profit —See UNREALIZED GAIN.

par —See PAR VALUE.

par bond A bond that sells at a price equal to its par value (usually $1,000).

parent company A company that controls or owns another company or other companies. For example, Santa Fe Industries is the parent company of the Atchison, Topeka, and Santa Fe Railway Company. —See also HOLDING COMPANY; SUBSIDIARY.

parity The state of an option when its premium plus the strike price is equal to the market price of the underlying stock. If GM stock is selling at $75 per share, an option to buy the stock at $70 would be selling at parity if its premium is $5. —See also CONVERSION PARITY.

parking The placement of idle funds in a safe, short-term investment while awaiting the availability of other investment opportunities. Many investors end up parking proceeds from a security sale in a money market account while searching for other securities to purchase.

partial delivery Delivery by a broker of less than the quantity stipulated in the contract. A broker delivering 200 shares of a stock when 500 shares are due is making a partial delivery.

partial execution Execution of less than the full amount of an order. An investor may place an order to buy 500 shares of GenCorp at $45 or less and get a partial execution if the broker is able to buy only 300 shares at that price. —Also called *partial fill*.

partial redemption Redemption by an issuer of less than an entire issue of its securities. For example, a corporation may redeem a portion of an outstanding bond issue. —See also BUYBACK; REDEMPTION.

partial spinoff Distribution to stockholders or sale to the public of shares representing a minority interest in a firm's subsidiary. A firm may undertake a partial spinoff when it feels the subsidiary is not properly valued by the public as part of the parent firm, or when it wishes to raise funds without giving up total control of the subsidiary. —See also SPINOFF.

participate but do not initiate A customer instruction on a large order to a broker when the customer does not want the order to affect the price of the security. The instruction indicates that the broker should handle the order in such a way that no price change will be initiated by the broker.

participating Designating or being an unusual class of preferred stock that participates with common stock in dividend increases according to a specified formula. For example, a participating preferred issue might require that any increases in dividends on common stock above $2 per share be shared equally with preferred. —See also NONPARTICIPATING.

participation certificate A certificate indicating ownership in a pool of assets, generally mortgages.

partner A member of a partnership.

partnership A business owned by two or more people who agree on the method of distribution of profits and/or losses, and the extent to which each will be liable for the debts of the other partner(s). A partnership permits pass through of income and losses direct to the owners. In this way they are taxed at each partner's personal tax rate. —See also CORPORATION; GENERAL PARTNERSHIP; LIMITED PARTNERSHIP; PROPRIETORSHIP; SILENT PARTNER.

partnership account A brokerage account in which two or more individuals are equally liable. A partnership account differs from a joint account in that the partnership account may include a written agreement defining the interest of each partner.

par value 1. The stated value of a security printed on its certificate. A bond's par value is the dollar amount on which interest is calculated and the amount paid to holders at maturity. Par value of preferred stock is used in a similar way in calculating the annual dividend. —Also called *face value; par.* —See also STATED VALUE. 2. The minimum contribution made by investors to purchase a share of common stock at the time of issue. Par value is of no real consequence to investors; in fact, many new common stock issues have no stated par value. —Also called *par.* —See also NO PAR.

passed dividend A regular dividend that is omitted by a firm's board of directors. Passed dividends on most issues of preferred stock, but not on common stock, eventually must be made up. —Also called *unpaid dividend.* —See also DIVIDENDS IN ARREARS.

passive investment management A method of managing an investment portfolio that seeks to select properly diversified securities which will remain relatively unchanged over long periods of time. Passive investment management involves minimal trading, based on the belief that it is impossible to beat the averages on a risk-adjusted basis consistently. —See also ACTIVE INVESTMENT MANAGEMENT.

passive portfolio A portfolio of securities that is altered only when another variable, such as market index, is altered.

pass-through security A security that passes through payments from debtors to investors. Packages of loans are assembled and sold to investors by private lenders. Although pass-through securities have stated maturities, the actual lives of the securities are likely to be shorter, especially during periods of falling interest rates when borrowers pay off mortgages early. The security derives its name from the fact that interest and principal payments made by borrowers are passed through monthly after deduction of a service fee. —Also called *pass through*. —See also GINNIE MAE PASS THROUGH; PRODUCTION RATE.

pattern —See CHART FORMATION.

payable That is owed to another party as a debt.

payback period The length of time needed for an investment's net cash receipts to cover completely the initial outlay expended in acquiring the investment.

paydown In a corporate or U.S. Treasury refunding, the amount by which the face value of the bonds being refunded exceeds the par value of the new bonds being sold. The paydown represents the amount by which the debt is reduced.

paying agent A financial institution that makes the payments to the holders of an issuer's securities. For example, an indenture will name a paying agent responsible for making interest and principal payments on a bond issue.

payment date The date on which a dividend will be paid to stockholders or on which interest will be paid to bondholders by the issuers' paying agents. In some cases, the issuers will have the payments made a day early so that the security holders will receive payment on the payment date.

Should investors seek companies with high payout ratios? If so, why? Why not?

Payout ratio is the percentage of reported aftertax earnings per share which is paid out in dividends per share. Most companies actually pay out a fairly constant percentage of their *previous* years' earnings. Earnings not paid out are reinvested in the business. Therefore, a company with a low or nonexistent payout ratio is assumed to have a high need for capital, either because of high debt or high prospective growth or both. Some advisors believe that, as both dividends and capital gains are now taxed to shareholders at the same rate, corporations should pay out more and reinvest less. PaineWebber believes that that is not true of companies capable of high growth. Investors should choose the combination of yield and growth which best meets their own objectives. Typically, one must be sacrificed for the other.

J. Kendrick Noble, Jr., First Vice President
PaineWebber Incorporated, New York, NY

---

payout ratio The percentage of net income a firm pays to its stockholders in dividends. Companies paying most of their earnings in dividends have little left for investment to provide for future earnings growth.

Stocks of firms with high payout ratios appeal primarily to investors seeking high current income and limited capital growth. —Also called *dividend payout ratio.* —See also DIVIDEND COVERAGE; RETAINED EARNINGS.

payup Additional funds required when an investor swaps a current holding for higher-value securities. For example, a person might swap low-interest bonds for higher-coupon bonds of equal face value but of higher market value.

PBW Exchanges —See PHILADELPHIA-BALTIMORE-WASHINGTON STOCK EX-CHANGES.

P-Coast —See PACIFIC STOCK EXCHANGE.

P/E ratio —See PRICE-EARNINGS RATIO.

peg **1.** To fix the price of a new security issue during the issuance period through buying and selling it in the open market in order to ensure that the price in the secondary market will not fall below the offering price. —Also called *holding the market; stabilize.* —See also STA-BILIZATION PERIOD; UNDERWRITE. **2.** To fix the rate at which foreign currencies exchange with one another.

penalty plan A mutual fund accumulation plan in which sales fees for the entire obligation are deducted from shares purchased in the first few years that the plan is in effect. In the event that the investors redeem the shares after a short time, only a small portion of the purchase price will be refunded. Sales charges and penalty plans are regulated by the Investment Company Amendments Act of 1970.

pennant —See TRIANGLE.

penny stock A low-priced, speculative stock. Although the maximum price at which a security may sell and still be classified as a penny stock is subject to individual interpretation, $1 is probably the most commonly recognized limit. Many penny stocks are traded in the over-the-counter market and on smaller exchanges.

Pension Benefit Guaranty Corporation A government agency that in-sures certain corporate pension funds. The Corporation, established un-der the Employee Retirement Income Security Act, is funded by charging companies a premium based on the number of covered employees.

pension cost The annual cost incurred by a firm in providing its em-ployees with a pension plan.

pension fund A financial institution that controls assets and disburses income to people after they have retired from gainful employment. Pen-sion funds, which invest in a variety of securities, control such enormous sums that their investment decisions can have significant impact on individual security prices.

pension parachute A pension agreement stating that, in the event of an unfriendly takeover, a firm can use any surplus pension assets to increase pension benefits. A pension parachute is used to make the firm less attractive to takeover, for it prevents the acquiring company from using the excess pension assets to help finance the acquisition.

pension plan An arrangement for paying death, disability, or retirement benefits to employees. Payments into the plan are ordinarily a tax-deductible expense for the firm but any contribution by employees may or may not be deductible on personal tax returns. Likewise, retirement benefits paid to employees will be wholly or partially taxable. —See also DEFINED-BENEFIT PENSION PLAN; DEFINED-CONTRIBUTION PENSION PLAN; VESTED BENEFITS.

pension rollover Reinvestment of a lump-sum pension payout into an individual retirement account. The rollover permits a pension beneficiary to defer taxation until funds are paid out of the individual retirement account. A pension rollover is an alternative to paying taxes on a lump-sum payout, either in one year or by averaging over a number of years. —See also IRA ROLLOVER; ROLLOVER.

PER POST EXECUTION REPORTING SYSTEM.

per capita debt The total debt of a municipality divided by the municipality's population. Financial analysts use per capita debt when evaluating a municipality's ability to repay its debt.

percentage depletion Depletion calculated as a percentage of gross income derived from a natural resource. Percentage depletion is independent of the cost of the resource. —See also DEPLETION.

percentage-of-completion method A method of recognizing revenues and costs from a long-term project in relation to the percentage completed during the course of the project. Thus, the percentage-of-completion method allows a business profits (or losses) on a project before its completion. —See also COMPLETED-CONTRACT METHOD.

perfect hedge A hedge that exactly offsets any gains or losses from an existing investment position. An example of a perfect hedge is the short sale of an owned security in order to lock in an existing profit and transfer it to a subsequent tax year. Since very few hedges are perfect, most of them operate merely to offset a portion of losses or gains. —See also RISK HEDGE.

performance audit —See MANAGEMENT AUDIT.

performance fee A fee paid to an investment manager based on the performance of a client's portfolio, determined by a specified standard. For example, an investment manager might be paid a regular fixed fee plus an incentive fee based on the change in value of the client's portfolio.

⚠️ In late 1985 the Securities and Exchange Commission (SEC) partially relaxed its long-standing prohibition against investment advisers' fees based on portfolio performance. Until that time, advisers could only charge a flat fee or a fee based on the amount of assets under their management. Performance fees permitted by the SEC apply only to institutional investors and wealthy investors, with *performance* being measured as the increased value in the investor's portfolio over a period of one year or more.

performance fund —See GO-GO FUND.

performance stock A stock that investors feel has an excellent chance for significant price appreciation. Performance stocks tend to be issued by growth-oriented firms that retain most or all income for reinvestment. The stocks usually sell at above-average price-earnings ratios and experience large price swings. Performance stocks are judged more on the basis of fundamental analysis than are glamor stocks and hot stocks, which are more subject to investor psychology.

periodic payment plan A plan in which an investor agrees to make monthly or quarterly payments to a mutual fund as a method of accumulating shares over a period of years. The periodic payment plan's stipulation of fixed periodic contributions results in dollar cost averaging for the investor. —See also PLAN COMPLETION INSURANCE.

periodic purchase deferred contract A deferred annuity purchased with a series of premium payments. For example, an individual might obtain a lifetime monthly income by making annual premium payments to an insurance company prior to retirement. —See also SINGLE-PREMIUM DEFERRED ANNUITY.

period of call protection —See DEFERMENT PERIOD.

permanent financing Long-term financing to support a long-term asset.

permanent insurance —See CASH-VALUE LIFE INSURANCE.

perpetual bond —See CONSOL.

perpetual warrant A warrant with no expiration date. Although many warrants have relatively long maturities, few are perpetual.

perpetuity A stream of payments expected to last indefinitely. —See also ANNUITY.

personal income Before-tax income of individuals and unincorporated businesses. Personal income is an inferior measure of the economy compared with disposable income; however, personal income is easier to compute and is made available on a monthly basis while disposable income is only calculated on a quarterly basis.

petrodollars Funds controlled by oil-exporting countries that have been used to pay for oil imports. Petrodollars are a huge pool of funds available for investment and the purchase of goods and services. Although stated in terms of dollars, the word *petrodollars* generally refers to all currencies.

pf —Used in stock transaction tables in newspapers to indicate that the stock is a preferred issue. Issues without any designation are common stock. A capital letter (i.e., A, B, or C) beside *pf* indicates the particular issue of preferred listed: *GaPc pfC2.24.*

phantom stock plan An incentive plan for a firm's executives in which the executives are offered bonuses based on increases in the market price of the firm's stock. A phantom stock plan is supposed to induce the executives to act in the best interests of the shareholders.

Philadelphia-Baltimore-Washington Stock Exchanges   A name formerly used for what is now the Philadelphia Stock Exchange.

Philadelphia Stock Exchange (PHLX)   A regional securities exchange that provides facilities for trading in a wide variety of financial instruments including stocks, bonds, stock options, foreign currency options, stock index options, and a precious metals index.

physical life   The potential service life of an asset before it physically becomes unable to produce a good or service. An asset is often physically able to continue operating but at a cost or rate rendering it economically obsolete. The economic life, as opposed to the physical life, is most important in valuing the asset.

pickup   A gain in yield from swapping bonds. For example, a pickup of 30 basis points comes about when bonds with a 9.70% basis are traded for bonds with a 10.00% basis.

pickup bond   A bond with a relatively high coupon and a short period remaining until it is likely to be called by the issuer. If interest rates fall and the bond is called, the investor will pick up a premium equal to the difference between the call price and the purchase price.

picture   The bid and ask price at which a dealer is willing to buy or sell a security.

piggyback registration   Registration of a new issue and already outstanding stock of the same issuer for a single public offering. Thus, a single registration suffices for the primary and secondary offering.

pink sheets   Daily sheets containing wholesale price quotations for thousands of over-the-counter stocks as listed by dealers acting as market makers in the individual securities. Pink sheets are published by the National Quotation Bureau for brokers and dealers but not for the general public. The name derives from the color of the paper on which the quotations are printed. —See also NATIONAL QUOTATION BUREAU; YELLOW SHEETS.

pipeline   The process through which security issues pass before distribution to the public. If securities are being readied for distribution, they are said to be in the pipeline.

pipeline theory   —See CONDUIT THEORY.

pit   A location on a commodities exchange trading floor where the futures of a particular commodity are traded. The name *pit* derives from the ring-shaped trading area. —Also called *ring*.

place   To sell a new securities issue.

placement ratio   The percentage of municipal bonds brought to market during the past week that have been sold by underwriters. Only issues of $1 million and over are included in this calculation published by the *Daily Bond Buyer.*

plan company   A company that receives customer payments and purchases mutual fund shares when the customers wish to purchase shares in a fund on a periodic payment plan. Thus, the plan company acts as middleman in collecting the payments and crediting customer accounts.

plan completion insurance A life insurance policy for people purchasing mutual fund shares as part of a periodic payment plan. In the event of the participant's death before completion of the contract, plan completion insurance pays an amount sufficient to complete the remaining payments.

plant and equipment Fixed assets used to produce the goods and services that a firm sells to its customers. On a corporate balance sheet, plant and equipment are valued at original cost. Plant and equipment become net plant and equipment when adjusted for accumulated depreciation.

play An investment. —See also DIRECT PLAY.

pledged asset An asset used as security for a loan.

plow back To reinvest earnings in additional income-producing assets. Firms that plow back earnings rather than paying the earnings in dividends tend to experience more rapid increases in earnings per share.

plus (+) **1.** —Used in the net change column of security transaction tables to indicate a closing price higher than the closing price on the last previous day on which the security was traded. **2.** —Used in reporting closed-end investment company share prices to indicate the percentage amount by which market price exceeds net asset value. —See also MINUS 2. **3.** An addition of $\frac{1}{64}$ either to the bid or to the ask price for a government bond. Government securities are normally quoted in 32nds; therefore, a quote of 91.03+ indicates a price of $91\frac{3}{32} + \frac{1}{64}$, or $91\frac{7}{64}$.

plus-cash convertible An unusual type of convertible security that requires a fixed cash payment in addition to surrender of the convertible in order to exercise the conversion privilege and obtain the shares of common stock. A plus-cash convertible has built-in leverage that produces relatively large price swings in the convertible compared with the underlying common stock.

plus tick —see UPTICK.

PN —See PROJECT NOTE.

point A measure of security price changes. In the case of stocks and stock averages, a point normally means a change of $1; for bonds, a point refers to a $10 movement for a $1,000 bond.

point-and-figure chart A graph, peculiar to securities, in which only the significant value changes of a security, a futures contract, or a market average are recorded. The vertical axis represents price, but unlike nearly all other charts, no variable, including time, is plotted on the horizontal axis. Entries on a point-and-figure chart are made only when a variable changes by a predetermined amount, e.g., by one point or two points. A period of days may pass before an entry is recorded. —See also BAR CHART; LINE CHART.

poison pill An antitakeover tactic in which warrants are issued to a firm's stockholders, giving them the right to purchase shares of the firm's stock at a bargain price in the event that a suitor hostile to management acquires a stipulated percentage of the firm's stock. The poison pill is intended to make the takeover so unpalatably expensive that any attempt to take control will be abandoned. —See also FLIP-OVER PILL; POISON-PUT BOND; SUICIDE PILL.

poison-put bond A bond that allows an investor to cash in a security before maturity if the issuer becomes the target of a takeover hostile to its management. Poison-put bonds make it expensive for the bidder to buy the target firm because the bidder will have to raise cash to pay off the owners of the bonds. The bonds can benefit the bondholders because they permit the holders to cash in the securities if the takeover spawns a new, more leveraged high-risk corporate entity. —See also POISON PILL; PUT BOND.

pollution control bond A municipal revenue bond in which debt service is secured by payments from a private firm using pollution control equipment that the bond was used to finance. Thus, the guarantee of repayment is made by the private firm rather than by the municipal issuer. For pollution control bonds issued before August 8, 1986, interest is free from federal taxation. Tax reform passed in 1986 eliminated this exemption: interest on pollution control bonds issued on or after August 8, 1986, is fully taxable.

Ponzi scheme —See PYRAMID.

pool 1. A temporary affiliation of two or more people in an attempt to manipulate a security's price and/or volume. The pool is necessary in order to acquire the capital needed to manipulate a stock having a large market value. Pools were especially popular in the 1920s and early 1930s but now have been regulated out of existence. —See also TRADING POOL. 2. —See MORTGAGE POOL.

pool financing —See BOND POOL.

pooling of interests An accounting method for combining the balance sheet items of two firms after a merger or combination. The original firm's assets, liabilities, and owners' equity are combined relatively unchanged from premerger values. —See also PURCHASE METHOD.

portfolio A group of investments. The more diversified the investments in a portfolio, the more likely the investor is to earn the same return as the market. —See also DIVERSIFICATION.

portfolio beta The relative volatility of returns earned from holding a specific portfolio of securities. A high portfolio beta indicates securities that tend to be more volatile in their price movements than the market taken as a whole. Portfolio beta is calculated by summing the products of each security's beta times the proportional weight of the security in the portfolio. For example, if a portfolio consists of two securities, one valued at $15,000 and having a beta of 0.9 and the other valued at $10,000 and having a beta of 1.5, the portfolio beta is $(.9)(\$15,000/\$25,000) + (1.5)(\$10,000/\$25,000)$, or 1.14.

portfolio dedication Synchronization of returns on an investment portfolio with known future liabilities. Portfolio dedication applies primarily to investment decisions by institutions such as pension funds and insurance companies. These institutions can estimate future liabilities fairly accurately; then try to minimize the outlay to satisfy the liabilities. —Also called *dedication; matching*.

portfolio dressing The addition and deletion of securities by an institutional investor before a financial reporting period in order to make the portfolio appear acceptable to investors. Typically, portfolio dressing involves the sale of big losers and the addition of big gainers to convey the impression that the portfolio manager is competent.

portfolio effect Reduction in the variation of returns on a combination of assets compared with the average of the variations of the individual assets. This effect measures the extent to which variations in returns on a portion of assets held are partially canceled by variations in returns on other assets held in the same portfolio.

portfolio manager A person who is paid a fee to supervise the investment decisions of others. The term is normally used in reference to the managers of large institutions such as bank trust departments, pension funds, insurance companies, and mutual funds. —Also called *money manager*.

portfolio theory The theory of selecting an optimal combination of assets such that the investor secures the highest possible return for a given level of risk or the least possible risk for a given level of return. Using portfolio theory, an investor assembles a group of assets on the basis of how the individual assets interact with one another. Thus, a security would be purchased not on the basis of how that security is expected to perform in isolation but rather on the basis of how that security can be expected to influence the risk and return of the investor's entire portfolio. Although individual investors can use some of the ideas of portfolio theory in putting together a group of investments, the theory and the literature relating to it are so complex and mathematically sophisticated that the theory is applied primarily by market professionals. —Also called *modern portfolio theory*.

position The ownership status of a person's or an institution's investments. For example, a person may own 500 shares of Exxon, 350 shares of Westinghouse, and a $10,000 principal amount of 9% bonds due in 2001. —See also LONG POSITION; SHORT POSITION.

position To buy or sell securities in order to establish a net long or a net short position. —Also called *take a position*.

position building The continual and gradual accumulation of a firm's shares for a long position or the borrowing and sale of the shares for a short position.

position day The day on which an investor with a short position in a commodity (i.e., the investor who must make delivery) declares an intention to make delivery if the day is other than the first day permitted. —See also FIRST POSITION DAY.

position limit In futures and options trading, the maximum number of contracts that an individual or a group of individuals working together may hold. The position limit is determined by the Commodity Futures Trading Commission for futures or by the exchange on which the particular contract is traded. —See also TRADING LIMIT.

position trader A security trader who holds a position overnight, and, in some cases, for even longer periods. Position traders are different from day traders and scalpers who operate within shorter time frames.

positive carry The current net income from an investment position when the current income from the investment exceeds the cost of carrying it. A Treasury bond with a current yield of 14% has a positive carry if its purchase can be financed at 12%. —See also CARRYING CHARGES 1; NEGATIVE CARRY.

positive covenant A clause in a loan agreement that requires a specified action by the borrower. For example, a positive covenant may mandate that the borrower maintain a specific level of working capital or issue periodic reports to creditors. —See also NEGATIVE COVENANT.

positive yield curve The normal relationship between bond yields and maturity lengths that results from higher interest rates on long-term bonds than on short-term bonds. The word *positive* refers to the slope of the curve drawn to depict this relationship. —See also FLAT YIELD CURVE; NEGATIVE YIELD CURVE; YIELD CURVE.

post A location on the floor of an organized exchange at which assigned securities are traded. Posts are numbered and staffed by specialists. A single location may accommodate the trading of a number of different securities. —Also called *trading post*.

post To enter information in an account. For example, if a customer sends money to a broker, the brokerage firm will post a credit to the customer's account.

Post Execution Reporting System (PER) An automated switching system on the American Stock Exchange that transmits orders electronically to the appropriate specialist on the exchange floor.

Post 30 stock A stock listed on the New York Stock Exchange that is traded in 10-share units. The name derives from the fact that these stocks are traded at Post number 30 on the Exchange floor.

pot Securities from a new issue that are returned to the lead underwriter by syndicate members for sale to institutional investors. —See also POT IS CLEAN.

potential dilution The decrease in the proportional equity position of a share of stock that will occur eventually if additional authorized shares are actually issued. This term generally refers to outstanding options and convertible securities likely to be exchanged for shares of common stock at a future time. —See also DILUTION.

pot is clean —Used as an indication from the lead underwriter of a new issue that the securities set aside for sale to institutional investors have been sold.

power of attorney A legal document in which a person gives another the power to act for him or her. The authority may be general or it may be restricted to activities such as the handling of security transactions.

Pr —Used on the consolidated tape to indicate preferred stock: *GMPr 80½.*

precedence The sequence in which orders are executed on an exchange floor. For example, the order with the lowest ask or highest bid has precedence over other orders. With orders at an identical price, the one entered earliest has precedence. The precedence of orders is established by the rules of each exchange. —See also PRIORITY.

preemptive right A stockholder's right to keep a constant percentage of a firm's outstanding stock by being given the first chance to purchase shares in a new stock issue in proportion to the percentage of outstanding shares already held. Not all firms provide the preemptive right, which is more important to stockholders owning a significant part of a company. —Also called *subscription privilege.* —See also PRIVILEGED SUBSCRIPTION; RIGHTS OFFERING; SPECIAL SUBSCRIPTION ACCOUNT.

preference stock —See PRIOR PREFERRED.

preferred call period —See DEFERMENT PERIOD.

preferred creditor A creditor having priority to payment over one or more other classes of creditors. For example, holders of first mortgage bonds must be paid by the borrower before payments are made to holders of second mortgage bonds on the same collateral. First mortgage bondholders are the preferred creditors.

preferred dividend coverage The measure of a firm's ability to meet its dividend obligations on preferred stock. The greater the coverage the less the chance that management will pass a dividend. This ratio is calculated by dividing fixed charges plus preferred dividends (divided by 1 minus the firm's tax rate) into earnings before taxes and fixed charges. —See also COVERAGE RATIO; DIVIDEND COVERAGE; FIXED-CHARGE COVERAGE.

⟨$⟩ One of the few advantages preferred stockholders have over common stockholders of the same company is that dividends to the preferred holders have priority over dividends to the common stockholders. Thus, if a firm is suffering through a difficult business climate, dividends to preferred stockholders usually will continue even after those for common stockholders have been curtailed. However, even the preferred dividend payments are sometimes omitted. In September of 1986 Allegheny International announced suspension of payment on its preferred stock, a suspension that not only permitted Allegheny to conserve needed cash but also signaled its creditors that it was serious about making adjustments favorable to its lenders. (Allegheny had suspended dividends on its common stock earlier in 1986.) Because Allegheny's two preferred stock issues were cumulative, omitted dividends on the preferred began accumulating and would have had to be paid up before resumption of dividend payments to its common stockholders.

What factors should be taken into account when purchasing preferred stock?
• •

Preferred stock tends to have the characteristics of both a bond and a common stock. It can offer the high yields of a bond but less safety of a bond and its participation in a company's growth may be limited by its less volatile share price versus common stock. Thus, preferred stock is generally bought for a combination of income *and* growth. Preferred stock is a security that has prior claim on dividends (and/or assets in the case of corporate dissolution), up to a certain amount before the common stockholders may claim entitlement. A bondholder's claim is legally enforceable. The preferred stockholder's is not. Investors therefore should make an effort to assess the sound financial condition of the issuer of the preferred stock.

George Domolky, Portfolio Manager
Fidelity Investments, Boston, MA

---

preferred stock   A security that shows ownership in a corporation and gives the holder a claim prior to the claim of common stockholders on earnings and also generally on assets in the event of liquidation. Most preferred stock issues pay a fixed dividend set at the time of issuance, stated in a dollar amount or as a percentage of par value. Since no maturity date is stipulated, these securities are priced on dividend yield and trade much like long-term corporate bonds. As a general rule, preferred stock has limited appeal for individual investors. —See also CALL-ABLE PREFERRED STOCK; CUMULATIVE; FLOATING-RATE PREFERRED STOCK; NEW MONEY PREFERRED; PARTICIPATING; PREFERRED DIVIDEND COVERAGE; PRIOR PREFERRED.

preferred stock ratio   The proportion of preferred stock, valued at par, in a firm's total capitalization. The preferred stock ratio is calculated by dividing the firm's net worth and long-term debt into the par value of its outstanding preferred stock.

preliminary prospectus   —See RED HERRING.

premature exercise   Exercise of an option by the owner before the expiration date. Although most options are exercised near expiration, an owner occasionally finds it advantageous to exercise prematurely. Such an action will often foul up the option writer's plan, in which instance the writer must sell (with a call) or purchase (with a put) the stock earlier than expected.

premium 1. The price at which an option trades. The size of the premium is affected by various factors including the time to expiration, interest rates, strike price, and the price and price volatility of the underlying asset. —Also called *option premium*. 2. The amount by which a bond sells above its face value. —See also ABOVE PAR. 3. The excess by which a warrant trades above its theoretical value.

premium bond A bond selling at a price above its par value. An investor must be careful about purchasing a bond selling at a premium because of the possibility of a call by the bond's issuer for sinking fund requirements or for refunding. Except for convertible bonds, the size of a bond's premium normally can be expected to decline as the bond approaches maturity, at which time it will be paid off at par.

premium income Income from premiums received by an investor writing put and call options. For example, an investor owning NCR stock might decide to write a call option. The premium received from the call is premium income to the writer.

premium put A put price on a bond that is above par value. An example would be a $1,000 principal amount bond with a put price of $1,100 ten years after issue. The purpose of including a premium put is to reduce the coupon rate of interest that must be paid to sell the issue. —See also YIELD TO PUT.

> ⚠ In late 1984 Insilco Corporation (formerly International Silver) issued $40 million of 9% coupon debentures convertible into Insilco common stock at $22.75, approximately 25% above the $18.25 market price. Although the bonds were to mature in the year 2010, investors could put (sell) the bonds back to Insilco at 110% of par 5 years from the issue date. Because of the premium put, Insilco was able to include a coupon significantly less than the 11%–12% coupon necessary to sell the same issue without a put feature. Even if an investor were unable to use the bonds' conversion feature in the intial 5 years, putting the bond at a 10% premium over the issue price would provide a yield to put (interest plus appreciation) of approximately 10.5%. Investors purchasing these bonds were giving up some current income for the added safety of being able to redeem them 20 years before scheduled maturity.

prenuptial agreement A written agreement by a couple to be married in which financial matters, including rights following divorce or the death of one spouse, are detailed.

preopening indication —See INDICATION 2.

prepaid expense An expenditure for an item that will provide future benefits. For example, a firm may pay an insurance premium only once a year, resulting in an expense that provides benefits over a 12-month period. The unexpired part of the premium is carried on the firm's balance sheet as a prepaid expense.

prepaid interest   Interest on a loan that has been paid but is not due until a following period. The Internal Revenue Service does not permit taxpayers to claim an itemized deduction on tax returns for prepaid interest.

prepayment   Payment before the day it is due. For example, sending a check on the transaction date for securities bought with regular-way delivery will almost surely result in prepayment.

prerefunded bond   A bond secured by an escrow fund of U.S. government obligations that is sufficient to pay off the entire issue of refunded bonds at maturity. The rating of the refunded bond generally assumes the rating of the government obligations (highest rating) at the time the fund is established. —See also ARBITRAGE BOND; NONREFUNDABLE.

prerefunding   Placement of funds with a trustee in order to retire a bond issue as a liability before the call date. —Also called *advance refunding*. —See also ARBITRAGE BOND.

presale order   An order to buy a portion of a new municipal bond issue before the time at which certain information concerning the issue, such as the coupon, has been determined. Presale orders are permitted with municipal bond issues, but not with other security issues because municipal bond issues are exempt from requirements of the Securities and Exchange Commission.

Prescribed Right to Income and Maximum Equity   —See PRIME.

present value (PV)   The current value of future cash payments when the payments are discounted by a rate that is a function of the interest rate. For example, the present value of $1,000 to be received in 2 years is $812 when the $1,000 is discounted at an annual rate of 11%. Conversely, $812 invested at an annual return of 11% would produce a sum of $1,000 in 2 years. —See also FUTURE VALUE; NET PRESENT VALUE.

president   A leading decision maker of a company. The president is sometimes the company's chief executive officer.

presidential election cycle   The tendency of the stock market to move in four-year cycles with rising markets occurring during the period before presidential elections. The presidential election cycle is based on observation of past market movements and on the theory that incumbent presidents manipulate the economy before elections in such a way that bull markets ensue. —Also called *election cycle*.

presold   Describing or being a new security issue that is sold out before all the specifics of the issue have been announced. In the case of a bond issue, this term normally means that sufficient orders for the issue have been placed before announcement of the coupon rate(s).

pretax income   Reported income before deducting income taxes. Pretax income is sometimes considered a better measure of a firm's performance than aftertax income because taxes in one period may be influenced by activities in earlier periods. —Also called *pretax*.

pretax writedown   An accounting reduction in the value of an asset, measured before any effect by income taxes.

pretax yield   The rate of return on an investment before taxes have been considered. As with other measures of yield, pretax yield is normally stated on an annual basis.

price   The dollar amount at which a security trades. Stocks are nearly always quoted fully (i.e., 25 means $25 per share), while bonds are ordinarily quoted as a percentage of par value (i.e., 98 represents $980 per $1,000 par bond).

price change   —See NET CHANGE.

price-earnings ratio (P/E)   A common stock analysis statistic in which the current price of a stock is divided by the current (or sometimes the projected) earnings per share of the issuing firm. As a rule, a relatively high price-earnings ratio is an indication that investors feel the firm's earnings are likely to grow. Price-earnings ratios vary significantly among companies, among industries, and over time. One of the important influences on this ratio is long-term interest rates. In general, relatively high rates result in low price-earnings ratios; low interest rates result in high price-earnings ratios. The reduction in interest rates was a prime factor in the bull market beginning in 1982 as investors valued firms' earnings at high multiples with the resulting rise in stock prices. —Also called *earnings multiple; market multiple; multiple; P/E ratio.*

price gap   —See GAP.

price limits   For a given futures contract, the maximum price change from the previous day's settlement price permitted during a trading session. These limits are sometimes adjusted in fast-moving markets.

price range   —See RANGE.

price-sales ratio (PSR)   A financial ratio that compares a firm's stock price with its sales per share (or its market value with total revenue). It is used by some analysts to find companies that may be temporarily undervalued in the stock market. A low PSR is thought to characterize a firm with the potential for a significant turnaround because sales are already being made and improvement need only take place in the margin the firm is able to earn on each dollar of sales.

price spread   —See MONEY SPREAD.

price stabilization   —See PEG 1; STABILIZATION PERIOD.

price target   The projected price of a security.

price-to-asset ratio   The ratio of a firm's stock price to its book value per share. A low ratio indicates that the firm's assets are not being fully valued by investors or that the assets are being overvalued on the firm's financial statements. If the former is the case, the company may be a candidate for a takeover attempt.

price-to-book-value ratio   —See MARKET TO BOOK.

price weighted average   A security average weighted by the market price of each security included in the average. Thus, securities with high market prices tend to be more heavily weighted and have more influence on changes in a price weighted average. The Dow Jones Averages are examples of price weighted averages. —See also MARKET VALUE WEIGHTED AVERAGE.

pricey   Pertaining to or being an unrealistically high offer. An offer to sell a security at $50 when the current market price is $47 is pricey. —See also LOWBALL.

pricing   Determination of the price at which stock will sell or the yield at which bonds will sell as new issues. If the price is set too high or the yield is set too low, the issue will not sell out. If the price is set too low or the yield is set too high, the issuer will pay more than necessary in dilution or interest to sell it.

primary dealer   A government securities firm to which the New York Federal Reserve Bank sells directly and from which it buys directly in an attempt to control the money supply. —See also OPEN-MARKET OPERATIONS; REPORTING DEALERS.

primary distribution   The sale of a new issue of securities with the funds going to the issuer. —Also called *primary offering*. —See also INVESTMENT BANKER; SECONDARY DISTRIBUTION.

primary earnings per share   Net income during a given period divided by the average number of shares of common stock and common stock equivalents outstanding during that period. —See also DUAL PRESENTATION; FULLY DILUTED EARNINGS PER SHARE.

primary market   The market in which new, as opposed to existing, securities are sold. Investors who purchase shares in a new security issue are purchasing them in the primary market. Investors who buy stocks and bonds in the primary market normally are not required to pay brokerage commissions because fees for selling the issue are built into its price and are absorbed by the issuer. —Also called *new issue market*. —See also SECONDARY MARKET.

primary offering   —See PRIMARY DISTRIBUTION.

primary trend   The main direction in which security prices are moving. An upward primary trend is a bull market while a downward primary trend is a bear market. —See also SECONDARY TREND.

prime   —See PRIME RATE.

PRIME   A unit investment trust providing its owner all dividends and appreciation up to a predetermined termination value. A PRIME is the result of breaking regular common stock down into income and appreciation components. PRIME, the income component of this breakdown, is traded on the American Stock Exchange. A PRIME is appropriate for investors willing to give up potential capital gains in return for higher current income. —Also called *Prescribed Right to Income and Maximum Equity*. —See also AMERICUS SHAREOWNER SERVICE CORPORATION; SCORE.

prime paper The highest grades of commercial paper, determined by the rating agencies. Prime paper includes those having Moody's ratings of P-3 and above.

prime rate A short-term interest rate quoted by a commercial bank as an indication of the rate being charged on loans to its best commercial customers. Even though banks frequently charge more and sometimes less than the quoted prime rate, it is a benchmark against which other rates are measured and often keyed. For various reasons, a rising prime rate is generally considered detrimental to security prices. —Also called *prime*.

⚠️ Although some people might view the prime as important only to Big Business, which can borrow money at this "most favorable" rate, movements in the prime rate can be very significant to individual investors. First of all, the prime is a crucial determinant of the rate that investors must pay on funds borrowed to finance the purchase of securities on margin. As the prime rises, the interest rate charged on borrowed funds in margin accounts rises in tandem, thereby increasing the cost of carrying the securities. Conversely, a fall in the prime reduces the cost of carrying securities purchased with borrowed funds and may stimulate increased demand for securities. Secondly, changes in the prime are important indicators of what is happening or what may happen to other interest rates. For example, lending institutions generally raise the prime in response to increases in their own cost of funds or in response to increases in customer demand for loans. Thus, a rising prime may signal a tightening of lendable funds and a probable rise in general interest rates. The prime rate generally moves more slowly than most other interest rates because of the control exercised over it by the lending institutions. While the federal funds rate may fluctuate wildly . even over the short term, the prime will remain relatively steady and will move usually by small increments of ¼ of 1%. It should be noted that the prime is a short-term interest rate: it is more comparable to the rate on U.S. Treasury bills than it is to the rate on long-term bonds. As a result, the prime is generally lower than the rates paid on corporate bonds. Nonetheless, a rising prime is almost always bad news for the bond market.

principal **1.** The face amount of a bond. Once a bond has been issued, it may sell at more or less than its principal amount, depending on changes in interest rates and the riskiness of the security. At maturity, however, the bond will be redeemed for its principal amount. —Also called *principal amount*. **2.** Funds put up by an investor. **3.** The person who owns or takes delivery of an asset in a trade. For example, an investor is the principal for whom a broker executes a trade.

principal amount —See PRINCIPAL 1.

principal market The main market in which a security trades. The principal market for the common stock of most large corporations in the United States is the New York Stock Exchange, even though most of these stocks also trade on one or more other exchanges and in the over-the-counter market. —See also CONSOLIDATED TAPE.

principal stockholder   A stockholder who owns a large number of voting shares in a firm. For Securities and Exchange Commission purposes, a person owning 10% or more of a firm's voting stock is considered a principal stockholder.

principal trade   A securities transaction in which the executing brokers are trading from inventory and are thus acting as dealers.

print   The appearance of securities transactions on the composite tape.

priority   The preference of the bid or offer entered first in an auction market. Regardless of size, the first offer has priority if a transaction occurs at the price specified by the order. —See also PRECEDENCE.

prior-lien bond   A bond with a priority claim over other bonds, both secured and unsecured, of the same issuer.

prior period adjustment   Correction of a material mistake in reported income in an earlier financial statement. Although prior period adjustments affect retained earnings, they are not used to alter income in the current period.

prior preferred   A class of preferred stock that has preference over one or more other classes of preferred stock of the same issuer. Preference may be with respect to payment of dividends and/or claims on assets. —Also called *preference stock*.

private activity bond   A bond issued by a municipality when the funds are to be used for a nonessential purpose. Private activity bonds pay taxable interest unless specifically exempted by the federal government. Private activities for which tax-exempt bonds may be issued include airports, electric and gas distribution systems, government mass transportation systems, hazardous waste disposal facilities, solid waste disposal facilities, and student loans. Small issues of industrial development revenue bonds and nonprofit college and hospital bonds are also permitted. Except for nonprofit college and hospital bonds, interest from tax-exempt private activity bonds is subject to the alternative minimum tax. —Also called *nonessential function bond*; *private purpose municipal bond*. —See also ESSENTIAL FUNCTION BOND; 501(C)(3) BOND; MUNICIPAL BOND; SMALL-ISSUE BOND.

privately-held company   A firm whose shares are held within a relatively small circle of owners and are not traded publicly.

private placement   The sale of an issue of debt or equity securities to a single buyer or to a limited number of buyers without a public offering. The placement is generally conducted by an investment banker who acts as an agent in bringing together the seller and the buyer(s).

private purpose municipal bond   —See PRIVATE ACTIVITY BOND.

privileged subscription   The issuance of new stock in which existing stockholders are given preference in purchasing new shares up to the proportion of shares that they already own. Thus, an owner of 5% of all the issuing firm's outstanding stock would be permitted to buy up to

5% of the new issue at a special price below the current market price. —See also PREEMPTIVE RIGHT; RIGHTS OFFERING.

probability distribution The distribution of possible outcomes to an event along with the probability of each potential outcome. This statistical tool is used to measure the risk associated with events such as shooting craps, playing cards, or investing in securities.

probate Proof that a will is valid and that its terms are being carried out. Probate is accomplished by an executor/executrix who is paid a fee based on the size of the estate that passes through the will. Certain trusts and jointly owned property pass to beneficiaries without being subject to probate and the attendant fee. —See also NONPROBATE PROPERTY.

proceeds The amount received from the sale of an asset. The word *proceeds* usually refers to the amount received before deduction of commissions or other costs related to the transaction. —See also NET PROCEEDS.

proceeds sale A transaction in which funds received from selling a security are immediately reinvested in another security. The National Association of Securities Dealers regards a proceeds sale as a single transaction; therefore, the member's commission or markup cannot exceed 5% of the principal of the trade.

producer price index A comprehensive index of price changes at the wholesale level. Since wholesale price changes eventually will find their way into consumer prices, the producer price index is closely watched as an early indicator of future retail price changes. —Formerly called *wholesale price index*. —See also CONSUMER PRICE INDEX; GNP DEFLATOR.

production rate The coupon rate of interest at which pass-through securities issued by the Government National Mortgage Association are issued. The production rate is set one-half percent less than the maximum rate permitted on residential mortgages insured by the Federal Housing Administration. —See also GINNIE MAE PASS THROUGH.

productivity The efficiency with which output is produced by a given set of inputs. Productivity is generally measured by the ratio of output to input. An increase in the ratio indicates an increase in productivity. Conversely, a decrease in the output/input ratio indicates a decline in productivity.

product mix The composition of goods and services produced and/or sold by a firm. A limited product mix tends to increase the firm's risk at the same time it increases the potential for large profits. Thus, a firm specializing in a niche market in electronics is likely to experience great success or large losses depending on how demand and competition develop for its specialized output. —Also called *sales mix*.

profit —See NET INCOME.

profitability ratio A comparison of two or more financial variables providing a relative measure of a firm's income-earning performance. Profitability ratios are of interest to creditors, managers, and especially owners. —See also COMMON-SIZE STATEMENT; GROSS PROFIT MARGIN; NET PROFIT

MARGIN; RETURN ON COMMON STOCK EQUITY; RETURN ON EQUITY; RETURN ON INVESTMENT; RETURN ON SALES.

profit and loss statement (P&L) —See INCOME STATEMENT.

profit center A segment of a business for which costs, revenues, and profits are separately calculated, with the manager of the segment being responsible for and judged on the performance of that segment. A large corporation with diversified interests in paper manufacturing, trucking, and fast food may regard each of these three businesses as a profit center.

profit margin **1.** The relationship of gross profits to net sales in a business. Net sales are determined by subtracting returns and allowances from gross sales, whereupon the cost of goods sold is then subtracted from net sales to obtain gross profit. Gross profit is divided by net sales to obtain the profit margin—an excellent indicator of a firm's operating efficiency, its pricing policies, and its ability to remain competitive. —See also GROSS PROFIT MARGIN. **2.** Net profit margin of a business, arrived at by deducting operating expenses and cost of goods sold and then dividing the result by net sales. *Profit margin* is less often used to indicate net profit margin.

profit range The range of potential profitable outcomes resulting from a given investment position. Profit range is used extensively in putting together complicated option strategies in which gains or losses or both are limited to an established level.

profit-sharing plan A savings plan offered by many firms to their employees in which a part of the firm's profits is funneled into a tax-deferred employee retirement account. These plans give employees additional incentive to be productive.

profit squeeze A reduction in earnings perhaps caused by a poor business climate, increased competition, or rising costs.

profit taking General widespread selling of securities or a particular security after a significant price rise as investors realize, or take, their profits. Although profit taking depresses prices, it does so temporarily. The term *profit taking* usually implies that the market is trending upward. —Also called *taking profits*.

When should I take profits?

Determine your goals before the investment is made. If you are a long-term investor, don't let short-term considerations tempt you to realize a gain if the positives are still in place. If you are a short-term investor and reach your target—take it. Don't allow greed to dictate your decisions.

Katherine L. Robinson, Assistant Vice President
Kidder, Peabody & Co., Boston, MA

pro forma financial statement A financial statement constructed from projected amounts. A firm might construct a pro forma income statement based on projected revenues and costs for the following year. Likewise, a firm may wish to develop a set of pro forma statements to determine the effect of a projected stock buyback.

program trading An arbitrage operation in which traders take a long or short position in a portfolio of stocks and the opposite position in one or more futures contracts on the same portfolio. Program trading is undertaken in order to take advantage of a difference in market values between two essentially identical portfolios of securities. Both sides of the trade are closed out on or near the day the futures contract expires when the values of the positions should be equal. Owing to the size of the trades and the complexity of the technique, program trading is practiced almost exclusively by large institutions. Program trading has been blamed for many of the occasionally occurring big movements in the market. —See also BASIS TRADING; TRIPLE WITCHING HOUR.

$ Program trading is the sophisticated trading of a large portfolio of securities in combination with an offsetting position in a futures contract. The ability to pursue this strategy for earning a risk free return depends on integrating computer programs with trades involving one of the many new products in the securities markets—stock index futures. High-powered computer programs determine the point at which the value of a portfolio of securities identical to the securities constituting a stock index is out of line with the value of a futures contract on that same stock index. Thus, the value of all the stocks included in the Standard & Poor's 100 Index may be determined to be either overvalued or undervalued relative to the price at which a futures contract on the index is selling. Program traders take one position in the securities constituting the index and at the same time, take an offsetting position in a futures contract on the index. Because the two positions must be of equal value on the date that the futures contract expires, the program trader profits by the difference in values when the position was established. The greater the initial divergence of values and the shorter the wait until the values converge, the more profitable the trade. The profitability of the trade must be compared with the rate of return that can be earned on other risk free investments to determine if the arbitrage operation is profitable enough to be worthwhile. Since most positions in program trading are closed out near the settlement date of the futures contract when the value of the securities is at or close to the value of the futures contract, considerable trading, volatility, and turmoil in the markets can occur on the expiration dates. Big price changes involving the stock included in the averages and indices frequently take place, especially late in the day on the settlement date. While there has been considerable criticism of program trading as the stimulus to volatility in the security markets, some analysts claim that program trading has a favorable effect in that it makes for more efficient markets. Program trading can be used profitably only when values in the market are out of line. Because program trading involves such huge sums and such sophisticated trading practices, it is generally undertaken only by a limited number of traders with access to large pools of capital: establishing a position at one time in 100 or more stocks is not small potatoes.

Offsetting the need for investing huge sums, however, is the fact that program traders establish what is essentially a riskless investment position. It is left to the remainder of the investment community to absorb the added risk of a more volatile market.

progressive tax   A tax with a rate that increases as the amount to be taxed increases. For example, a taxing authority might levy a tax of 10% on the first $10,000 of income and increase the rate by 5% per each $10,000 increment up to a maximum of 50% on all income over $80,000. A progressive tax often uses high rates on relatively large incomes and tends to encourage tax shelters. The federal income tax and the unified gift-estate tax are progressive taxes. —See also FLAT TAX; MARGINAL TAX RATE; REGRESSIVE TAX.

project note (PN)   A short-term debt security issued by a municipality to finance a federally sponsored real estate project with repayment guaranteed by a pledge from the United States Department of Housing and Urban Development. These securities are considered very high-grade.

promissory note   —See NOTE 1.

property dividend   A stockholder dividend paid in a form other than cash, scrip, or the firm's own stock. For example, a firm may distribute samples of its own product or shares in another company it owns to its stockholders. In general, a property dividend is taxable at its fair market value.

property tax   —See AD VALOREM TAX.

proportionate redemption   A partial stock buyback in which a stockholder maintains the same ownership percentage after selling a portion of his or her shares back to the issuer.

proprietor   The owner of a one-person business.

proprietorship   A firm with a single owner, chiefly one who acts as the manager of the business. Income, expenses, taxes, liability for debts, and contractual obligations are inseparable with respect to differentiating the owner from the business. —See also CORPORATION; PARTNERSHIP; UNLIMITED LIABILITY.

pro rata   —Used to refer to something on a proportional basis. For example, in a rights offering, rights are distributed to stockholders on the basis of the number of shares already held by each stockholder. Thus, the pro rata distribution enables the stockholders to purchase new shares in proportion to the old shares that they already own.

proratable factor   The proportion of shares tendered by each stockholder that will be accepted for purchase or exchange.

prospect   To look for customers. For example, a registered representative may join a civic organization to prospect for new customers.

prospect list   A list of prospective customers. A broker might acquire a list of physicians, dentists, or owners of private aircraft, assuming that at least some of these people have money to invest and would consider becoming customers.

prospectus A formal written document relating to a new securities offering that delineates the proposed business plan or the data relevant to an existing business plan—information needed by investors to make educated decisions whether or not to purchase the security. The prospectus includes financial data, a précis of the firm's business history, a list of its officers, a description of its operations, and mention of any pending litigation. A prospectus is an abridged version of the firm's registration statement, filed with the Securities and Exchange Commission. —See also OFFERING CIRCULAR; RED HERRING.

protected strategy An investment strategy with a goal of limiting risk. For example, purchasing a stock and a put on the stock establishes a limit on the amount of money that may be lost since the put protects against losses derived from a declining value of the stock. Although protected strategies limit losses, they also generally penalize potential profits.

protectionism Establishment of barriers to the importation of goods and services from foreign countries in order to protect domestic producers. Protectionism generates higher consumer prices. It is also likely to penalize domestic exporters since foreign countries are apt to retaliate with trade barriers of their own.

protective covenant —See COVENANT.

proved reserves The quantity of minerals expected to be recoverable under current economic and operating conditions. The amount of proved reserves is important in valuing the stock of a company with significant holdings in natural resources.

provisional rating A bond rating conditional upon the successful completion of a specific project or the fulfillment of a stipulated condition. —Also called *conditional rating*.

proxy Written authority to act or speak for another party. Proxies are sent to stockholders by corporate management in order to solicit authority to vote the stockholders' shares at the annual meetings. —See also VOTING RIGHTS.

proxy fight A contest among two or more opposing forces to solicit stockholders' proxies and, in effect, gain control of the firm through the election of directors. It is normally quite difficult to wrest control from the existing management through a proxy fight, but the tactic has been used, for example, by some suitors in takeover attempts.

proxy statement The material accompanying solicitation of a proxy from stockholders. The proxy statement lists the items to be voted on including nominees for directorships, the auditing firm recommended by directors, the salaries of top officers and directors, and resolutions submitted by management and stockholders. Proxy statements are required by the Securities and Exchange Commission.

prudent man rule A federal and state regulation requiring trustees and portfolio managers to make financial decisions in the manner of a prudent man, e.g., with intelligence and discretion. The prudent man rule requires care in the selection of investments but does not limit investment alternatives. —See also INVESTMENT-GRADE; LEGAL LIST.

PSE —See PACIFIC STOCK EXCHANGE.

PSR —See PRICE-SALES RATIO.

public distribution The sale of a new securities issue to individual investors. The sales fee for the distribution, normally absorbed by the issuer, is included in the offering price.

public housing authority bond A bond issued by a local public housing agency with proceeds utilized to construct or repair low-rent housing. Public housing authority bonds are backed by the federal government and pay federally tax-exempt interest.

publicly held 1. Pertaining to or being securities that are freely transferable among investors. For example, stock owned by institutional investors is publicly held, but unregistered stock held by a firm's founder is not publicly held. 2. Of, relating to, or being a publicly traded company.

publicly traded company A company whose shares of common stock are held by the public and are available for purchase by investors. The shares of publicly traded firms are bought and sold on the organized exchanges or in the over-the-counter market. Such companies are regulated by the Securities and Exchange Commission.

publicly traded fund —See CLOSED-END INVESTMENT COMPANY.

public offering Sale of an issue of securities to the public, an activity normally occurring with the assistance of an investment banker that purchases the securities from the issuer and then resells them to the public. —Also called *distribution; offering.*

public offering price The price at which securities are offered for sale to the public. The price normally includes any sales commission.

public power bond Debt issued by a public power agency such as Washington Public Power System and the Municipal Electric Authority of Georgia. Interest is normally tax-exempt federally. Interest and principal payments are derived from revenues generated by the sale of electricity.

Public Securities Association A trade group of banks, brokers, and dealers engaged in underwriting and trading federal, state, and local government securities.

Public Utility Holding Company Act A 1935 act giving the Securities and Exchange Commission authority over the security issues, the accounting systems, the corporate structures, and the intercompany transactions of public utilities. This Act was a response to serious abuses of utility managements uncovered during the depression years.

purchase and sales department (P & S) The department of a brokerage firm that compares details of a trade with the firm identified on the other side of the transaction. In addition, it processes and mails confirmations to customers.

purchase group —See SYNDICATE.

purchase method A method of accounting for a merger or combination in which one firm is considered to have purchased the assets of the other firm. If the price paid for the acquired firm exceeds the market value of the acquired firm's assets, the difference is recorded as goodwill on the acquiring firm's balance sheet. The goodwill must be written off over a period of years. —See also POOLING OF INTERESTS.

purchasing power 1. Consumer ability to purchase goods and services. Increased purchasing power represents proportionately larger increases in income than increases in the cost of goods and services. 2. The ability to purchase goods and services with a fixed amount of money. With this narrower definition, purchasing power is inversely related to the consumer price index. Increased purchasing power is a signal that future increases in economic activity are likely.

purchasing power risk The risk that unexpected changes in consumer prices will penalize an investor's real return from holding an investment. Since investments from gold to bonds and stock are priced to include expected inflation rates, it is the unexpected changes that produce this risk. Fixed income securities such as bonds and preferred stock subject investors to the greatest amount of purchasing power risk since their payments are set at the time of issue and remain unchanged regardless of the inflation rate.

pure play An investment concentrated in a particular industry or operation. An investor who believes that snowmobiles are the wave of the future will search for a pure play in snowmobiles. In other words, the investor seeks out a company that does nothing other than manufacture and sell snowmobiles. Likewise, Cracker Barrel Old Country Stores is more of a pure play in restaurants than is Pepsico, even though Pepsico owns Taco Bell and Pizza Hut. Reason: Pepsico generates much of its revenues from its other operations.

purpose loan A loan using securities as collateral with proceeds from the loan being used to purchase additional securities. —See also NON-PURPOSE LOAN.

purpose statement A written document reporting the use to which proceeds of a loan backed by securities is to be put. The borrower agrees not to use the funds to purchase securities in violation of Federal Reserve credit regulations.

put 1. An option that conveys to the owner (option holder) the right, but not the obligation, to sell a specific asset at a predetermined price until a certain date. In most cases, puts have 100 shares of stock as the underlying asset. For example, an investor may purchase a put option on GenCorp common stock that confers the right to sell 100 shares at $80 per share until September 21. Puts are sold for a fee by other investors who incur an obligation to purchase the asset if the option holder decides to sell. Investors purchase puts in order to take advantage of a decline in the price of the asset. —Also called *put option*. —See also CALL 1;

GUARANTEE LETTER; SYNTHETIC PUT. **2.** The forcing of the seller (writer) of a put option to purchase shares of stock at the stipulated price. Puts are exercised by the owner only when the market price of the underlying stock is less than the strike price. —Also called *put to seller*. **3.** The forcing of the issuer of a bond to repurchase the security at par before maturity. Few bond issues permit the holder this option.

Putting things into perspective: how to hedge, using puts. How to speculate, using puts.
• •

A put option has an inverse relationship to the underlying security. As the value of the stock increases, the value of the put decreases. Like calls, puts can be used for both hedging and speculation. Puts can be purchased in conjunction with stock ownership as a form of insurance (i.e., a hedge) against downside loss on a stock. If the stock price declines, the put holder can either sell the put and keep the stock, or exercise the put and sell the stock at the put's strike price. In either case, the increased value of the option will offset the stock loss to some degree. If the stock price rises beyond a certain level, the put will expire worthless. In this case, the put holder will lose the premium paid for the option but will still participate in the upward stock movement. The breakeven point occurs when the stock price advances beyond the put's strike price plus the premium. Puts also can be used speculatively without a position in the underlying security. Instead of selling a stock short, an investor who anticipates a decline in the price of a stock can buy an at-the-money-put. If the stock price rises, causing the put to expire worthless, the maximum loss is the premium paid for the put. But if the stock price declines substantially, the investor could make profits that far exceed the initial cost of the put.

Henry Nothnagel, First Vice President—Retail Marketing
Chicago Board Options Exchange, Chicago, IL

---

put bond A relatively unusual bond allowing the holder to force the issuer to repurchase the security at specified dates before maturity. The repurchase price, usually at par value, is set at the time of issue. A put bond allows the investor to redeem a long-term bond before maturity but the yield generally equals the one on short-term rather than long-term securities. —Also called *multimaturity bond; option tender bond*. —See also POISON-PUT BOND; PREMIUM PUT; YIELD TO PUT.

put-call ratio The ratio of trading volume in put options compared with trading volume in call options. Technicians use the put-call ratio to forecast market turns. A high ratio with heavy trading in puts indicates strong bearish sentiment and the possibility of a market bottom. A relatively low put-call ratio with heavy trading volume in calls indicates very bullish sentiment and a probable market top. As with many other technical indicators, use of the put-call ratio assumes that most investors are wrong.

put option —See PUT 1.

put spread An option position in which a put option is purchased while another put option on the same security is sold short. The two puts have different strike prices, different expiration dates, or both.

put to seller —See PUT 2.

PV —See PRESENT VALUE.

pyramid A classic investment fraud in which the operator pays promised high returns to current investors from the contributions made by new investors. Thus, funds are never invested in any productive assets but are simply paid out as a return to existing owners. The operator must continue to attract more and more investors in order to pay a return to those who have already committed their funds. —Also called *Ponzi scheme.*

pyramid To use profits derived from a profitable security position in combination with borrowed money in order to acquire an even larger investment position. Pyramiding allows an investor the possibility of greater profits by using a given amount of funds to control the maximum amount of securities. It is also very risky.

q —Used directly before the firm name in over-the-counter stock transaction tables in newspapers to indicate that the firm is in bankruptcy proceedings: *qSykes Data.*

QTIP trust A marital-deduction trust in which the surviving spouse receives income from the trust's assets for life but the trust's principal is left to someone else (usually children). A QTIP trust controls the eventual beneficiaries while at the same time taking advantage of the marital deduction, and providing an income for the surviving spouse.

qualified opinion The opinion of a Certified Public Accountant that a firm's financial statements deviate in some respect from a clean opinion according to generally accepted accounting principles. —See also AD-VERSE OPINION; CLEAN OPINION; DISCLAIMER OF OPINION; SUBJECT TO OPINION.

qualifying annuity An annuity approved by the Internal Revenue Service in which the contributions may be deducted from taxable income. The effect of contributing to a qualifying annuity is deferred taxes on the contributions from the time that the contributions are made to the time that any withdrawals are made. Qualifying annuities are used for individual retirement accounts, Keogh plans, and profit-sharing plans. —See also NONQUALIFYING ANNUITY.

qualifying dividends   Dividends that meet Internal Revenue Service regulations for exclusion or partial exclusion from federal income taxation. For example, corporations are permitted to exclude a portion of all of the qualifying dividends received from stock owned in domestic corporations. There are no qualifying dividends for calculating individual income taxes.

quality of earnings   —See EARNINGS QUALITY.

quant   A person with strong skills in mathematics, engineering, or computer science, who applies those skills to the securities business. For example, a pension fund may employ a quant to put together an optimal portfolio of bonds to meet the fund's future liabilities. —Also called *rocket scientist*.

quarter   **1.** One quarter of a point. For stock quotes, a quarter represents one quarter of $1, or 25¢. For bond quotes, a quarter represents one quarter of 1% of par, or $2.50. Thus, a bond quoted at 91¾ is being offered for $917.50. For option quotes, a quarter of a point represents $25.   **2.** A 3-month period representing 25% of a fiscal year.

quasi-public corporation   A privately operated firm with legislatively mandated public responsibilities. A quasi-public corporation may have publicly traded shares of stock. The Federal National Mortgage Association is a quasi-public corporation established to make a secondary market in mortgages. The firm is privately owned but publicly traded and its shares of common stock are listed on the New York Stock Exchange.

quick asset   A current asset that is quickly convertible into cash with no loss of value. Quick assets are often calculated as current assets less inventories. —See also NET QUICK ASSETS.

quick ratio   A relatively severe test of a company's liquidity and its ability to meet short-term obligations. The quick ratio is calculated by dividing current liabilities into all current assets with the exception of inventory. (Inventory is excluded on the basis that it is the least liquid current asset.) A relatively high quick ratio indicates conservative management and the ability to satisfy short-term obligations. —Also called *acid-test ratio*. —See also CASH RATIO; CURRENT RATIO; LIQUIDITY RATIO 1; NET QUICK ASSETS; WORKING CAPITAL.

quick turn   The purchase or short sale of a security followed in a short time by a closing transaction. A quick turn is intended to earn a relatively small profit in a short period of time.

quid pro quo   Something that a person or firm gives another person or firm in return for something else received. In the securities industry institutional investors provide orders to brokerage firms as a quid pro quo for in-depth research.

quota A maximum or minimum limit on quantity. Applied to imports, a quota designates the maximum quantity of a product that may be brought into a country during a specified period of time. Quotas can have significant impact on certain industries and companies. The establishment of a quota or a change in an existing quota can influence the price of the affected firm's securities. —See also TARIFF; TRIGGER PRICE.

quotation A statement or listing of the price at which a security trades. A quotation is often the last price at which the trade took place, but occasionally it is the current bid and ask. For example, a quotation of 15–15¼ means that the market maker is willing to buy at $15 per share (the bid) and sell at $15.25 per share (the ask). —Also called *quote*.

Quote Rule A Securities and Exchange Commission rule requiring specialists and market makers to maintain and provide continuous, firm quotations for the securities in which they make a market.

R

r **1.** —Used in the dividend column of stock transaction tables in newspapers to indicate the amount of dividends declared or paid in the preceding 12 months plus a stock dividend: *PE Cp .25r.* **2.** —Used in option transaction tables in newspapers to indicate that the option was not traded: *Lilly 65 11 r r.* **3.** —Used in mutual fund transaction tables in newspapers to indicate funds that levy a redemption charge when shares are sold: *IDS Inc r.* **4.** —Used in bond transaction tables in newspapers to indicate a registered security. Although most bonds are registered, this symbol is used when a distinction is necessary, as when a bond trades in registered and in bearer form: *NoPac 3.47r.*

R4 —See REGISTERED REPRESENTATIVE RAPID RESPONSE SERVICE.

raider A person or firm attempting a takeover of a company. —Also called *corporate raider.* —See also DEFENSIVE ACQUISITION; GREENMAIL; JUNK FINANCING; SHARK REPELLENT; TARGET COMPANY; WHITE KNIGHT.

raiding An attempt to purchase a sufficient number of shares of a company's stock through a tender offer such that control of the target's operations can be taken away from its current management. —Also called *venture arbitrage.*

rally A fairly sharp, short-term general rise in security prices after a period of little movement or of declining prices.

RAN —See REVENUE ANTICIPATION NOTE.

R & D costs —See RESEARCH AND DEVELOPMENT COSTS.

random-walk hypothesis The hypothesis that past stock prices are of no value in forecasting future prices because past, current, and future prices merely reflect market responses to information coming into the market at random. In short, price movements are no more predictable than the pattern of the walk of a drunk. This controversial hypothesis, if valid, implies that technical analysis is useless in its attempts to predict future price movements in the market. —See also EFFICIENT MARKET.

range The high and low prices reached by a security over a given period of time. A large range in relation to a security price tends to indicate greater price volatility, making the security a better candidate for trading purposes but not necessarily for investment purposes. —Also called *price range*.

rate anticipation swap The sale of one bond combined with the purchase of another bond of different maturity in order to take maximum advantage of expected changes in interest rates. For example, an investor would want to trade short-term bonds for long-term bonds if interest rates were expected to fall, because the price of the long-term bonds would rise more than the price of the short-term bonds.

rate base The value of a utility's assets for the purpose of determining the rates the utility is permitted to charge its customers. Exactly what a utility should be permitted to include in its rate base is often a point of contention between it and its customers.

rate case A hearing before a state public service commission during which a public utility's application for new rates is approved, altered, or denied. For stockholders of a regulated company such as an electric utility or a telephone company, the outcome of a rate case is of major importance in determining the value of their shares.

rate covenant A provision for a municipal revenue bond issue setting requirements for charging revenue on the facility that is being financed by the bond issue. For example, a rate covenant might require that the rates from customers of a city sewage plant be sufficient to ensure adequate maintenance and repair for the facility. A rate covenant is included in a bond agreement to protect the bondholders' interests.

rate of return 1. —See CURRENT YIELD; TOTAL RETURN. 2. —See RETURN ON INVESTMENT.

rate relief The granting to a regulated company (as a utility) higher rates (i.e., the prices charged to its customers) so that it can generate greater revenues. Public utilities frequently seek rate relief by filing a request for rate increases with public regulatory bodies. The utility's success in obtaining rate relief has a very heavy impact on the value of its shares.

rate shock Electric utility customers' dismay when their bills suddenly jump because of sharply higher rates. The term is nearly always used in reference to utilities that bring a new, large, costly (often nuclear) plant on stream. The big rise occurs because most regulatory commissions do not allow a utility to include new plant costs in its rates until the plant actually begins generating electricity. Rate shock can be just as detrimental to a utility's investors because the regulatory commission may not allow the utility to earn the rate of return to which it is entitled for fear of causing public outrage with even greater rate increases.

rating   The grading of a security with respect to a characteristic or a set of characteristics such as safety and growth. Rating is most often applied to debt securities which are graded according to the issuer's ability to pay interest and principal when due. —See also BOND RATING; DOWN-GRADING; MOODY'S INVESTMENT GRADE; NOT RATED; STOCK RATING; UPGRAD-ING 1.

rating agencies   Companies that grade securities so as to indicate the quality of the securities for investors. The two major rating services are Moody's Investor Services and Standard & Poor's Corporation. Two lesser known rating firms are Duff & Phelps and Fitch Investors Service.

ratio   A comparison of one amount to another amount. For example, the most frequently used ratio among investors is the price-earnings ratio. Financial analysts, investors, and managers use ratios to evaluate many factors such as the attractiveness of a stock or the operating efficiency of a company. —Also called *financial ratio.* —See also ACTIVITY RATIO; DEBT MANAGEMENT RATIO; LIQUIDITY RATIO; PROFITABILITY RATIO.

ratio analysis   Study of the relationships of financial variables. Ratios of one firm are often compared with the same ratios of similar firms or of all firms in a single industry. This comparison indicates if a particular firm's financial statistics are suspect. Likewise, a particular ratio for a firm may be evaluated over a period of time to determine if any special trend exists. —See also HORIZONTAL ANALYSIS; TREND ANALYSIS; VERTICAL ANALYSIS.

ratio writing   —See VARIABLE RATIO OPTION WRITING.

raw material   Goods used in the manufacture of a product. For example, a furniture manufacturer is likely to have raw materials such as hardware, lumber, and metal tubing on hand. Raw material is carried as an inventory item in the current assets section of a firm's balance sheet.

reaction   A decline in security prices following a period of rising security prices.

read the tape   To observe security price and volume information as it appears on the consolidated tape. Some traders read the tape in an attempt to spot irregular trades or price movements that signal buying or selling opportunities. —See also TAPE READER.

Reaganomics   The economic plan instituted by President Ronald Reagan that called for reduced tax rates, increased defense spending, decreased social spending, and reduced growth of the money supply. This plan, which was essentially passed in Reagan's first term, initially resulted in a serious recession accompanied by high interest rates. Falling interest rates and rising economic output then followed. In addition the President's policies brought about massive government deficits and major reductions in inflation.

real asset   A physical asset such as gold or timber. Real assets tend to be most desirable during periods of high inflation. —See also FINANCIAL ASSET.

real estate   Land, buildings, and improvements thereto. —Also called *real property*.

real estate certificate of deposit   A certificate of deposit providing a guaranteed rate of interest in combination with the possible return from rent and capital gains derived from the property the funds from the certificate are used to acquire. The guaranteed rate of interest is normally lower than the rate paid on regular certificates of deposit. —See also EQUITY KICKER.

real estate investment trust (REIT)   A company that purchases and manages real estate and/or real estate loans. Some REITs specialize in purchasing long-term mortgages, while others actually buy real estate. Income earned by a trust is generally passed through and taxed to the stockholders rather than to the REIT. —See also EQUITY REIT; MORTGAGE REIT.

real income   Income, as that of a person, group, or country, adjusted for changes in the prices of goods and services. Real income measures purchasing power in the current year after an adjustment for changes in prices since a selected base year. If money income increases more than consumer prices, real income increases. If money income increases less than consumer prices, real income declines. Declines in real income are unfavorable for those suffering the declines and for firms selling goods and services to them.

real interest rate   The nominal current interest rate less the rate of inflation. For example, an investor holding a 10% certificate of deposit during a period of 6% annual inflation would be earning a real interest rate of 4%. The real interest rate is a more valid measure of the desirability of an investment than the nominal rate is.

realization principle   The accounting standard that recognizes revenue only when earned. Generally, realization occurs when goods are sold or a service is rendered.

realized gain   The amount by which the net proceeds from the sale of an asset exceed its cost of acquisition. When gains are realized, they become income for tax purposes. —See also UNREALIZED GAIN.

realized loss   The amount by which an investment's acquisition cost exceeds the net proceeds from its sale. A realized loss, as opposed to a paper loss, may be used to reduce taxable income. —See also UNREALIZED LOSS.

real market   Quotes from a dealer willing to buy and sell a security in relatively large volume. Dealers uninterested in trading a security may provide quotes but do not expect anyone to act on them.

real property   —See REAL ESTATE.

real return   The inflation-adjusted rate of return on an investment. If an investor earns a return of 12% during a year when inflation is 4%, the real return is 8%. —See also NOMINAL RETURN.

recapitalization   A change in the long-term financing mix used by a company. For example, a firm may borrow long-term funds (i.e., it may sell bonds) in order to acquire the money needed to repurchase a block of its outstanding stock. Since recapitalization will often affect the level and the volatility of earnings per share, it is of interest to stockholders. Recapitalization often occurs when a firm attempts to reorganize while in bankruptcy proceedings. —See also CAPITALIZATION.

recapture of depreciation   The extent to which the price received from selling a depreciated asset represents recovery of depreciation taken in prior years. For example, an asset purchased for $10,000, depreciated to a book value of $6,000, and sold for $9,000 would result in a recapture of $3,000. —Also called *depreciation recapture*.

receivables   —See ACCOUNTS RECEIVABLE.

receivables turnover   —See ACCOUNTS RECEIVABLE TURNOVER.

receiver   A person assigned by a court to handle affairs and assets of a business in bankruptcy proceedings. The receiver is charged with overseeing the firm for the benefit of its creditors and stockholders.

receiver's certificate   Short-term debt issued by the receiver of a firm in bankruptcy proceedings. Receivers' certificates are of high quality because they have first claim on the bankrupt firm's assets.

receive versus payment (RVP)   A settlement procedure in which a customer instructs that security delivery will be made immediately upon receipt of proceeds from the sale of the security. —See also DELIVER VERSUS PAYMENT.

recession   An extended decline in general business activity. The National Bureau of Economic Research formally defines a recession as three consecutive quarters of falling real gross national product. A recession affects different securities in different ways. For example, holders of high quality bonds stand to benefit since inflation and interest rates may decline. Conversely, stockholders of manufacturing firms will probably see company profits and dividends drop.

reciprocal immunity   The tax immunity that interest payments on federal securities have against state and local authorities and that interest payments on state and local securities have against federal authorities. While not specifically stated as such in the U.S. Constitution, reciprocal immunity has been recognized by the U.S. Supreme Court.

reclamation   Recovery of losses by either party in a securities transaction in which there has been a bad delivery.

record date   The date on which a firm's books are closed during the process of identifying the owners of a certain class of securities for purposes of transmitting dividends, interest, proxies, financial reports, and other documentation to them. For example, only the common stock-holders who are listed on the record date will receive the dividends that are to be mailed on the payment date. —See also EX-DIVIDEND; INTEREST DATES.

recoup   To sell an asset at a price sufficient to recover the original outlay or to offset a previous loss.

recourse loan   A loan in which the lender can claim more than the collateral as repayment in the event that payments on the loan are stopped. Thus, a recourse loan places the borrower's personal assets at risk. —See also NONRECOURSE LOAN.

recovery   1. The rising price of an asset. For example, following an extended decline in the price of precious metals, investor expectations of future inflation may generate recoveries in gold and silver prices. 2. Increased economic activity during a business cycle, resulting in growth in the gross national product.

rectangle   In technical analysis, a chart formation in which the price of a security bounces back and forth between two horizontal lines. Since a rectangle is thought to occur when stock is being distributed or accumulated by knowledgeable investors, a major price movement is expected once the stock breaks out of the rectangle formation. —See also ACCUMULATION AREA; DISTRIBUTION AREA; REVERSAL PATTERN.

red   Pertaining to a firm or the operations of a firm deemed unprofitable. The term *red* derives from the red ink used to show losses on financial statements. —See also BLACK.

redemption   The retirement of a security by repurchase. While generally used in reference to the repurchase of a bond before maturity, the term also applies to stock and mutual fund shares. —See also PARTIAL REDEMPTION.

redemption charge   —See DEFERRED SALES CHARGE.

redemption price   1. The price at which an open-end investment company will buy back its shares from the owners. In most cases, the redemption price is the net asset value per share. 2. —See CALL PRICE.

red herring   A prospectus that is given to potential investors in a new security issue before the selling price has been set and before the issuer's registration statement has been approved for accuracy and completeness by the Securities and Exchange Commission (SEC). This document, which provides details of the issue and facts concerning the issuer, is so named because of a statement on it, printed in red, that the issue has not yet been approved by the SEC. —Also called *preliminary prospectus*.

rediscount   To discount a negotiable instrument a second time.

refinance   1. To extend the maturity of a loan. 2. —See REFUND.

refund   To retire securities with the funds that have been raised through the sale of a new security issue. Refunding normally occurs after a period of falling interest rates when firms issue new debt in order to retire existing debt having high coupon rates of interest. Refunding works to the disadvantage of existing bondholders who must sell their securities before maturity (usually at a slight premium over face value) when proceeds can only be reinvested at a reduced yield. —Also called *refinance*. —See also CALL PROVISION; NONREFUNDABLE; PREREFUNDED BOND.

refund annuity An annuity that provides fixed payments as long as the annuitant lives, and that guarantees repayment of the amount paid in. If the annuitant dies before receiving the amount paid in for the annuity, the balance is paid to the beneficiary.

refunding bond A bond issued for the purpose of retiring an outstanding bond.

regional exchange A securities exchange that specializes in the stocks and bonds of companies with a regional, rather than a national, interest. The regional exchanges provide the only organized trading in many of these securities. They also list and trade many of the securities traded on one or more of the national exchanges, and in recent years the majority of trading on the regional exchanges has been in these dual listed securities. The major regional exchanges in the United States are the Boston, Cincinnati, Midwest, Pacific, and Philadelphia stock exchanges.

registered bond —See REGISTERED SECURITY.

registered company A corporation that has filed a Securities and Exchange Commission registration form and that is subject to the Commission's reporting requirements.

registered competitive market maker **1.** A dealer who is registered with the National Association of Securities Dealers to make a market in one or more securities. A registered competitive market maker must supply firm bid and ask prices to the market. **2.** A floor trader on the New York Stock Exchange.

registered competitive trader —See FLOOR TRADER.

registered equity market maker A floor trader on the American Stock Exchange.

registered exchange A securities exchange that has filed, and has had accepted, a registration statement with the Securities and Exchange Commission (SEC). All the larger securities exchanges in the United States are registered with the SEC as required by the Securities Exchange Act of 1934. —See also UNREGISTERED EXCHANGE.

registered options trader A member of an organized options exchange who is a market maker in certain options assigned by the exchange. A registered options trader holds a position similar to a specialist on a stock exchange.

registered representative An employee or a partner in a brokerage firm who is registered to handle customer accounts. —Also called *account executive; broker; customer's man*.

Registered Representative Rapid Response Service (R4) An automated stock trading system used on the New York Stock Exchange that provides immediate execution for a limited list of stocks at the best quoted price.

registered retirement savings plan (RRSP) A personal tax-sheltered retirement plan for Canadians that is similar to individual retirement accounts offered in the United States. Contributions may be deducted from taxable income, and earnings on contributions are exempt from taxation until withdrawals are made.

registered secondary distribution The sale of a block of previously issued securities following registration with the Securities and Exchange Commission. Securities sold in a registered secondary offering are likely to come from an institutional investor that acquired the securities in a private placement. —See also SECONDARY DISTRIBUTION; SPOT SECONDARY DISTRIBUTION.

registered security A security, the certificate of which is imprinted with the owner's name on its face. A record of current owners is kept by the issuer for purposes of transmitting checks, proxies, reports, and so forth. Nearly all securities are registered. —Also called *registered bond*. —See also BEARER FORM.

registered trader —See FLOOR TRADER.

registrar A firm that updates stock records through information sent by the transfer agent. Essentially, the registrar makes certain that the issued certificates correspond with those that have been canceled.

registration The preparation of a security issue for public sale. Normally, registration involves the issuer's employment of an underwriting firm to prepare a registration statement to be submitted to the Securities and Exchange Commission or to a state authority. As part of this process, an investment banker will also bring in a public accounting firm to audit the issuer's financial condition. —See also COOLING-OFF PERIOD; GUN JUMPING; PIGGYBACK REGISTRATION.

registration fee The fee paid to the Securities and Exchange Commission by a firm issuing securities.

registration statement A document filed with the Securities and Exchange Commission containing detailed information about a firm that plans to sell securities to the public. Required data include financial statements, the reason for the issue, details on the firm's business, etc. Certain issues (such as under $500,000, intrastate sales only, private placements, and bank securities) are exempt from this requirement. —See also DEFICIENCY LETTER; OFFICIAL STATEMENT; PROSPECTUS.

regression analysis Measurement of the change in one variable as a result of changes in one or more variables. Regression analysis is used frequently in an attempt to identify the variables that affect a certain stock's price.

regression coefficient A mathematical measure of the relationship between a dependent variable and an independent variable. For example, a financial theorist might attempt to determine the effect of increased dividends on a stock's price by calculating the regression coefficient between the price of the stock and its dividends per share. In this instance, the stock price is the dependent variable and the dividend payment is the independent variable.

regressive tax   A tax having a rate that declines as the amount to be taxed increases. In terms of income, federal and state taxation of cigarettes is regressive because low-income smokers pay a higher rate of taxation in terms of their income than high-income smokers do. A system of regressive taxation tends to free more funds for investment because high-income individuals tend to save a greater portion of their income. However, a regressive tax is often considered socially and politically unacceptable. —See also FLAT TAX; PROGRESSIVE TAX.

regular member   A full member of a securities exchange, entitled to all privileges and subject to all regulations of the exchange. —See also ASSOCIATE MEMBER.

regular-way contract   A security transaction in which delivery of the certificate by the selling broker and delivery of cash by the buying broker are to occur five business days after the trade date. A regular-way contract is the normal method for handling stock and corporate and municipal bond transactions. Government securities and options settle one business day following the trade date. —See also CASH CONTRACT; SELLER'S OPTION CONTRACT.

regulated investment company   An investment company that meets certain standards and, as a result, does not have to pay federal income taxes on distributions of dividends, interest, and realized capital gains. Essentially, this income is passed through to the stockholders who, in turn, are taxed. To qualify as a regulated investment company a firm must derive at least 90% of its income from dividends, interest, and capital gains. It also must distribute at least 90% of the dividends and interest received. It must have a minimum diversification of its assets.

Regulation A   A Securities and Exchange Commission (SEC) regulation partially exempting small new security issues from certain SEC registration requirements.

Regulation A issue   A new security issue that requires a much shorter prospectus and that carries with it reduced officer and director liability for misleading and/or false statements.

Regulation G   A Federal Reserve regulation extending control over credit to purchase and carry listed stocks to firms other than brokers, dealers, and banks.

Regulation Q   A Federal Reserve regulation setting the maximum rates of interest that savings institutions were legally permitted to pay on time and savings deposits. This control was gradually phased out beginning in 1980. While Regulation Q was in effect, it tended to penalize savers and subsidize borrowers. —See also CREDIT CRUNCH.

Regulation T   A Federal Reserve regulation specifying the maximum initial credit extension to investors in securities. The initial margin requirement has varied from 40% to 100% since the Regulation was established under provisions of the Securities Exchange Act of 1934. Listed stocks, convertible bonds, and many over-the-counter stocks are covered by Regulation T. —See also FREERIDING 2; FROZEN ACCOUNT; SPECIAL MISCELLANEOUS ACCOUNT.

Regulation U   A Federal Reserve regulation controlling bank loans to customers for the purpose of purchasing and carrying listed stocks.

regulatory climate   The extent to which a regulated firm or industry is permitted to earn an adequate return on the stockholders' investment. This term is nearly always used in reference to utilities, which are required to obtain approval for rate changes. A favorable regulatory climate generally causes investors to value a company more highly because they expect its earnings to be bigger.

rehypothecate   To repledge stock as collateral for a loan. In practice, this term means to pledge securities (by a brokerage firm) for a bank loan when the securities have already been pledged to the firm by one of its customers. The brokerage firm essentially passes along the collateral in order to obtain a loan to finance the customer's account. —See also HYPOTHECATE.

reinsurance   The insuring of part or all of the risk on a policy written by one insurance company for another insurance company. Reinsurance is a method by which an insurance company spreads risks among other insurance companies.

reinvestment plan   —See DIVIDEND REINVESTMENT PLAN.

reinvestment privilege   The prerogative of a mutual fund shareholder to have dividends used to purchase additional shares in the fund. Most mutual funds give their shareholders reinvestment privileges and most do not charge fees for the purchase of the new shares.

reinvestment rate   The annual yield at which cash flows from an investment can be reinvested. The reinvestment rate is of particular interest to people holding short-term investments (e.g., certificates of deposit or Treasury bills) or long-term investments that produce large annual cash flows (e.g., high-coupon bonds).

reinvestment risk   The possibility that cash flows produced by an investment will have to be reinvested at a reduced rate of return. For example, the owner of a certificate of deposit faces the risk that lower interest rates will be in effect when the certificate matures and the funds are to be reinvested.

REIT   —See REAL ESTATE INVESTMENT TRUST.

rejection   Refusal to accept a security delivered by a customer or broker. A questionable certificate or an improper endorsement are reasons for rejection.

relationship trading   —See BASIS TRADING.

relative strength   The price strength of an individual stock compared with the strength of an industry index or a general market index. In general, a stock acting stronger than its industry or the market as a whole is a bullish sign for that stock. Likewise, an industry index acting stronger than a market index is bullish for stocks in that industry. Relative strength is typically measured for calculating an index of a stock's price to its industry or market index over a period of time. —Also called *strength*.

remainderman The person or organization that is to receive the remaining interest in a property or estate after prior interests have been satisfied.

remargin To deposit additional cash or securities in a margin account when equity in the account is insufficient to meet the maintenance margin requirement.

remit To send payment for goods or services.

reopen an issue In U.S. Treasury financing, to sell additional securities of an existing issue rather than to offer a new issue with different terms. If the market for debt has changed since the existing issue was sold, reopening the issue will require a revised selling price to make the securities competitive in the current market environment.

reopening The opening of trading in a security or futures contract in which trading was earlier suspended. For example, exchange officials may suspend trading in a security until certain information is made public. Following a public announcement of the information, trading in the security will resume.

reorganization The restatement of assets to current market value along with a restructuring of liabilities and equity to reflect the reduction in asset values and negotiations with creditors. Reorganization is used as an attempt to keep a financially troubled firm viable. —See also BANKRUPTCY; CHAPTER 11.

reorganization plan A plan filed with a bankruptcy court judge by a company in Chapter 11 proceedings in which the disbursement of assets is stipulated. The plan must be approved by the firm's creditors and by the court. A reorganization plan results in new securities being given to creditors in a trade for old securities.

repatriate To bring home assets currently held in a foreign country. Domestic corporations are frequently taxed on the profits that they repatriate, a factor inducing the firms to leave overseas the profits earned there.

repeat prices omitted A notice on the consolidated tape that only the initial trade at a given price will be reported. Subsequent trades in a security are reported only when there is a price change. Repeat prices omitted is used when heavy trading volume requires increased speed in reporting transactions.

replacement cost The current cost of replacing an asset with another equivalent asset.

replacement cost accounting An accounting system valuing assets and liabilities at replacement cost rather than at historical cost. Replacement cost accounting incorporates the effects of changing prices and the resultant changing values of the items that are listed in the firm's financial statements.

repo —See REPURCHASE AGREEMENT.

repo rate The rate of interest (annualized) on a repurchase agreement.

report A confirmation of a transaction at the time of execution.

reporting dealers Independent dealers in government securities that report their trading activity and security positions to the Federal Reserve. Since the Federal Reserve uses purchases and sales to influence the money supply, information from reporting dealers plays an important part in monetary policy. —See also OPEN-MARKET OPERATIONS; PRIMARY DEALER.

repurchase agreement (RP) The sale of an asset at the same time an agreement is made to repurchase the asset at a specified price on a given date. Essentially, this process involves taking out a loan and using the asset as collateral. The opposite side of the transaction is called a reverse repurchase agreement. —Also called *repo*. —See also OVERNIGHT REPO.

required rate of return 1. The minimum rate of return that an investment must provide or must be expected to provide in order to justify its acquisition. For example, an investor who can earn an annual return of 11% on certificates of deposit may set a required rate of return of 15% on a more risky stock investment before considering a shift of funds into stock. An investment's required return is a function of the returns available on other investments and of the risk level inherent in a particular investment. 2. The minimum rate of return required by an investor, which limits the types of investments the investor can undertake. For example, a person with a required rate of return of 15% would generally have to invest in relatively risky securities.

required reserves The reserves against deposits that commercial banks and thrifts are required to hold either in cash or in deposits at the Federal Reserve. —See also EXCESS RESERVES; RESERVE REQUIREMENT.

research and development costs (R & D costs) Costs incurred to develop and bring new products to market or to improve existing products. Although R & D costs tend to penalize current profits, they eventually benefit the firm's future profits when new products developed as a result of the research become profitable themselves. Many analysts regard a high proportion of sales revenue devoted to R & D as a positive sign relative to a firm's profit potential and future stock price.

research department The section of a brokerage firm or institutional investment house in which companies, economic matters, and securities are analyzed. The research departments in institutional investment houses assist in selecting investments and devising investment strategies. Brokerage firm research departments assist the registered representatives in making customer purchase suggestions.

What are the things to look for in research reports, and what kinds of research should I ask for from my broker?
••

Since most Wall Street research reports are buy recommendations, I will assume that we are discussing a buy recommendation research report. You should look for a number of things in the research reports from your broker, including the following:

1. The first thing the investment firm making the research recommendation should provide the reader with is a brief overview of its assumptions on the outlook for the economy and the securities markets for the next one to two years. This outlook should include a forecast for real GNP growth, inflation, corporate earnings, interest rates and the bond market, and equity prices.

2. The first objective of the research report should be a reflection of the type of investment recommendation. Is this recommendation for high and secure current income? For moderate growth of principal and a moderate level of current income? For long-term growth of principal? Or for aggressive growth? The report also should define the quality of the issue being recommended, i.e., highest quality, high quality, above-average quality, average quality, special situation/higher risk, small emerging growth company, or speculative. The readers may then quickly determine if the recommendation is suitable for their investment objective and for their time horizons.

3. Next, the report should discuss the outlook for the industry within the economic environment anticipated by the firm writing the report.

4. How does the recommended company compare with other companies in the same industry? It is an absolute must that the research report contain an industry group comparison to enable a relative evaluation on the particular stock being recommended. One must always compare apples to apples. The report should include a comparison of growth in sales, cash flow, earnings per share, dividends per share, book value per share, return on equity, and other income comparisons. Comparisons should also be shown for various balance sheet items including capitalization. The report should provide a history of price ranges and price-earnings ratios along with an explanation of any large dissimilarities in the price-earnings ratios of various companies in the same industry.

5. Why is this company recommended? What is unique about the company that makes it attractive for purchase?

6. What are the major risks associated with an equity investment in this company? This discussion should include government regulations, any pending legislation, or new tax laws that could affect the company. *(continued)*

(continued)

7. The analyst should also discuss the management of the company in some detail. This information would include the backgrounds of two or three key executives, top management depth, their ages, their ownership of the equity securities of the company, their compensation, and management turnover.

8. One of the most important aspects of the report should be an indication whether the investment firm has had an investment banking relationship with the company in question during the past several years. Securities law requires the disclosure of such a relationship. Though it is not always a negative factor, if the firm recommending the company has an existing or past investment banking relationship with it, the investment banker may have a certain preference for the company that it has underwritten. Investment banking fees are the most profitable area of an investment firm's business.

9. Make sure that the report is dated and that it uses current price levels. Many times Wall Street firms will have significant lags between the printed date and the written date on such reports. In periods of price acceleration the time of executing an investment idea is very critical.

10. Last, but certainly not the least important, the report should display a bar chart showing the price history of the stock for a minimum of the last three years. The report should also include a technical analyst's opinion on the price trend of the stock with price support levels and price resistance levels. In addition, long-term point-and-figure chart counts should be given to provide the reader with an approximate indication of the long-term price objectives from the technical aspect. Any large purchases or sales of the stock by corporate insiders should be listed along with appropriate comments on these large purchases or sales.

J. Blaine Reeve, CFA, Senior Vice President
Commerce Union Bank, Nashville, TN

reserve Funds earmarked by a firm from its retained earnings for future use, as for the payment of likely-to-be-incurred bad debts. The existence of such a reserve informs readers of the firm's financial statements that at least a part of the retained earnings will not be available to the stockholders. —See also ALLOWANCE FOR DOUBTFUL ACCOUNTS; RESERVE FOR CONTINGENCIES.

reserve deficiency A shortage in funds set aside as a reserve for a specific purpose. For example, during a recession a firm may find the reserve fund covering allowance for bad debts deficient when the amount of bad debts exceeds expectations. A reserve deficiency will penalize the firm's profits if the firm has to set aside additional funds to offset the deficiency.

reserve for bad debts —See ALLOWANCE FOR DOUBTFUL ACCOUNTS.

reserve for contingencies A part of retained earnings set aside for potential future losses. For example, a firm may establish a reserve account to cover the possibility of losing a lawsuit to which it is a party.

reserve requirement The required percentage of deposits that banks and thrifts must hold in cash or in deposits at the Federal Reserve. This requirement is set by the Fed. Any changes in the required percentage are used to influence credit conditions. An increased percentage requirement means fewer funds available for lending and a resultant rise in interest rates. —See also MONETARY POLICY; REQUIRED RESERVES.

reset note A debt security with terms that can be reset on one or more dates during the life of the note. At the time the terms are changed, the holder normally has the right to redeem the security.

residual security A security with the potential for diluting earnings per share. A convertible bond is a residual security because conversion of the bond by an investor will result in more shares of common stock outstanding and a reduction in earnings per share.

residual value The price at which a fixed asset is expected to be sold at the end of its useful life. Residual value is used in calculating some types of depreciation. —Also called *salvage value; scrap value.*

resistance Increased supply of a security. —See also SUPPORT.

resistance level A price at which a security or the market itself will encounter considerable selling pressure. A resistance level is formed when investors purchase large amounts of a security just before a decline and then resolve to sell the security should it again reach the level at which it was purchased. Technical analysts believe that an additional supply of a security will tend to keep its price from rising above the resistance level. —Also called *overhead resistance level.* —See also OVER-HANGING SUPPLY; SUPPORT LEVEL.

resource recovery revenue bond A debt obligation, normally issued by a municipality or local government agency, with the proceeds used to construct a facility that converts solid waste into some sort of salable item. Debt service is generally covered through fees paid by firms disposing of garbage and through revenues from the sale of an end product such as energy or fuel.

restatement The altered presentation of a portion or all of an earlier financial statement. For example, a firm may issue a restatement of its previously published balance sheet and income statement because it has discovered some heretofore unknown information that should have been included on it.

restricted account A margin account in which the customer cannot purchase any additional stock on margin without putting up more equity. An account is restricted when its debit balance is greater than the loan value of the securities within the account. —Also called *blocked account.*

restricted option An option in which an uncovered opening transaction cannot be made. An option becomes restricted when it closes at a price under $50 (½ point) and is out-of-the-money by over 5 points. Restricted options are not prohibited for covered transactions or spreads.

restricted retained earnings Retained earnings unavailable for the payment of dividends to common stockholders. For example, dividend arrearages on cumulative preferred stock must be paid before any dividend payments can be made to common stockholders. Thus, the arrearages result in restricted retained earnings.

restricted security A security that has not been registered with the Securities and Exchange Commission and therefore may not be sold publicly. These securities frequently enter portfolios of institutional investors through private placements and are sometimes registered at a later date. —Also called *letter bond; letter security; letter stock; unregistered security.* —See also INVESTMENT LETTER.

restrictive covenant —See COVENANT.

restructuring —See DEBT RESTRUCTURING.

retail The sale of securities to individual investors, as opposed to sales to institutions and transactions among broker-dealer firms for eventual sale to retail clients. —See also WHOLESALE.

retail house A brokerage firm that primarily attracts individual investors. A retail house frequently has numerous offices, research reports targeted to individuals, large office staffs, high overhead, and relatively high commissions.

retail market A market composed of price quotes for a security made by a broker or a dealer to an individual investor. A quote at the retail level entails a higher ask and a lower bid than a quote on the same security for another dealer. —See also INSIDE MARKET.

retained earnings Accumulated net income that has been retained for reinvestment in the business rather than being paid in dividends to stockholders. Net income that is retained in the business can be used to acquire additional income-earning assets that result in increased income in future years. Retained earnings is a part of the owners' equity section of a firm's balance sheet. —Also called *earned surplus; surplus.* —See also ACCUMULATED EARNINGS TAX; PAYOUT RATIO; RESTRICTED RETAINED EARNINGS; STATEMENT OF RETAINED EARNINGS.

retained earnings statement —See STATEMENT OF RETAINED EARNINGS.

retention Securities distributed to members of an underwriting syndicate after accounting for the portion of the new issue retained for sales to institutions and members of the selling group who are not also part of the syndicate.

retirement **1.** The disposal of a fixed asset at the end of its useful life. Retirement may result in a gain or loss depending on any compensation received for the asset and whether or not the asset is carried at a positive book value. **2.** The voiding of a firm's own stock that has been reacquired and is being held as treasury stock.

retractable bond *Canadian.* A put bond.

return —See YIELD.

return of capital —See CAPITAL DIVIDEND.

return on assets (ROA) —See RETURN ON INVESTMENT.

return on common stock equity A measure of the return that a firm's management is able to earn on common stockholders' investment. Return on common stock equity is calculated by dividing owners' equity less the par value of any preferred stock outstanding into net income less preferred dividends. For firms with no preferred stock, return on common stock equity is identical to return on equity. —See also PROFITABILITY RATIO.

return on equity (ROE) A measure of the net income that a firm is able to earn as a percent of stockholders' investment. Many analysts consider ROE the single most important financial ratio applying to stockholders and the best measure of performance by a firm's management. Return on equity is calculated by dividing owners' equity into net income after taxes. —See also PROFITABILITY RATIO; RETURN ON COMMON STOCK EQUITY.

return on investment (ROI) A measure of the net income that a firm's management is able to earn with the firm's total assets. Return on investment is calculated by dividing total assets into net profits after taxes. —Also called *return on assets.* —See also PROFITABILITY RATIO.

return on sales The portion of each dollar of sales that a firm is able to turn into income. Because of severe competition, regulation, or another factor, some firms or industries have low returns on sales. This is generally the case for grocery chains, for example. In some instances, a low return on sales can be offset by increased sales. Return on sales varies significantly from industry to industry. —See also GROSS PROFIT MARGIN; NET PROFIT MARGIN; PROFITABILITY RATIO.

revenue The inflow of assets resulting from sales of goods and services and earnings from dividends, interest, and rent. Revenue is often received in the form of cash but also may be in the form of receivables to be turned into cash at a later date.

revenue anticipation note (RAN) A short-term municipal obligation with repayment to be made from a revenue source other than taxes.

revenue bond A municipal debt on which the payment of interest and principal depends on revenues from the particular asset that the bond issue is used to finance. Examples of such projects are toll roads and bridges, housing developments, and airport expansions. Revenue bonds are generally considered of lower quality than general obligation bonds, but there is a great amount of variance in risk depending on the particular assets financed. —See also AUTHORITY BOND.

revenue enhancement An increase in revenues, especially by way of increased taxes. Revenue enhancement includes reducing taxpayer deductions and eliminating tax credits.

revenue ruling Written guidance provided by the Internal Revenue Service (IRS) to taxpayers. Although revenue rulings apply to individual situations, they are often of general interest because of the manner in which the IRS interprets a particular tax problem. —Also called *letter ruling; ruling.*

reversal pattern In technical analysis, a chart formation indicating a market top or a market bottom. A reversal pattern, which normally occurs after a major movement in the price of a stock or in the entire market, indicates that investors should adjust their positions to take advantage of the coming change in market direction. A saucer and a head-and-shoulders are reversal patterns.

reverse —See REVERSE REPURCHASE AGREEMENT.

reverse annuity mortgage A mortgage in which a homeowner's equity is gradually depleted by a series of payments from the mortgage holder to the homeowner. Thus, a reverse annuity mortgage increases in size as the annuity payments continue. A reverse annuity mortgage is used primarily by elderly homeowners wishing to convert the equity in their homes into a stream of retirement income payments.

reverse crush A combination commodity trade in which soybean meal and oil futures are purchased and soybean futures are sold. —See also CRUSH.

reverse repurchase agreement The purchase of an asset with a simultaneous agreement to resell the asset on a given date at a specified price. The result is simply a loan at a prescribed rate for a predetermined period of time while holding the asset as collateral. The opposite is called a *repurchase.* —Also called *reverse.*

reverse stock split A proportionate decrease in the shares of stock held by stockholders. For example, a one-for-three split would result in the stockholders' owning one share for every three shares owned before the split. A company generally institutes a reverse split in order to increase the market price of its stock. Such an act is quite unusual. —Also called *split down.* —See also SPLIT.

reverse swap The exchange of one bond for another such that an earlier investment position is reestablished to the investment position that existed before an earlier swap. For example, an investor might swap intermediate-term bonds for long-term bonds to take advantage of a steeply sloped yield curve. As the yield curve flattens, the investor might engage in a reverse swap by exchanging the long-term bonds for intermediate-term bonds. —See also BOND SWAP.

reversing trade In futures trading, a trade that brings an investor's position in a particular contract back to zero. For example, the purchase of a stock index contract that has previously been sold short is an example of a reversing trade.

revisionary trust A trust that is irrevocable for a predetermined period (at least ten years or until the death of the beneficiary), after which it becomes revocable. During the time the trust is irrevocable it will not be included as part of the donor's estate for tax purposes.

revocable trust   A trust that may be terminated by the grantor or that is set up to terminate automatically at a specific date. Revocable trusts are often used to turn daily decisions regarding certain assets over to someone else. They are also used to reduce probate fees, to reduce delays in distributing assets, and to keep assets from becoming a matter of public record. A revocable trust—an important estate-planning tool—may serve to reduce federal estate taxes but generally will have no effect on income taxes. —See also IRREVOCABLE TRUST.

revolver   —See LINE OF CREDIT.

revolving credit agreement   —See LINE OF CREDIT.

rich   Pertaining to or being a security price judged by some investors to be too high. For example, a new issue of stock may carry an offering price that many analysts consider rich. If too many investors and analysts believe the price is rich, the offering may be unsuccessful.

riding the yield curve   The purchase of a security with a longer term to maturity than the investor's expected holding period in order to produce increased returns by taking advantage of a positive yield curve. For example, a $10,000 twenty-six-week Treasury bill yielding 10% annually will sell for $9,524 while a 13-week bill yielding 9% will sell for $9,780. Buying the longer-term security, holding it for 13 weeks, and selling it at the existing 13-week bill price will produce a profit of $256 for an annualized yield of ($256/$9,524) × 4 = 10.75%. This yield is considerably higher than what might be obtained by simply purchasing a 13-week bill. But riding the yield curve increases yield only when longer-term interest rates are higher than shorter-term rates.

Should rights be sold or used?

Rights offerings refer to the right of an investor to maintain his or her percentage ownership in the company when the company decides to issue new stock. Generally it will do so at a discount to its market price to attract buyers so the existing stockholders' rights have value. The decision the rights holder must make is whether to put more money into the stock of this company, or to sell the rights in the open market as compensation for the dilution of their percentage ownership in the company. TIP: Such a purchase depends completely on the individuals' circumstances, goals, prejudices, and objectives, just as in any other stock purchase, and should be approached accordingly.

Thomas J. McAllister, CFP
McAllister Financial Planning, Indianapolis, IN

---

right   A certificate permitting the owner to purchase a certain number of shares, or, frequently, a fractional share of new stock from the issuer at a specific price. Rights are issued to existing stockholders in proportion to the number of shares the stockholders already own. Rights then may be combined with cash to purchase the new shares or they may be sold to other investors. Rights normally have value because they permit the owner to purchase shares of stock at less than the market price. A right is indicated in stock transaction tables by the symbol *rt*, appearing after the stock's name. —Also called *stock right*; *subscription right*. —See also EX-RIGHTS; PREEMPTIVE RIGHT.

right of accumulation The right that is granted to buyers by some mutual funds permitting the buyers to count existing holdings of the fund along with new purchases in determining the size of the sales fee on the new shares. This right applies to funds that charge fees on a sliding scale, whereby the more shares that are purchased, the lower the fee that is charged on a percentage basis. Thus the fee charged on succeeding purchases is determined by all purchases, past and present, not just by new purchases. —See also BREAKPOINT; LETTER OF INTENT; LOAD.

right of survivorship —See JOINT TENANCY WITH RIGHT OF SURVIVORSHIP.

rights off —See EX-RIGHTS.

rights offering Distribution to existing owners of rights to purchase shares of stock as part of a new stock offering. A company uses a rights offering when it sells new shares to existing shareholders rather than selling new shares to the entire investment community. The rights are used as a means to distribute new shares to existing holders on the basis of the shares each holder already owns. —See also OVERSUBSCRIPTION PRIVILEGE; PREEMPTIVE RIGHT; SUBSCRIPTION PRICE.

rights on Pertaining to stock that trades so that new buyers, rather than sellers, will receive rights that have been declared but not yet distributed. —Also called *cum rights*. —See also EX-RIGHTS.

ring —See PIT.

rising-coupon security —See STEPPED COUPON BOND.

risk The variability of returns from an investment. The greater the variability (i.e., of dividend fluctuation or of security price) the greater the risk. Since investors are generally averse to risk, investments with greater inherent risk must promise higher expected yields. —See also COVARIANCE; STANDARD DEVIATION.

risk adjusted Pertaining to a variable, such as the return on an investment, that has been altered in order to account for the differences in risk among variables of the same type. For example, financial managers adjust expected returns on various investment projects for risk in order to make them comparable.

risk arbitrage The simultaneous purchase and sale of assets that are potentially, but not necessarily, equivalent. For example, Firm A may make an offer to acquire Firm B by exchanging one share of its own stock for two shares of Firm B's stock. If the stock of Firm A is trading at $50 and the stock of Firm B is trading at $23, the risk arbitrager would buy shares in Firm B and sell short one-half this number of shares in Firm A. If the buyout offer is approved, the two stocks will exchange on a one-for-two basis and the arbitrage position will be profitable. The risk is that the buyout will be unsuccessful and the exchange of stock will not take place. Risk arbitrage is also used in situations involving reorganizations and tender offers. —Also called *equity arbitrage*.

risk aversion   The tendency of investors to avoid risky investments. Thus, if two investments offer the same expected yield but have different risk characteristics, investors will choose the one with the lowest variability in returns. If investors are risk averse, higher-risk investments must offer higher expected yields. Otherwise, they will not be competitive with the less risky investments.

risk-free return   The annualized rate of return on a riskless investment. This is the rate against which other returns are measured. —See also EXCESS RETURN.

risk hedge   The taking of an offsetting position in related assets so as to profit from relative price movements. For example, an investor might purchase futures contracts on gold and sell futures contracts on silver in the belief that gold will become relatively more valuable compared with silver over the life of the contracts. —See also PERFECT HEDGE.

riskless investment   An investment with a certain rate of return and no chance of default. Although various investments (e.g., savings accounts and certificates of deposit at insured institutions) meet these requirements, a Treasury bill is the most common example of a riskless investment.

riskless transaction   A dealer transaction in which the dealer makes a purchase or sale to offset a customer order. Thus, if a customer wishes to purchase 500 shares of Rushville Exterminators, Inc. at $80 per share, the dealer may purchase the 500 shares from another source at $79¼ and resell the stock to the customer at a markup of 75¢. The dealer has entered into a riskless transaction because the purchase will be offset by an existing customer order. The markup on riskless transactions is regulated by the National Association of Securities Dealers. —Also called *simultaneous transaction*. —See also FIVE-PERCENT RULE.

risk premium   The extra yield over the risk-free rate owing to various types of risk inherent in a particular investment. For example, any issuer other than the U.S. government normally must pay investors a risk premium in the form of a higher interest rate on bonds to account for the fact that the risk of default is less on U.S. government securities than on securities of other issuers. —Also called *bond premium risk*.

ROA   —See RETURN ON ASSETS.

rocket scientist   —See QUANT.

ROE   —See RETURN ON EQUITY.

ROI   —See RETURN ON INVESTMENT.

roll   —See ROLL OVER.

rolling down   Liquidation of an option position by an investor at the same time that he or she takes an essentially identical position with a lower strike price.

rolling forward   Liquidation of one option position by an investor at the same time that he or she takes an essentially identical position with a more distant maturity. An example would be repurchasing an option with a May expiration and selling an option on the same asset with an identical strike price but with a November expiration date.

rolling stock   Readily movable transportation equipment such as automobiles, locomotives, railroad cars, and trucks. Rolling stock generally makes good collateral for loans because the equipment is standardized and easily transportable among firms or locations. —See also EQUIPMENT TRUST CERTIFICATE.

rolling up   Liquidation of an option position by an investor at the same time that he or she takes an essentially identical position with a higher strike price.

roll over   To reinvest funds from a maturing security into a similar security. —Also called *roll*.

rollover   Reinvestment of money received from a maturing security in another similar security. Rollover normally applies to short-term investments such as certificates of deposit, commercial paper, and Treasury bills. For example, investors often desire a rollover of the proceeds from a maturing certificate of deposit into a new certificate of deposit. —See also IRA ROLLOVER; PENSION ROLLOVER.

roll-up   A master limited partnership in which a number of existing limited partnerships are pooled into a single partnership.

rounded bottom   —See SAUCER.

rounded top   —See DOME.

round lot   The standard unit of trading in a particular type of security. For stocks, a round lot is 100 shares or a multiple thereof, although a few inactive issues trade in units of 10 shares. For corporate, municipal, and government bonds, a round lot is normally considered to be $100,000 of principal amount of securities per trade. Customers involved in security transactions in lots other than round lots are often penalized somewhat because the trades require more broker and dealer effort. —Also called *even lot; normal trading unit.* —See also ODD LOT.

round trip   The purchase and sale of the same security. Some brokerage firms offer a discounted commission if a round trip is completed within a certain length of time. —Also called *round turn*.

royalty   Compensation paid to the owner of an asset based on income earned by the asset's user. For example, an oil company pays royalties to the owners of mineral rights, and a book publisher compensates its authors with royalty payments.

royalty interest   Proportional ownership interest by the owner of oil and gas rights in income produced by the asset. —See also OVERRIDING ROYALTY INTEREST.

royalty trust An ownership interest in certain assets, generally crude oil or gas production and real estate. Unlike the normal corporate organization, a trust arrangement permits income and tax benefits to flow through to the individual owners. Thus, some investors argue that a trust produces more value for the owners.

RP —See REPURCHASE AGREEMENT.

RRSP —See REGISTERED RETIREMENT SAVINGS PLAN.

r
t —Used on the consolidated tape to indicate the transaction of a right: *AEP ⸍ 50s¼.*

rt —Used in stock transaction tables in newspapers to indicate a listing for rights. No dividend, yield, or price-earnings ratio is listed for a right since dividends are not paid and earnings are not applicable: *Contll rt.*

Rule 3b–3 The Securities and Exchange Commission rule defining short sales.

Rule 5 A rule of the American Stock Exchange that prohibits members of the Exchange from trading listed stocks off the Exchange floor. —See also RULE 19C3; RULE 390.

Rule 10a–1 A 1939 Securities and Exchange Commission rule that prohibits the short sale of a security below the last price at which that security was traded or at the last price unless the last price was higher than the previous different price. Rule 10a–1 was instituted to keep short sellers from battering down the price of a stock.

Rule 10b–2 A Securities and Exchange Commission rule that prohibits firms engaged in a primary or secondary distribution from soliciting orders for the security in distribution by any means other than by the prospectus.

Rule 10b–4 A Securities and Exchange Commission rule that prohibits the tendering of stock by means of a short sale. —See also SHORT TENDER.

Rule 10b–6 A Securities and Exchange Commission rule that prohibits brokers, dealers, issuers, or underwriters participating in a securities distribution from purchasing the securities before they have been offered to the public.

Rule 10b–7 A Securities and Exchange Commission rule that limits the use of stabilizing bids by underwriters of a new security issue.

Rule 10b–10 A Securities and Exchange Commission rule that sets disclosure requirements for confirmations sent by broker-dealers to customers.

Rule 10b–13 A Securities and Exchange Commission rule that prohibits persons making a tender or an exchange offer from acquiring the security from other sources until the offer has expired.

Rule 10b–16 A Securities and Exchange Commission rule that sets minimum disclosure requirements for margin accounts opened by brokerage firms.

Rule 11A　A Securities and Exchange Commission rule that establishes requirements for trades made on the floor of an exchange by exchange members.

Rule 13d　A Securities and Exchange Commission rule that establishes disclosure requirements for investors acquiring a beneficial interest of 5% or more of an equity issue registered with the SEC.

Rule 13e　A Securities and Exchange Commission rule that regulates repurchase by a corporation of its own securities.

Rule 14a　A Securities and Exchange Commission rule that sets minimum standards for proxy materials distributed by a corporation to its shareholders.

Rule 15c2–1　A Securities and Exchange Commission rule that regulates the safekeeping of a customer's securities by the broker-dealer.

Rule 15c3–1　A Securities and Exchange Commission rule that sets minimum net capital requirements for broker-dealers. Firms are expected to have liquid assets equal to or greater than a certain percentage of total liabilities. If the ratio falls below this minimum the broker-dealer may face restrictions on soliciting new business or on keeping existing business.

Rule 15c3–2　A Securities and Exchange Commission rule that requires broker-dealers to inform customers with free credit balances that their balances can be withdrawn.

Rule 15c3–3　A Securities and Exchange Commission rule that regulates the way by which broker-dealers handle customers' fully paid securities and security values in excess of margin requirements. Fully paid securities must be segregated by the broker-dealers. —See also SEGREGATION.

Rule 17f–1　A Securities and Exchange Commission rule that requires financial institutions processing securities to report promptly counterfeit, lost, missing, or stolen securities to the proper authorities.

Rule 19b–3　A Securities and Exchange Commission rule that prohibits the fixing of commission rates.

Rule 19c3　A Securities and Exchange Commission rule that permits exchange member firms to trade stocks listed after April 26, 1979 off the exchange. Rule 19c3, which became effective in 1980, is supposed to promote competition among market makers. —See also 19C3 STOCK; OFF-BOARD TRADE.

Rule 104　The New York Stock Exchange rule that prohibits specialists from trading for their own accounts except when such trades are necessary to maintain a fair and orderly market.

Rule 105　The New York Stock Exchange rule that prohibits specialists from having an interest in a pool involving a stock in which the specialists are registered.

Rule 144　A Securities and Exchange Commission rule stipulating that a corporate executive who owns a large amount of his or her firm's stock that has not been bought in the open market be permitted to sell a portion of the stock every six months following a holding period of two years without having to file a formal registration statement with the SEC.

Rule 145   A Securities and Exchange Commission rule that permits investors who acquire certain securities from consolidations, mergers, or reclassifications to transfer those securities without having them registered.

Rule 156   A Securities and Exchange Commission rule that regulates investment company sales literature. Essentially, investment companies are prohibited from distributing sales literature containing false or misleading statements.

Rule 209   The New York Stock Exchange rule that requires all signatures on a security certificate to be guaranteed by a bank, trust company, or Exchange member when the certificate is presented for registration.

Rule 254   A Securities and Exchange Commission rule that established simplified registration requirements for issuers selling relatively small amounts of a security.

Rule 390   The New York Stock Exchange rule stipulating that, unless exempted by the Exchange, members must receive permission before trading an Exchange-listed security off the Exchange floor. The Exchange argues that the rule is necessary in order to ensure a fair and liquid market in its listed securities. —See also RULE 5; RULE 19C3.

Rule 396   —See NINE BOND RULE.

Rule 405   The "know your customer" rule of the New York Stock Exchange that requires member firms to obtain significant facts from customers when opening new accounts. These facts are supposed to give the broker and the firm some background on the customers.

Rule 415   A 1982 Securities and Exchange Commission rule that permits corporations to register a security issue and then sell the securities piecemeal over a two-year period as conditions and needs warrant. —See also SHELF REGISTRATION.

rule of 72   The mathematical rule of approximating the number of years it takes a given investment to double in value. The number of years to double an investment is calculated by dividing 72 by the annual rate of return. Thus, an investment expected to earn 10% annually will double the investor's funds in 72/10, or 7.2 years. Dividing 72 by the number of years in which the investor wishes to double his or her funds will yield the necessary rate of return.

Rules of Fair Practice   Rules of conduct for members of the National Association of Securities Dealers (NASD) which require, among other things, fair prices, reasonable charges, firm quotations, and ethical practices. Failure to follow these rules may result in fines or expulsion from NASD.

ruling   —See REVENUE RULING.

run   **1.** A dealer's list of security offerings with respective bid and ask quotes. —See also OFF-THE-RUN ISSUE. **2.** A sequence of security price movements in the same direction. Five straight days in which a stock price closed higher is an example of a run. Runs have been evaluated in order to determine if the charting of stocks is a worthwhile way to earn an above-average return.

runaway gap   In technical analysis, a gap in a chart caused by the rapid price movement of a security including a range of prices in which no trading occurs. Runaway gaps occur during strong bull or bear movements on high volume. In general, technical analysts believe that a security's price will return to the price range at which a gap occurs to fill in the missing prices. Thus, a strong upward movement with a runaway gap is likely to be followed by a downward correction to the price at which the gap occurred. A downward runaway gap signals the opposite correction. —See also BREAKAWAY GAP; EXHAUSTION GAP.

rundown   A list of available bonds in a municipal issue of serial bonds.

running ahead   The purchase or sale of a security by a broker for his or her personal account before execution of customer orders in the same security. If a brokerage firm issues a negative report on a company, a broker acting on the report for his or her own account before telling clients about the report would be running ahead. Running ahead is illegal. —See also FRONT RUNNING.

running yield   —See CURRENT YIELD.

runup   A sharp, short-term increase in the price of a stock or the stock market.

Rust Bowl   The geographic area of the United States from New Jersey to Illinois in which manufacturers are going out of business or are moving south or west, leaving their older plants to deteriorate. Some analysts believe that firms still operating primarily in the Rust Bowl have limited growth prospects. The term *Rust Bowl* is also applied to similar areas of Europe, specifically to Germany's Ruhr valley, at this writing.

RVP   —See RECEIVE VERSUS PAYMENT.

S

s   **1.** —Used immediately following a stock name in stock transaction tables in newspapers to indicate that the stock has been split or that the firm has paid a stock dividend of at least 25% within the last 52 weeks: *Getty s*.   **2.** —Used in option transaction tables in newspapers to indicate that no option of that strike price and expiration date is offered: *RoyDut 80 s*.   **3.** —Used on the consolidated tape to indicate the size of a transaction as a multiple of 100 shares: *Gy 9s81*.   **4.** —Used in bond transaction tables in newspapers to separate a bond's coupon and year of maturity: *Deere 9s01*.

safe harbor   **1.** A regulation that protects individuals or corporations undertaking certain actions from subsequent legal consequences. For example, firms filing forecasts with the Securities and Exchange Commission have a safe harbor from individuals or businesses that use the forecasts and are subsequently damaged (i.e., they lose money), as long as the forecasts were prepared in good faith.   **2.** A tactic in which the target of a takeover hostile to its management makes itself less attractive by taking a specific action.

safekeeping   The keeping of assets, including securities, by a financial institution.

salary reduction plan   A retirement plan that permits an employee to set aside a portion of salary in a tax-deferred investment account selected by the employer. Contributions made to the account and income earned by the contributions are sheltered from taxes until the funds are withdrawn. —Also called *401(K) plan.*

sale and leaseback   The sale of a fixed asset that is then leased back by the former owner from the new owner. A sale and leaseback permits a firm to withdraw its equity in an asset without giving up use of the asset. —Also called *leaseback.*

> ⚠ Sale and leaseback permits a company to control and use an asset without actually owning the asset. For instance, a firm might have a building constructed to its own specifications. The finished building is then sold to another party and simultaneously leased back. The firm initiating the construction is therefore able to use the asset for a long period of time without having any of its own funds tied up in it. The same procedure is used for owned assets when the owner wishes to get its money out of the asset without losing the use of the asset. If the asset can be sold at a price above book value, the transaction produces a profit that can be used to offset losses in other segments of the business or to supplement other profits. In 1986 Atlantic Richfield (Arco) and BankAmerica sold a large Los Angeles office complex to a Japanese real estate developer even though both firms intended to continue using space in the complex under a lease arrangement. The $620 million sale price produced an $80 million net gain for Arco and a $190 million pretax gain for BankAmerica. BankAmerica had previously sold its own San Francisco headquarters building at a substantial gain in another sale and leaseback.

sales   Revenue from the sale of goods and services. Sales exclude other types of revenue such as dividends, interest, and rent.

sales load   —See LOAD.

sales mix   —See PRODUCT MIX.

Sallie Mae   The Student Loan Marketing Association, a government-chartered, privately owned corporation providing a secondary market in government-guaranteed student loans. Sallie Mae sells government-guaranteed bonds to investors to raise funds for purchasing student loans from financial institutions.

salvage value   —See RESIDUAL VALUE.

same-day substitution   The buying and selling of equal dollar values of securities on the same trading day.

Samurai bond   A yen-denominated bond issued by a non-Japanese firm or institution.

S & L —See SAVINGS and LOAN ASSOCIATION.

S & P —See STANDARD & POOR'S.

S & P 400 —See STANDARD & POOR'S 400 STOCK INDEX.

S & P 500 —See STANDARD & POOR'S 500 STOCK INDEX.

Santa Claus rally   Rising security prices during the last week of the calendar year and during the first few days of the new year. —Also called *year-end rally.*

saucer   In technical analysis, a U-shaped chart formation indicating a market bottom for the security or market index being graphed. —Also called *rounded bottom.* —See also REVERSAL PATTERN.

savings and loan association (S & L)   A deposit-gathering financial institution that is primarily engaged in making loans on real estate. Although many S & Ls are owned by their depositors, some are organized as profit-making institutions with stock that is publicly traded. S & Ls may be state or federally chartered with most having deposits insured by the Federal Savings and Loan Insurance Association. These institutions are very susceptible to financial damage from rising interest rates. —Also called *thrift.*

savings bank —See MUTUAL SAVINGS BANK.

savings bond   A nonmarketable security issued by the U.S. Treasury in relatively small denominations for individual investors. Two categories of bonds are available. Interest on them is exempt from state and local (but not federal) taxation. —Also called *United States savings bond.* —See also SERIES EE SAVINGS BOND; SERIES HH SAVINGS BOND.

Do U.S. savings bonds have a place in a portfolio?

Probably not, at least for most serious investors. Higher yields are available in various other government obligations which also offer marketability with no penalties if one wants one's money. TIP: For a beginning investor or for people of modest means, U.S. savings bonds are often a better investment than certificates of deposit, for taxes are not due until the bonds are redeemed.

Thomas J. McAllister, CFP
McAllister Financial Planning, Indianapolis, IN

---

scale   The schedule of yields (or prices) at which a serial bond issue is offered to the public by the underwriter. The schedule reflects yields at the various maturities being offered. —Also called *offering scale*. —See also INVERTED SCALE.

scale order A specialized brokerage order requesting multiple executions at varying prices for the same security, e.g., when an investor wishing to liquidate a security position in a rising market spaces orders to sell specified numbers of shares at half-point price intervals.

scalper 1. A market maker who assigns excessive markups or markdowns on security transactions. 2. An investment adviser who takes a position in a security before publicly recommending the security for purchase. The scalper then sells the security at a profit after the recommendation has caused investors to buy the security and push its price higher. 3. An in-and-out trader who attempts to profit on relatively small price changes.

Schedule B The federal income tax schedule for listing gross dividends and/or gross taxable interest income payments that total over $400 during the tax year.

Schedule D The federal income tax form on which individuals list gains and losses from capital assets which have been sold (or bought, in the case of a short sale) during the tax year. —See also 1099–OID.

Schedule 13D A Securities and Exchange Commission (SEC) form required of anyone acquiring ownership of 5% or more of any publicly traded corporation's equity securities. The schedule must be filed with the SEC within 10 business days of the date on which the 5% threshold has been reached.

Schedule 13E–3 A Securities and Exchange Commission form to be filed when a company is taken private. —See also GOING PRIVATE.

Schedule 13E–4 A Securities and Exchange Commission form to be filed by issuers making a tender offer for their own securities.

Schedule 14B A Securities and Exchange Commission form to be filed by participants in a proxy contest.

Schedule 14D–1 A Securities and Exchange Commission form required of an individual making a tender offer for securities, if a successful tender would result in the individual's ownership of over 5% of the class of securities.

scorched earth An antitakeover strategy in which the target firm disposes of those assets or divisions considered particularly desirable by the raider. Thus, by making itself less attractive, the target discourages the takeover attempt. Such a strategy is almost certain to penalize the shareholders of the target firm. —See also CROWN JEWEL.

SCORE A unit share providing its owner with no dividends but all appreciation above a predetermined level. A SCORE is the appreciation component resulting from the artificial division of regular common stock into income shares and appreciation shares that trade on the American Stock Exchange. Since SCORE pays no current income and may have no value at the end of the trust period, it is a relatively risky investment.

—Also called *Special Claim on Residual Equity.* —See also AMERICUS SHARE-OWNER SERVICE CORPORATION; PRIME.

SCOREX^(SM) —See SECURITIES COMMUNICATION ORDER ROUTING AND EXECUTION^(SM).

scrap value —See RESIDUAL VALUE.

screen To examine various securities with the goal of selecting a limited number that meet certain predetermined requirements. For example, an investor might screen all electric utilities for stocks offering a dividend yield of 8% or more and a price-earnings ratio of 8 or less.

scrip A certificate exchangeable for a fractional share of stock. Scrip is distributed as the result of a spinoff, a stock dividend, or a stock split, in which the stockholder would be entitled to a fractional share of stock. For example, the owner of a single share would receive scrip for one-half a share in the event the issuer declared a three-for-two stock split.

scrip dividend An unusual type of dividend involving the distribution of promissory notes calling for some type of payment at a future date. Scrip dividends generally signal that a firm is short of cash. —See also LIABILITY DIVIDEND.

scripophily The collecting of old security certificates. Certificates are often valuable as collectors' items apart from any redemption value they may have.

seasonal variation A regularly recurring change in the value of a variable. For example, electric utilities generally experience significant seasonal sales variations in electricity. Likewise, toy manufacturers have sales increases before Christmas.

seasoned Referring to or being a security issue that has traded in the secondary market long enough to establish a track record for price variability and trading volume.

seat Membership on an organized securities exchange. Since the number of seats on an exchange is generally fixed, membership may be acquired only by purchasing a seat from an existing owner at a negotiated or an offered price.

SEC —See SECURITIES AND EXCHANGE COMMISSION.

SEC fee The Securities and Exchange Commission fee levied on sellers of listed equity securities.

secondary distribution The sale of a large block of existing, not newly issued, securities with the proceeds going to the present holders rather than to the issuing firm. An especially large secondary distribution may put pressure on the security's price until the additional shares or bonds have been assimilated in the market. —Also called *secondary offering.* —See also PRIMARY DISTRIBUTION; REGISTERED SECONDARY DISTRIBUTION; SPECIAL OFFERING; SPOT SECONDARY DISTRIBUTION.

secondary market The market in which existing securities are traded among investors through an intermediary. Organized exchanges such as the New York Stock Exchange facilitate the trading of securities in the secondary market. —Also called *aftermarket*. —See also FOURTH MARKET; PRIMARY MARKET; THIRD MARKET.

secondary offering —See SECONDARY DISTRIBUTION.

secondary stock The stock of a smaller firm listed on the New York Stock Exchange or nearly any stock traded on the American Stock Exchange, the regional exchanges, or in the over-the-counter market. These generally volatile stocks often exhibit price movements different from those of the large blue chips. —Also called *second-tier stock*.

secondary trend A movement of a security or of the entire market that is opposite the primary trend. For example, even during a bull market when the primary trend of stock prices is upward, secondary downward trends frequently occur. While it is easy to differentiate primary and secondary trends in graphs illustrating past price changes, it is much more difficult, and some people believe impossible, to determine if a trend is of a primary or secondary nature during the period in which it is being established.

second mortgage A real estate mortgage with a subordinate claim to another mortgage on the same property. The second mortgage is more risky than the first mortgage; thus, it carries a higher rate of interest.

second-tier stock —See SECONDARY STOCK.

Section 1256 contracts Options and futures contracts subject to a special tax rule of the Internal Revenue Service. Prior to enactment of the Tax Reform Act of 1986 an investor buying a Section 1256 contract realized any gain or loss as 60% long-term capital gain or loss and 40% short-term capital gain or loss irrespective of the duration of the contract. A Section 1256 contract held at the end of the tax year is deemed to be sold for tax purposes. Section 1256 contracts (named for the section of the Internal Revenue Code addressing these contracts) include nonequity options and exchange-traded futures contracts.

sector A group of securities (as airline stocks) that share certain common characteristics. Stocks that are particularly interest-sensitive are considered a sector.

sector fund An investment company that concentrates its holdings among securities or other assets sharing a common interest. For example, a sector fund (e.g., Korea Fund or Pacific Fund) may limit its holdings to foreign securities from a particular country or geographic region. Likewise, it may specialize in the securities of energy-related firms or in companies that produce precious metals. Sector funds permit investors to concentrate on a specific investment segment and yet diversify their investments among various issuers. Sector funds entail more risk but offer greater potential returns than funds that diversify their portfolios. —Also called *special-purpose fund; specialty fund*.

Are sector funds too risky?
● ●

These are funds that concentrate their holdings in the securities of companies within a specific industry like computers, health care, or food. Because of industry cycles, sector funds are more volatile than diversified mutual funds which spread their holdings across a broad range of industries. While the risks associated with sector funds may be greater than diversified funds, so may the rewards. Sector investing has emerged as an innovative way for aggressive investors to target their investment dollars more specifically to the industry sectors they feel have the greatest growth potential. The funds are managed by industry experts, thus alleviating the need for investors to research and then choose from a wide range of individual stocks.

George Domolky, Portfolio Manager
Fidelity Investments, Boston, MA

sector swap A bond trading strategy used to gain profit by changing yield spreads among different sectors of the bond market. The sectors may be defined by type of industry, public vs. private issuer, coupon size, and so forth. With a sector swap, one trades a type of bond currently in favor for a type currently out of favor on the belief that the yield differences are only temporary. The sale of utility bonds and subsequent use of the funds for the purchase of industrial bonds is a sector swap.

secular trend Relatively consistent movement of a variable over a long time period. A stock in a secular uptrend is an indicator that the security has experienced an extended period of rising prices.

secured bond A bond guaranteed with a pledge of assets. A bond might be secured with real estate.

secured creditor A creditor with a claim that is protected by specific assets. For example, the owner of a mortgage bond can force the sale of or can take possession of a particular asset if the borrower fails to meet the terms of the lending agreement. —See also UNSECURED CREDITOR.

secured liability A debt for which specific assets have been pledged to guarantee repayment.

Securities Act Amendments of 1975 Legislation that gave the Securities and Exchange Commission authority to develop a national market in securities, thereby making the system more competitive and more efficient. The Amendments have had only limited success in producing a fully integrated market system.

Securities Act of 1933 A landmark securities law intended to improve the flow of information to potential investors in new security issues and to prohibit certain selling practices relating to those issues. Issuing firms are required to register their securities with the federal government, and investment bankers must provide investors with a prospectus. Secondary issues, private offerings, and certain small issues are normally exempted from requirements of the Act.

Securities and Exchange Commission (SEC)   The federal agency that administers U.S. securities laws. The SEC, headed by five appointed members, was created under the Securities Exchange Act of 1934.

Securities Communication Order Routing and Execution (SCOREX)Ⓢᴹ   A service mark for stock exchange services with the added features of monitoring quotations of all markets, expediting the transactions, and providing for odd-lot transfers. This automatic order execution system is owned by the Pacific Stock Exchange.

securities exchange   A facility for the organized trading of securities. The major national exchanges are the American Stock Exchange, Chicago Board Options Exchange, and New York Stock Exchange. In addition, a number of regional exchanges are to be found throughout the country. —Also called *exchange; organized securities exchange; stock exchange.*

Securities Exchange Act of 1934   Landmark legislation that established the Securities and Exchange Commission and gave it authority over proxy solicitation and registration of organized exchanges. In addition, the Act set disclosure requirements for securities in the secondary market, regulated insider trading, and gave the Federal Reserve authority over credit purchases of securities. The Act reflected an effort to extend and overcome shortcomings of the Securities Act of 1933. These two pieces of legislation are the basis of securities regulation in the twentieth century. —See also FOREIGN CORRUPT PRACTICES ACT; WILLIAMS ACT.

Securities Industry Association (SIA)   A trade group of broker-dealers whose primary function is to lobby for its members' interests in Congress and before the Securities and Exchange Commission. The SIA is the successor to the Association of Stock Exchange Firms and the Investment Bankers Association.

Securities Industry Automation Corporation (SIAC)   A firm that processes and checks clearing data on securities transactions sent by purchase and sales departments of member brokerage firms. SIAC, owned by the exchanges, is supposed to alleviate much of the confusion and paperwork ordinarily resulting from independent actions of the individual brokerage firm. —See also CONTRACT SHEET.

Securities Investor Protection Act of 1970   An act that established the Securities Investor Protection Corporation, which shields investors against financial losses caused by brokerage house failures. The legislation responded to the generally unstable condition of the brokerage industry in the late 1960s.

Securities Investor Protection Corporation (SIPC)   A government-sponsored organization created in 1970 to insure investor accounts at brokerage firms in the event of the brokerage firms' insolvency and liquidation. The maximum insurance of $500,000, including a maximum of $100,000 in cash assets per account, covers customer losses due to brokerage house insolvencies, not customer losses caused by security price fluctuations. SIPC coverage is similar in concept to Federal Deposit Insurance Corporation coverage of customer accounts at commercial banks.

securities loan **1.** A loan made to an investor for the purpose of buying securities. The loan is secured by the securities. **2.** The lending of securities by one broker-dealer to another broker-dealer. Securities loans generally occur when broker-dealers need to borrow securities for delivery on customers' short sales.

securitized Being debt securities that are secured with assets. For example, mortgage purchase bonds are secured by mortgages that have been purchased with the bond issue's proceeds.

security **1.** An instrument (as a stock, a bond, or an option) that shows ownership in a firm, that indicates a creditor relationship with a firm or with a federal, state, or local government, or that signifies other rights to ownership, respectively. **2.** Collateral used to guarantee repayment of a debt.

security depository A centralized location in which security certificates are placed and stored for later transfer. (Transfers normally take place by book entry rather than by physical movement.) —Also called *depository.* —See also DEPOSITORY TRUST COMPANY.

security market line A line used to illustrate the relationship between risk and return for individual securities. The security market line shows a positive linear relationship between returns and systematic risk as measured by beta.

security valuation model A series of mathematical relationships that is used to determine the price at which a security should sell. Accuracy using a model depends not only on the validity of the relationships, but also on the precision of the estimates of other variables required by the model. One widely-used security valuation model discounts estimated cash flows (e.g., dividends or interest) from holding an investment.

seek a market To search for someone to complete a transaction, as when a buyer searches for a seller or a seller searches for a buyer.

segment An identifiable part of a business organization. For example, a large corporation might have a number of segments including industrial, aerospace, and leisure products.

segment reporting Financial reporting in which the firm discloses information by identifiable industry segments. For example, Union Pacific Corporation reports revenues, income, assets, depreciation, and capital expenditures for each of four segments: transportation, oil and gas, mining, and land. Segment reporting is required by the Securities and Exchange Commission in an attempt to provide stockholders and the public with better financial data. —Also called *line-of-business reporting.* —See also INDUSTRY SEGMENT.

segregation The safekeeping of a customer's securities in a separate location when the securities have been fully paid for. Segregated securities may not be commingled with the securities of the broker-dealer and they may not be used by the broker-dealer to collateralize loans. —See also RULE 15C3-3.

selected dealer agreement An agreement by members of a selling group that specifies the rules under which the group will operate in selling an issue of securities.

self-correcting Pertaining to or being a security price movement that is excessive and likely to be at least partially retraced.

self-directed IRA An individual retirement account that permits its owner to have wide latitude as to types of assets and control over the investments within the account. A self-directed IRA generally refers to IRAs established at brokerage firms in which customers may buy and sell securities. Most brokerage firms charge an annual fee of up to $50 in addition to commissions on any trades in an account.

self-tender An offer by a firm to repurchase some of its own securities from stockholders, generally on a pro rata basis from those shares offered for sale. A self-tender may be preferable to purchase of the securities in the open market because a self-tender is quicker and will not disrupt public trading in the securities. Firms frequently repurchase their own stock from investors holding fewer than a set number of shares in order to eliminate the high cost of servicing small stockholders. A self-tender is similar to a buyback except that buybacks often refer to repurchases from special groups or a few large holders. —Also called *stock repurchase plan*. —See also TENDER OFFER.

sell To dispose of an asset. —See also BUY.

sell a spread In options trading, to establish a spread position in which the premium on the option sold exceeds the premium on the option purchased. The spread may be on the basis of a difference in expiration or a difference in strike price. An example of selling a spread would be to sell an August call ($20 strike) on Firestone for a premium of $137 and to buy a February call ($20 strike) for $25.

sellers' market A market in which the demand for an asset swamps supply to the point that prices rise above the level that would have been expected under more normal circumstances. A new issue in great demand by investors is an example of a sellers' market. Underwriters may have to allocate available shares of the issue to their clients, resulting in sharply higher prices once the shares begin trading in the secondary market. —See also BUYERS' MARKET.

seller's option contract A security transaction in which the date of settlement is delayed beyond the normal five business days in a regular-way contract. This very unusual transaction is generally caused by the unavailability of a certificate for regular delivery. The settlement date will be specified. —See also CASH CONTRACT; REGULAR-WAY CONTRACT.

selling climax A period of sharp downward movement in the stock market accompanied by very high volume. A selling climax generally signals the end of a prolonged bear market. —See also BUYING CLIMAX.

selling concession —See CONCESSION.

selling group A group of investment bankers that assists a syndicate or an underwriter in the sale of a new security issue, but that is not responsible for any unsold securities. Since the members of a selling group do not assume the risk of syndicate members, their fees are correspondingly lower than the fees of the syndicate members. —See also SELECTED DEALER AGREEMENT.

selling panic A period of rapidly falling stock prices on very large volume as investors, speculators, traders, and institutions attempt to liquidate investment positions without regard to price. Selling panics occur when individuals and institutions believe they must sell securities at once before prices fall further. —See also BUYING PANIC.

selling short —See SHORT SALE.

selling short against the box —See SHORT AGAINST THE BOX.

sell-off A general decline in security prices. This term generally refers to a short- or intermediate-term decline rather than to an extended period of falling prices.

sell out To liquidate a client's investment position because the client fails to respond to a margin call or fails to pay for securities purchased for the account.

sellout Distribution of all the securities in a new issue by the selling group.

sell plus A customer order to sell a security only at a price higher than the last preceding price. Thus, the order is to be executed only on an uptick.

sell side The portion of the securities business in which orders are transacted. The sell side includes retail brokers, institutional brokers and traders, and research departments. If an institutional portfolio manager changes jobs and becomes a registered representative, he or she has moved from the buy side to the sell side. —See also BUY SIDE.

sell signal An indication provided by a technical tool, such as a chart of a stock's price, that the stock should be sold. For example, the fall of a stock below its upward trendline is often interpreted as a sell signal. —See also BUY SIGNAL.

sell stop order A customer order to a broker to sell a security if it sells at or below a stipulated price. (The stipulated price is known as the *stop price*.) A sell stop order can be used to protect an existing profit or to limit the potential loss on an owned security. —See also BUY STOP ORDER; STOP ORDER 1.

sell the book A customer order to a broker to sell as much of a security as possible at the current bid. Purchases also may be made by the specialist or other interested broker-dealers. The phrase derives from the book of existing orders that a specialist keeps.

semistrong form A component of the theory of efficient markets holding that security prices adjust nearly instantaneously to publicly available information relevant to valuation of securities. If security markets are efficient in the semistrong form, investors cannot earn extraordinary returns by activities such as perusing financial reports, investigating financial ratios, or reading investment newsletters. —See also STRONG FORM; WEAK FORM.

senior debt A class of debt that has priority with respect to interest and principal over other classes of debt and over all classes of equity by the same issuer. In the event of financial difficulties or liquidation of the borrower's assets, holders of senior debt will have a priority claim. Most loans from financial institutions and certain high-grade debt securities such as mortgage bonds are senior debt. Because senior debt has a relatively secure claim, it is less risky from the point of view of the lender and it pays a lower rate of interest compared with debt of the same issuer having a subordinate claim. —See also JUNIOR DEBT.

seniority The condition or status of a security that has priority with respect to the payment of income (i.e., interest or dividends) and repayment of principal. As an example, for the same issuer, bonds have seniority over preferred stock and preferred stock has priority over common stock. —See also JUNIOR SECURITY.

sentiment index A numerical measure of investor feeling toward the securities markets, constructed to determine whether certain segments of the investment community are bullish or bearish. The index is used by technical analysts to determine whether stocks should be bought or sold. Sentiment is measured in a variety of ways including short sales by specialists, mutual fund cash positions, and the amount of margin debt. —See also ADVISORS' SENTIMENT.

SEP —See SIMPLIFIED EMPLOYEE PENSION PLAN.

separate customer For purposes of insurance coverage by the Securities Investor Protection Corporation, an account entitled to full insurance coverage. A husband and wife, each with individual accounts and also a joint account, are viewed as three separate customers for insurance purposes. Each one of the accounts, including the joint account, is covered in full.

separate property Property that is entirely owned by one spouse, even in a community property state. Separate property generally includes property received as an inheritance or as a gift or property owned by one spouse before marriage.

separate return A tax return filed separately by each spouse, in which income and deductions attributable to that spouse are listed. Spouses may choose to file separate returns or to file a joint return combining incomes and deductions. —See also JOINT RETURN.

Separate Trading of Registered Interest and Principal of Securities (STRIPS) Treasury securities that have had their coupons and principal repayments separated into what effectively becomes zero-coupon Treasury bonds. The parts, issued in book-entry form, carry the full backing of the U.S. Treasury. Like other zero-coupon bonds, these securities are subject to wide price fluctuations. They also subject the owner to a yearly federal income tax liability even though no direct interest is paid.

serial bonds Bonds issued under a single indenture simultaneously with groups of the bonds that are scheduled to mature periodically. For example, a municipality may issue $40 million of bonds with $2 million scheduled to mature each year for 20 years. Many bond issues are a combination of serial bonds and term bonds.

serial correlation The extent to which one event is related to a series of past events. In technical analysis, serial correlation is used to test whether or not various chart formations are useful in projecting a security's future price movements.

series —See OPTION SERIES.

Series EE savings bond A U.S. Treasury obligation that pays a variable interest rate and is sold to investors in amounts as low as $50 at a 50% discount from face value. The interest rate is set at 85% of the rate paid on 5-year Treasury securities with a minimum rate guaranteed if the bonds are held at least 5 years. Federal income taxes on interest earned may be paid each year or may be deferred until the savings bond reaches maturity. Although savings bonds cannot be resold, they can be redeemed before maturity.

Series HH savings bond A U.S. Treasury obligation issued in multiples of $500 that pays interest every 6 months. The security has a maturity of ten years but may be redeemed after being held six months. This security has not been as popular as the Series EE bond. Now it may be obtained only by swapping the Series EE at its maturity.

Series 7 An examination required of potential registered representatives, intended to test the candidates' basic understanding of the securities industry. The multiple-choice test, developed by the New York Stock Exchange, is administered by the National Association of Securities Dealers. —Also called *General Securities Registered Representative Examination.* —See also UNIFORM SECURITIES AGENT STATE LAW EXAMINATION.

settlement Transfer of the security (for the seller) or cash (for the buyer) in order to complete a security transaction. —See also DELAYED SETTLEMENT.

settlement date The date on which either cash (for a buyer) or a security (for a seller) must be in the hands of the broker in order to satisfy the conditions of a security transaction. —See also DELAYED SETTLEMENT; TRADE DATE.

settlement month The month in which delivery is to take place in a futures contract. Most futures positions are reversed (long positions sold; short positions covered) before their respective settlement months.

settlement period The period between the trade date and the settlement date. The settlement period on most securities is five business days.

settlement price In futures trading, an official price established at the end of each trading day by using the range of closing prices for a particular contract. This price, similar to the closing price for stocks, is used to determine margin requirements and the following day's price limits.

seven sisters The seven large international oil companies: British Petroleum, Chevron, Exxon, Gulf, Mobil, Shell, and Texaco. Although this list was accurate for a long period of time, Chevron has since acquired Gulf and Royal Dutch Petroleum has acquired Shell; thus, only five of the original seven firms remain as separate entities.

severally and jointly —See JOINTLY AND SEVERALLY.

severally but not jointly Pertaining to a security offering in which individual underwriters are responsible for selling their initial allocations but are not responsible for any unsold securities allocated to other underwriters. —See also JOINTLY AND SEVERALLY.

shadow calendar Security issues in the Securities and Exchange Commission registration process with no firm offering date.

shakeout A reduction in the number of firms operating in a particular industry. An example of a shakeout is the decline in the number of companies developing computer software in the United States. Shakeouts often occur after an industry has experienced a period of rapid growth in demand followed by overexpansion by manufacturers. Large, diversified companies able to survive a weak business climate tend to benefit from shakeouts.

share 1. A single unit of a class of ownership in a corporation, represented by a stock certificate. 2. A single unit of ownership in a mutual fund. 3. The portion of a market controlled by a particular firm.

shareholder —See STOCKHOLDER.

shareholder derivative suit A special type of class action lawsuit filed by one shareholder or by a limited number of shareholders on behalf of all of the other shareholders in a firm. An example is such a suit filed against a mutual fund's management, in which the litigants claim excessive management and distribution fees.

shareholder proposal A proposal submitted by a shareholder for action at a forthcoming annual meeting. If the holder gives timely notice of his or her intentions, the firm's management must include the proposal in the proxy statement and must give the other shareholders a chance to vote for or against the proposal. Typical shareholder proposals involve voting rights, management compensation, and corporate charitable contributions.

shareholders' equity —See OWNERS' EQUITY.

share repurchase plan A corporation's plan for buying back a predetermined number of its own shares in the open market. Institution of a share repurchase plan derives from management's view that the company has limited outside investment opportunities and that its shares are undervalued. Repurchase of the shares will decrease the amount of outstanding capital stock, will increase earnings per share, and, it is hoped, will result in an increase in the price of the stock.

shares authorized —See AUTHORIZED CAPITAL STOCK.

shares outstanding —See OUTSTANDING CAPITAL STOCK.

shark A firm or an investor that is hostile to the target firm's management and that is interested in taking over the firm.

shark repellent A strategy used by corporations to ward off unwanted takeovers. Examples of shark repellents include a major acquisition, the issuance of new shares of stock or securities convertible into stock, and the staggered election of directors. Shark repellents often benefit corporate officers more than the stockholders. —Also called *takeover defense.* —See also ANTITAKEOVER MEASURE; POISON PILL; SHOW STOPPER.

shelf registration A simplified method of registering securities that permits corporations to file a relatively uncomplicated registration form with the Securities and Exchange Commission (SEC), and over the subsequent two years, issue the securities. Shelf registration is supposed to provide more flexibility for corporations when raising funds in the capital markets. Shelf registration is permitted by SEC Rule 415.

shell corporation A corporation that has no active business operations and few or no assets.

shelter —See TAX SHELTER.

shelter To protect one's income from taxation. Some taxpayers shelter their income by investing in oil drilling ventures, among others.

Sherman Antitrust Act An 1890 federal law intended to control or prohibit monopolies by forbidding certain practices that restrain competition. In the early 1900s, the U.S. Supreme Court ruled that the Act applied only to unreasonable restraints of trade and thus could be used only against blatant cases of monopoly. —See also ANTITRUST LAWS; CLAYTON ACT; FEDERAL TRADE COMMISSION ACT OF 1914.

Shogun bond A bond denominated in currency other than yen and issued in Japan by a non-Japanese borrower. For example, a U.S. firm issuing dollar-denominated bonds in Japan would be selling Shogun bonds.

shop A dealership in securities.

shop To get in touch with a number of dealers in a security in order to obtain the most advantageous bid or ask price.

short —See SHORT POSITION; SHORT SALE.

short against the box To sell an owned security short, normally in order to carry a profit on the security into the next tax year. Delivery may be made by using the owned shares or by purchasing new shares in the market. —Also called *against the box; selling short against the box.*

short bond A debt security with a short period remaining until maturity. —See also INTERMEDIATE BOND; LONG BOND.

short coupon   **1.** —See SHORT BOND. **2.** The first interest payment on a newly issued bond that includes less than the normal six months' worth of interest. For example, a bond issued on February 1 with interest payment dates of June 1 and December 1 would make an initial interest payment equal to four months' interest.

short cover   To purchase a security that has previously been sold short in order to close out the position. While short covering may occur at any time, the term is often used in reference to investors with short positions who repurchase stock in strongly rising markets in order to cut their losses or protect their profits. This procedure produces even more strength in the market. —Also called *cover*. —See also SHORT SQUEEZE.

short exempt   A short sale exempt from the rule that short sales must occur on upticks. Short exempts include some arbitrage transactions. Owning a security that will be converted into the common stock which will be sold allows a short exempt sale.

short hedge   An investment transaction intended to provide protection against a decline in the value of an asset. For example, an investor who holds shares of General Motors and expects the stock to decline may enter into a short hedge by purchasing a put option on GM stock. If GM does subsequently decline, the value of the put option should increase.

short interest   The number of shares of a particular stock that have been sold but have not yet been repurchased. Many analysts consider a large short position in a given stock bullish, since it represents future demand for the security as purchases are made to replace borrowed certificates. —See also CUSHION THEORY.

> ⚠️ Short interest on the New York Stock Exchange hit a record 387 million shares for the month ending September 15, 1986, an increase of over 50% from short interest a year earlier. While the record short interest represented 2.80 times average daily volume for the entire Exchange, short interest for particular stocks varied significantly. For example, short interest in Continental Illinois was 14 times the stock's average daily volume, but short interest in Niagara Mohawk Power was only .4 times its average daily volume. Relatively high short interest in stocks generally represented a bearish stance on the part of investors who had sold stock short, although certain individual stocks had high short interest because of arbitrage operations in which one stock was sold short and a related stock bought.

short-interest ratio   The ratio of short interest divided by average daily volume. Technicians use the short-interest ratio as a tool to determine market direction. A relatively high ratio is generally considered bullish because it indicates significant future buying pressures as short sellers cover their short positions. A low ratio is considered bearish.

short leg   The side of an option spread that has been sold short. With a spread made up of owning a September 30 call and being short a December 30 call, the December 30 call is the short leg. —See also LONG LEG.

short position   **1.** A net investment position in a security in which the security has been borrowed and sold but not yet replaced. Essentially, it is a short sale that has not been covered. —See also LONG POSITION. **2.** An investment position in which the investor either has written an option or has sold a commodity contract, with the obligation remaining outstanding.

short sale   The sale of a security that must be borrowed to make delivery. Short sales normally, but not always, entail the sale of securities that are not owned by the seller in anticipation of profiting from a decline in the price of the securities. —Also called *selling short.* —See also FICTITIOUS CREDIT; GHOST STOCK; LENDING AT A PREMIUM; LENDING AT A RATE; ODD-LOT SHORT SALES; RULE 10A–1; SHORT AGAINST THE BOX; SHORT COVER; SYNTHETIC SHORT SALE.

short squeeze   The pressure on short sellers to cover their positions as a result of sharp price increases or difficulty in borrowing the security the sellers are short. The rush to cover produces additional upward pressure on the price of the stock, which then causes an even greater squeeze. —Also called *squeezing the shorts.*

short tender   Capitalizing on a tender offer by using borrowed shares acquired through a short sale. A short tender is prohibited by Securities and Exchange Commission Rule 10b–4.

short-term   **1.** Designating a gain or loss on the value of an asset that has been held less than a specified period of time. The Tax Reform Act of 1986 eliminated the difference between short-term and long-term realized gains or losses for individual tax purposes. —See also HOLDING PERIOD; LONG-TERM 1.   **2.** Describing a debt security in which a short period of time remains until the face value is paid to the investor. Exactly what constitutes *short-term* is a subjective judgment, although five years and under may be the norm.

short-term discount notes   Promissory notes issued by municipalities at a discount from face value. Essentially, short-term discount notes are a form of tax-exempt commercial paper.

short-term municipal bond fund   —See TAX-EXEMPT MONEY MARKET FUND.

short-term trading index   A technical trading indicator calculated by dividing the number of advancing stocks relative to the number of declining stocks into the volume of advancing stocks relative to the volume of declining stocks. An index value above 1.30 is considered a buy signal, while a value below .70 is a sell signal.

show stopper   A legal barrier to a takeover attempt that is virtually impossible for the suitor to overcome. For example, a target company might convince state legislators to pass various antitakeover laws that would preclude the takeover. —See also ANTITAKEOVER MEASURE; SHARK REPELLENT.

shrinkage   Loss of inventory encountered in the normal course of business. A firm engaged in transporting grain can expect to lose part of its product to weather, careless handling, and various other factors.

shrinking asset —See WASTING ASSET.

SIA —See SECURITIES INDUSTRY ASSOCIATION.

SIAC —See SECURITIES INDUSTRY AUTOMATION CORPORATION.

SIC —See STANDARD INDUSTRIAL CLASSIFICATION SYSTEM.

side-by-side trading Simultaneously making a market in a stock and in its associated options. The Securities and Exchange Commission has long frowned on this practice because of the possibility of price manipulation inherent in it. —Also called *integrated market making.*

sideline —See ON THE SIDELINES.

sideways market —See FLAT MARKET.

sight draft A draft payable on demand. —See also TIME DRAFT.

signature guarantee A written guarantee by a financial institution (nearly always a commercial bank or stock exchange member firm) that a particular signature is valid. A signature guarantee is often required on a certificate or other official document to be mailed.

silent partner A member of a partnership who does not take active part in management and who is not publicly recognized as a partner.

simple interest Interest paid on an initial investment only. Simple interest is calculated by multiplying the principal times the annual rate of interest times the number of years involved. —See also COMPOUND INTEREST.

simplified employee pension plan (SEP) A special type of joint Keogh-individual retirement account created for employees by employers and permitting contributions from each party. The SEP was developed to give small businesses a retirement plan easier to establish and administer than an ordinary pension plan.

simulation A mathematical exercise establishing a model of a system and then altering the model's variables to determine effects on other variables. For example, a financial analyst might construct a model for predicting a stock's market price and then manipulate various determinants of the price including earnings, interest rates, and the inflation rate to determine how each of these changes affects the market price.

simultaneous transaction —See RISKLESS TRANSACTION.

single-premium deferred annuity A deferred annuity purchase with one lump-sum premium payment. Single-premium deferred annuities offer the tax benefit of building up in value tax-free until distribution takes place. Thus, an investor could pay a large single premium, have the investment build up free of taxes over a period of years, and then receive partially taxable annuity payments at retirement. A single-premium deferred annuity is more flexible than an individual retirement account (IRA), but unlike contributions by some individuals to an IRA, a premium to purchase a deferred annuity is not deductible for tax purposes. —See also PERIODIC PURCHASE DEFERRED CONTRACT.

single state municipal bond fund —See DOUBLE-EXEMPT FUND.

sinker —See SINKING FUND BOND.

sinking fund Assets set aside for the redemption of stock, the retirement of debt, or the replacement of fixed assets.

sinking fund bond A bond issue for which the issuer is required to establish a sinking fund to provide for the orderly retirement of the bonds. —Also called *sinker.*

> ⚠💲 On November 1, 1980, Eastern Air Lines issued an 11¾% coupon bond with a November 1, 2005 maturity. The bond's indenture contained a sinking fund provision in which Eastern was required to pay the trustee each year before November 1, commencing in 1991, 3% of the principal amount originally issued until November 1, 1997. Subsequently, Eastern was required to increase the annual payment to 5% of the original issue. Thus, by the time the bonds were to mature in 2005, the trustee would have used proceeds of the sinking fund to redeem 56% of the original issue. Redemptions to meet a sinking fund requirement may be made by forcing the holders to sell (normally, at face value), or by purchasing bonds in the open market. Opinion is mixed as to whether a sinking fund works to the advantage of investors of a bond issue. On the one hand, a sinking fund may cause the investor to have to sell the bond back to the issuer before the maturity date. On the other hand, the fact that the issuer is in the market repurchasing bonds provides added liquidity for the bond in the securities market.

sinking fund call An issuer's call of a portion of an outstanding bond issue to satisfy the issue's sinking fund requirement. A sinking fund call is generally at par value with the bonds to be called determined by lot. Most bond issues provide investors with a period of protection between the date on which the issue is originally sold and the date on which the first sinking fund call takes place. For low-coupon bonds selling at discount from par value, issuers will normally satisfy sinking fund requirements by purchasing bonds in the open market rather than calling them from investors. —See also CALL 3; CALL PRICE; EXTRAORDINARY CALL; OPTIONAL CALL.

sinking fund provision A stipulation in many bond indentures that the borrower retire a certain proportion of the debt annually. The retirement may be effected by calling the bonds from the investors (if interest rates have declined) or by purchasing the bonds in the open market (if interest rates have increased). This orderly retirement may be advantageous to a bondholder because it creates some liquidity; however, it also may cause the holder to give up a high-yielding bond at the call price (often at par) during a period of reduced interest rates. —Also called *bond sinking fund.* —See also DOUBLING OPTION; FUNNEL SINKING FUND.

SIPC —See SECURITIES INVESTOR PROTECTION CORPORATION.

sixteenth One sixteenth of a point. For stock quotes, a sixteenth represents ¹⁄₁₆ of $1, or 6.25¢. For option quotes, a sixteenth represents $6.25. For bond quotes, a sixteenth represents ¹⁄₁₆ of a percent. Thus, a bond quoted at 98¹⁄₁₆ would indicate a price of 98¹⁄₁₆% of par, or $980.62. The smallest price interval for most quotations is an eighth, with sixteenths used primarily on very low-priced stocks or bonds nearing maturity. —Also called *steenth; teenie.*

size **1.** The market for a security in which a relatively large volume is being offered for sale or in which a large volume can be absorbed. Size in a security is more important for institutional investors than it is for individuals, since most individuals normally do not trade in sufficiently high volume to warrant concern about the size of the market. **2.** The number of units bid for and offered in the current quote, usually expressed in abbreviated form, e.g., Texaco 32¼–½, 2,000 by 1,000.

sizing Determination of the number of shares or bonds to be included in a new issue.

skip-day settlement Settlement of a security trade one business day beyond the normal settlement date. For example, a trade that normally requires next-day settlement would require payment and delivery two business days following the trade date using skip-day settlement.

SLD **1.** —Used on the consolidated tape to indicate a transaction that is reported out of sequence. For example, a transaction that occurred earlier in the day may be reported late: *IBM.SLD 6s35.* **2.** —Used on transaction slips to indicate the side of a trade in which securities are sold. —See also BOT.

SLD LAST SALE —Used on the consolidated tape to indicate a large price change in the indicated security since the time at which the security was last traded.

sleeping beauty A firm with valuable assets not effectively utilized by its management. Such a firm has high profit potential and value. It is a prime candidate for takeover for these reasons.

How to find firms with undervalued assets—the real sleeping beauties.

Choosing sleeping beauties requires expertise but an investor may be aware of such companies in the industry in which he or she works. Another indication may be that a given company's earnings and market price are consistently weaker than those of comparable companies. Be cautious of arbitrary asset valuations in making such judgments unless you trust the source.

J. Kendrick Noble, Jr., First Vice President
PaineWebber Incorporated, New York, NY

SMA —See SPECIAL MISCELLANEOUS ACCOUNT.

small-capitalization stock The stock of a relatively small firm with little equity and few shares of common stock outstanding. Small-capitalization stocks tend to be subject to large price fluctuations; therefore, the potential for short-term gains and losses is great.

small-firm effect   The theory that stocks of small firms tend to outperform the stocks of large firms. Some analysts attribute the small-firm effect to the fact that small firms have more room to grow than large firms do.

small investor   A person of modest financial means who occasionally buys and sells securities, generally in relatively small amounts. —See also ODD-LOTTER.

small-issue bond   A bond that is part of a small-sized municipal bond issue for private purposes such that interest on the bond qualifies for federal tax exemption. Municipalities are limited as to the size of such an issue and the total number of issues if the bonds are to pay tax-exempt interest. —See also PRIVATE ACTIVITY BOND.

Small Order Execution System   —See SOES.

smart money   Funds controlled by investors who should have special knowledge of the right kinds of investments to make. Essentially, *smart money* refers to funds controlled by insiders or to institutional money. The implication is that if the individual investor can figure out where the smart money is going, he or she can follow suit and make above-average profits. Many researchers believe that smart money is no more likely to earn above-average returns than the funds invested by typical investors.

smokestack industry   A basic manufacturing industry (as the automobile, rubber, and steel industries) having limited growth potential and earnings and revenues that vary cyclically with general economic activity.

social investing   Limiting one's investment alternatives to securities of firms whose products or actions are considered socially acceptable. For example, an investment manager might decide to eliminate from consideration the securities of all firms engaged in the manufacture of tobacco or liquor products. —Also called *ethical investing.*

SOES   A National Association of Securities Dealers computer linkup of market makers that allows the trading of securities without the services of a broker. Traders post the prices at which they are willing to buy or sell. The best price can then be called up on a computer by another subscriber interested in making a trade. —Also called *Small Order Execution System.*

soft dollars   Payment for brokerage firm services via commissions generated from trades. Thus, an investor who does significant trading might be provided with "complimentary" subscriptions to market letters or an at-home quote system. Payment is disguised in the form of large commissions paid to the brokerage firm. —See also HARD DOLLARS.

soft market   A securities market with declining prices and little trading.

solvent   Being able to meet debts or discharge liabilities. —See also INSOLVENT.

sources and uses of funds statement —See STATEMENT OF CHANGES IN FINANCIAL POSITION.

sovereign risk The risk of owning the security of an issuer in a country other than the one in which the investor lives. For example, an investor residing in the United States incurs sovereign risk in purchasing a bond issued by the government of Brazil. This risk stems from the fact that a foreign country may nationalize its private businesses, stop paying interest, or repudiate its debt.

special arbitrage account A brokerage account in which a customer is limited to hedged positions requiring significantly lower margin than ordinary unhedged positions do.

special assessment bond A municipal bond with debt service limited to revenues from assessments against those who directly benefit from the project the funds have been used to finance. This type of bond is more risky than a general obligation bond of the same issuer if it is not also secured by a full-faith-and-credit pledge.

special bid A bid by an exchange member to fill an order to buy a large block of a security. The member generally must find a number of sellers to accrue the required amount of the security. —See also EXCHANGE ACQUISITION.

special bond account A brokerage account in which a customer is limited to transactions in bonds. Special low margin requirements apply to a special bond account because bond prices are generally less volatile than those of most other securities.

special call —See EXTRAORDINARY CALL.

special cash account —See CASH ACCOUNT.

Special Claim on Residual Equity —See SCORE.

special dividend —See EXTRA DIVIDEND.

specialist A member of a securities exchange who is a market maker in one or more securities listed on the exchange. The specialist is the person on the exchange floor to whom other members go when they wish to transact or leave an order. Specialists are assigned securities by the exchange and are expected to maintain a fair and orderly market in them. —See also BOOK 1; RULE 104.

specialist's book —See BOOK 1.

specialists' sentiment The view of specialists as to the future direction of a stock or the stock market itself. Some investors, believing that the specialists have an inside, or a particularly informed, view of the market, try to make their own investment decisions based on their perceived interpretation of specialists' sentiment, in hopes of gaining above-average profits. Specialists' sentiment is sometimes measured by studying the specialists' short sales.

specialists' short-sale ratio The ratio of specialists' short sales to total short sales. Technical analysts use the ratio to measure the market sentiment of the specialists. A high ratio indicates that the specialists are bearish.

specialist unit   A group of people or firms acting together to maintain an orderly market in securities assigned by an exchange. Specialist units may act as agent or as principal in executing trades on the floor of the exchange.

special miscellaneous account (SMA)   An account in which balances in excess of the amount required under Regulation T are placed. Funds in an SMA may be used to purchase more securities on margin or they may be withdrawn in cash. Suppose a customer purchases $10,000 of securities and puts up the minimum 50% margin required by the Federal Reserve under Regulation T. If the securities subsequently rise in value to $14,000, the new $7,000 loan value (50% of the market value) is $2,000 more than is currently borrowed on the securities. The $2,000 in the special miscellaneous account may be withdrawn in cash as a loan or it may be used to purchase up to $4,000 in additional securities. —See also ADJUSTED DEBIT BALANCE; EXCESS MARGIN.

special offering   A secondary distribution on the floor of the New York Stock Exchange by an Exchange member. A special offering is generally priced at the current market price of the security being offered, with the seller absorbing all costs. Thus, members buying parts of the offering for their clients or their own inventory can avoid any fees. The selling member is able to sell a large block of stock without having to give a price concession to buyers.

special-purpose fund   —See SECTOR FUND.

special situation   A currently undervalued stock that can suddenly increase in value because of imminently favorable circumstances. For example, a firm may be about to bring a new, potentially profitable product to market. If everything turns out favorably, the gains in the firm's stock could be quite large. Another special situation might derive from the impending liquidation of a company. Special situations are normally quite risky.

special subscription account   A brokerage account opened to purchase stock issued by use of preemptive rights.

special tax bond   A municipal bond with debt service limited to the revenues generated by a special tax. A bond issue to finance a convention center with the interest and principal payments limited to taxes received from a levy on motel and restaurant sales is an example of a special tax bond. Certain special tax bonds are also secured by the full faith and credit of the issuer; they have the additional security of being general obligations.

specialty fund   —See SECTOR FUND.

spectail   A securities dealer who undertakes speculative trading for his or her own account while at the same time handling retail accounts.

speculation   The taking of above-average risks to achieve above-average returns, generally during a relatively short period of time. Speculation involves buying something on the basis of its potential selling price rather than on the basis of its actual value.

speculator A person who is willing to take large risks and sacrifice the safety of principal in return for potentially large gains. Certain decisions regarding securities clearly characterize a speculator. For example, purchasing a very volatile stock in hopes of making a half a point in profit is speculation, but buying a U.S. Treasury bond to hold for retirement is an investment. It must be added, however, that there is a big gray area in which speculation and investment are difficult to differentiate.

spike A sudden, short-term change in the price of a security that just as suddenly returns close to its previous level. For example, a stock that has consistently traded in a $10 to $12 per share range may suddenly move to a price of $14 and then return to $12. The sudden rise to the $14 price is a spike.

spinoff Distribution to stockholders of the stock of a subsidiary held by a parent company. Normally the distribution is not taxable to the stockholders until the new shares have been sold. —See also PARTIAL SPINOFF; SPLITOFF.

⚠️ In 1985, Amoco distributed shares in one of its subsidiaries, Cyprus Minerals Company, to Amoco shareholders. As of June 19, the Amoco shareholders had received one share of Cyprus for every 10 shares of Amoco owned. The new Cyprus shares, which had traded in the over-the-counter market in the $12 to $13 range on July 1, approximately doubled in value within a year. Before the spinoff, Amoco stockholders had had no choice but to be owners of Cyprus because Cyprus was a 1979-acquired subsidiary of Amoco. Following the spinoff, however, Amoco owners could choose to remain stockholders in the minerals business or they could opt to sell their Cyprus shares. Amoco's stated objectives were to allow its management to concentrate on its core businesses in oil and gas and to divest itself of an investment with relatively poor earnings.

split A proportionate increase in the number of shares of outstanding stock without a corresponding increase in assets or in funds available, as would be the case in a new stock offering or in an acquisition using stock as payment. Essentially, a firm splits its stock to reduce the market price and make the shares attractive to a larger pool of investors, although it is questionable if the firm's stockholders actually benefit from a split since share prices are reduced proportionately with the increase in shares outstanding. A 4-for-1 split would result in an owner of 100 shares receiving 300 additional shares, or a total of 4 shares after the split for every single share owned before the split. —Also called *stock split*. —See also REVERSE STOCK SPLIT.

⚠️ In 1986, American Brands announced that it would split its common stock on a 2-for-1 basis. As a result, American Brands stockholders were to receive an additional share for each share already owned as of a specific date. As is often the case with a stock split, the firm also announced a slight increase in the dividend. The directors of American

Brands declared a quarterly dividend on the new shares of 52¢ (equivalent to $1.04 on the presplit shares), an increase from $1.01 on the presplit shares. Thus, the owner of 100 shares before the split would receive annual dividends of $4.04 per share, or a total of $404. After the split in which the owner would receive an additional 100 shares, the annual dividend would amount to $416 (52¢ × 4 quarters × 200 shares).

split commission   A sales fee divided among two or more people.

split down   —See REVERSE STOCK SPLIT.

split funding   The purchase of more than one financial product with the same payment. For example, some financial programs combine life insurance and a mutual fund into the same package with each customer payment being split between the two.

split gift   A gift from one partner in a marriage to someone else outside the marriage when one-half of the gift is assumed by law to have been made by each spouse. A split gift permits the $10,000 annual gift tax exclusion per recipient to effectively be $20,000 per recipient when the gift originates from a married couple.

splitoff   An exchange of the stock of a subsidiary for a pro rata surrender of stock in the parent corporation. A splitoff is similar to a spinoff but in the case of the splitoff a smaller (or no) decline in the stock of the parent corporation should take place. —See also SPINOFF.

split offering   1. The sale of a new bond issue composed of serial bonds and term bonds. Many municipal issues are sold as split offerings. 2. A security offering consisting of new and previously issued securities of the issuer. For example, a corporation may undertake an issue of common stock composed of new shares and shares being held as treasury stock.

split rating   A condition that occurs when the same bond is rated differently by the rating agencies. An example is a bond rated AA by one agency and A by another agency. A split rating may occur because one rating agency places a different emphasis on certain variables or because it views a particular item (such as a recent acquisition by the issuer) differently than the other rating agency does.

split up   —See SPLIT.

split-up value   The aggregate dollar value of a firm's various parts if they were to be sold separately. Many takeovers occur because of a difference between the stock market values and the split-up values of the target companies.

sponsor   1. An institutional investor or a brokerage firm that has a position in a security and influences other investors also to establish a position in that security. 2. —See UNDERWRITER.

spot commodity   A commodity available for immediate delivery.

spot market   —See CASH MARKET.

spot month   The nearest month in which a currently traded futures contract is due for delivery.

spot price —See CASH PRICE.

spot secondary distribution A secondary distribution by security holders not affiliated with the issuer such that the distribution does not require registration with the Securities and Exchange Commission. —See also REGISTERED SECONDARY DISTRIBUTION.

spousal IRA An individual retirement account in the name of a nonworking spouse. A spousal IRA may be funded by the working spouse up to a maximum amount established by law. There is also a limit on annual contributions to the combination of the IRAs of the working and nonworking spouses.

spousal remainder trust An irrevocable trust that may be set up for any length of time in order to pass assets to a spouse. Between the time that the trust becomes effective and the time that the assets are passed, income earned by the trust is taxable to a named beneficiary at the beneficiary's tax rate.

spread 1. A position taken in two or more options or futures contracts to profit through a change in the relative price relationships. Purchasing an option to expire in October and selling an option on the same asset expiring three months earlier is one example of a spread. 2. The difference in price between two futures contracts that are identical except for delivery date. 3. The difference between the bid and ask prices for a particular security. A large spread often indicates inactive trading of the security. —Also called *markup*. —See also GROSS SPREAD; NARROW THE SPREAD. 4. The difference in yields between two fixed-income securities. —See also BASIS POINT.

spreading The establishment of a long position in an option and a short position in another option of the same class but with a different strike price or expiration date, or both. Spreading is supposed to achieve profit from a difference in relative price movements of two options of the same class.

spread-load contractual plan A contractual plan for purchasing shares of a mutual fund in which sales charges are not concentrated in the first payment or in the first few payments made by the investor.

spread order An order to buy and to sell options of the same class but with different strike prices and/or expiration dates in which the customer specifies a spread between the option sold and the option purchased. For example, an investor might enter a spread order to buy a March call and sell a September call, both on General Motors and with a strike price of $80, if a spread of $6 can be obtained. The order will be executed only if a floor broker can sell the September call for $6 more than the price at which the March call can be purchased.

spreadsheet A worksheet on which financial data are laid out in rows and columns for comparative purposes. For example, a financial analyst might use a spreadsheet to determine how a firm's sales and profit margins have varied over a period of quarters or years.

springing convertible A convertible security that includes warrants to purchase additional shares of the issuer's common stock. Certain prescribed events, such as a hostile tender offer or the accumulation of a large block of stock by a single group, cause the exercise price of the warrants to drop or spring. This unusual security is issued primarily to deter a corporate takeover by making the takeover more expensive.

sprinkling trust A family trust in which the trustee has the power to distribute income to the beneficiaries according to their individual needs rather than according to a specified formula.

squeeze-out The forcing of stockholders to sell their stock. Majority holders of a company's stock may attempt a squeeze-out of minority stockholders in order to take complete control of the firm. —See also FAIRNESS OPINION.

squeezing the shorts —See SHORT SQUEEZE.

s
s —Used on the consolidated tape to indicate a transaction of less than a round lot: *AEPPr 5⅜47.*

stabilization period The time elapsing between the offering of a security issue for sale and its final distribution, during which the underwriter enters the secondary market in order to stabilize the price of the security. The underwriter attempts to keep the secondary market price of the security from falling below the offering price.

stabilize —See PEG 1.

stagflation An economic condition characterized by slow growth, rapidly rising consumer prices, and relatively high unemployment.

staggered maturities Bonds with differing maturity dates in an investor's portfolio. For example, an investor may accumulate a $250,000 portfolio of bonds such that $10,000 face value of bonds matures each year for 25 years.

staggered terms Membership terms for a firm's directors that expire in different years. A firm with 12 directors might have 4-year terms with 3 seats up for election each year. Staggered terms make it more difficult for a raider to gain control of a board.

STAIRS® —See MUNICIPAL CONVERTIBLE.

stand-alone company An independent operating firm. For example, a large diversified company may consider spinning off a subsidiary because, as a stand-alone company, the subsidiary would command a higher price-earnings ratio than the parent.

Standard & Poor's℠ (S & P) A registered service mark for a service furnishing financial and statistical data derived from computer tapes and punch cards for use in computers to the specification and/or order of others. Standard & Poor's Corporation is an investment advisory service that publishes financial data. This subsidiary of McGraw-Hill also rates debt securities and distributes a series of widely-followed stock indices. Major publications include *The Outlook, Stock Reports, Industry Survey,* and *Stock Guide.*

Standard & Poor's Confidence Indicator A measurement of investor confidence in the securities markets calculated by constructing an index of low-priced to high-grade common stocks. A rising index indicates increased investor willingness to assume risk and therefore indicates increased investor confidence. —See also BARRON'S CONFIDENCE INDEX; CONFIDENCE INDICATOR.

Standard & Poor's 400 Stock Index (S & P 400) A broad-based index of 400 industrial stock prices weighted on the basis of market value (stock price times shares outstanding). It includes listed and over-the-counter stocks but is heavily influenced by stocks of large corporations. The Index is based on a value of 10 during the period 1941–43.

Standard & Poor's 500 Stock Index (S & P 500) An inclusive index made up of 500 stock prices including 400 industrials, 40 utilities, 20 transportation, and 40 financial issues. The Index is constructed using market weights (stock price times shares outstanding) to provide a broad indicator of stock price movements.

standard deduction The minimum deduction from income allowed a taxpayer for calculating taxable income. Individuals with few itemized deductions elect the standard deduction in place of itemizing deductions. —Formerly called the *zero bracket amount*, even though the two varied slightly in application.

standard deviation A statistical measure of the variability of a distribution. An analyst may wish to calculate the standard deviation of historical returns on a stock or a portfolio as a measure of the investment's riskiness. The higher the standard deviation of an investment's returns, the greater the relative riskiness because of uncertainty in the amount of return. —See also RISK; VARIANCE.

standard industrial classification system (SIC) A classification of businesses and business units by type of economic activity. The system uses from a one-digit to a four-digit classification depending on how narrowly the business unit is defined. There are 11 one-digit groupings and over 1,000 four-digit groupings.

standard opinion —See CLEAN OPINION.

standby underwriting An agreement by underwriters to purchase the portion of a new securities issue remaining after the public offering. Standby underwriting eliminates the issuer's risk of not selling the issue out but it increases the investment bankers' risk.

standstill agreement A written agreement between two firms whereby the actions of one firm with respect to the other are limited until a specified date. For example, Firm A may sell Firm B a large block of Firm A's stock with the stipulation that Firm B will acquire no additional shares in Firm A for five years.

stapled stock —See PAIRED SHARES.

start-up company A new business.

stated capital —See LEGAL CAPITAL.

stated value A value assigned to common stock by the firm's management for purposes of financial statements. Stated value, used in place of par value, is calculated on a per-share basis by dividing the stated capital resulting from a new issue of common stock by the number of new shares issued. Stated value is unrelated to the stock's market price and is of little importance to the shareholders.

statement A written presentation, as of financial data. —See also AC-COUNT STATEMENT; FINANCIAL STATEMENT.

statement analysis Analysis of an organization's financial and operating condition through the use of financial statements. Statement analysis is used by financial analysts in an attempt to determine the value of a firm's securities.

statement of changes in financial position A financial statement listing how a firm has obtained its funds and how it has spent them over a period of time. This statement, developed from changes in balance sheet entries between two dates, provides insights as to the ways in which the firm's management raises and invests money. —Also called *application of funds statement; flow of funds statement; funds statement; sources and uses of funds statement.*

statement of financial condition —See BALANCE SHEET.

statement of financial position —See BALANCE SHEET.

Statement of Policy Securities and Exchange Commission regulations as to the ways in which investment company shares may be sold to the public. For example, investment companies are prohibited from distributing deceptive sales literature containing intentional omissions. The Statement of Policy was repealed in 1979.

statement of retained earnings A financial statement listing a firm's accumulated retained earnings and net income paid as dividends to stockholders in the current period. —Also called *retained earnings statement.*

statutory investment —See LEGAL INVESTMENT.

statutory voting —See MAJORITY VOTING.

steenth —See SIXTEENTH.

stepped coupon bond A bond with interest coupons that change to predetermined levels on specific dates. Thus, a stepped coupon bond might pay 9% interest for the first 5 years after issue and then step up the interest every fifth year until maturity. —Also called *rising-coupon security; step-up coupon security.*

step-up A scheduled increase in the exercise or conversion price at which a warrant, an option, or a convertible security may be used to acquire shares of common stock. For example, a warrant may permit its owner to purchase 10 shares of stock at $20 per share up to a specified date, and at $22.50 per share thereafter until the warrant expires. The step-up works to the disadvantage of the holder, however. It is not a feature of most of these securities.

step-up coupon security —See STEPPED COUPON BOND.

sticky deal A new securities issue that an investment banker may find difficult to sell.

stock An ownership share or ownership shares in a corporation. —See also BEARER STOCK; COMMON STOCK; PREFERRED STOCK; STOCK CLASS.

stock ahead —Used to describe limit orders that have been placed earlier and that take precedence over subsequent orders at the same price. An investor may find that a limit order has not been executed even though the specified price has been reached because orders with the same limit have been placed earlier than his or hers. Limit orders at a specific price are executed in the sequence in which they are received.

stock appreciation right Executive compensation permitting an employee to receive cash or stock equal to the amount by which the firm's stock price exceeds a specified base price.

stock average —See AVERAGES.

stock certificate —See CERTIFICATE.

stock class A category of capital stock with specific rights or characteristics. Most firms have only a single class of stock outstanding. Thus, every share has exactly the same rights as every other share. But some companies have two or more classes of capital stock designated as class A, class B, and so forth. For example, one class may have controlling voting rights but both classes may share equally in dividends. In general, a firm issues different classes of stock when it wishes to sell one class to the public and reserve a second class for its founders. —Also called *class*. —See also COMMON STOCK.

> ⚟ In 1986, Chris-Craft Industries management proposed a new class of common stock to its shareholders. The new class B stock would be distributed on the basis of two new shares for each share of common stock already owned. Each class B share had supervoting rights that would allow its holder ten votes (with the regular common stock continuing to have one vote per share), and transfer limitations. However, class B shares would have equal dividend rights and could be exchanged for regular common stock on a share-for-share basis. Existing class B stockholders would have to exchange their class B shares for regular common stock before selling the stock to another party. The net effect of the new class B shares was to concentrate voting in the hands of existing shareholders because future purchasers of Chris-Craft stock could buy only the regular common shares having relatively weak voting rights.

stock company A company owned by stockholders, with the ownership evidenced by transferable certificates. —See also MUTUAL COMPANY.

stock dividend A dividend made up of shares of the paying firm's stock. A stock dividend is often used in place of or in addition to a cash dividend if the firm wishes to conserve cash. Unlike a cash dividend, a stock dividend is normally not taxable to the shareholder when it is received, but rather when it is sold. Stockholders who are supposed to receive a fractional share will often receive a check for the amount equal to the market value of the fractional share. Payment of a stock dividend is indicated in stock transaction tables in newspapers by the symbols *b* and *t*. —See also SCRIP DIVIDEND.

stock exchange —See SECURITIES EXCHANGE.

stockholder An individual or organization owning common stock or preferred stock in a corporation. —Also called *shareholder*.

stockholder derivative suit A lawsuit by one or more of a company's stockholders in the name of the company. A derivative suit is filed when the firm's management will not or cannot sue in the name of the company. For example, a stockholder may enter a derivative suit against the firm's chief executive officer to recover funds from a questionable or an improper act by that officer. —Also called *derivative suit*.

stockholder of record —See HOLDER OF RECORD.

stockholders' equity —See OWNERS' EQUITY.

stock index —See INDEX.

stock index future A contract for the future delivery of a sum of money based on the value of a stock index (in most cases, 500 times the index). Unlike other futures contracts in which a given commodity is specified for delivery, stock index futures call for cash settlements since it is not possible actually to deliver an index. This future can be used to speculate on the future direction of the stock market (rather than just a few stocks) or to hedge a portfolio of securities against general market movements. —See also SECTION 1256 CONTRACTS.

stock index option A contract that gives its owner the right to buy (call option) or sell (put option) a stock index at a fixed value until a specified date. Options are traded on the Standard & Poor's 500, the Standard & Poor's 100, the Value Line Index, the New York Stock Exchange Index, and the AMEX Major Market Index, along with specialized indices. These options work exactly like regular stock options except that an index rather than a particular stock is the underlying asset. As with stock index futures, delivery must be in cash since it is not possible to deliver an index. —See also SECTION 1256 CONTRACTS.

stock list The department of a securities exchange that takes care of new listings and delistings of securities on the exchange. —Also called *listing department*.

stock option An option to buy or sell a specific number of shares of stock at a fixed price until a specified date. —See also CALL 1; INCENTIVE STOCK OPTION; PUT 1.

stock outstanding —See OUTSTANDING CAPITAL STOCK.

stock power A form, separate from a stock certificate, that can be used to transfer stock. A stock power is useful when an investor wishes to deliver an unsigned certificate in one envelope and the power to transfer the certificate in another envelope. —See also BOND POWER.

stock rating　The grading of a stock, generally with respect to its expected price performance or safety. A number of publications, such as *Value Line* and *Financial World*, publish stock ratings regularly. Of the major ratings firms only Standard & Poor's rates stocks. —See also BOND RATING.

stock record　An account of the securities being held by a brokerage firm.

stock register　A record listing the issues, transfers, and retirements of a firm's stock.

stock repurchase plan　**1.** —See BUYBACK.　**2.** —See SELF-TENDER.

stock right　—See RIGHT.

stock split　—See SPLIT.

stock symbol　The letter or sequence of letters used to identify a security. For example, on the consolidated tape, C is used for Chrysler Corporation, FIN for Financial Corporation of America, and X for USX Corporation. Symbols are also used to identify securities on videodisplay terminals.

Stock Watch　A New York Stock Exchange system to monitor trades on the floor of the Exchange and flag those trades exceeding predetermined parameters. Essentially, Stock Watch is designed to spot unusual activity in a security's trading pattern so that Exchange officials can investigate the cause of the activity.

stop-and-go tactic　The tax reduction or deferment technique of moving income and deductions from one year to another. This technique involves advancing deductions and delaying income. For example, an investor may pay for a subscription to an investment-related magazine just before the end of the year or may wait to recognize gains from a stock by selling it early in the next year.

stop-limit order　A specialized order in which a limit order and a stop order are combined. Once the specified stop price has been reached or exceeded, the stop-limit order becomes a limit order. A stop-limit order differs from a stop order, which becomes a market order when the stop price has been reached or exceeded. A stop-limit order to buy must have a stop-limit price above the market price; conversely, a stop-limit order to sell must have a stop-limit price below the security's market price. In response to a stop-limit order specifying "sell 100 GY 70 stop limit," once the stock sells at or below $70, the order becomes a limit order to sell 100 shares at a price of $70. A variation of the stop-limit order specifies a limit price lower than the stop price.

stop-limit price　The price specified in a stop-limit order at which the order becomes a limit order. A stop-limit order to buy must have a stop-limit price above the security's current market price and a stop-limit order to sell must have a stop-limit price below the security's current market price. —See also STOP PRICE.

stop order   **1.** An order to buy or to sell a security when the security's price reaches or passes a specified level. At that time the stop order becomes a market order and the executing broker, usually the specialist, obtains the best possible price. A stop order to buy must be at a price above the current market price and a stop order to sell must have a specified price below the current market price. —See also BUY STOP ORDER; ELECTING SALE; SELL STOP ORDER; STOP-LIMIT ORDER; STOP PRICE; TRAILING STOP.   **2.** An order from the Securities and Exchange Commission suspending a registration statement when an omission or a misstatement has been found.

stop-out price   The lowest price (highest yield) accepted for new securities issued in a U.S. Treasury auction.

stopped out   Having an order executed at a specified stop price. Suppose Cincinnati Bell stock currently trades at $65 and an investor enters a stop order to sell 500 shares at $62. If the stock subsequently rises and the order is executed at $62, the customer is stopped out.

stopped stock   A broker's order with a specialist in which the specialist guarantees a specific price or better.

stop price   The price specified in a stop order at which the stop order becomes a market order. A stop price at which to buy is entered above the current market price and a stop price at which to sell is entered below the current market price.

stop transfer   An order to stop the transfer of ownership of a particular stock or bond certificate, a situation that generally occurs after an investor has notified a transfer agent that a certificate has been lost or stolen.

story bond   A bond so unusual or having such complicated features that salespeople are frequently called on to explain its intricacies to customers. Story bonds sometimes offer slightly higher yields than ordinary bonds as a way to convince investors that they are worth holding.

straddle   A combination of a put option and a call option. The buyer of a straddle will profit from large price fluctuations in the underlying asset, regardless of whether the price change is up or down.

straight debt   Debt that cannot be exchanged for another asset. Since most bonds are not convertible, they are examples of straight debt. —See also CONVERTIBLE SECURITY.

straight life annuity   An annuity that makes payments to the recipient only for the duration of his or her lifetime. No minimum number of payments and no minimum sum to be paid are guaranteed. All payments end upon the recipient's death. This annuity is desirable for someone with no dependents who wishes to obtain the largest possible payments.

straight-line depreciation   A method of recording depreciation such that the original cost less the estimated salvage value of an asset is written off in equal amounts during each period of the asset's life. For example, a machine costing $10,000 with an estimated life of 5 years and no salvage value would be depreciated $2,000 ($10,000/5 years) annually, using straight-line depreciation. If the machine had an estimated salvage of $4,000, annual straight-line depreciation would amount to $1,200. —See also ACCELERATED COST RECOVERY SYSTEM; ACCELERATED DEPRECIATION.

strangle strategy   The strategy of selling both an out-of-the-money call and an out-of-the-money put. Profits are greatest when relatively small price movements occur in the underlying asset and neither option is exercised. In case the value of the underlying asset moves in one direction, the loss on one side of the spread is at least partially offset by a gain on the other side.

strap   A combination option made up of two calls and one put. The buyer of a strap profits from large variations in the price of the underlying asset, especially if it moves upward.

(the) Street   —See WALL STREET.

street name   —Used to describe registration of a customer-owned security in the name of the brokerage firm holding the certificate. A security is held in street name to simplify trading because no delivery of or signature on the certificate is required, or because the certificate is being used as collateral in a margin account. —See also DELIVERY INSTRUCTIONS.

street-side trade   A security trade between brokers.

strength   —See RELATIVE STRENGTH.

strike price   Exercise price at which the owner of a call option can purchase the underlying stock or the owner of a put option can sell the underlying stock. —See also EXERCISE PRICE.

strike spread   —See MONEY SPREAD.

strip   A combination of two put options and a call option. The buyer of a strip profits from large variations in the price of the underlying asset, especially if it is moving downward.

stripping   —See COUPON STRIPPING.

STRIPS   —See SEPARATE TRADING OF REGISTERED INTEREST AND PRINCIPAL OF SECURITIES.

strong dollar   A dollar that is valuable relative to foreign currencies. A strong dollar exchanges for more units of other currencies compared with the units for which it could be exchanged in the past. A strong dollar tends to hurt U.S. firms that rely heavily on foreign sales because the firms' products will cost more in terms of the foreign currencies. —See also EXCHANGE RATE; WEAK DOLLAR.

strong form   A component of the theory of efficient markets holding that security prices fully incorporate all public and most private information relevant to valuation of securities. The strong form component, if true, infers that professional portfolio managers and insiders are consistently unable to earn extraordinary returns in the security markets. —See also SEMISTRONG FORM; WEAK FORM.

Student Loan Marketing Association   —See SALLIE MAE.

Subchapter M   The portion of the Internal Revenue Service Code addressing the ways by which investment companies and investment trusts may pass income through to owners in order to avoid double taxation. —See also CONDUIT THEORY.

subject   A quotation that must be confirmed by the broker-dealer before execution.

subject quote   —See NOMINAL QUOTE.

subject to opinion   An audit opinion by a Certified Public Accountant that a firm's financial statements are fairly presented subject to the outcome of an uncertain future event. A major lawsuit, the outcome of which could significantly affect the firm, may be unresolved at the time of the audit; such a situation is an example of a factor influencing the opinion.

subordinated debenture   An unsecured bond with a claim to assets that is subordinate to all existing and future debt. Thus, in the event that the issuer encounters financial difficulties and must be liquidated, all other claims must be satisfied before holders of subordinated debentures can receive a settlement. Frequently, this settlement amounts to relatively little. Because of the risk involved, the issuers have to pay relatively high interest rates in order to sell these securities to investors. Many issues of these debentures include a sweetener such as the right to exchange the securities for shares of common stock. The sweeteners are included so that interest rates on the subordinated debentures can be reduced below the level that would be required without them. Subordinated debentures without the conversion option appeal to risk-oriented investors seeking high current yields. —See also CONVERTIBLE SECURITY; DEBENTURE.

subscribe   To use rights for ordering securities sold as a new issue.

subscription period   The period of time during which a new issue of securities may be bought by investors. A subscription period will typically last a week or two, after which the rights to subscribe will expire at no value.

subscription price   The price at which rights holders may acquire shares in a new securities issue. The subscription price is normally set at slightly less than the market price so as to ensure that it will be successfully sold. —See also OVERSUBSCRIPTION PRIVILEGE; RIGHTS OFFERING.

subscription privilege   —See PREEMPTIVE RIGHT.

subscription ratio   The number of rights required to purchase a single share of a security in a rights offering.

subscription right   —See RIGHT.

subscription warrant   —See WARRANT.

subsidiary   A company controlled or owned by another company. For example, the Atchison, Topeka and Santa Fe Railway Company is a wholly-owned subsidiary of Santa Fe Industries. If a subsidiary is wholly owned, all its stock is held by the parent company. —See also HOLDING COMPANY; PARENT COMPANY.

substitute   —See SWAP.

substitution bond swap   The sale of one bond combined with the purchase of another virtually identical bond that offers a slightly higher yield.

suicide pill   A poison pill provision so devastating to the target of a takeover attempt that the target company may have to be liquidated to satisfy its creditors. For example, the company's directors may institute a suicide pill giving stockholders the right to exchange their stock for debt if a raider acquires more than a specified percentage of the company's outstanding shares. The tremendous increase in debt will effectively doom the target company if the takeover attempt is successful.

suitor   A company that offers to purchase another firm.

sum-of-the-years' digits depreciation (SYD)   A method of accounting for the wear-and-tear on an asset such that large deductions are recorded in the early years of the asset's life and small deductions are recorded in later years of the asset's life. The annual rate of recorded depreciation is calculated by dividing the sum of all the years in the asset's life into the number of years of the asset's life remaining. The rate times the asset's cost minus salvage value equals annual depreciation. Thus, a 5-year asset would be depreciated at a rate of $\frac{5}{15}$ during its first year of acquisition. —See also DOUBLE-DECLINING-BALANCE DEPRECIATION.

sunk cost   A past outlay or loss that cannot be altered by current or future actions.

Super Bowl rule   The technical indicator that if a team from the American Football Conference wins the Super Bowl, the stock market will decline during the year, but if a team from the National Football Conference wins the Super Bowl, the stock market will experience an up year.

SuperDOT   A New York Stock Exchange system for automatically routing market and limit orders to the appropriate specialist. SuperDOT eliminates the need for clerks and floor brokers to handle modest-size orders.

supermajority provision   A part of a corporation's by-laws that requires an abnormally high percentage of stockholder votes in order to bring about certain changes. For example, a firm may require that 80% of shares approve a resolution to call a meeting of stockholders for any purpose other than the annual meeting. This provision makes a corporate takeover more difficult.

super NOW account   An interest-bearing checking account that pays a higher return and requires a greater balance than a standard NOW account. These accounts have not gained much popularity.

super sinker   A housing revenue bond issue in which mortgage prepayments are used to retire a specified maturity. Although this particular maturity is far in the future, the bond is likely to be paid off in a relatively short period. Even though an investor in the specified maturity bond is unsure when the security may be retired, the annual return is likely to be relatively high for a short- to intermediate-term holding period.

supervoting stock   A class of stock that provides its holders with larger than proportionate voting rights compared with another class of stock issued by the same company. For example, the holders of Wang Laboratories class C stock have the votes to elect 75% of the company's directors. Supervoting stock permits a limited number of stockholders to retain or gain control over a company without having to own over 50% of all common stock outstanding. —Also called *control stock*. —See also LIMITED-VOTING STOCK.

supply-demand analysis   A technical evaluation of securities on the basis of factors affecting the supply of and demand for a particular security or securities in general. Supply-demand analysis is supposed to determine if an imbalance exists or will exist between supply and demand for securities. For example, if the supply of a security is expected to exceed demand, the security should be sold or not purchased because its price can be expected to decline. Supply-demand analysis incorporates information on new stock offerings, government borrowing, contributions to pension funds, mutual fund cash balances, and a number of other similar factors.

supply-side economics   The branch of economics that concentrates on measures to increase output of goods and services in the long run. The basis of supply-side economics is that marginal tax rates should be reduced to provide incentives to supply additional labor and capital, and thereby promote long-term growth.

support   Increased demand for a security. —See also RESISTANCE.

support level   A price at which a security or the market will receive considerable buying pressure. Technical analysts believe demand at the support level will tend to keep a stock's price from falling below the support-level price. A support level develops as investors miss purchasing a stock just before a price rise and resolve to buy the stock if it again reaches that level. —See also RESISTANCE LEVEL.

surety bond   An insurance fee required before a duplicate security is issued to replace one that has been lost. The fee is approximately 4% of the market value of the security to be replaced.

surplus   **1.** Equity in excess of par value. Surplus includes additional paid-in capital and retained earnings. **2.** —See RETAINED EARNINGS.

surrender value   —See CASH SURRENDER VALUE.

surviving company   The company that emerges in control following a business combination. The surviving company is generally one of the firms entering the combination but may be a new company formed by the combination.

suspended trading   Temporary suspension of trading in a security. Trading in a security may be suspended if, for instance, a major announcement by the issuing company is expected to influence significantly the security's price. The temporary halt in trading is intended to give the financial community enough time to hear the news. —Also called *trading halt*.

swap   To trade one asset for another. —Also called *exchange; substitute; switch.*

swap order   A specialized security order in which a customer specifies that two transactions be made only if a given price differential can be achieved. For example, an investor might specify that 500 shares of one security be purchased and 500 shares of another security be sold only if the former can be executed for $5 per share less than the latter. —Also called *switch order.*

Please explain the central assets, or sweep, accounts and the reasons for their popularity.

• •

The first central assets account, introduced in the late 1970s by Merrill Lynch, was quickly hailed as revolutionizing the way Americans look at and manage their cash and credit. It was designed to attract investors interested in consolidating their stock and bond trading, money market investing, and borrowing into a single account, covered by one monthly statement. Since that time, other firms have developed their own versions of the popular account, and Merrill Lynch itself has developed separate Cash Management Accounts for different groups of investors (overseas, business, startup, retirement planners). An important feature of a central assets acccount is its "sweep" feature. Instead of remaining idle, dividends and income in the account are swept into a choice of money market funds, where they immediately start to earn interest. The account also allows immediate access to one's assets, and borrowing power through checks and credit/debit cards. The convenience features offered by central assets accounts vary with the offering company. They may include access through cash machines, direct deposit of payroll and government checks, and the ability to code checks by expense categories which are reviewed on an annual statement. A central assets account with a full-service company can provide a window on a wide range of financial products and services and an easy way to monitor one's resources.

Mitchell S. Farkas
Vice President, Manager, CMA Marketing
Merrill Lynch, Pierce, Fenner & Smith Inc.
New York, NY

---

sweep account   An account in which all funds or all funds above a specified minimum are automatically transferred from the account. In brokerage accounts, the sweep feature transfers cash items into an interest-earning money market account. Brokerage sweep accounts also generally incorporate checking, a debit or credit card, and margin loans.

Examples of trademarked names of brokerage sweep accounts include Cash Management Account by Merrill Lynch, Financial Management Account by Shearson Lehman, Schwab One by Charles Schwab, and Ultra Service Account by Fidelity. —Also called *central assets account.*

sweetener An addition to a security that makes it more appealing to investors. One popular sweetener is the addition of warrants (options to buy stock) to a bond in order to make the bond marketable with a lower interest cost.

sweetheart deal A collusive, unethical transaction between two parties.

swing loan —See BRIDGE LOAN.

switch **1.** —See SWAP. **2.** To move funds out of one mutual fund and into another mutual fund. —See also TELEPHONE SWITCHING.

switch order —See SWAP ORDER.

SYD —See SUM-OF-THE-YEARS' DIGITS DEPRECIATION.

syndicate A combination of investment banking firms that bids on a new security issue and then sells it if the bid is successful. The syndicate disbands when the security offering has been completed. Syndicates are needed to spread the risk and obtain greater financial and marketing resources for large issues. —Also called *purchase group; underwriting syndicate.* —See also AGREEMENT AMONG UNDERWRITERS; BREAKING THE SYNDICATE; SELLING GROUP.

syndicate To distribute shares of ownership in a partnership or joint venture. For example, a brokerage firm may syndicate ownership in certain oil and gas properties.

syndicate manager A major underwriting firm that forms a syndicate in order to distribute a security issue to the public. The manager allocates the securities among other firms in the group but is itself generally responsible for the largest share of the issue.

synergy An increase in the value of assets as a result of combining the assets. Expected synergy is the justification behind most business mergers. For example, General Motors purchased Electronic Data Systems in 1984 with the expectation that considerable synergy would result. —See also MERGER.

synthetic asset The combination of securities and/or assets in such a way that they produce the same financial effect as the ownership of an entirely different asset would. For example, selling a put option and buying a call option on a commodity produce the same financial effect as actually owning the underlying commodity.

synthetic call The combination of a commodity and a put option on the commodity with the effect being the same as owning a call option.

synthetic put The short sale of a commodity and the purchase of a call option on the same commodity with the effect being the same as the purchase of a put option.

synthetic short sale The purchase of a put and the simultaneous sale of a call on the same security. This combination produces the same results as a short sale of the underlying stock: that is, unlimited potential gains for a downward price movement of the stock and unlimited potential losses for an upward movement of the stock.

synthetic stock The purchase of a call and simultaneous sale of a put on the same stock. This combination produces unlimited potential gains if the stock rises but unlimited potential losses if the stock falls—the same results as if the stock were owned.

systematic risk Risk caused by factors that affect the prices of virtually all securities, although in different proportions. Examples include changes in interest rates and consumer prices. Although it is not possible to eliminate systematic risk through diversification, it is possible to reduce it by acquiring securities (i.e., those of utilities and many blue chips) that have histories of relatively slowly changing prices. —Also called *market risk; nondiversifiable risk*. —See also BETA; UNSYSTEMATIC RISK.

t **1.** —Used in the dividend column of stock transaction tables in newspapers to indicate the market value as of the distribution date of stock dividends paid during the preceding 12 months. Stocks with this listing paid no cash dividends: *Jetron .71t*. **2.** —Used in bond transaction tables in newspapers to indicate a floating-rate bond or note: *Amoco 8.05s89t*.

T —Used in earnings reports in newspapers to identify the Toronto Stock Exchange as the primary market of a firm's common stock.

TAB —See TAX ANTICIPATION BILL.

tag ends The remaining securities in a new issue that has been largely sold.

tail **1.** In a bid for a new security issue, the portion of the bid price following the decimal. For example, a bid of $92.125 has a tail of .125. **2.** The difference between the average bid and the lowest bid at an auction for Treasury securities.

tailgating Placement of an order by a registered representative for the registered representative's own account on the basis of an order that has been received from a client. Suppose a customer calls a registered representative with an order to sell 1,000 shares of stock. If the representative sells the stock for the customer and follows it by selling additional shares of the same stock for his or her own personal account, the representative is tailgating.

take To accept the price at which a dealer offers a security.

take a bath To lose a large portion of the money invested in a particular asset, as during a prolonged bear market.

take a position —See POSITION.

take delivery **1.** To accept a commodity to be delivered as part of a long futures contract. For example, the buyer of a gold futures contract who will need the metal on the delivery date may plan to take delivery rather than close out the contract. **2.** To accept certificates for securities that have been purchased.

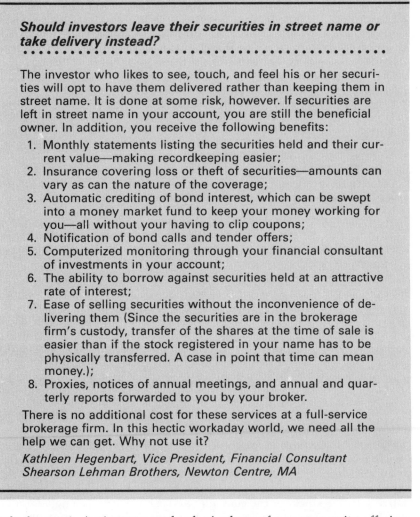

Should investors leave their securities in street name or take delivery instead?

The investor who likes to see, touch, and feel his or her securities will opt to have them delivered rather than keeping them in street name. It is done at some risk, however. If securities are left in street name in your account, you are still the beneficial owner. In addition, you receive the following benefits:

1. Monthly statements listing the securities held and their current value—making recordkeeping easier;
2. Insurance covering loss or theft of securities—amounts can vary as can the nature of the coverage;
3. Automatic crediting of bond interest, which can be swept into a money market fund to keep your money working for you—all without your having to clip coupons;
4. Notification of bond calls and tender offers;
5. Computerized monitoring through your financial consultant of investments in your account;
6. The ability to borrow against securities held at an attractive rate of interest;
7. Ease of selling securities without the inconvenience of delivering them (Since the securities are in the brokerage firm's custody, transfer of the shares at the time of sale is easier than if the stock registered in your name has to be physically transferred. A case in point that time can mean money.);
8. Proxies, notices of annual meetings, and annual and quarterly reports forwarded to you by your broker.

There is no additional cost for these services at a full-service brokerage firm. In this hectic workaday world, we need all the help we can get. Why not use it?

Kathleen Hegenbart, Vice President, Financial Consultant
Shearson Lehman Brothers, Newton Centre, MA

takedown **1.** An investment banker's share of a new security offering. **2.** The price paid by an underwriter for securities to be sold as part of a new issue.

take-or-pay agreement A contractual agreement in which one party agrees to purchase a specific amount of another party's goods or services or to pay the equivalent cost even if the goods or services are not needed. Take-or-pay contracts are frequently employed by electric utilities which use the agreements as collateral for loans to build electric generating plants.

take out **1.** The extra funds generated in an account when an investor sells one block of securities and buys another block at a lower total cost. For example, a customer may sell $50,000 face amount of bonds at 85 and then purchase $50,000 face amount of a different bond at 80. **2.** A bid for a seller's remaining position in a security.

Is a takeover good or bad for the stockholders of the acquired firm? What types of companies would benefit from a takeover?
••

If you look at the actual results—and we have plenty of results now—you can see that a takeover is decidedly to the advantage of the stockholders of the acquired company. For instance, Harvard professor Michael C. Jensen's study on how the stockholders of an acquired company came out showed something between a 30% and a 40% runup in the value of the stock. I'll just take Jensen's findings and go with those.

Of course, the only reason a company is vulnerable to takeover to begin with is that its management has done a poor job: the stock is selling at a discount to the appraised value of the assets. For instance, if a company's stock sells at $30 in the marketplace and the appraised value of the assets is $60, it is an invitation for somebody to come in and challenge the management for corporate control. A lot of times it's just a fight for who's going to run the company and manage the assets. A manager who's doing a good job will have the stock price up and close to the appraised value of the assets. Therein, they're not vulnerable to takeover.

T. Boone Pickens, Jr.
Founder and General Partner, Mesa Limited Partnership,
Amarillo, TX; and Founder and Chairman,
United Shareholders Association, Washington, DC
In a March 18, 1987, interview at Houghton Mifflin Company.

---

takeover Acquisition of controlling interest in a firm. Although the term is often used to refer to acquisition by a party hostile to the target's management, many takeovers are friendly. —See also FRIENDLY TAKEOVER; RAIDER; UNFRIENDLY TAKEOVER.

⚠️ In May of 1986, Sperry Corporation agreed to be acquired by Burroughs Corporation in a major computer industry takeover. The agreement called for Burroughs to pay $76.50 for each of Sperry's 31 million common shares. Slightly over half the shares would be purchased for cash and each of the remaining shares for $76.50 worth of Burroughs securities. Burroughs pursued Sperry for over a year during which time Sperry held merger talks with a number of potential white knights. Sperry finally agreed to the takeover when Burroughs consented to increase the value of its offer. The total value of the takeover was nearly $4.5 billion. The Burroughs takeover was just one of many such takeovers taking place during the Reagan administration. Takeovers that once would have been considered anticompetitive became commonplace in the 1980s when many government officials began to believe that U.S. firms needed to be big in order to compete with foreign corporations.

takeover defense —See SHARK REPELLENT.

takeover stock A stock that, for various reasons, has good potential for being taken over by another firm. In 1985, companies engaged in radio and television broadcasting were considered potential takeover targets; as a result, their stocks achieved significant price gains. —See also IN PLAY; SPLIT-UP VALUE.

takeover target —See TARGET COMPANY.

taking off a leg —See LEG LIFTING.

taking profits —See PROFIT TAKING.

TAN —See TAX ANTICIPATION NOTE.

tandem Entering into two trades at the same time. An investor selling a July futures contract and buying a September futures contract is engaging in a tandem trade.

tangible asset An asset such as a building or piece of equipment that has physical properties. —Also called *hard asset*. —See also INTANGIBLE ASSET; NET TANGIBLE ASSETS PER SHARE.

tape —See TICKER TAPE.

tape racing A registered representative's taking advantage of a large customer order by transacting business for a personal account before transacting the customer's order. A registered representative with a significant order likely to affect the price of a security can take personal advantage of that situation by tape racing. Tape racing is illegal.

tape reader A trader who observes stock price and volume reports on the consolidated tape and uses this information to make trading decisions. —See also READ THE TAPE.

target company A firm that is the object of a specific action unwanted by its management, such as a takeover attempt or an antitrust suit. —Also called *takeover target*. —See also DEFENSIVE ACQUISITION; IN PLAY; RAIDER; TAKEOVER; TOEHOLD PURCHASE.

target fund A specialized self-liquidating mutual fund that invests in bonds maturing around a specific date. After the last maturity, the fund distributes its assets to the owners and ceases business. The limited life of the fund makes it much like a unit trust except that the portfolio is managed. An annual management fee is charged.

target price 1. The price that an investor or a security analyst expects a security to achieve. Generally, when a security achieves the target price it is time to close out a position in it. 2. The price at which an investor hopes to purchase an asset. For example, a company desiring to take over another firm may set a target price for the firm.

tariff A tax levied on a good imported into a country. In most instances, tariffs are intended to make imported goods more expensive and thus less competitive with domestic products. —Also called *duty*. —See also DRAWBACK; GENERAL AGREEMENT ON TARIFFS AND TRADE; TRIGGER PRICE.

taxable income Income that is subject to taxation. Taxable income remains after accounting for adjustments and deductions.

taxable municipal bond A municipal bond in which interest paid to the bondholder does not qualify as tax-exempt for federal tax purposes because of the use to which the bond proceeds are put by the municipal borrower. Taxable municipal bonds were issued in 1986 for the first time since 1913 because of limitations placed on municipal obligations by tax reform. Although taxable municipal bonds are subject to federal taxation, most are not subject to taxation by the state in which the municipal issuer is located. Taxable municipal bonds are generally more appropriate for pension funds and other tax-exempt investors than for individual investors.

tax anticipation bill (TAB) A short-term U.S. Treasury obligation that is issued at a discount and that may be used at face value upon maturity or a few days before to pay a federal tax obligation. These securities appeal primarily to corporations and relatively large investors with significant tax obligations.

tax anticipation note (TAN) A short-term municipal obligation that is sold to provide funds for government operations until taxes have been received. At that time the receipts are used to repay the debt. These generally low-risk securities appeal primarily to larger investors.

tax avoidance Reduction of a tax liability by legal means. For example, high-income individuals avoid significant federal income taxes by purchasing and holding municipal bonds. Likewise, investors who itemize deductions may avoid some taxes by deducting the cost of this book and others like it. —See also TAX EVASION.

tax base The resources that are available for taxation. An evaluation of the tax base is of particular importance in certain municipal bond issues secured by tax revenues.

tax basis —See BASIS 2.

tax bracket —See MARGINAL TAX RATE.

Tax Court A federal court established to resolve disputes between taxpayers and the Internal Revenue Service.

Some ways of keeping the Star-spangled Wolf out of your till—tax avoidance tips.
· ·

While it is true that the Tax Reform Act of 1986 eliminated a number of tax-saving investment opportunities, several remain:

1. If you are not covered by a qualified retirement plan or if your income falls below a specific level, you will be able to receive a full deduction for your IRA contribution. Those with higher incomes may be able to receive a partial deduction.
2. Although the maximum contribution to 401(k) plans has been reduced to $7,000, they still remain an attractive way to accumulate retirement funds as well as reduce your current tax liability.
3. Persons who are self-employed or who receive directors' fees should consider establishing a Keogh account. The tax law did not lower the maximum contribution of $30,000 which may be made to this type of plan. Contributions are fully deductible no matter what your income level is.
4. Insurance remains one of the few tax-advantaged investments not impacted by tax reform. Tax-deferred annuities and single premium whole life policies provide the benefits of tax-deferred compounding. However, deductions are not generated by the initial investment.
5. Investment in tax-free municipal bonds may be appropriate, based on your investment alternatives and your marginal tax rate. The interest paid is not subject to federal tax and, in some cases, it also may escape state taxes.

Michele R. Bourgerie, CPA
Arthur Young, New York, NY

---

tax credit   A reduction in the amount of taxes owed. For example, corporations are permitted a credit on U.S. taxes for taxes paid to foreign governments, and individuals could, for a number of years, claim a tax credit for a portion of expenditures for certain energy-saving home improvements. A tax credit is more valuable than a deduction of an equal amount because the credit results in a reduction in tax owed rather than a reduction in taxable income. —See also FOREIGN TAX CREDIT.

tax deduction   —See DEDUCTION.

tax deferral   The delay of a tax liability until a future date. For example, an IRA may result in a tax deferral on the amount contributed to the IRA and on any income earned on funds in the IRA until withdrawals are made. At the corporate level, accelerated depreciation of assets results in a delay in tax liabilities. Tax deferral, which is legal, means a postponement, not an elimination, of a tax liability.

tax-deferred annuity —See TAX-SHELTERED ANNUITY.

tax-deferred income Income that is earned but neither received nor taxed until a later date. For example, interest earned on U.S. Treasury bills is received and taxed at maturity. Likewise, U.S. savings bonds provide appreciation of value on which holders may defer paying taxes until the security is cashed in. —See also TAX-FREE INCOME; TAX-SHELTERED INCOME.

Tax Equity and Fiscal Responsibility Act (TEFRA) A 1982 act that provided for a 10% federal tax withholding by institutions paying interest and dividends and that scaled back some of the preferences enacted under the Economic Recovery Tax Act of 1981. Essentially, TEFRA was a Reagan administration attempt to raise tax revenues and reduce the size of the government deficit.

tax evasion Illegal avoidance of taxes. The intentional omission of a gain from the sale of stock in reporting income to the Internal Revenue Service is an example of tax evasion. —See also TAX AVOIDANCE.

tax-exempt bond —See MUNICIPAL BOND.

tax-exempt money market fund An open-end investment company that invests in short-term tax-exempt securities. These funds normally pay relatively low current income (free of federal taxes) but are very liquid. They appeal to higher-income investors who seek a temporary investment. —Also called *short-term municipal bond fund*. —See also DOUBLE-EXEMPT FUND; MUNICIPAL BOND FUND.

tax-free exchange An exchange of assets between taxpayers in which any gain or loss is not recognized in the period during which the exchange takes place. Rather, taxpayers are required to adjust the basis of assets exchanged.

tax-free income Income received but not subject to income taxes. For example, interest from most municipal bonds is free of federal income taxes and often from state and local income taxes as well. —See also TAX-DEFERRED INCOME; TAX-SHELTERED INCOME.

tax haven A country or other political entity that offers outside businesses and individuals a climate of minimal or nonexistent taxation. In some cases, the low taxes apply not only to those levied by the tax haven itself, but also to the possibility of reducing or avoiding taxes levied in the investor's home country.

tax indexing —See INDEX.

tax loss carryback —See CARRYBACK.

tax loss carryforward —See CARRYFORWARD 1.

tax-loss selling The sale of securities that have declined in value in order to realize losses that may be used to reduce taxable income. Tax-loss selling occurs near the end of a calendar year so that the loss can be used in that tax year to offset ordinary income or gains on other security transactions. Thus, tax-loss selling occurs mainly among stocks that have declined in price. —See also TAX SELLING.

> ## When should an investor consider tax-loss selling?
> ●
>
> All other investment considerations being equal, there are
> times when it will be advantageous to sell an investment that
> produces a tax loss. The usual reason for taking a tax loss is to
> offset another gain and eliminate the tax burden on the gain. In
> such case the loss is said to "shelter" the gain. Long-term capi-
> tal losses resulting from the sale of securities can, to a limited
> degree, shelter even ordinary income such as wages.
>
> *Anthony L. Bartolini, Esq.*
> *Dechert Price & Rhoads, Philadelphia, PA*

tax preference item An item that can be legally omitted in order to
reduce taxable income when calculating an individual's tax liability by
ordinary means. However, the item must be included when calculating
the individual's alternative minimum tax. For example, interest paid by
certain municipal bonds that is ordinarily omitted in calculating taxable
income must be included when calculating the alternative minimum tax.

tax rate The proportional amount of taxes paid on a given income or
the given dollar value of an asset. If the tax is calculated on the basis of
total income, it is the average tax rate. If the tax is calculated only on
extra units of income, the rate is the marginal tax rate.

Tax Reform Act of 1986 Major tax legislation that significantly reduced
marginal income tax rates for individuals and corporations while at the
same time curtailing many deductions and eliminating numerous preference items. The Act was designed to be revenue-neutral and, in general, it benefited high-income and low-income individuals and corporations that do not spend large amounts of money on long-lived
equipment. While an original goal had been to simplify the tax system,
no simplification was evident in the final legislation.

  $\boxed{\$}$ The Tax Reform Act of 1986 was a significant event for investors.
  The Act eliminated the exclusion that had previously applied to long-
  term gains and long-term losses with the result being that these gains
  and losses were treated like other forms of income for tax purposes.
  Therefore, it was no longer expedient to hold appreciated securities over
  six months before selling them in order to receive favorable tax treatment
  on any gains. Most analysts expected that this change would tend to
  favor those securities providing investors with high current income in
  the form of interest and dividend payments. Another important change
  was a reduction in the maximum marginal individual income-tax bracket
  from 50% to 28% (actually 33% if a surtax was taken into account). The
  reduction in marginal rates tended to make tax shelters less attractive;
  at the same time it favored investments providing higher current income. The Act produced some major restrictions as to who qualified for
  favorable tax treatment when contributing to individual retirement ac-

counts (IRAs), and it stripped tax-shelter benefits from real estate investments. Many higher-income taxpayers could no longer deduct annual contributions to an IRA although income earned in the accounts would continue to be tax deferred. Other restrictions had to do with taxpayer income and whether or not the taxpayer was involved in another qualified retirement plan. The longer depreciation schedules for real estate and the inability of many investors to use losses created by real estate investment to offset other forms of income produced a negative impact on real estate investments. Deductions for various investment-related expenses were curtailed under the Act. Interest deductions were limited to interest expenses incurred on a primary residence and second home, and to interest incurred so as to finance investment income to the extent of the investment income earned. Deductions for things such as expenses for investment-related publications and advice, now classified as miscellaneous, could be used only by taxpayers who itemized their deductions and only to the extent that total miscellaneous deductions exceed 2% of adjusted gross income. The Act had some restrictions on the exclusion from taxation of municipal bond interest. Interest on certain municipal issues became subject to the alternative minimum tax, while interest on other municipal bonds became fully taxable. However, in general, the Tax Reform Act permitted municipal bonds to survive as a tax shelter.

tax selling   Sales of securities to establish gains or losses for income-tax purposes. Significant tax selling often occurs in December, especially following a bear market, as investors seek losses to offset previous gains or other income. An investor may engage in tax selling to establish gains when he or she expects to be paying a higher marginal tax rate the following year. —See also TAX-LOSS SELLING.

tax shelter   An investment that produces relatively large current deductions which can be used to offset other taxable income. Popular tax shelters include real estate projects and gas and oil drilling ventures. —Also called *shelter*. —See also ABUSIVE TAX SHELTER.

tax-sheltered annuity (TSA)   A retirement plan that permits an employee of a tax-exempt charitable, educational, or religious institution to contribute a certain portion of wages or salary into a tax-sheltered fund. Contributions serve to reduce taxable income in the year they are contributed. Taxes on income earned in the plan are deferred. Both past contributions and income are fully taxable when withdrawals are made. —Also called *403(b) plan; tax-deferred annuity.*

tax-sheltered income   Income received that would ordinarily be taxable, but because of certain noncash deductions such as depreciation, is protected from taxation. For example, rent received from a rental property is generally sheltered by depreciation on the property. —See also TAX-DEFERRED INCOME; TAX-FREE INCOME.

tax straddle   A combination of two similar futures contracts (one bought and one sold) that tend to move in opposite directions so that a loss on one is offset by a gain in the other. The contract showing the loss is sold in the current year (shortly before year's end) while the contract showing the gain is sold in the next year. The net effect is to push taxes back one year. This practice was ended with a new law that requires all gains and losses in futures contracts to be realized for tax purposes at the end of each year. —See also MARK TO THE MARKET.

tax swap   The sale of a security that has declined in price since the purchase date and the simultaneous purchase of a similar, but not substantially identical, security. The purpose of the swap is to achieve a loss for tax purposes while continuing to maintain market position. —See also WASH SALE 1.

tax umbrella   A corporation's tax loss carryforwards that may be used to shelter profits in future years.

tax year   The 12-month period for which tax is calculated. For most individual taxpayers the tax year is synonymous with the calendar year.

T bill   —See TREASURY BILL.

tear sheet   A page from one of the security reports published by Standard & Poor's in loose-leaf binders. Customers frequently ask registered representatives to send them tear sheets on particular securities.

technical analysis   Study of relationships among security market variables such as price levels, trading volume, and price movements so as to gain insights into the supply and demand for securities. Rather than concentrating on earnings, the economic outlook, and other business-related factors that influence a security's value, technical analysis attempts to determine the market forces at work on a certain security or on the securities market as a whole. —See also FUNDAMENTAL ANALYSIS.

technical correction   A temporary downturn in the price of a stock or in the market itself following a period of extensive price increases. A technical correction takes place in a generally increasing market when there is no particular reason that the increases should be interrupted, other than the fact that investors have temporarily slowed securities purchases.

technical indicator   A variable used in technical analysis to provide assistance in determining when to invest and which stocks to select. Technical indicators include chart formations, volume, odd-lot sales, and many other variables.

technically strong   —Used to describe a security or the whole market when most technical indicators point toward a price rise. For example, a stock may be technically strong because it has twice attempted and failed to break through a support level.

technically weak   —Used to describe a security or the whole market when technical indicators point toward declining prices. For example, small investors may step up odd-lot purchases of securities, the number of stocks hitting new highs may be small, and market volume on days the averages are rising may be light. All these things together indicate a technically weak stock market.

technical rally   A temporary rise in a security price or in the general market during a downward trend. Technical rallies are considered interruptions to a general trend.

technician   A person who uses technical analysis to determine the selection and timing of security purchases and sales. —Also called *market technician.* —See also CHARTIST; FUNDAMENTALIST.

TEDIS   —See MUNICIPAL CONVERTIBLE.

teenie   —See SIXTEENTH.

TEFRA   —See TAX EQUITY AND FISCAL RESPONSIBILITY ACT.

telephone booth   One of a series of cubicles around the perimeter of the trading floor of the New York Stock Exchange. Telephone booths are used by member firms to receive orders that are to be executed on the floor. Once the orders have been executed, the booths are used to transmit information back to the members' offices.

telephone switching   The movement of an investor's funds from one mutual fund to another mutual fund on the basis of an order given via telephone.

tenancy by the entirety   A type of asset ownership limited to married couples in which each spouse holds an equal share of the asset but neither may sell or give away an interest without the other's permission. If one spouse dies, the deceased's share automatically passes to the surviving spouse. —See also JOINT TENANCY WITH RIGHT OF SURVIVORSHIP; TENANCY IN COMMON.

tenancy in common   A type of asset ownership for two or more persons in which, upon the death of one owner, his or her share passes to heirs if a will is left or to the estate if no will is left, rather than to the co-owners. Transactions involving the property require written permission of all owners. —See also JOINT TENANCY WITH RIGHT OF SURVIVORSHIP; TENANCY BY THE ENTIRETY.

ten-day window   The period of time between the point when an individual or a company buys 5% or more of a firm's stock and the time at which the purchase must be publicly reported.

tender   To offer a security for sale to a party that is making an offer to buy it. For example, a stockholder may decide to tender shares to the issuing firm as part of the company's buyback. —See also HEDGED TENDER.

tender offer   An offer made directly to stockholders to purchase or trade for the stockholders' securities. A tender offer often contains restrictions such as the minimum number of shares required to be tendered for the offer to be effective or the maximum number of tendered shares that will be accepted. A tender offer may be made by a firm to its own shareholders to reduce the number of outstanding shares or it may be made by an outsider wishing to obtain control. —See also CREEPING TENDER OFFER; EXCLUSIONARY TENDER OFFER; HOSTILE TENDER OFFER; SELF-TENDER; TWO-TIER TENDER OFFER; WILLIAMS ACT.

⚠️ In the fall of 1986, Union Pacific Corporation agreed to make a major acquisition when it offered $1.2 billion to the stockholders of Overnight Transportation. In its tender offer to Overnight's stockholders, Union Pacific agreed to pay $43.25 for each of their 27.7 million shares. The price was approximately $12 per share above the price at which Overnight's stock had traded on the New York Stock Exchange the day before the announcement of the offer. Both companies' boards approved the offer, which was intended to extend Union Pacific's presence to the eastern United States and to form a significantly more integrated transportation company.

10–K An annual report of a firm's operations filed with the Securities and Exchange Commission. Compared with the typical annual report sent to stockholders, a 10–K is much less physically attractive; however, it contains many more detailed operating and financial statistics, including information on legal proceedings and management compensation. A firm's stockholders may obtain a free copy of the 10–K by writing to the corporate treasurer. —Also called *form 10–K*.

10–Q A quarterly unaudited financial report filed by firms having securities listed with the Securities and Exchange Commission. The 10–Q is a less detailed, more frequently filed version of the 10–K. —Also called *form 10–Q*.

1099–DIV An annual statement to investors and to the Internal Revenue Service by payers of dividends listing the amount of taxable dividend payments for the year. Also included, if appropriate, is any backup withholding required by law.

1099–INT An annual statement to savers and the Internal Revenue Service showing the amount of taxable interest payments from an institution during the year. Interest included on 1099–INT forms includes interest paid on savings accounts, money market funds, interest-bearing checking accounts, and taxable bonds. Municipal bond interest is not included on a 1099–INT form.

1099–OID An annual report sent to investors and the Internal Revenue Service listing interest income from taxable original-issue discount securities. The form, which originated during the 1984 tax year, reports the amount of implied and real income derived from original-issue discount securities such as Treasury bills, zero-coupon bonds, and commercial paper. Income shown on a 1099–OID is to be included on Part I in Schedule D of an investor's federal income tax return.

tentative order A customer order for part of a new securities issue before all the terms of the issue have been set. Underwriters take tentative orders to determine investor interest in a new issue. This practice assists the underwriters in pricing and sizing the issue.

term 1. The period of time during which a bond will remain outstanding. 2. The length of time that a person is to serve in a usually official capacity. For example, a firm's directors may be elected for terms of three years each.

term bonds Bonds that all mature on the same date. Corporate bond issues are often of the term variety since all the bonds of a given issue are scheduled to mature simultaneously. Municipalities often issue a combination of serial and term bonds with periodic retirements of serial bonds and then a redemption of a large block of term bonds during the final year. —See also SERIAL BONDS.

term certificate A certificate of deposit with a maturity of one year or more.

terminable marital trust A trust in which the surviving spouse has use of the income but may not touch the trust's assets. These assets will pass to others (most likely children) at the death of the spouse.

terminal value The dollar value of an asset at a specific future time. For example, a $1,000 certificate of deposit earning an annual return of 9% has a terminal value of $1,539 in 5 years.

termination fee The one-time charge for terminating or transferring an individual retirement account. If a financial institution charges a termination fee, the fee must be spelled out in the original agreement that is signed when the account is opened. Some institutions, particularly banks and savings and loans, often do not charge termination fees.

term insurance Life insurance in which the insurance company pays a specified sum if the insured dies during the coverage period. Term insurance includes no savings, cash values, borrowing power, or benefits at retirement. On the basis of cost, it is the very least expensive insurance available, although policy prices can vary significantly among firms. —See also CASH-VALUE LIFE INSURANCE.

term structure of interest rates —See YIELD CURVE.

term to maturity The number of years over which the issuer of debt promises to meet the requirements of an indenture agreement. Bonds with longer terms to maturity are subject to greater price fluctuations than short-term securities. —See also YIELD CURVE.

territory bond A bond issued by a U.S. territory such as Guam, Puerto Rico, and the Virgin Islands. Interest from territorial bonds is generally exempt from taxation by federal, state, and local authorities anywhere in the United States.

testamentary trust A trust created by a person's will, thereby not effective until the death of the testator. Testamentary trusts are used chiefly by wealthy individuals who are concerned about their beneficiaries' ability to administer large amounts of assets.

theoretical value The mathematically calculated price at which a security should sell. Depending on investor expectations and market imperfections, a security may sell at a price above or below its theoretical value.

thinly traded security A security that trades with little volume. Institutional investors normally exclude these securities from their portfolios because of the large price changes that would occur if trades of any significant size took place.

thin market A market for a security in which there are relatively few offers and bids. A thin market causes reduced liquidity and makes it more difficult to buy or sell the security without affecting its price. —See also DEEP MARKET; TIGHT MARKET.

third market The over-the-counter dealer market in stocks listed on organized exchanges such as the New York Stock Exchange. The third market developed in the 1960s when institutional investors became dissatisfied with the liquidity and brokerage commissions for large security trades on the exchanges. —See also FOURTH MARKET.

thirty-day visible supply Municipal securities that will be issued within 30 days.

thrift A financial institution that derives its funds primarily from consumer savings accounts. The term originally referred to those institutions offering mainly passbook savings accounts. But the industry has evolved through financial deregulation to the point that these accounts often provide only a small source of funds for many thrifts. The word *thrift* often refers to savings and loan associations, but it also can mean credit unions and mutual savings banks.

throwaway —See FOR YOUR INFORMATION.

Thundering Herd Merrill Lynch, Pierce, Fenner and Smith, Inc. The term derives from the firm's large size and the use of bulls in its advertising.

tick A movement in the price or price quotation of a security or contract. —See also DOWNTICK; MINIMUM TICK; UPTICK.

ticker An automated quotation system on which security transactions are reported after they occur on an exchange floor. Even though the newer systems are electronic and no longer actually tick, the name of the old mechanical device has stuck.

ticker symbol The abbreviation by which a security appears on stock quotation machines. For example, XON represents Exxon, GY represents GenCorp, X represents USX Corporation, and AN represents Amoco. Booklets containing the symbols are available at most brokerage offices.

ticker tape The narrow continuous rolls of paper on which stock transactions were printed before the electronic age made the old system obsolete. The term now refers to the flow of prices appearing on the boards of brokerage firms. —Also called *tape*.

ticket —See ORDER TICKET.

tick test A test to measure the extent to which a floor trader has stabilized security prices by trading against market trends, e.g., the extent to which transactions have been made against the trend as measured by purchases on downticks and sales on upticks.

tier A grouping of securities, usually by company size or security quality. —See also SECONDARY STOCK.

tiered market A securities market in which investors favor certain groups or types of stock with the result being that the favored securities sell at higher price-earnings ratios than do other securities with similar characteristics. Favored groups tend to rotate as investors' interests and perceptions change.

tight market   A market for securities in which competition is intense and spreads are narrow. In a tight market, dealers must make up in volume what they lose on a narrowing of the spread. —See also DEEP MARKET; THIN MARKET.

tight money   Restricted credit creating a period of relatively high interest rates. Tight money generally has a negative effect on security prices, at least in the short run. —See also EASY MONEY.

TIGR⊙   A registered service mark of Merrill Lynch for financial investment services, namely, providing zero-coupon obligations evidencing an interest in U.S. government bonds. —See also COUPON STRIPPING.

time deposit   An interest-bearing savings deposit or certificate of deposit at a financial institution. Although the deposits formerly included only deposits with specific maturities (i.e., certificates of deposit), they now are generally considered to include virtually all savings-type deposits. —See also DEMAND DEPOSIT.

time draft   A draft payable a certain number of days after being presented. —See also SIGHT DRAFT.

time horizon   The time interval over which an investment program is to be completed. An investor's time horizon is very important in determining the types of investments that should be selected. For example, investments that would be appropriate for an individual's retirement in 30 years are seldom suitable for reaching a short-term goal. —Also called *horizon.*

time series   A set of variables with values related to the respective times the variables are measured. Thus, a weekly record of a stock's price over a period of years is an example of a time series. Time series are often used to project future values by observing how the value of a variable has changed in the past.

times fixed charges   —See FIXED-CHARGE COVERAGE.

times interest earned   —See INTEREST COVERAGE.

time spread   —See CALENDAR SPREAD.

time stamping   The stamping of order tickets with the time of entry and execution. For example, options exchanges require stamping of order tickets with the times of execution to the nearest minute.

time value of money   The concept that a specific sum of money is more valuable the sooner it is received. Time value of money is dependent not only on the time interval being considered but also the rate of discount used in calculating current or future values.

time-weighted return   A rate-of-return measure of portfolio performance that gives equal weight to each period included in the study regardless of any differences in amounts invested in each period.

timing difference The time difference between the point when a transaction affects items for financial reporting purposes and the point when it affects the same items for tax purposes. For example, purchase of a fixed asset depreciated by an accelerated method for tax purposes but by straight-line for reporting purposes creates a timing difference for depreciation expense.

tip Information unavailable to the general public that, if accurate, could produce extraordinary profits for an investor who acts on it in a security transaction.

tippee A person who is given inside information.

tipster A person who provides inside information.

toehold purchase The purchase of under 5% of the outstanding common shares of a target company before establishing a much larger stake. A toehold purchase allows a party to buy stock in a company without filing a notice with the Securities and Exchange Commission and with the target company.

Tokyo Stock Exchange The world's second-largest organized securities exchange. Trading on the Tokyo Stock Exchange takes place through the matching of buy and sell orders.

tombstone An advertisement for a securities issue. The ad lists the security, some of the security's specifics, and the members of the syndicate selling the issue in the order of the members' importance. The term *tombstone* derives from the fact that the notice appears as a matter of record after the sale has been completed. —See also BRACKETING.

top The highest level to which a stock, a market index, or some other asset will rise. A top may be short-term or long-term, depending on the type of price movement being evaluated. —See also BOTTOM.

top a bid To make a bid higher than the prevailing bid.

Toronto Stock Exchange The major Canadian stock exchange on which over 1,000 issues are listed. The organization of the Exchange is similar to that of the U.S. exchanges except that a specialist system is not used.

total asset turnover A financial ratio indicating the effectiveness with which a firm's management uses its assets to generate sales. A relatively high ratio tends to reflect intensive use of assets. Total asset turnover is calculated by dividing the firm's total assets into annual sales. Assets are listed on the firm's balance sheet and sales are listed on the income statement. —Also called *asset turnover*. —See also ACTIVITY RATIO; FIXED ASSET TURNOVER.

total capitalization —See CAPITALIZATION.

total cost The total amount of money expended to establish an investment position. Total cost includes commissions, accrued interest, and taxes in addition to the principal amount of securities traded.

total return Dividend or interest income plus any capital gain, generally considered a better measure of an investment's return than dividends or interest alone.

total volume The aggregate amount of trading in a security on a particular security exchange, or in a specific type of security such as stocks, bonds, options, or futures contracts.

Totten trust A trust in which the assets are deposited for a beneficiary but the grantor has complete control over the trust including the right to reclaim the assets. The assets pass to the beneficiary upon the death of the grantor but are taxed as part of the grantor's estate.

tout To foster interest in a particular company or security. For example, a broker might tout a security to a client in hopes the client will purchase the security.

trade The purchase or sale of an asset. —Also called *transaction*.

trade To buy or sell an asset, frequently with only short intervals of ownership.

trade date The date on which an order is executed. Payment or delivery must be made within five business days of the trade date. —Also called *transaction date.* —See also SETTLEMENT DATE.

trade deficit The excess of goods and services that a country buys from abroad over goods and services sold to other countries. Large trade deficits may result in unemployment and a reduction in economic growth in the country with the deficit. —See also TRADE SURPLUS.

trademark A distinctive proprietary emblem, insignia, or name identifying a particular product or service. A trademark is an intangible asset that may be protected from use by others.

trader A person who buys and sells securities with the goal of profiting from short-term price swings.

trade surplus The excess of exported goods and services over imported goods and services. A trade surplus increases economic activity in a country but also may result in higher prices and interest rates if the economy is already operating at near capacity. —See also TRADE DEFICIT.

trade through To transact an order on an exchange when a more advantageous price is available through another source.

trading authorization A written document that gives another party the power to enter orders for an investor's account. The other party may be an employee of the broker-dealer handling the account, a spouse, or someone else designated by the client in the trading authorization.

trading dividends The purchase and sale of equity securities with the goal of maximizing dividend income. This practice is used primarily by corporate investors for which 80% of dividend income is tax-exempt.

trading gap A period of time during which a security is not traded because of a wide gap between the bid and ask or because of an official halt triggered by a technical factor, such as the expected release of a major news story relating to the security.

trading halt —See SUSPENDED TRADING.

trading limit   The number of commodity contracts that a person may trade during a single day. The limit is established by the Commodity Futures Trading Commission or by the exchange on which the particular contract is traded. —See also POSITION LIMIT.

trading on the equity   Use of borrowed money to increase the return on an investor's capital. Suppose an investor is able to borrow 50% of the funds required for a $10,000 investment returning 16% annually. If interest on the loan is 12%, the investor can earn $1,600 ($10,000 @ 16%) less interest of $600 ($5,000 @ 12%), or $1,000 on an investment of $5,000 ($10,000 less $5,000 borrowed), for a return of 20% ($1,000/$5,000).

trading on the perimeter   Trading of a security in the crowd around a specialist's post. When trading in a security becomes particularly active and floor brokers are unable to gain access to the specialist, trading on the perimeter may occur.

trading pattern   The systematic movement of a security's price over a period of time. Traders attempt to discover trading patterns and profit from them when buying and selling.

trading pool   A pool in which the stock is manipulated by purchases and sales in the open market. For example, pool operators affect a stock's price and volume by making purchases in the open market, thereby attracting the interest of other investors.

trading post   —See POST.

trading profit   Income derived from buying and selling a security at a profit over a relatively short-term period.

trading range   The high and low prices between which a specific stock or some stock average has been traded, or is expected to trade. —See also HISTORICAL TRADING RANGE.

trading ring   The area in the bond room of the New York Stock Exchange within which trading in bonds must take place.

trading unit   —See UNIT OF TRADING.

trading variation   —See MINIMUM TICK.

traditional governmental purpose bond   —See ESSENTIAL FUNCTION BOND.

trailing stop   A stop order to sell (buy) a security in which subsequent stop orders are placed at progressively higher (lower) levels as the stock price increases (decreases). For example, an investor may purchase shares of Zayre Corporation at $60 and simultaneously place a stop order to sell the stock if it drops to $58 or below. If the stock rises to $63 without going through the $58 stop price, the investor raises the stop price to $61. Thus, the stop price trails the market price of the stock.

transaction   —See TRADE.

transaction costs   The expense incurred in buying or selling a security. Transaction costs include commissions, markups, markdowns, fees, and any direct taxes. Transaction costs, of special significance to investors who frequently trade securities, can vary substantially depending on the firm with which the investor conducts business. —See also DISCOUNT BROKERAGE FIRM.

transaction date —See TRADE DATE.

transfer **1.** To record a change of ownership in a security on the issuer's books. **2.** To deliver a security to the buyer's broker by the seller's broker.

transfer agent A company, generally a bank or trust company, appointed by a firm to transfer that firm's securities. Security holders may send the security certificates directly to the transfer agents by registered mail. The security should be endorsed, with a letter of instruction included. The firm's agent is listed on its certificates. The transfer agent is also likely to maintain the current record of security owners for transmitting dividends, reports, security distributions, and so forth.

transfer notice —See DELIVERY NOTICE.

transfer of account An authorization by a customer to transfer the assets of his or her brokerage account at one firm to a brokerage account at another firm. It is generally easier and safer for one to transfer securities this way instead of requesting delivery and then sending the certificates to the new firm by oneself.

transfer price The price at which an item is transferred internally between two units of the same company. An oil company engaged in drilling, refining, and marketing must determine the price of the product as it is passed through the chain from oil field to service station in order to determine the profitability of each stage.

transfer tax **1.** A tax on the transfer of securities, paid by the seller. The Securities and Exchange Commission also imposes a small fee (1¢ per $500 value) on securities that are sold. **2.** A tax on the transfer of assets by gift or by death.

translation Use of the rate at which two currencies exchange in order to express amounts denominated in one currency in terms of the other currency. For example, a firm with foreign operations might express sales made in German marks in terms of U.S. dollars. —Also called *foreign currency translation.*

translation gain The gain resulting from translation of one currency to another currency. A U.S. company that translates German marks into U.S. dollars following a period of a weakening dollar will report a translation gain because the marks exchange for a greater number of dollars.

translation loss The loss that results when a firm translates amounts stated in one currency into terms of another currency. The loss is incurred when the firm translates from a currency that has declined in value relative to the currency into which the amounts are being converted.

treasurer A corporate financial officer who often has the responsibility for preparing financial reports, releasing financial information, and filing tax returns. The treasurer may or may not be the firm's main financial decision maker.

Treasuries   All bonds backed by the U.S. government that are issued through the Department of the Treasury. The safety of Treasuries is the benchmark against which all other debt securities are measured.

Treasury bill   A short-term debt security of the U.S. government that is sold in minimum amounts of $10,000 and multiples of $5,000 above this. Bills with 13-week and 26-week maturities are auctioned each Monday, and 52-week bills are sold every four weeks. These obligations, which are very easy to resell, may be bought through brokers, commercial banks, or directly from the Federal Reserve. —Also called *T bill*. —See also BANK DISCOUNT BASIS; CERTIFICATE OF INDEBTEDNESS; COUPON-EQUIVALENT YIELD; FORM PD4633–1.

How can an investor purchase T bills direct from the Fed?

Investors can purchase U. S. Treasury bills from a Federal Reserve Bank or Branch in person or by mail. Currently, there is no charge for such transactions. Thirteen-week and 26-week bills are offered once a week; 52-week bills are offered once every 4 weeks. The minimum denomination for a Treasury bill is $10,000, with $5,000 increments thereafter. Before purchasing Treasury bills, the investor must first establish a Treasury Direct account with the Federal Reserve. This account contains information such as social security number, tax backup withholding status, and a checking or savings account number at a financial institution to which direct deposit payments due the investor can be sent.

Having opened a Treasury Direct account, an investor submits a completed, signed tender form to purchase a Treasury bill. On this tender form, the investor specifies either a noncompetitive bid (an agreement to accept the average rate established in the bill auction) or a competitive bid (a specific yield desired). Noncompetitive tenders are accepted in full up to $1,000,000. Competitive tenders may be rejected if the desired yield is too high. Tenders delivered in person must arrive at the Federal Reserve by the cutoff hour on the auction date. Noncompetitive tenders submitted by mail are accepted if they are postmarked no later than the day prior to the auction and are received by the issue date. Full payment, in the form of a bank check, a certified personal check, maturing securities, or cash (delivered in person only), must accompany the tender. Investors can call or write to their nearest Federal Reserve Bank or Branch for the Treasury Direct account application form, tender forms, and for more information on the Treasury Direct program.

Herbert F. Wass, Vice President
Federal Reserve Bank of Boston, Boston, MA

Treasury bill auction   The weekly Monday auction for 13-week and 26-week Treasury bills and the monthly auction for 52-week Treasury bills. The auctions are conducted on a competitive-bid basis by the Federal Reserve. Securities are also set aside for investors who do not wish to enter a specific bid but who will purchase the securities at the average price paid by competitive bidders. —See also FORM PD4632.

Treasury bond   Longer-term, interest-bearing debt of the U.S. Treasury. Treasury bonds are quoted and traded in 32nds of a point.

Treasury Bond Receipts   —See COUPON STRIPPING.

Treasury note   Intermediate-term (1–10 years) interest-bearing debt of the U.S. Treasury, purchasable through a bank or brokerage firm or directly from the Federal Reserve. An active secondary market makes it easy to resell a Treasury note.

treasury stock   Shares of a firm's stock that have been issued and then repurchased. Treasury stock is not considered in paying dividends, voting, or calculating earnings per share. It may be eventually retired or reissued. —See also RETIREMENT 2.

trend   Relatively constant movement of a variable during a period of time. The period may be short-term or long-term, depending on whether the trend itself is short-term or long-term. For example, a rising market is taken to mean that prices of most stocks are in an upward trend.

trend analysis   Analysis of a variable's past value changes to determine if a trend exists and, if so, what the trend indicates. A technical analyst may graph a stock's price over a period of time to determine if a trend has been established. Analysts often attempt to determine if trends exist for a firm's earnings per share. —See also RATIO ANALYSIS.

trendline   In technical analysis, a straight line or two parallel straight lines indicating the direction in which a security has been moving, and, many chartists believe, will continue to move. When a security price breaks through a trendline, the beginning of a new trend is indicated.

triangle   In technical analysis, a chart formation in which successive high and low prices move closer together, forming a pattern that appears as a triangle turned on its side. A triangle indicates a period of combat between bulls and bears with the technical analyst having to determine the winner. If prices break out of the triangle on the upside, it is a bullish sign. A breakout on the downside indicates that the bears are winners. The closer the breakout occurs to the point of the triangle, the less conclusive the signal to buy or sell. —Also called *coil; flag; pennant; wedge.* —See also ASCENDING TRIANGLE; DESCENDING TRIANGLE.

trigger price   The specific price of an imported item below which a quota or tariff will be put into effect. A trigger price is imposed to keep foreign competitors from undercutting prices charged by domestic companies in the domestic firm's home market.

triple A   —See AAA.

triple bottom In technical analysis, a chart formation of a stock or a market index that has attempted to penetrate a lower price level on three different occasions. If the stock price or index actually breaks through on the downside during the third attempt, it is a bearish signal and the investor should sell or sell short the stock or index. If the stock or index is unable to penetrate the price level, it is a bullish sign that the price is at a strong support level. —See also TRIPLE TOP.

triple tax exempt Pertaining to or being a municipal bond, trust, or fund paying interest that is free of federal, state, and local income taxation for individuals residing in certain localities. This situation results from the fact that most but not all states and localities exempt municipal bond interest from taxation if the bonds are issued within that particular state. Triple tax exemption is of particular interest to investors residing in the high-tax states and localities, such as New York City.

triple top In technical analysis, a chart formation of a stock or a market index that has attempted to penetrate an upper price level on three different occasions. If the stock price or index actually breaks through on the upside during the third attempt, it is a bullish signal. If the stock price or index fails on the third attempt and pulls back, it is a bearish signal. —See also TRIPLE BOTTOM.

triple witching hour The hour before the market closing when options and futures on stock indices expire on the same day, thereby setting off frenzied trading in futures, options, and underlying securities. Traders and arbitrageurs unwind investment positions and produce large price movements in securities. The triple witching hour occurs on the third Fridays of March, June, September, and December. —See also EXPIRATION EFFECT; EXPIRATION FRIDAY; PROGRAM TRADING.

⚠️ On September 10, 1986, following very large price swings during each quarter's triple witching hour, the Securities and Exchange Commission issued instructions that traders placing orders for executions at the market's close on triple witching days should do so at least one-half hour before the market's close. The order was supposed to give investors and members 30 minutes in which to take care of order imbalances. The subsequent triple witching hour on September 19 exhibited relatively evenly matched orders and only a small fluctuation in the Dow Jones Industrial Average.

troubled debt restructuring —See DEBT RESTRUCTURING.

truncation The process of terminating the routing of a check at a point before it reaches the person who wrote it. Truncation generally occurs at the financial institution on which the check was written. Financial institutions view truncation as a method of reducing the costs of operating checking accounts. They frequently offer their customers a lower monthly fee to accept an account in which monthly statements are not accompanied by canceled checks.

trust A legal arrangement whereby control over property is transferred to a person or organization (the trustee) for the benefit of someone else (the beneficiary). Trusts are created for a variety of reasons, including tax savings and improved asset management. —See also CHARITABLE LEAD TRUST; CHARITABLE REMAINDER TRUST; CLIFFORD TRUST; MARITAL DEDUCTION TRUST; QTIP TRUST.

trust deed —See INDENTURE.

trustee An appointed person or institution that manages assets for the benefit of someone else. Trustees are most often trust corporations or trust departments of commercial banks that manage the assets for a fee based on a percentage of the size of the trust (usually under 1%). A trust may be very restrictive or it may allow the trustee wide discretion, depending on the grantor's wishes.

Trust Indenture Act of 1939 Legislation that established rights for security holders under indenture agreements. The Act sets standards for trustees, requires financial reports by the issuers to the trustees, and mandates disclosure of owners' rights under the indenture agreements.

TSA —See TAX-SHELTERED ANNUITY.

turkey An investment that has performed poorly.

turnaround 1. The process of moving from a period of losses or low profitability into a more profitable stage. A turnaround may be triggered by a number of factors including a better use of assets or the development of new products and services. 2. A security that is in the process of reversing a declining price trend. 3. The purchase and sale of a security on the same day.

turnover 1. The trading volume of the market or of a particular security. 2. The number of times that an asset is replaced during a given period. For example, an inventory turnover of 5 indicates that the firm's inventory has been turned into sales and has been replaced 5 times.

turnover rate 1. The trading volume in a particular stock during a time period (generally one year) as a percentage of the total number of shares of that stock outstanding. The turnover rate adjusts for the differences in outstanding shares and provides a measure of the relative activity in a stock. 2. For an investment company, the volume of shares traded as a percentage of the number of shares in the company's portfolio. A high turnover rate may indicate excessive trading and commissions.

12–b plan A type of mutual fund in which the fund's operators are permitted to cover marketing expenses by using the fund's assets. This fee becomes a hidden load charge in that the cost to the buyer is not spelled out as clearly as the sales charge in a load fund is. Thus, a fund classified as no-load may take a fee out of assets rather than charge the buyer directly.

twenty-day period —See COOLING-OFF PERIOD.

twenty-five percent rule A guideline for municipal bond buyers holding that if a municipality's total long-term debt exceeds 25% of its annual budget, the debt is excessive.

twisting An attempt to convince an individual to sell one product and purchase another product, primarily so that the salesperson can earn additional commissions. In the brokerage business, twisting is usually called *churning. Twisting,* the more general term, applies to the sale of other products as well, such as insurance policies.

two-dollar broker   A member of a securities exchange who executes orders for other members. A two-dollar broker performs essentially the same function as a commission broker except that he or she is independent rather than a representative of a specific firm. —Also called *independent broker.*

200-day moving average   A statistical series of a security's closing prices over 200 consecutive trading days. A 200-day moving average is a technical indicator designed to discover changes in a trend. Generally, a moving average is superimposed on a stock's line chart. If the stock price penetrates the moving average on the upside after a downward trend, the penetration is a signal to buy. But if the stock price penetrates the moving average on the downside following an upward trend, the penetration is a bearish sign.

two-sided market   The market for a security in which a bid price and an ask price are both quoted. —Also called *two-way market.* —See also ONE-SIDED MARKET.

two-tier tender offer   An offer to purchase a sufficient number of stockholders' shares so as to gain effective control of a firm at one price per share and then to make a lower offer at a later date for the remaining shares. For example, an investor may offer $50 per share for up to 51% of a firm's outstanding stock and then, having gained control, offer $40 for each of the remaining shares. —See also FAIR PRICE AMENDMENT.

two-way market   —See TWO-SIDED MARKET.

U

u   —Used in the daily or weekly high column of stock transaction tables in newspapers to indicate that the price of a security has reached a new 52-week high: *u75.*

UGMA   —See UNIFORM GIFTS TO MINORS ACT.

un *or* **ut**   —Used in stock transaction tables in newspapers to indicate unit shares: *WebD un.*

unamortized bond discount   When a bond is originally sold at a discount from par value, the difference between the par value and the proceeds from selling the bond that has not yet been calculated as an interest expense for the borrower. A firm issuing a bond at below par value must charge off the difference to interest expense over the issue's life. Unamortized bond discount is the portion of the discount that has not yet been shown as an expense. —Also called *bond discount*.

unamortized bond premium When a bond is originally sold at a premium to par value, the difference between the par value and the proceeds from selling the bond that has not yet been subtracted from interest expense.

unaudited statement A financial statement prepared by an auditor but not in accordance with generally accepted auditing standards. Unaudited statements are prepared to less rigorous standards than audited statements.

unbundling The separation and separate pricing of products and services by financial institutions. When deregulation resulted in price competition and the introduction of new products, financial institutions found it increasingly necessary to offer and price each product separately.

uncollected funds A deposit or a portion of a deposit that has not yet been collected by a financial institution. Financial institutions typically prohibit customers from writing checks on uncollected funds.

uncovered option —See NAKED OPTION.

underbanked Pertaining to or being a new security issue for which the managing underwriter has difficulty obtaining commitments from other underwriters.

underbooked Pertaining to or being a new security issue in which investment bankers find a general lack of interest among investors before the issue date. —See also INDICATION OF INTEREST.

undercapitalized Pertaining to or being a firm that has insufficient long-term equity to support its assets. A rapidly growing firm that finds itself financing its operations primarily with short-term loans may be undercapitalized.

underdepreciation 1. Depreciation that is insufficient to allow for the eventual replacement of the asset being depreciated. Underdepreciation is generally caused by rising prices on replacement assets. —See also OVERDEPRECIATION 1. 2. Depreciation that causes an asset to be carried on a firm's books at a greater value than it would be worth if it were sold. Underdepreciation results in overstated earnings and assets on the firm's financial statements. —See also OVERDEPRECIATION 2.

underleveraged Of, relating to, or being a firm that has insufficient debt in its capital structure. Because bond interest is deductible for tax purposes and is generally fixed in amount over a long period of time, some use of debt can often result in greater earnings per share for stockholders. Whether or not a company is underleveraged is usually a matter of opinion.

underlying asset 1. The physical and financial asset to which a security holder or a class of security holders has a claim. An analyst may feel that a stock is underpriced on the basis of the value of the firm's underlying assets and the potential earning power of these assets. 2. The asset that underlies and gives value to a security. The underlying asset of a stock option is the stock that the option can be used to purchase. Likewise, the underlying asset of a convertible bond is the stock for which the bond can be exchanged. The market value of a security is directly affected by changes in the value of any underlying asset into which it may be exchanged. —See also DERIVATIVE INSTRUMENT.

underlying debt   Debt of a municipal organization for which a higher municipal organization is at least partially responsible. For example, debt of a hospital authority may be guaranteed by a county such that the hospital debt is underlying the debt of the county. —See also OVERLAPPING DEBT.

underperforming asset   An asset that earns a lower rate of return than it would be capable of earning if it were properly used. A firm with underperforming assets is a prime target for takeover. —See also NONPERFORMING ASSET.

underpricing   The pricing of a new security issue at less than the prevailing price of the same security in the secondary market. Underpricing helps to ensure a successful sale.

undervalued   Pertaining to or being a security that trades at a price lower than it logically should be. Whether or not a security is undervalued is a subjective judgment. —See also OVERVALUED.

undervalued company   A firm whose assets and potential earning power are not adequately reflected in its stock price. Although such firms are more likely to be subject to takeover attempts than others, determining if a particular firm is actually undervalued can be quite difficult. —See also ASSET VALUE.

underwrite   To assume the risk of securities' sale by purchasing the securities from the issuer for resale to the public. Investment bankers often assume this underwriting function in order to guarantee that the issuer will receive all the funds needed from the sale. —See also BEST-EFFORTS BASIS 1; FREED UP; HOT ISSUE; INVESTMENT BANKER; PEG 1; STANDBY UNDERWRITING.

underwriter   An investment banker that acts to guarantee the sale of a new securities issue by purchasing the securities for resale to the public. —Also called *sponsor 2.* —See also AGREEMENT AMONG UNDERWRITERS; INVESTMENT BANKER; LEAD UNDERWRITER.

underwriting agreement   —See AGREEMENT AMONG UNDERWRITERS.

underwriting spread   —See GROSS SPREAD.

underwriting syndicate   —See SYNDICATE.

undivided profit   Undistributed net income not yet included as part of retained earnings.

unearned income   Individual income, such as dividends, pension payments, and capital gains, derived from something other than personal services. —See also EARNED INCOME.

unencumbered　Pertaining to an owned asset without a claim against it. Real estate not being used as collateral for a loan and on which all taxes are current is unencumbered. —See also ENCUMBRANCE 1.

unfriendly takeover　Acquisition of a firm in spite of resistance by the target firm's management and board of directors. —Also called *hostile takeover.* —See also FRIENDLY TAKEOVER; HOSTILE TENDER OFFER; KILLER BEE; RAIDER.

unified credit　A credit used against federal taxes due on estates and large gifts. Under current law, the unified credit is sufficient to offset taxes on values of up to $600,000 in estates and large gifts. Thus, the combination of estate value and large gifts must exceed $600,000 during a person's lifetime before any taxes must be paid to the federal government.

Uniform Gifts to Minors Act (UGMA)　Uniform state laws that facilitate irrevocable gifts to a minor by eliminating the requirement of a guardian or trust. A custodian, who may be the donor, is appointed to manage the gift but full rights to the principal and income reside with the minor. Under 1986 tax reform, only the first $1,000 of income from these custodial accounts will be taxed at the child's rate if the child is under 14 years of age. Income above $1,000 is taxed at the donor's rate. When the child turns 14, income from the trust is taxed at the child's rate. Individuals can put as much as $10,000 annually ($20,000 with a joint gift) into an UGMA account without incurring a gift tax consequence.

Uniform Practice Code　A set of standards for members of the National Association of Securities Dealers in settling securities transactions. The Code covers technical items such as the ways by which interest is computed, the times at which settlements are to occur, and so on.

Uniform Securities Act　A 1956 act designed to bring uniformity to state regulation of securities. The Act deals with fraud and the registration of securities and dealers. States are free to adopt all, parts, or none of the Act.

Uniform Securities Agent State Law Examination　A test required by many states of people who want to become registered representatives. In addition to passing this test, the National Association of Securities Dealers requires candidates to pass the Series 7.

unissued capital stock　Corporate capital stock that has been authorized but not yet issued. Management of a firm will often ask its stockholders to authorize many more shares of stock than are actually needed in order to provide flexibility for the issuance of more shares later without stockholders' approval.

unit　—See SPECIALIST UNIT; UNIT OF TRADING; UNIT SHARE.

unitary tax　A state corporate income tax on worldwide income. Although they are unpopular with corporations, unitary taxes are instituted by governments to foil firms that use creative accounting techniques to transfer their income to states or countries with low income-tax rates.

unit convertible A security that is convertible into a package of assets or securities rather than into a specified number of shares of a single common stock.

United States government securities —See GOVERNMENTS.

United States savings bond —See SAVINGS BOND.

unit growth Growth in sales in terms of the actual number of units, as opposed to the dollar value of the units that have been sold. Measuring growth in units, rather than in dollars, eliminates the effects of inflation and shows real growth.

unit investment trust An unmanaged portfolio of investments put together by an investment adviser and sold in units to investors by brokers. Units of a trust usually sell for $1,000 including a sales commission of approximately 4% at the time of the initial offering. Sponsoring brokers normally maintain a secondary market for the units, the value of which depends on the value of the securities held by the trust. Because of the initial sales charge, unit investment trusts are normally not attractive for short-term trading. —Also called *fixed trust.*

unit of trading The minimum quantity of a security required for normal trading purposes. The unit of trading for most stocks is 100 shares. —Also called *trading unit.*

unit sales Sales measured in terms of physical units rather than in dollars. Unit sales data are often used by financial analysts in evaluating the health of a company.

unit share A combination of securities traded as a single package. For example, a share of common stock and a warrant may be traded as a unit.

universal life insurance A combination of term insurance and a tax-deferred savings plan paying a variable return. This combination was developed during the early 1980s when interest rates rose to very high levels and caused the public to view regular whole life policies unfavorably.

unlimited liability The liability of the owner of a business for all the obligations of the business. An owner's personal assets can be seized if the business's assets are insufficient to satisfy claims against it. The placement of personal assets at risk is a great disadvantage of proprietorships and general partnerships. The ability to limit the amount of liability to which an owner is subject is a major reason for the formation of corporations and limited partnerships. —See also LIMITED LIABILITY.

unlisted security A security that trades only in the over-the-counter market. —See also LISTED SECURITY.

unlisted trading Trading a security on the floor of an exchange when the security is not listed for trading on that exchange. Unlisted trading occurs when members of an exchange wish to trade the security but the issuing company has not applied for listing. Unlisted trading requires approval of the Securities and Exchange Commission.

unload To sell an investment, generally at a loss.

unpaid dividend **1.** A declared dividend that has not yet been paid. **2.** —See PASSED DIVIDEND.

unqualified opinion —See CLEAN OPINION.

unrealized gain The increased market value of an asset that is still being held, compared with the asset's cost of acquisition. Unrealized gains are not normally taxable. —Also called *paper gain; paper profit.* —See also REALIZED GAIN.

unrealized loss The reduction in value of an asset that is being held compared with the original cost. An unrealized loss normally must be realized by closing out the position before it can be recognized for tax purposes. —Also called *paper loss.* —See also REALIZED LOSS; WASH SALE 1.

unregistered exchange A securities exchange that has been exempted from registration by the Securities and Exchange Commission. Unregistered exchanges are generally quite small and trade local issues in moderate volume. The Honolulu Stock Exchange is unregistered. —See also REGISTERED EXCHANGE.

unregistered security —See RESTRICTED SECURITY.

unsecured creditor A creditor with a claim for which no specific assets are pledged. A debenture holder is an unsecured creditor. —See also SECURED CREDITOR.

unsecured liability A liability for which no specific collateral is held by a creditor. Essentially, payment on an unsecured liability is assured by the promise of the borrower.

unsystematic risk Risk that is specific to an industry or firm. Examples of unsystematic risk include losses caused by labor problems, nationalization of assets, or weather conditions. This type of risk can be reduced by assembling a portfolio with significant diversification so that a single event will affect only a limited number of the assets. —Also called *diversifiable risk.* —See also SYSTEMATIC RISK.

unwelcome assignment Assignment of an option to a writer when the writer does not yet wish to fulfill the terms of the contract. For example, for tax reasons, an option writer may want assignment to occur near the expiration. Unwelcome assignment is a possibility for calls when the underlying asset sells at or above the strike price, and it is a possibility for puts when the underlying asset sells at or below the strike price. Unwelcome assignment can be avoided by purchasing an offsetting contract and closing out a position.

unwind **1.** To close out a relatively complicated investment position. For example, an investor who practices arbitrage by taking one position in stocks and the opposite position in option contracts would have to unwind by the date on which the options would expire. **2.** To rectify a transaction in which a mistake has been made. For example, because of a misunderstanding, a brokerage firm may have bought the wrong stock for a customer. The firm must then unwind the erroneous trade by selling the stock just purchased and buying the correct stock.

upgrading 1. An increase in the quality rating of a security issue. An upgrading may occur for a variety of reasons, including an improved outlook for a firm's products, increased profitability, or a reduction in the amount of debt the firm has outstanding. As circumstances change, upgrading or downgrading of a security takes place once the issue has been initially rated and sold. An upgrading generally can be expected to have a positive influence on the price of the security. —See also DOWN-GRADING. 2. An increase in the quality of securities held in a portfolio.

upside potential The potential price or gain that may be expected in a security or in a security average, generally stated as the dollar price or the dollar amount of gain that may reasonably be expected in the particular security or security average. For example, an analyst may feel that a stock currently selling at $25 per share has an upside potential of $40. —See also DOWNSIDE RISK.

upstairs market The trading of securities within a broker-dealer firm rather than taking a trade to an exchange floor or trading with another broker-dealer in the over-the-counter market. In the upstairs market, the broker-dealer acts as a dealer or as an agent for both parties.

upstream Pertaining to earnings or operations at a firm that are near or at the initial stages of producing a good or service. For example, exploration and production are upstream operations for a large integrated oil company. —See also DOWNSTREAM.

> In its September 1986 quarterly financial statements, Amoco (formerly Standard Oil of Indiana) reported that because of lower energy prices, its upstream operations in exploration and production lost $49 million during the period. At the same time low energy prices penalized upstream operations, however, they helped downstream operations to the extent that Amoco earned $173 million from refining, marketing, and transportation. Thus, Amoco was able to balance losses in one segment of its business against profits in another segment. During this time of falling oil prices, firms that were engaged solely in production and exploration failed in record numbers.

uptick An upward price movement for a security transaction compared with the preceding transaction of the same security. The short sale of a security is permitted only when the security's most recent price change is an uptick. —Also called *plus tick*. —See also DOWNTICK.

uptrend A series of price increases in a security or in the general market. Some investors feel that securities tend to take on a certain inertia; as a result, these investors search for stocks in an uptrend, thinking that they will probably continue to move in the same direction. —See also DOWN-TREND.

usable bond A bond that may be used at face value in combination with a warrant to purchase shares of common stock. Essentially, the issuer allows warrant owners to substitute the bond for cash when the warrants are exercised. Ownership of this type of bond is, like ownership of a convertible bond, a speculation on the direction of interest rates and on the direction of the price of the underlying stock.

Please compare the risk and return on utility bonds vis-à-vis risk and return on industrial bonds.

Utility bonds, like industrial bonds, range the full spectrum with regard to credit quality. Some utility companies have been able to overcome successfully more difficult times associated with bringing large construction projects into their ratepayers' rate base, thus enabling the companies to pass on to these ratepayers the costs of constructing the projects. Other companies have been forced to pass some or all of these costs on to their stockholders instead, meaning that these companies' earnings have been hurt severely. (The harm to earnings, of course, also adversely affects the utilities' bondholders because these companies' financial ratios, i.e., interest-coverage ratios and debt to equity ratios, are reduced and credit rating agencies are likely to reduce credit ratings as a result. Lower credit ratings translate into higher bond yields and lower bond prices for bondholders.) This is an extremely abbreviated and simplistic explanation of why utility bonds at one time traded at relatively wide yield spreads to industrial bonds; the utility companies' financial ratios were influenced by political factors such as whether the elected public utility commissioners would permit their re-election chances to be harmed by passing on unpopular rate increases to those same ratepayers who elected them, besides all the other factors which were almost beyond the control of the utilities, e.g., high interest costs, energy conservation efforts, and environmental concerns, to name just a few. These factors all contributed to the market's perception of greater risk in the utility industry. Some of the factors have changed; others have been overcome by time, as projects have been completed and put into the rate bases of the utility companies of our nation. Still other very positive trends have occurred (such as high interest costs having been reduced through refinancing at lower interest costs). Now we observe that many utility companies are becoming cash cows. The excess cash flows generated by some of them have enabled them to buy companies in nonregulated industries, thus reducing their vulnerability to political influences and allowing them to participate in more growth-oriented businesses. In short, utility companies are turning the corner on their past problems in many cases, and their bonds are trading more and more like industrial bonds in those selected cases.

Stephanie R. Goldsborough, Treasury Officer
Maryland National Bank, Baltimore, MD

ut —See UN.

utility A business providing an essential service, generally under government regulation. Electric companies, gas transmission firms, and local telephone companies are utilities.

utility bond A long-term debt security issued by a utility.

value-added tax (VAT) A tax levied on increases in a product's value at each stage of production and distribution. The value-added tax, essentially an invisible sales tax included in the final price, is ultimately paid by consumers. For example, a candy maker paying $10,000 for ingredients used in the manufacture of chocolate bars resold for $15,000, would be required to pay a tax on the $5,000 of value added to the product. Proponents of the value-added tax argue that it should be substituted for the current federal income tax to stimulate consumer saving. —See also CONSUMPTION TAX.

value investing The selection of securities to be bought and sold on the basis of the value of the firms' assets. For example, an investor may look for a stock in which current assets exceed total liabilites on a per share basis by more than the market price of the stock. Value investing emphasizes asset value more than earnings projections.

Value Line Composite Index An overall measure of stock price movements that is calculated using 1,700 stocks listed on the New York Stock Exchange, the American Stock Exchange, the regional and Canadian exchanges, and the over-the-counter market. Unlike most other popular indices, this average gives equal weight to each of the stocks. It is a relatively good indicator of the price movements of low-priced stocks and speculative securities.

Vancouver Stock Exchange The smallest of the three main exchanges in Canada. The Vancouver Stock Exchange, which specializes in speculative mining stocks, attracts significant interest from investors in the United States.

variable Something (as stock prices, earnings, dividend payments, interest rates, and gross national product) that has no fixed quantitative value. —See also DEPENDENT VARIABLE; INDEPENDENT VARIABLE.

variable annuity An annuity with payments to the annuitant that vary depending on the investment success of a separate investment account underlying the annuity. Since the invested funds are primarily in common stocks, this annuity offers greater potential rewards and greater attendant risks than annuities supported by fixed-income securities. —See also FIXED ANNUITY; HYBRID ANNUITY.

variable cost Costs of production that vary directly in proportion to the number of units produced. Variable costs often include labor expenses and raw material costs because labor and raw material normally must be increased to increase output. Firms for which variable costs represent a high proportion of total costs are normally less likely to experience large fluctuations in earnings because changes in sales and revenues are accompanied by nearly equal changes in costs. —See also AVERAGE COST; FIXED COST; MARGINAL COST.

variable coupon renewable note (VCR) A renewable note on which interest is reset on a weekly basis according to a predetermined formula. A VCR continues to renew at quarterly intervals unless the owner directs the issuer to repay the principal.

Is variable life insurance right for me?

Variable life insurance (VLI) may not be for everyone. However, if you're comfortable with the idea of your money riding the fortunes of the stock and bond markets, then it's definitely worth considering. After all is said and done, there are only two types of cash-value life insurance—the fixed kind, where the insurance company promises a rate of return on the investment account, and the variable kind, where the policyowner directs the investment course. Here are some tips:

- VLI policies come in two basic varieties: Annual pay VLI allocates a higher percentage of each yearly premium dollar to pay for insurance protection. Use it for your protection needs. Single premium VLI, on the other hand, puts most of its one-time premium into an investment fund. Use it to fill small gaps in your insurance program, to build a retirement nest egg, to build a college fund, to fund a nonqualified deferred compensation agreement, or as a charitable gift. In short, use it for any purpose wherein you wish to accumulate money on a tax-favored basis.

- VLI should only be purchased from companies rated A or A+ by A.M. Best Company, the insurance rating company. It is also a good idea to deal with insurance companies licensed to do business in New York State, the state with the toughest insurance laws.

RECAP: VLI properly understood and applied can be an excellent financial planning tool.

Rudolph D. Watz, CLU, ChFC
Vice President, Director, Retirement Plans
Value Line Securities, Inc., New York, NY

variable life insurance Life insurance that relates benefits to the value of the separate investment account underlying the annuity. This insurance is designed to prevent erosion of benefits by inflation. The size of the benefits will vary.

variable-rate certificate of deposit A certificate of deposit that pays a rate of interest which changes at predetermined intervals according to a specified formula or a key interest rate. This savings instrument is most appropriate if the investor expects short-term interest rates to rise before the certificates mature.

variable-rate note —See FLOATING-RATE NOTE.

variable ratio option writing The writing of options when only some of the underlying assets that may be called for delivery are owned by the writer. Professional option writers use variable ratio option writing to generate profits if the underlying asset price moves within an established range. —Also called *ratio writing*.

variance A statistical measure of the variability of measured data from the data's average value. A high variance, indicating relatively great variability, also indicates that the average is of minimal use in projecting future values for the data. Standard deviation is the square root of variance. Financial analysts use both statistical measures to weigh investment risk. —See also COVARIANCE; RISK.

VAT —See VALUE-ADDED TAX.

VCR —See VARIABLE COUPON RENEWABLE NOTE.

venture arbitrage —See RAIDING.

venture capital A pool of risk capital, typically contributed by large investors, in which money is made available to young, small companies that have good growth prospects but are short of funds. Small investors can buy new issues or participate in mutual funds specializing in the supply of venture capital.

venture-capital fund An investment company that invests its shareholders' money in new, very risky, but potentially very profitable, business ventures. —See also NONDIVERSIFIED MANAGEMENT COMPANY.

vertical analysis Comparison of an item on a financial statement with a different item on the same statement. For example, an analyst may study a firm's balance sheet to compare the level of current assets with the level of current liabilities in order to measure liquidity. Analysts often study a firm's income statement to compare net income with total sales. —See also HORIZONTAL ANALYSIS; RATIO ANALYSIS.

vertical line chart —See BAR CHART.

vertical merger A merger between two firms involved in the same business but on different levels. As an example, an automobile company may purchase a tire manufacturer or a glass company. The merger permits the firm to gain more control over another level of the manufacturing or selling process within that single industry. —See also HORIZONTAL MERGER.

vertical security exchange   The exchange of one security for a different security (i.e., stock for debt or debt for stock). Exchange offers involving unlike securities are generally tax-free unless the investor only receives debt in exchange for stock.

vertical spread   —See MONEY SPREAD.

vested benefits   Pension benefits belonging to an employee independent of his or her future employment. An employee normally becomes vested after five years of employment with the same firm, although there are numerous exceptions requiring longer employment. —See also PENSION PLAN.

V-formation   In technical analysis, a chart formation caused by a sharp extended decline followed by a sudden upward movement. Some chartists believe a V-formation is not generally a good indicator of a major change of direction in a security's price. These people feel that a major price reversal requires a period of testing low prices with succeeding price advances and declines. Only after this consolidation phase can a new bull movement be assured.

vi   —Used in listed stock and bond transaction tables in newspapers to indicate that the firm issuing the stock is in bankruptcy or receivership or that the firm is being reorganized under bankruptcy. It also indicates securities assumed by such companies: *vi Robbins.*

visible supply   New security issues, primarily bonds, scheduled for sale during the next month.

volatile   Subject to large price fluctuations. Traders generally prefer volatile securities if they buy and sell on short-term price movements. —See also BETA.

volume   The amount of trading sustained in a security or in the entire market during a given period. Especially heavy volume may indicate that important news has just been announced or is expected.

volume deleted   —Used on the consolidated tape to mean that volume data for trades of 10,000 shares and fewer will be omitted until further notice. The deletion of volume, the next step following the deletion of certain price information, is intended to speed the reporting of trades during periods of very heavy volume. With volume and all data but the digits and fractions having been deleted, a trade that ordinarily appears as XON 5s52½ will be reported as XON 2½. —See also DIGITS DELETED; LATE TAPE.

voluntary accumulation plan   A plan to acquire additional shares in a mutual fund on a more or less regular basis, at the discretion of the shareholder.

voluntary bankruptcy   Bankruptcy initiated by the organization entering the bankruptcy rather than by that organization's creditors. Organizations generally enter voluntary bankruptcy to protect themselves from creditors' claims. —See also CHAPTER 7; CHAPTER 11; INVOLUNTARY BANKRUPTCY.

voting rights The type of voting and the amount of control held by owners of a class of stock. —See also CUMULATIVE VOTING; MAJORITY VOTING; NONVOTING STOCK; PROXY.

voting stock Stock for which the holder has the right to vote in the election of directors, in the appointment of auditors, or in other matters brought up at the annual meeting. Most common stock is voting stock. —See also NONVOTING STOCK.

voting trust certificate A trust-issued certificate that evidences stock ownership but reserves voting rights for the trust. Voting trust certificates are exchanged for stock when voting power must be consolidated. Thus, holders of certificates have all the normal rights of stockholders with the exception of voting rights.

vulture fund A pool of investment money used to purchase distressed real estate at bargain prices. Vulture funds are relatively risky but offer large potential profits. The performance of a vulture fund is dependent upon the skill of the fund's managers in identifying and purchasing undervalued real estate that can be turned into profitable investments.

waiting period —See COOLING-OFF PERIOD.

walk-in A new brokerage customer who simply walks into the office. Although walk-ins are generally assigned to brokers, they have the right to specify a preferred broker.

Are wallflowers good to buy or sell?

A wallflower is essentially stock in which there is little or no investor interest. In a group that is doing well overall, it may be a sleeping beauty. If it is part of a stock group in which few stocks are doing well, its problem is likely one tied to industry fundamentals such as declining demand, foreign competition, or the like. Betting on one specific wallflower is speculative without good understanding of its environment. However, studies have shown that truly long-term investments in a highly diversified portfolio of wallflowers are likely to prove rewarding on a multiyear basis. Some wallflowers eventually blossom.

J. Kendrick Noble, Jr., First Vice President
PaineWebber Incorporated, New York, NY

wallflower An out-of-favor security, company, or industry.

Wall Street The main street in New York City's financial district. *Wall Street* is often used to denote the entire financial district in New York or the world of U.S. finance and investments. —Also called *the Street.*

wanted for cash A notice on the ticker tape that an investor is interested in purchasing a particular security for immediate delivery and payment, in contrast with a normal transaction in which five business days are permitted for delivery and payment.

warrant A security that permits its owner to purchase a specific number of shares of stock at a predetermined price. For example, a warrant may give an investor the right to purchase 5 shares of XYZ common stock at a price of $25 per share until October 1, 1997. Warrants usually originate as part of a new bond issue, but they trade separately after issuance. Warrants normally have limited lives. Their values are considerably more volatile than the values of the underlying stock. Thus, investment in warrants is not for the timid. —Also called *subscription warrant.* —See also PERPETUAL WARRANT; USABLE BOND.

warrant agreement A written statement of the terms of a warrant issue. While the information in these agreements is quite important, their technical nature is such that they are more appropriate for use by financial analysts and sophisticated traders than by individual investors.

warrant leverage ratio An indication of the degree of change in a warrant price for a given change in the price of the underlying stock. If a warrant doubles for a 50% increase in the stock that the warrant can be used to purchase, the warrant leverage ratio is 100%/50%, or 2. A warrant with a high leverage ratio offers large potential profits at the expense of relatively large potential losses because the leverage operates in both directions.

warrant premium The excess of a warrant's market price over its minimum value in exchange for shares of common stock. For example, a warrant to purchase 3 shares of stock at $10 each has minimum value of $45 if the shares trade at a price of $25 (3 × $15). If the warrant has a market price of $55, the premium will be equal to $10 ($55 − $45). Although a warrant normally trades at a premium, the size of the premium declines as its price climbs and as it approaches expiration.

Washington Public Power Supply System (WPPSS) A huge public utility system established in 1957 to construct and operate electric power plants. The construction and partial construction of five large nuclear plants during the 1970s and early 1980s incurred massive cost increases and a surplus capacity for electricity, resulting in the biggest municipal default in U.S. history. —Also called *Whoops.*

wash sale **1.** The illegal purchase or repurchase of an asset within 30 days of the sale date of a basically identical asset that was sold in order to take a tax loss. For example, if an investor sold a security at a loss and then immediately repurchased the same security or a basically identical security, the Internal Revenue Service would consider the transaction a wash sale. (Wash sales are prohibited by the Internal Revenue Service.) **2.** An illegal trade in which no change in ownership takes place.

wasting asset   An asset that tends to decline in value over time as its expected life is used up. A factory machine or an automobile is a wasting asset. Some individuals also consider options or warrants wasting assets since they have a limited life after which they are valueless. —Also called *shrinking asset*.

watch list   A roster of securities under scrutiny for a special reason. For example, a watch list may be established for stocks that have exhibited unusual trading volume or for debt securities that have reduced quality ratings.

water and sewer bond   A revenue bond issued by a municipality to finance the building or extension of water and sewer systems. Interest and principal payments on the bond are derived from and are limited to revenues received from charges to the users of the systems.

watered stock   Stock issued with a value considerably in excess of the value of the assets supporting the stock. The term *watered stock* may be derived from the practice of feeding cattle salt to induce them to drink large amounts of water just before they are sold, thereby increasing their weight. Thus, the buyer—whether of stock or of livestock—pays for more than is actually received.

wd   —Used in stock and bond transaction tables in newspapers to indicate that a security is trading on a when-distributed basis: *ColgP wd.*

WD   —Used on the consolidated tape to indicate that a stock is trading on a when-distributed basis: *GY.WD 52.*

weak dollar   A dollar that is of smaller value relative to foreign currencies. A weak dollar exchanges for fewer units of other currencies compared with the units for which it could have been exchanged in the past. A weak dollar tends to help U.S. firms that rely heavily on foreign sales because the firms' products will cost less in terms of the foreign currencies. A weak dollar hurts consumers of foreign goods because these goods cost more in terms of U.S. dollars. —See also EXCHANGE RATE; STRONG DOLLAR.

weak form   A component in the theory of efficient markets holding that successive changes in security prices are independent of one another. If security markets are efficient to the extent of the weak form, existing prices reflect all the information contained in historical market data. Therefore, the charting of security prices and volume is not useful in projecting future price movements. The weak form of efficient markets supports the random-walk hypothesis. —See also SEMISTRONG FORM; STRONG FORM.

wedge   —See TRIANGLE.

weekend effect The tendency of securities to perform better on Fridays than on Mondays. Some technical analysts contend the weekend effect is primarily the result of the Monday auctions of U.S. Treasury securities.

weighting The assigning of a measure of relative importance for each of a group of variables that are combined. If an investor has 70% of his or her invested funds in stock A, which provides a current yield of 6%, and the remaining 30% of the invested funds in stock B, which provides a current yield of 12%, the weighted current yield of both securities is (.70)(6%) + (.30)(12%), or 7.8%.

W formation In technical analysis, a chart formation caused by a sharp decline, a sharp upward movement, and then a repeat of these two moves. The resultant chart pattern is similar to the letter *w*. In general, if the second upward movement surpasses each of the two previous high points, the W formation is a bullish sign.

when-distributed —Used to refer to a security that trades after the date of issue but before the time at which the certificates are delivered.

when-issued —Used to refer to a security that has not yet been issued but that will be issued in the future. Trading in when-issued securities often occurs between the time a new security is announced (e.g., the time when a stock is split) and the time the certificates are actually issued.

whipsaw A quick price movement followed by a sharp price change in the opposite direction. An investor expecting a continuation in the direction of a security's price movement is likely to experience whipsaw in a volatile market. This risk is very important to short-term traders but inconsequential to long-term investors.

white knight A person or company that rescues a target firm from a takeover attempt by buying the firm. —See also HOSTILE TENDER OFFER; RAIDER; SHARK REPELLENT; WHITE SQUIRE.

white squire An investor sympathetic with management who holds a large block of stock in a company that is or could be subject to a takeover unwanted by the management. —See also WHITE KNIGHT.

white squire defense An antitakeover strategy in which a takeover target places a large block of its stock in the hands of an investor deemed sympathetic to management. Having a white squire decreases the possibility of a takeover because the suitor must acquire a significantly greater proportion of the remaining shares in order to complete the takeover. However, the white squire may become disenchanted and put its block of stock up for sale or it may itself mount a takeover attempt.

⚠️ In late 1985 following speculation about takeover attempts, CBS Inc. asked its major stockholder, Loews Corporation, to increase its ownership of CBS stock from the then current 12% to as much as 25%. CBS's goal was to have Loews accumulate such a large block of CBS stock that Loews would become a white squire able to discourage any offers for CBS deemed unfriendly by CBS's management. The white squire defense had been used previously by Walt Disney Productions with the Bass family as the white squire and by Warner Communications with

Chris-Craft Industries as its white squire. One danger of this defense is that the white squire, having acquired such a large block of the threatened firm's stock, can itself attempt a takeover. At the least, the white squire normally will seek a voice in the management of the target firm to protect its large investment and to ensure orderly management. In the CBS matter, Loews Corporation chairman Lawrence Tisch was elected to the CBS board of directors and undertook an important role in running the company. Afterward, CBS management made some significant changes in its operations including the sale of a publishing group that had provided 15% of its sales revenues.

White's Ratings   A rating service for tax-exempt bond issues in which a relative market value index is constructed from bond trading patterns rather than from credit analysis. A bond's yield is scaled in an index from 1 to 100.

whole life insurance   —See CASH-VALUE LIFE INSURANCE.

wholesale   The sale of securitiés among broker-dealers and to large institutional investors. Securities sold at wholesale go for slightly lower prices than those paid by individual investors. —See also INSIDE MARKET; RETAIL.

wholesale price index   —See PRODUCER PRICE INDEX.

Whoops   —See WASHINGTON PUBLIC POWER SUPPLY SYSTEM.

^w_i —Used on the consolidated tape to indicate the transaction of a security on a when-issued basis: *GMPrE ^w_i 10s47½*.

wi   —Used in stock transaction tables in newspapers to indicate securities traded on a when-issued basis: *BltGE wi*.

wide basis   A market condition in which there is a relatively large difference between a spot price and futures prices for the same type of contract. —See also NARROW BASIS.

widow-and-orphan stock   A stock characterized by smaller than average price movements, a relatively high dividend, and little likelihood of dividend reduction or serious financial problems. Widow-and-orphan stocks are conservative investments with limited possibility for large gains or losses.

Williams Act   A 1968 addition to the Securities Exchange Act of 1934 that requires investors owning or tendering for over 5% of a firm's stock to furnish certain information to the Securities and Exchange Commission. Required information includes the reason for the acquisition, the number of shares owned, and the source of the funds used for the purchase. —See also CREEPING TENDER OFFER.

Wilshire 5000 Equity Index   A very comprehensive measure of stock prices made up of all stocks listed on the New York Stock Exchange and the American Stock Exchange as well as most active over-the-counter stocks. Stocks are weighted by market value.

windfall   An unexpected profit or gain. An investor holding a stock that increases greatly in price because of an unexpected takeover offer receives a windfall.

Now that AT&T has undergone breakup, are there any good widow-and-orphans left? Are they safe?
• •

Widow-and-orphans are believed to typify those with a high need for safety and yield. Stocks believed to offer such characteristics are therefore sometimes described, jokingly, as "suitable for widows and orphans." Actually, the safest securities for such investors are probably U.S. government notes or bonds with staggered maturities. Unfortunately, all investors like safety, and stocks considered relatively safe are usually priced to offer low yields by the market. In general, stocks in this category are semimonopolies with good earnings and dividend track records (preferably unbroken) such as utilities without nuclear reactors. However, conditions change and a diversified portfolio of low multiple defensive stocks would probably best meet the requirements of such investors.

J. Kendrick Noble, Jr., First Vice President
PaineWebber Incorporated, New York, NY

---

window   A period of time when an action can be expected to generate a successful result. For example, underwriters may have a window for corporate debt issues sandwiched between two periods of heavy U.S. Treasury offerings.

window dressing   Adjustment of a portfolio or financial statement to create false appearances. For example, a manager may decide to provide window dressing to a portfolio by selling stocks that have declined in value and by replacing them with stocks that have increased in value. Such activity creates the impression of successful portfolio management.

window settlement   The physical settlement of transactions between dealers. Window settlement is used when one or both participants are not members of a clearing firm such as the National Clearing Corporation. Settlement entails an actual physical comparison.

wire house   A relatively large, multioffice brokerage firm using electronic communications to transmit customer orders for execution.

wire room   The area in a broker-dealer firm in which customer orders are received from retail offices and are relayed to an exchange floor for execution. Following execution, that information is relayed from the wire room back to retail offices.

wire transfer   —See ELECTRONIC FUNDS TRANSFER.

withdrawal plan   An option offered by some open-end investment companies whereby an investor can receive payments at regular intervals. Withdrawal plans are generally used by people who wish to use their accumulated funds for retirement purposes.

withholding   1. The holding back of a portion of wages, dividends, interest, pension payments, or various other sources of income for payment of taxes to the U.S. Treasury.   2. The illegal holding back of a portion of securities allocated as part of a new issue to a member of an underwriting syndicate. The underwriter may wish to keep the securities or resell them to a designated party so as to profit from an expected price rise soon after the issue has been offered to the public.

with or without (WOW)   —Used to designate an odd-lot order in which the customer asks for an immediate execution. An odd-lot purchase order marked *WOW* will be executed at the current offering price plus any odd-lot differential, and an odd-lot sell order will receive the current bid price less any odd-lot differential. An odd-lot order marked *with or without* is likely to result in a lower sale price or in a higher purchase price than an ordinary odd-lot order.

without   —Used to indicate that no quotation is offered. For example, a dealer might quote a security as a $45 bid without, which means that the dealer is willing to buy at $45 but no ask price is currently available. A dealer quotation including a without indicates a one-sided market.

with warrants   —Used to designate a stock that trades with the right to a declared distribution of warrants. The buyer of a stock trading with warrants will be entitled to receive them if the stock is held until traded ex-warrants. The warrants will later trade separately from the stock.

worker capitalism   A system in which employees own part or all of the firm for which they work. Proponents of worker capitalism believe that employees will be more productive if they have a stake in the profits resulting from their labor. Employee Stock Ownership Plans (ESOP) were developed on this premise.

working capital   The excess of current assets over current liabilities. Working capital is frequently used to measure a firm's ability to meet current obligations as they come due. A high level of working capital indicates significant liquidity. —Also called *net current assets; net working capital.* —See also CURRENT RATIO; LIQUIDITY RATIO 1; QUICK RATIO.

working control   Ownership of a sufficient block of a firm's voting stock (not necessarily over 50%) to determine corporate policy. —See also MAJORITY STOCKHOLDER.

work in progress   Partially finished goods held in inventory for completion and eventual sale. —Also called *goods in process.*

workout 1. The process of a debtor's meeting a loan commitment by satisfying altered repayment terms. For example, a firm in Chapter 11 bankruptcy proceedings might reach an agreement with its creditors for ways in which the firm's obligations can be worked out over time.   2. A range of prices over which a transaction or a series of transactions is likely to take place. For example, a market maker might quote a price range over which he or she would attempt to buy or sell a large order of securities.

WOW —See WITH OR WITHOUT.

WPPSS —See WASHINGTON PUBLIC POWER SUPPLY SYSTEM.

wraparound annuity An annuity contract in which the investor has a measure of control as to the investments that are in the plan, while at the same time the income provided by the investments is sheltered from taxation until withdrawal. Tax deferral through a wraparound annuity is no longer permitted by the Internal Revenue Service.

wrinkles —See BELLS AND WHISTLES.

writedown A reduction in the value of an asset carried on a firm's financial statements. For example, the firm's accountants, feeling that the inventory is overvalued, may decide to take a writedown by reducing inventory valuation. Unlike a writeoff, a writedown does not result in elimination of the asset.

write off To reduce the balance (i.e., the book value of an asset or a group of assets) in an account to zero by recognizing the recorded value as an expense. For example, a firm may write off a technologically obsolete asset shown on its balance sheet as having monetary value. The asset will then be deleted from the balance sheet and income during the period will be reduced (or losses will be increased) by a like amount. —Also called *charge off*.

writeoff A reduction to zero in the value of an asset carried on a firm's financial statement. Companies often hesitate to make writeoffs because profits reported to stockholders are reduced.

writer The person who creates an option by selling an option contract in an opening transaction. An investor may be the writer of a call or a put. —See also NAKED WRITER.

writeup An accounting increase in the book value of an asset without an accompanying expenditure of funds. For example, if a firm accounts for inventory on the basis of market value, the firm may need a writeup of inventory during a period of price inflation.

writing The sale of an option in an opening transaction. The option writer incurs a potential obligation to buy (if a put is written) or to sell (if a call is written) an asset at a particular price.

WS —Used on the consolidated tape to indicate a warrant: *G.WS 23½*.

wt —Used in stock transaction tables in newspapers to indicate that the security is a warrant to buy shares of the common stock: *AExp wt*.

ww —Used in stock and bond transaction tables in newspapers to indicate a security traded with warrants: *RokInd ww*.

X

x —Used in stock transaction tables in newspapers to indicate a stock that trades ex-dividend or ex-rights. Usually the symbol immediately precedes sales volume: *Gencp x212*.

XD —Used on the consolidated tape to indicate a stock that is trading ex-dividend: *GY.XD 52*.

XDIS —Used on the consolidated tape to indicate a stock that is trading ex-distribution: *WX.XDIS 73*.

XRT —Used on the consolidated tape to indicate a stock that is trading ex-rights: *GY.XRT 52*.

xw —Used in stock and bond transaction tables in newspapers to indicate securities that are trading ex-warrants: *RokInd xw*.

Y

y —Used in stock transaction tables in newspapers to indicate a stock that began trading ex-dividend with sales listed in full: *y7100*.

Yankee bond A dollar-denominated bond sold in the United States by a foreign-domiciled issuer. U.S. investors can therefore purchase the securities of foreign issuers without being subject to price swings caused by variations in currency exchange rates. Yankee bond prices are influenced primarily by changes in U.S. interest rates and the financial condition of the issuer.

year bill A 12-month U.S. Treasury bill. Unlike 13- and 26-week Treasury bills, which are auctioned weekly, year bills are auctioned only once a month.

year-end dividend —See FINAL DIVIDEND 2.

year-end rally —See SANTA CLAUS RALLY.

yellow sheets Daily sheets containing wholesale bid and ask price quotations on over-the-counter bonds as listed by dealers who make markets in the individual securities. The sheets, which are published by a subsidiary of Commerce Clearing House, are for use inside the trade. —See also PINK SHEETS.

yield The percentage return on an investment. A given investment can have a wide variety of yields because of the many methods used to measure yield. For example, a bond's yield may be stated in terms of its returns if held to maturity, if held to the call date, if held to the put date;

or the yield may be calculated simply on the basis of the interest the bond pays compared with its current market price. —Also called *return*. —See also CURRENT YIELD; DIVIDEND YIELD; YIELD TO AVERAGE LIFE; YIELD TO CALL; YIELD TO MATURITY; YIELD TO PUT.

yield advantage The additional current return from holding a convertible security as opposed to owning the stock into which the convertible can be exchanged.

yield basis A method of quoting a bond's price in terms of its yield rather than in terms of its dollar value. Since bonds are bought and sold on the basis of yield, yield is generally a more informative measure of value than a bond's dollar price is. Treasury securities are normally auctioned on a yield basis.

yield curve At any particular time, the relation between bond yields and maturity lengths. The yield curve normally has a positive slope because yields on long-term bonds generally exceed yields on short-term bonds. The shape of a yield curve is influenced by a number of factors including the relative riskiness between long-term and short-term securities and by investors' expectations as to the level of future interest rates. —Also called *term structure of interest rates.* —See also FLAT YIELD CURVE; NEGATIVE YIELD CURVE; POSITIVE YIELD CURVE; RIDING THE YIELD CURVE.

yield curve note A floating-rate note in which yields increase when interest rates decline and yields decline when interest rates increase. Yield curve notes appeal to investors who want to hedge falling interest rates.

yield equivalence Equal aftertax returns on different investments. As an example, for an investor in a 25% marginal tax bracket, a corporate bond with a taxable return of 8% has yield equivalence with a tax-free bond returning 6%.

yield spread The difference in yield, at a given time, between two bonds or between different segments of the bond market. For example, the yield spread between AAA-rated bonds and A-rated bonds may be ½ of 1% at a particular time. Likewise, the yield spread between long-term taxable and nontaxable bonds may be 2%. Yield spread may be caused by any of various factors including maturity difference, risk difference, taxability difference, and so forth.

yield to average life The average yield on a fixed-income security assuming an average life for the security. In the case of bonds, average life may be significantly less than the number of years until maturity because of sinking fund requirements. Thus, the investor may be forced to sell the bond back before maturity.

yield to call The annual return on a bond, assuming that the security will be redeemed at the call price on the first date permitted. This measure of yield includes interest payments and price depreciation since bonds are quoted in this way only if they sell above the call price.

yield to maturity (YTM) The annual return on a bond held to maturity when interest payments and price appreciation (if priced below par) or depreciation (if priced above par) are considered. When a bond sells at par, the yield to maturity is the same as the current yield because price appreciation or depreciation is zero if the security is held to maturity. Bond quotations are generally on a yield-to-maturity basis although an investor selling a bond before maturity may earn a yield different from the yield to maturity as calculated at the time the security was purchased. —See also INTERNAL RATE OF RETURN; MATURITY BASIS.

When is yield to call more relevant than yield to maturity?
• •

Yield to call is more relevant than yield to maturity is when interest rates are declining and you are concerned about the yield on a premium-priced bond. What you really want to know is how much you will make on an investment that is going to pay you an above-market rate of income for some period of time but then may result in only a partial return of your original principal at a later date when the bond is called. If the income flow to you is sufficiently above the going rate for par-priced bonds, and if it lasts long enough, then the loss of principal that might result from a bond being called is not a problem. In any case, the yield to call formula takes this principal loss into account; the shorter the time period a premium-priced bond has before its first call date versus its maturity date, the greater the disparity between the bond's yield to call and its yield to maturity.

Stephanie R. Goldsborough, Treasury Officer
Maryland National Bank, Baltimore, MD

---

yield to put The annual yield on a bond, assuming that the security will be put (sold back to the issuer) on the first permissible date after purchase. Bonds are quoted in this manner only if they sell at a price less than the put price. Therefore, the yield includes interest and price appreciation. —See also PREMIUM PUT.

YTM —See YIELD TO MATURITY.

Z

z **1.** —Used in stock transaction tables in newspapers to indicate that the volume reported is the actual number of shares transacted, not the number of round lots: z150. **2.** —Used in over-the-counter stock transaction tables to indicate that no representative quote is available: z.

zero —See ZERO-COUPON BOND.

zero bracket amount —See STANDARD DEDUCTION.

zero-coupon bond A bond that provides no periodic interest payments to its owner. A zero-coupon bond is issued at a fraction of its par value (perhaps at $3 to $5 for each $100 of face value for a long-term bond) and increases gradually in value as it approaches maturity. Thus, an investor's income from a zero-coupon bond comes solely from appreciation in value. Zero-coupon bonds are subject to very large price fluctuations. The tax consequences of taxable issues often make zero-coupon bonds more suitable for tax deferred accounts such as IRAs than for regular investments. —Also called *capital appreciation bond; zero.* —See also ORIGINAL-ISSUE DISCOUNT BOND.

> ⑂ In 1984, the California Housing Finance Authority issued $300 million worth of home mortgage revenue bonds including $15.5 million worth of zero-coupon bonds. One type of zero in the offering was a bond maturing at a $5,000 face value in the year 2016. The bond paid no semiannual interest, but sold at an offering price of $142 per $5,000 face value. Thus, an investor purchasing one of the zero-coupon bonds in the offering and holding it until maturity would earn a return of 11.5% annually. The value of the bond at each semiannual date as listed in the prospectus included $427.10 on August 1, 1994 (10 years after issue), $1306.72 on August 1, 2004 (20 years after issue), and $3997.96 on August 1, 2014 (30 years after issue). Of course, the selling price an investor could obtain would depend on various factors including the market level of interest rates, existing tax laws, and the quality of the repayment guarantee at the time of the attempted sale.

zero-coupon certificate of deposit A certificate of deposit (CD) that pays no periodic interest and that is sold at a discount from face value (i.e., maturity value). A zero-coupon CD is essentially the same as any other CD in which the investor leaves interest to compound.

zero-minus tick The sale of a security when the price is the same as the security's preceding sale price but is below the last different sale price. A short sale of a security is not permitted on a zero-minus tick.

zero-plus tick The sale of a security when the price is the same as the security's preceding sale price but is above the last different sale price. A short sale of a security is permitted on a zero-plus tick.

What are the advantages and disadvantages of buying zero-coupon bonds? Who should buy them?

Zero-coupon bonds are quite useful in financial planning because they permit you to plan with certainty for specific rates of growth on the monies invested in zero-coupon bonds, provided that the monies will be left intact until maturity. If, however, you need to liquidate your zero-coupon bonds before their maturity, you will find that their prices will have moved dramatically in the opposite direction from where interest rates will have moved since you bought your bonds. These bonds have the most volatile price movements of any bonds in their respective credit quality and maturity group because they pay no coupon interest to cushion the blow of any change in interest rates. Another important aspect of zero-coupon bonds relates to their taxation. Income is accrued on zero-coupon bonds even though they do not pay any interest before maturity. If the bond is taxable (i.e., it is a U.S. Treasury bond or a corporate bond), you will have to pay annual federal income tax on the accrued income even though you did not receive any cash flow from the bond before maturity. The income is based on the accretion of the bond from the discount price at which you bought it to the par value it will grow to be at maturity. If your bond is a municipal zero-coupon, the accretion is still calculated each year, but the bond's accretion is not taxed at the federal level. (Consult your state's tax laws regarding the taxation of the accretion.) This accretion affects the municipal bond's book value, however, which in turn influences the portion of any capital gain subject to federal income tax. Taxable zero-coupon bonds are often used in retirement plans and in children's custodial accounts because of the predictability of their values at maturity and the fact that income earned in accounts of this sort is generally able to grow tax-deferred or is taxed at a low federal income tax rate. Tax-exempt zero-coupon bonds are often used to form a "Side-IRA," which means that a pool of money is able to grow, free of taxation, with its anticipated use being to enhance the pool of money that is allowed to grow within an IRA. The obvious result is that more money will be available at the time of retirement because of careful planning for tax savings and the continuous compounding of the tax-favored rate of return.

Stephanie R. Goldsborough, Treasury Officer
Maryland National Bank, Baltimore, MD

---

zero-sum game A situation in which one person's gain must be matched by another person's loss. Without considering taxes and transaction costs, many types of investing, such as options and futures, are examples of zero-sum games.

zero tick   A security transaction when the sale price is identical to the price of the immediately preceding transaction in the same security.

zr   —Used in bond transaction tables in newspapers to indicate a zero-coupon bond. No coupon is listed, since a zero-coupon bond makes no annual interest payment to its holders: *CitSvc zr89.*

Technical Analysis Chart Patterns

Typical Examples

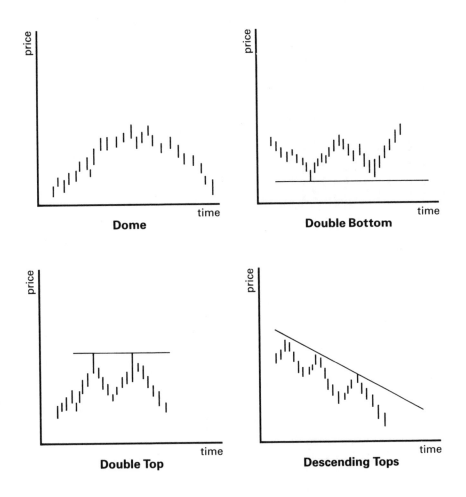

Dome

Double Bottom

Double Top

Descending Tops

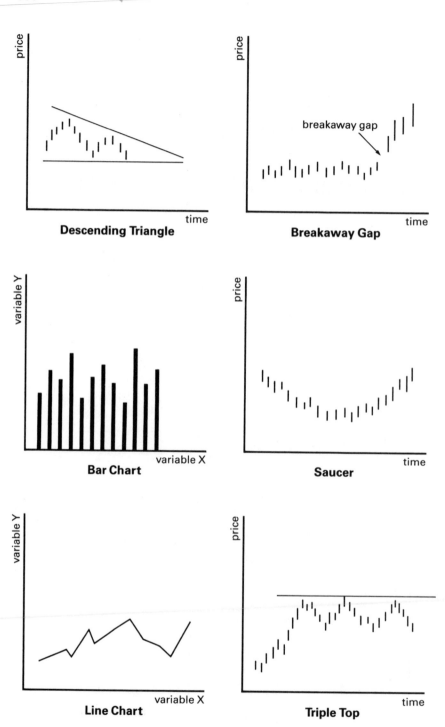

Descending Triangle

Breakaway Gap

Bar Chart

Saucer

Line Chart

Triple Top

Triangle

Point-and-figure Chart

Head-and-shoulders

Exhaustion Gap

Rectangle

Runaway Gap

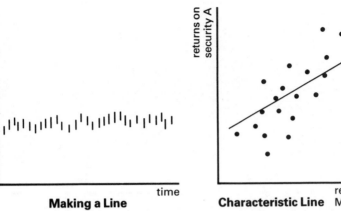

Making a Line

Characteristic Line   returns on Market Index

Used in fundamental analysis

Selected Bibliography

Andrew, John. *Buying Municipal Bonds: A Commonsense Guide to Tax-free Personal Investing.* New York: Macmillan, Free Press, 1987. An easy-to-understand book on an investment that has become increasingly popular among individual investors.

Edwards, Robert D., and John Magee. *Technical Analysis of Stock Trends,* 5th ed. Springfield, Mass.: John Magee, 1968. The classic that remains a must for investors with even a passing interest in technical analysis. Expensive but worth it.

Galbraith, John K. *The Great Crash of Nineteen Twenty-nine.* New York: Avon Books, 1980. The most understandable, insightful, and entertaining book written on the Great Depression. Can it happen again? Read the book and decide for yourself.

Graham, Benjamin. *The Intelligent Investor: A Book of Practical Counsel,* 4th rev. ed. New York: Harper and Row, 1986. Advice from a master in the field of investments. Concentrates on investigating the principles and psychology of investing.

Graham, Benjamin, David L. Dodd, and Sidney Cottle. *Security Analysis: Principles and Technique,* 4th ed. New York: McGraw-Hill, 1962. The pathbreaking book on value investing and fundamental analysis that has set the standard by which other investment books are judged. Originally published in 1934 and still belongs on every investor's bookshelf.

Malkiel, Burton G. *A Random Walk down Wall Street,* 4th ed. New York: W. W. Norton, 1985. A book that untangles modern investment theory and makes it understandable to the occasional investor.

Pessin, Allan H. *Fundamentals of the Securities Industries,* rev. ed. New York: New York Institute of Finance, 1985. A comprehensive look at the internal workings of the securities business. An excellent reference book.

Scott, David L. *The Investor's Guide to Discount Brokers*. New York: Praeger, 1983. A listing of approximately 100 discount brokerage firms including commission schedules, addresses, and phone numbers. Rates are somewhat dated but in a relative sense are still useful.

Smith, Adam [George Jerome Waldo Goodman]. *The Money Game*. New York: Random House, Vintage Books, 1976. My all-time favorite book on the stock market. Humorous and full of insights still applicable today.

Teweles, Richard J., and Edward S. Bradley. *The Stock Market*, 4th ed. New York: John Wiley, 1982. A well-written overview of the operations of securities exchanges. Includes information on how the exchanges function, regulations that affect investors, the over-the-counter market, and investment practices.